Reality TV

Reality TV

Remaking Television Culture

|||||||||||||||||||||||||||||||||||||||||||||||||||

Second Edition

|||||||||||||||||||||||||||||||||||||||||||||||||||

EDITED BY

Susan Murray and Laurie Ouellette

NEW YORK UNIVERSITY PRESS

NEW YORK AND LONDON

NEW YORK UNIVERSITY PRESS
New York and London
www.nyupress.org

Library of Congress Cataloging-in-Publication Data

Reality TV : remaking television culture /
Edited by Susan Murray and Laurie Ouellette. — 2nd ed.
p. cm.
Includes bibliographical references and index.
ISBN-13: 978–0–8147–5733–8 (cl : alk. paper)
ISBN-10: 0–8147–5733–2 (cl : alk. paper)
ISBN-13: 978–0–8147–5734–5 (pb : alk. paper)
ISBN-10: 0–8147–5734–0 (pb : alk. paper)
1. Reality television programs—United States.
I. Murray, Susan, 1967– II. Ouellette, Laurie.
PN1992.8.R43R45   2008   2009
791.45'6—dc22   2008036855

New York University Press books are printed on acid-free paper,
and their binding materials are chosen for strength and durability.
We strive to use environmentally responsible suppliers and materials
to the greatest extent possible in publishing our books.

Manufactured in the United States of America
c 10 9 8 7 6 5 4 3 2 1
p 10 9 8 7 6 5 4 3 2 1

Contents

Acknowledgments

The editors are indebted to the authors of this volume, and to Eric Zinner and New York University Press, who guided the manuscript to fruition in an exceptionally professional and timely manner. The editors also thank the contributors. We are honored to have worked with such a dedicated and insightful group of scholars. Susan Murray thanks her colleagues in the Department of Media, Culture and Communication at New York University for their encouragement and generosity. Laurie Ouellette thanks the College of Liberal Arts and her colleagues in the Department of Communication Studies at the University of Minnesota for supporting this project.

Grateful acknowledgment is made to the following for granting permission to reprint in this volume:

Jump Cut for the "Political Economy of Reali-TV" by Chad Raphael, originally published in 1997, volume 41, pages 102–9

New York University Press for "Buying into *American Idol*: How We Are Being Sold on Reality TV" by Henry Jenkins, originally published in 2006 in *Convergence Culture*

Sage Publishing for "Performing the Real: Documentary Diversions" by John Corner, originally published in *Television and New Media* in August 2002, no. 3, pages 255–69.

Introduction

Laurie Ouellette and Susan Murray

In May 2007, the Dutch public television network BNN announced that it would soon air *The Big Donor Show,* a reality program in which a 37-year-old woman who is dying from a brain tumor agrees to donate her kidney to one of three contestants. She will choose the recipient by watching interviews with the contestants' families and by considering the opinions of the audience, which votes on its choice by SMS (short message service) text message. The declaration triggered a contentious debate about the current state of TV, in which critics across the globe pondered the (to some) outrageous premise of *The Big Donor Show* and members of the Dutch Parliament considered banning its broadcast altogether. When the program did appear on television, its creators at the production company Endemol upped the ante on the controversy by eventually revealing that the woman who was "playing" the terminally ill donor was really an actress and the contestants vying for a new kidney were in on the hoax. When the revelation generated even more accusations of ratings-driven sensationalism, Endemol claimed that the goal of the faux reality TV program was to cast a critical eye on the legal issues and patient "reality" surrounding organ transplants.

The prospect of reality television claiming to provide gripping "real life" entertainment as well as public service in the form of an elaborate ruse points to some of the overlapping institutional, technological, ethical, and cultural developments addressed by this updated version of *Reality TV: Remaking Television Culture.* When our original collection of essays was published in 2004, reality TV was just beginning to take form, and few scholars had evaluated what some saw as a passing fad in media culture. The situation has changed, in part because few would now contest reality TV's reach and longevity. Across the globe, popular reality TV has become more pervasive and diversified, and popular nonscripted formats have become increasingly specialized and stylistically sophisticated. *The Big Donor* speaks to this shift, not only by narrowing and refining the generic premise of the gamedoc but also by self-consciously manipulating reality TV's (by now) established cultural conventions and further collapsing television's historic roles as a technology of truth, fiction, public service, and corporate gain. *The Big Donor Show*'s unapologetic play with "reality" also evokes other TV programs that have pretended to be unscripted, including *The Joe Schmo Show* (FX), *The Assistant* (MTV), and *My Big Fat Obnoxious Fiancé* (FOX). While these programs tested reality TV's programmatic rules and conventions for a range of dramatic, humorous, commercial, ideological, and ethical purposes, their overall emergence as a metanarrative about reality TV indicates the genre's maturation as a distinct, and widely recognized, cultural form.

Reality TV, as we predicted, has also remained on the cusp of developments in media convergence, interactivity, user-generated content, and greater viewer involvement in television. Since 2000, when *Big Brother* pioneered the use of wireless participation and 24/7 web streams, the Internet and mobile phones have become much more integral to the marketing, promotion, "mass customization," and delivery of all broadcast and cable television. From *Queer Eye* to *The Apprentice*, reality TV continues to serve as the principal testing ground for emerging convergence strategies such as podcasting, user-generated content, webisodes, and interactive computer games. As a number of essays in this edition demonstrate, however, the cultural and political possibilities of convergence have taken shape within a broader climate of corporate synergy, consumer profiling, and integrated advertising. TV viewers of *The Big Donor* who wished to vote for the most deserving kidney recipient were caught within this commercial matrix, as sophisticated marketing techniques converged with interactivity and "public service," and voters were required to pay a fee to participate in the game via their cell phones. *The Big Donor*'s gesture toward a form of "do goodism" points to another new development in reality TV: From *American Idol*'s foray into charitable activities to programs like *Extreme Makeover Home Edition* and Oprah Winfrey's *Oprah's Big Give* that provide privatized social services to the needy, the TV industry has found that there is money to be made by taking on the duties of the philanthropist, the social worker, the benefactor, and the "guardian angel." While such programming is often totted out to redeem reality TV's cultural reputation, experiments like *The Big Donor* have also emerged within the context of privatization and market liberalization examined in this book.

As reality TV has proliferated and evolved, critical scholarship has followed suit. When we began assembling the original essays for this book, the few existing studies of reality TV were narrowly rooted in the documentary film tradition. Today, scholars in media studies, film studies, TV studies, and communication are engaging with reality TV, often taking our volume as a starting point for critical research and analysis. This volume supplements the foundational essays featured in the 2004 edition with some of the best of the current scholarship on reality TV, specifically commissioned for this collection. These new essays address recent generic developments and configurations, update industrial happenings and responses to reality TV, work through current social and political issues that surround the genre, and explore the consequences of technological convergence and interactivity. In conjunction with the foundational essays, these new works reveal the extent to which reality TV has altered not only the business and culture of television but also the direction of television studies.

Situating Reality Television

What is reality TV? The classification of generic labels is always contextual and historical, as several essays in this volume demonstrate. While there are certain characteristics (such as minimal writing and the use of nonactors) that cut across many reality programs, we are ultimately more concerned with the cultural and "branding" discourses that have coalesced to differentiate a particular stage in television culture. We define "reality television" as an unabashedly commercial genre united less by aesthetic rules or certainties than by the fusion of popular entertainment with a self-conscious claim to the discourse of the real. This coupling, we contend, is what has made reality TV an important generic forum for a range of institutional and cultural developments that include the merger of marketing and "real life" entertainment, the convergence of new technologies with programs and their promotion, and an acknowledgement of the manufactured artifice that coexists with truth claims.

We have seen the rapid proliferation of television programming that promises to provide nonscripted access to "real" people in ordinary and extraordinary situations. This access to the real is presented in the name of dramatic uncertainty, voyeurism, and popular pleasure, and it is for this reason that reality TV is unlike news, documentaries, and other sanctioned information formats whose truth claims are explicitly tied to the residual goals and understandings of the classic public service tradition. Although the current wave of reality TV circulates ideologies, myths, and templates for living that might be called "educational" in nature, it eschews the twin expectations of unpopularity and unprofitability that have historically differentiated "serious" factual formats and popular entertainment. If the reality programming that we examine here celebrates the real as a selling point, it also distances itself from the deliberation of veracity and the ethical concerns over human subjects that characterize documentary programming in its idealized modernist form. For even those programs that claim to improve the lives of their participants, such as *Extreme Makeover Home Edition*, do not carefully consider the ethics and responsibility that come with the representation of "real" people and, as a result, are commonly charged with exploitation of their subjects.

While the convergence of commercialism, popularity, and nonscripted television has clearly accelerated, much of what we call popular reality TV can be traced to existing formats and prior moments in U.S. television history. The quiz formats of the late-1950s represent an early incarnation of highly profitable TV programming that hinged on the popular appeal of real people placed in dramatic situations with unpredictable outcomes. Other precursors include the staged pranks pioneered by *Candid Camera,* makeovers and charity games (*Queen for a Day, Strike It Rich, Glamour Girl*), celebrations of ordinary people in unusual or unusually contrived situations (*It Could Happen to You, That's Incredible, Real People*), and the amateur talent contest first brought to television by *Star Search.* The landmark cinema verité series *An American Family,* which is often cited as the first reality TV program, also provides an important reference point, as does low-budget, nonprofessionally produced television, from the activist and amateur programming shown on cable access stations to the everyday home video excerpted on *America's Funniest Home Videos.*

Daytime talk shows, the favored reality format of the late-1980s and early-1990s, anticipated the confessional ethos and cultivation of everyday drama that permeates contemporary reality TV. Yet, it wasn't until the premiere of *The Real World* on MTV in 1991 that we began to witness the emergence of many of the textual characteristics that would come to define the genre's current form. By casting young adults in a manner intended to ignite conflict and dramatic narrative development, placing the cast in a house filled with cameras and microphones, and employing rapid editing techniques in an overall serial structure, the producers created a text that would prefigure programs such as *Survivor* and *Big Brother*. It could also be argued that *The Real World* trained a generation of young viewers in the language of reality TV.

Today, reality TV encompasses a variety of specialized formats or subgenres, including most prominently the gamedoc (*Survivor, Big Brother, The Apprentice, America's Next Top Model, Project Runway*), the dating program (*Joe Millionaire, The Bachelor, next, Beauty and the Geek*), the makeover program (*What Not to Wear, Queer Eye for the Straight Guy, Extreme Makeover, The Swan*), and the docusoap (*The Real World, The Real Housewives of Orange County*). Other subgenres include the ever-popular talent contest (*American Idol, Dancing with the Stars*), popular court programs (*Judge Judy, Court TV*), reality sitcoms (*The Simple Life, The Osbournes, Family Jewels*), and celebrity variations that tap into many of the conventions for presenting "ordinary" people on television (*Celebrity Boxing, Celebrity Fit Club, Surreal Life*).

Since 2004, these subgenres have been joined by updated, high-profile versions of the charity program (*Extreme Makeover Home Edition, Pimp My Ride, Three Wishes, Oprah's Big Give*), as well as by a whole array of lifestyle games that fuse the conventions of gaming with expert guidance in parenting, nutrition, domesticity, and other everyday activities (*Wife Swap, Supernanny, The Biggest Loser, Honey We're Killing the Kids*). Everyday investigation and micro surveillance have become an expected generic convention of many subgenres, as well narrative focus of reality investigations (*To Catch a Thief, Room Raiders*). And, we have seen emergence of spoof shows that satirize reality TV's conventions, while simultaneously capitalizing on the genre's voyeuristic tendencies and popular appeal (*The Assistant, The Joe Schmo Show, My Big Fat Obnoxious Fiancé*). The most sophisticated examples of this strand of faux reality programming fuse the boundaries of comedy, performance, and nonfiction in ways that potentially disrupt the conventions of reality TV, as well as the conventions of gender and other identities.

What ties together all the various formats of the reality TV genre is their professed abilities to more fully provide viewers an unmediated, voyeuristic, and yet often playful look into what might be called the "entertaining real." This fixation with "authentic" personalities, situations, problems, and narratives is considered to be reality TV's primary distinction from fictional television and also its primary selling point. However, viewers have certainly been well trained in the ways of reality TV since its initial emergence and are therefore quite savvy and skeptical when it comes to how much is actually "real" in these programs. So, while the promise of the real is what might hook audiences from the outset, the ways in which authenticity is promised by producers and received or questioned by audiences is a complex interplay of a variety of factors, many of which are explored in this volume.

Beyond increasingly sophisticated textual characteristics and the appearance of new subgenres, what differentiates today's cultural moment is a heightened promotion of the "entertaining real" that cuts across prime time and daytime, network and cable programming. For a variety of complex reasons that the authors examine, reality TV has moved from the fringes of television culture to its lucrative core as networks continue to adopt reality formats to recapture audiences and as cable channels formulate their own versions of reality formats geared to niche audiences. Consequently, not since the quiz show craze of the 1950s have nonfiction entertainment programs so dominated the network prime-time schedule. Talk shows and game shows have historically been relegated to daytime or late-night hours, while networks have relied on dramas and sitcoms to secure their evening audience base.

While cable stations were the first to begin airing reality programs during prime time, the success of CBS's *Survivor* eventually led the networks to follow suit. By early 2003, the staying power of the genre and the success of hit shows like *American Idol, The Bachelorette,* and *Joe Millionaire* convinced networks to make long-term plans for reality TV and its accompanying business strategies. In a front-page story on the topic in the *New York Times,* president of CBS Television Leslie Moonves proclaimed, "The world as we knew it is over."[1] By January 2003, one-seventh of all ABC's programming was reality-based. ABC executives, along with those from NBC, FOX, and CBS, promised to bring even more reality to their schedules in the coming season and cut back on scripted fictional drama series and sitcoms.[2] A few months later, the first "reality movie," *The Real Cancun,* was released in theaters, and by 2004, the round-the-clock reality network "Reality Central" began airing on cable systems throughout the United States; it was soon followed by the more successful FOX Reality Channel (which boasted over 35 million subscribers in early 2007).

Even more noticeable perhaps than the movies and dedicated reality channels has been the fact that reality TV has become the go-to genre for cable and broadcast networks alike over the past few years. Far from the passing fad that some predicted it would be, reality television has changed business practices and audience expectations to such an extent that it is difficult to imagine television without it. Motivated in large part by witnessing these changes, we have commissioned new essays for this collection that address the reasons behind and the implications of reality TV's considerable influence.

Is Reality Television Real?

Reality TV's staying power renders an investigation of its relationship to truth and authenticity even more urgent. Many reality formats maintain noticeable connections to the documentary tradition. In particular, the use of handheld cameras and lack of narration found in many reality programs is reminiscent of observational documentaries and carries with it an implicit reference to the form's original promise to provide direct access to the experience of the observed subject. This has the effect of bolstering some of reality TV's claims to "the real."

Scholarly discussions of documentaries have tended to turn on issues of ethics of representation and the responsibilities associated with truth telling and mediation. In *New Documentary: A Critical Introduction*, Stella Bruzzi points out that at the root of these discussions is a naive belief in a future in which "documentaries will be able to collapse reality and fiction" by "bypass[ing] its own representational tools" with the help of particular techniques such as those commonly associated with cinema verité.[3]

The reception of reality TV programming evokes similar questions and concerns as critics (but not necessarily audiences) wring their hands over the impact that editing, reconstruction, producer mediation, and prefab settings have on the audience's access to "the real." However, despite such similarities in claims and critical concerns, reality TV also establishes new relationships between "reality" and its representation.

Although reality TV whets our desire for the authentic, much of our engagement with such texts paradoxically hinges on our awareness that what we are watching is constructed and contains "fictional" elements. In a highly provocative and influential article in the *Television and New Media* special issue on *Big Brother,* which we have reprinted here, John Corner claims that the commingling of performance with naturalism is a defining element of what he calls television's "postdocumentary context."[4] In this contradictory cultural environment, critics like Corner contend that viewers, participants, and producers are less invested in absolute truth and representational ethics and more interested in the space that exists between reality and fiction.

This is borne out by a 2005 Associated Press/*TV Guide* poll, in which "participants indicated that they did not believe reality TV was real, but they also didn't care that much." In fact, 25 percent of those polled said that reality shows are totally made up, and 57 percent said that they show some truth but are mostly distorted. And only 30 percent said that it mattered to them that reality shows were really truthful.[5] (Interestingly, the same poll indicates the public feels there is too much reality TV as well, which can help explain why reality producers are working so hard to reinvent the genre at every turn with spoofs, generic blends, and "do good" formats.)

Reality TV promises its audience revelatory insight into the lives of others as it withholds and subverts full access to it. What results is an unstable text that encourages viewers to test out their own notions of the real, the ordinary, and the intimate against the representation before them. Far from being the mind-numbing, deceitful, and simplistic genre that some critics claim it to be, reality TV provides a multilayered viewing experience that hinges on culturally and politically complex notions of what is real and what is not. Moreover, reality TV enlists people in activities and practices (text messaging, accessing online material such as video clips, games, and self-help resources, and applying to be on shows) that challenge the primacy of the television program and further complicate text-based notions of meaning and truth. As several new essays commissioned for this volume indicate, reality TV demands a new level of cultural participation on the part of TV viewers. While the political implications of this interactivity are debatable, there is no doubt that the genre has pushed television culture—and television studies—in new directions.

Central to what is "true" and "real" for reality TV is its connection to new forms of governing at a distance, including the private surveillance of "ordinary" individuals. In an era in which a "total information awareness" of all U.S citizens has been made a top governmental priority, the recording and watching of others—and ourselves—has become a naturalized component of our everyday lives. Surveillance cameras are everywhere in the United States. In fact, the American Civil Liberties Union found in 1998 that, in New York City alone, 2,397 cameras (both privately and governmentally operated) were fixed on public places such as parks, sidewalks, and stores.[6] By 2001, a company providing security services, CCS International, reported that the average New Yorker was recorded 73 to 75 times a day.[7] Since the events of September 11, 2001, even more cameras have been installed.

Reality TV mitigates our resistance to such surveillance tactics. More and more programs rely on the willingness of "ordinary" people to live their lives in front of television cameras. We, as audience members, witness this openness to surveillance, normalize it, and, in turn, open ourselves up to such a possibility. We are also encouraged to participate in self-surveillance. Part of what reality TV teaches us in the early years of the new millennium is that in order to be good citizens we must allow ourselves to be watched as we watch ourselves and those around us, and then modify our conduct and behavior accordingly. Our promised reward for our compliance within and support of such a panoptic vision of society is protection from both outer and inner social threats.

Surveillance is just one of the questionable promises of "public service" that reality TV makes. Reality TV is cheap, common and entertaining— the antithesis of the public service tradition in broadcasting and a threat to the well-informed citizenry that it promises to cultivate, according to conventional wisdom. And yet, a closer look at reality TV forces us to rethink the changing meanings of public service, democracy, and citizenship in the age of neoliberalism, deregulation, conglomeration, and technological convergence. Reality TV's growing preoccupation with formats that assess and test people's capacities (and capacities for self-improvement) has emerged at a historical juncture marked by the dismantling of public welfare programs and an emphasis on private and personal initiative as an alternative to the state's role in managing social needs and risks.

The proliferation of charity-themed productions, as well as lifestyle programs in which experts offer real people and families on air guidance in the "correct" ways of parenting, nutrition, body management, housecleaning, marriage, and personal appearance, speaks to this sociopolitical context. For better or worse, reality TV enacts a highly visible new form of market-based social welfare, as commercial lifestyle experts, product sponsors, and TV networks pick up where the state, in its role of public service provider, has left off.[8]

The Commercialization of the Real

If reality TV raises cultural and ethical questions, it also points to the medium's changing industrial context. In the late 1980s, a shifting regulatory climate, network financial troubles, and labor unrest forced the television industry to reconsider their current programming strategies. Finding reality formats cheap to produce, easy to sell abroad, and not dependent on the hiring of unionized acting and writing talent, they began to develop more programs like *Unsolved Mysteries, Rescue 911,* and *America's Most Wanted.* In Europe, public television stations also embraced reality programming, mainly as a financial survival mechanism. Faced with deregulatory policies and heightened pressures to compete with commercial channels that aired popular (and often U.S.-produced) programs, public stations in the United Kingdom, the Netherlands, and other European countries developed the reality genre.

The explosion of reality programming in the 1990s was also the product of a changing industrial environment—both in the United States and abroad. Feeling threatened by new recording devices such as TIVO and Replay (which contained commercial-skipping features) and an ever-increasing number of cable stations, U.S. television networks were open to the possibility of new production and financing models including the purchasing and selling of formats rather than completed programs, the expansion of merchandising techniques, an increased emphasis on audience interactivity, and the insertion of commercial messages within the program. (This last strategy isn't entirely new, of course, but is a variation on the indirect sponsorship model used in the 1950s and revived within the deregulated policy milieu of the 1990s.)

If reality TV is at the center of major shifts within the television industry, its proliferation has also corresponded with the rapid development of new media technologies. Much of reality TV in the late 1980s and early 1990s, such as *Cops* and *America's Funniest Home Videos,* depended on the availability and portability of handheld video cameras. The most recent wave of reality programs has relied on small microphones and hidden cameras to capture private moments such as those that occur on *Big Brother* and *The Real World.* Yet, the marketing and distribution of reality TV has also developed in particular ways in its use of the Internet, streaming video, cell phone technology, radio, mobile digital video players, and digital television. Viewers are no longer limited to just viewing the completed text but can keep in touch with the show through SMS updates sent to their cell phones, can access live 24-hour footage on the website, and can call to cast their eviction votes.

New technologies have also facilitated new advertising strategies that enable sponsors to cut through the clutter of traditional television advertising. In addition, reality TV is proving itself to be an ideal format for video-sharing sites such as YouTube and Revver as members share memorable clips from the most recent episode of their favorite reality show or even produce reality shorts based on their own lives. In May 2007, VH1 made a move to more formally interlock reality TV and YouTube by producing a program, called *Acceptable TV*, that fuses the interactivity of the Internet with the formal strategies of television. Viewers submit their own amateur shorts on YouTube and those that become the most popular with other viewers are shown on the program, along with professionally produced shorts. The result is part reality gamedoc played out on the Internet and part sketch comedy program.

One of the most compelling aspects of reality TV is the extent to which its use of real people or nonactors contributes to the diversification of television culture. *Survivor*, for example, has made a point to use people from diverse age, racial, geographical, class, and sexual backgrounds. Reality TV opens up new possibilities and limitations for representational politics, as the authors in this volume demonstrate.

The 15 minutes of fame that is the principal material reward for participating on the programs limits the selection of "real people" to those who make good copy for newspaper and magazine articles and desirable guests on synergistic talk shows and news specials. Indeed, many of the participants on *Survivor* and other successful reality programs have gone on to star in Hollywood films, host television programs like MTV's *Spring Break*, and appear as contestants on new reality programs. While participation in reality TV doesn't seem to lead to an acting career, it does seem to provide a continuation of the observed life, as former participant/players' off-screen behavior is tracked by the media even after their show airs. The celebrification of "average" folk further complicates the contours of television fame and the way that its star personas have been constructed as existing in a space between the ordinary and the extraordinary.

For some critics, reality TV's commercial orientation has co-opted its democratic potential. The dream of "the people" participating directly in television culture can be traced to the alternative video movements of the 1960s and 1970s, which sought to collapse the hierarchy between producers and receivers and empower everyone to participate in electronic imagemaking. Influenced by the writings of Hans Enzenberger and Bertold Brecht, video pioneers sought to remake television as a democratic endeavor, bypassing one-way transmission for a participatory model that allowed a full range of people to tell their stories and document their struggles "unfiltered" by the demands of convention, stereotyping, and commercial sponsorship.[9]

While this philosophy lives on in the alternative productions of Paper Tiger TV, Deep Dish, and Free Speech TV, it is now more commonly associated with the television industry itself, which emphasizes the democratic potential of reality TV by promising unscripted programs filled with (and sometimes made by) "real" people from all walks of life.

Reaching out to a generation raised with reality TV, shows such as Nickelodeon's *ME:TV,* which airs videos made by its kid viewers, and TLC's *My Life as a Child,* which gives kids cameras to document their lives, have become increasingly popular. *Current TV,* the cable network/website cofounded by former Vice President Al Gore, allows viewers to "vote" on their favorite user-generated videos, which are then shown on television. Even advertisers have jumped on the trend, as the Gap uses "real" people to sell jeans and the Subway sandwich chain claims that a television commercial was "shot by real teenagers." User-created advertising also thrives on the web, providing much of the content of Current TV and other sites where viewers use low-tech equipment to re-create the aesthetics of Madison Avenue in the hopes of breaking into the culture industries.

Only complicating matters even more was the revelation in 2006 that the web's own Sadie Benning–like Lonelygirl15, who had some of the most tracked and talked about first-person videos ever on YouTube,[10] was actually an actress reading lines scripted for her by a professional screenwriter. Her private video diaries were not done via webcam but were actually shot by an aspiring Los Angeles filmmaker. The hoax reveals the complicated nexus of factors that are at play in user-generated videos that seek to mimic the aesthetics of documentary and reality TV; the story of Lonelygirl15's creation and reception intersects with our hopes and fears about amateur-created video in an age of reality TV.

However opportunistic, the commercial embrace of popular "reality" programming does signal representational shifts and, with them, some opportunities that warrant special consideration. The reality boom has spawned an opportunity in which to wrest control of television images and discourses away from the culture industries. This space cannot be fully contained by producers, or can it? The authors in this book grapple with that question and ultimately demonstrate that "access" and "authenticity" are tenuous and contingent, created in an ongoing cultural struggle between producers, participants, and television viewers.

From historical precedents and political economic impetuses to aesthetic issues and representational politics, the essays assembled here present a multilayered examination of reality TV in its various incarnations and forms. In addition to situating the reality TV phenomenon within contexts that highlight its economic, cultural, generic, representational, and reception dimensions, the chapters in this book point to the need to update television scholarship. The theoretical assumptions and methodological principles on which we have come to depend are no longer sufficient tools to analyze an increasingly complex televisual environment.

As these chapters demonstrate, television has become more sophisticated not just in the presentation of reality programming that simultaneously claims authenticity yet rewards savvy viewers for recognizing constructed or fictional elements but in its reliance on interactive technologies, novel commercial strategies, and an intertextual environment in which "real" people slip and out of the roles of celebrities and vice versa. The global context in which reality programs are produced and shared is changing, too. As media conglomerates become international entities and television formats are exchanged and revamped across national boundaries, we need to revise our political-economic frameworks and ways to understand how meaning can be both culturally specific and globally relevant.

Genre

The essays that make up part I of this book consider the question of genre from a variety of perspectives. In chapter 1, Anna McCarthy takes a historical approach, tracing the roots of reality television to an affinity among liberal cultural reformers, cold war social scientists, and *Candid Camera* producer Alan Funt. If reality television is now dismissed as cheap and lowbrow, its "first wave" was championed by the prestigious Ford Foundation, highbrow TV critics, and behaviorist researchers, who saw the representation of "real life" in Funt's work as both a respectable genre and a boon to liberal democracy. While reality television's high cultural status has slipped, McCarthy shows that today's programs bear the traces of the affinity between reality TV producers and social scientists set into motion during the medium's early years.

In one of the most frequently cited and most talked about essays on reality TV, John Corner places the most recent wave of reality television within the context of the functions and modes of nonfiction television and documentary. Originally published in *Television and New Media* in 2002, this essay raised the possibility that we might be moving toward a "post-documentary" moment in our culture. As Corner notes in his afterword, written especially for chapter 2 in this volume, his use of this term led many to mistakenly believe that he was claiming that the death of documentary was nigh. Yet, as Corner points out, he was working to name something far more complex, dynamic, and still in process in audiovisual culture.

In chapter 3, Susan Murray compares the packaging of two genres, documentary and reality TV, and argues that their perceived differences are often based on aesthetic hierarchies, brand images, and audience expectations, as much as on generic conventions. Taking the HBO documentary series *America Undercover* and the cancelled FOX program *American High,* which later appeared on public television, as twin case studies, Murray grapples with the question of what, exactly, reality TV is and how it differs discursively from traditional notions of documentary. In this way, Murray's essay demonstrates how cultural labels intersect with aesthetic hierarchies, "brand" images, and audience expectations and competencies as much as generic conventions.

Nick Couldry's essay, chapter 4, moves us away from specific questions of form and conventions and focuses instead on how reality TV reformulates documentary reality claims. In performing a ritual analysis of a particular subgenre, Couldry shows how British gamedocs like *Big Brother, Castaway,* and *The Experiment* work as technologies of surveillance, reproducing power relations and enlisting viewers to participate in the mobilization of societal myths. Although Couldry claims that every gamedoc has its own specific myth or way of representing the world, all gamedocs reinforce the idea that "mediated reality is somehow 'higher' than, or more significant than, nonmediated reality."

Derek Kompare revisits the legacy of *An American Family* in the final essay of this section, chapter 5, comparing the documentary portrait of an upscale California family to *The Osbournes.* The creation and reception of both programs, he contends, hinges on their abilities to navigate the "normative" parameters of both genre and family. *An American Family* sought to capture "fly on the wall" reality but was criticized for mediating the truth by monitoring (and exploiting) the liberal, upper-class California Loud family. *The Osbournes,* in contrast, has been praised for reworking the fictions and conventions of the TV family sitcom. Tracing the shifting meanings of reality over three decades, Kompare shows that these programs are simultaneously alike and unalike, to the extent that the "real" family is produced and understood within shifting codes and conventions.

Industry

The essays in part II of this book look at the industrial and commercial contexts that spawned and spread the reality TV genre. In chapter 6, Chad Raphael explores the economic origins of reality TV by revisiting the specific factors—union battles, deregulation, increasing competition from cable stations, and financial scarcity—that led networks in the 1980s to air more nonfiction programs such as *COPS* and *Unsolved Mysteries.* Tracing such factors through the 1990s, Raphael disputes the myth that audience demands are responsible for the growth of reality TV and demonstrates just how central political-economic forces have been in its development.

In chapter 7, Ted Magder picks up where Raphael leaves off, focusing on the wave of reality programs that first appeared in the summer of 2000 and their effect on the television industry. Updating his original 2004 essay, Magder identifies three unique reality business strategies that have altered the logic of TV production: the increased use of product placement, a strategy that aims to "brand" entertainment by inserting commercial messages within the television program; the expansion of merchandising tie-ins, such as the reality TV–inspired theme park attraction Fear Factor Live at Universal Studios Florida and Nestle's *American Idol* candy bars; and the extension of the program outside the confines of the television set through the use of the World Wide Web, iPods, DVRs, and other digital technologies. Magder also underscores the importance of European program suppliers who have provided the American market with many of the most successful multiplatform reality formats.

In chapter 8, Alison Hearn looks more in depth at the promotional logic of reality TV by analyzing the metanarrative running through hoax reality shows such as *Joe Schmo* and *My Big Fat Obnoxious Fiance,* which feature unwitting participants in "fake" reality programs set up to humiliate them. While these programs provide rich and often troubling social lessons and models of cultural power, Hearn focuses on how they also work as stories about the production of television itself and therefore reveal the medium's mode of production, commercial and promotional functions, and mechanism for the making of celebrities in an age of reality TV.

John McMurria in chapter 9 examines the global business of reality TV, tracing transnational majors behind its production and tracing the international flow of North American and European reality formats to

Asia, Africa, Latin America, and the Middle East. McMurria situates reality TV as a product of first-world commodity capitalism and a "global modernity" in which wealthy countries leverage economic and cultural power. At the same time, he documents the local and regional specificities of reality TV, showing how stock competitions like *Who Wants to Be a Millionaire* failed in Japan because they clashed with that country's values and how countries from China to Iraq have created their own deeply local reality shows, and how these cultural productions sometimes openly protest global geopolitics.

Culture and Power

In part III, we examine the power dynamics of reality television programming. Jon Kraszeweski's essay, chapter 10, situates reality television as a site of ideological maneuvers that, because they are couched in the discourse of the "real," can be difficult to discern. Focusing on the construction of racism in *The Real World*, Kraszewski contends that MTV's embrace of racial diversity is mediated and contained by an ideology of "enlightened racism." While the program invites racial controversy by casting politicized African Americans as housemates, the attempts of these characters to force awareness of structural inequalities are managed through editing and narrative conventions that emphasize personal friendships and confine the problem of racism to the ignorance of rural whites.

Laurie Ouellette's essay, chapter 11, analyzes reality TV as a technology of citizenship that governs indirectly, in sync with neoliberal discourses and policies. She argues that court programs like *Judge Judy* exemplify this trend by taking lower-income women caught in the drama of everyday life as the raw material from which to train television viewers to function without direct state intervention, as self-disciplining and "self-enterprising" citizens. Linking reality TV to a neoliberal conception of public service, Ouellette argues that programs like *Judge Judy* do not subvert elusive democratic ideals as much as they construct templates for citizenship that complement the privatization of public life, the collapse of the welfare state, and the discourse of individual choice and personal responsibility. In that way, *Judge Judy* established a "governmental" template for the numerous lifestyle interventions and makeovers in which judges evaluate and attempt to correct real people's everyday conduct and behavior.

In chapter 12, Heather Hendershot analyzes the labor politics of reality TV, extending the concern with the invisible production workers examined in part II to the celebrities and cultural intermediaries who perform on reality shows. From a "strategic" hot tub soak on a dating competition to the mental tasks performed on *The Apprentice,* reality TV participants are compelled to turn every dimension of their on-camera lives into labor. Paris Hilton and Nicole Ritchie of *The Simple Life* are important exceptions; as representatives of the celebrity leisure class, their job is to model the antithesis of a "belabored" work ethic. If *The Simple Life* reeks of static class privilege, talent-based programs like *Project Runway* exploit the "passion" associated with cultural and creative labor to reaffirm the myth of American meritocracy.

In chapter 13, Jonathan Gray details other myths at work in American culture and found in reality TV: those of heterosexual romance, gender, and dating. In placing current reality dating shows within a history of televised dating, Gray is able not only to reveal common features of the format across historical moments but also to explore the unique meanings and functions of shows such as *The Bachelor* and *Joe Millionaire.* Finding these programs to contain a complex interplay of gender performance, fairy tale, unruly women, and camp vulgarity, Gray argues that many viewers read these programs as carnivalesque, distancing themselves from the often repressive stereotypes of men, women, and romance that lie within.

The articulations of gender in reality TV is also a focus for Heather Osborne-Thompson in chapter 14. In reviewing reality-hybrid shows, such as *Fat Actress* and *Kathy Griffin: My Life on the D-list,* Osborne-Thompson finds that these programs tap into a long-standing connections between female comedians and the humiliation that is often inherent in their on-screen personae. After reviewing the complex history of female television comedians, Osborne-Thompson goes on to investigate the ways in which the generic hybridity of these recent texts works to further elucidate and complicate the relationship between gendered performance, humor, and the "real lives" of celebrities.

Interactivity

The essays assembled in part IV are united by a concern with reality TV's promise of turning viewers into active and "interactive" participants. Although written from different viewpoints, each essay takes the audience as the starting point from which to assess the meanings and implications of reality television.

In chapter 15, Amber Watts reminds us that interactivity is not a new thing for television, and neither are reality shows that focus on misery, pathos, or even humiliation. Watts details the history of postwar "audience participation shows" such as *Queen for a Day, The Big Payoff,* and *Strike It Rich,* which showcased struggling contestants who shared their hard-knock life stories in hopes of receiving consumer goods and services in exchange. Watts argues that the "lessons in self-reliance" that result from these shows serve to buttress particular social and political directives of the postwar period and played on anxieties about consumerism and financial security.

Mark Andrejevic in chapter 16 challenges the notion that reality TV "democratizes" culture by inviting the masses into the historically guarded realm of cultural production. Focusing on reality TV's confluence with on-air and off-air strategies of personal detection and surveillance, Andrejevic argues that the current wave of interactivity has been fused to voyeuristic practices that complement neoliberal security regimes. Reality TV shows like *Room Raiders, One Bad Trip,* and *Spying on Myself* invite us to play voyeuristic games of mutual monitoring, enlisting a new generation of digital devices to bring "do-it-yourself" policing techniques into our dating, parental, and other personal relationships. What Andrejevic calls the investigative subgenre of reality TV invites us to feel as if we are "savvy" and empowered individuals who are not duped by television or other powerful cultural institutions. At the same time, they bind us to new forms of surveillance and the governing rationalities they promote.

In chapter 17, Henry Jenkins demonstrates how developments in interactivity and branding have developed hand in hand, taking *American Idol* as a case study. According to Jenkins, TV executives and brand marketers covet "loyal" viewers who are deeply invested in a particular TV program, in the hopes that they will not channel surf and will develop similarly intense relationships to sponsored products. *American Idol* encourages such loyalty by allowing viewers to become active as contestants and as judges, and by integrating the serialized pleasures of the talent show with the branded "culture" of Coca-Cola, Ford, and other sponsors. Viewers are promised a meaningful stake in the cultural production of *American Idol* and other reality TV programs, and for this reason they may tolerate product placements and other integrated marketing ploys. By the same token, when interactivity is curtailed by corporate control (as was the case in the voting irregularities on *American Idol*), viewers may extend their frustrations to the corporate sponsors who comprise the "integrated" entertainment brand.

Together, the essays that follow enhance our understanding of reality television as a cultural form, an institutional and sociopolitical development, a representational practice, and a source of meaning and pleasure. Using various approaches, the authors in this book come to terms with these developments, enhancing our understanding not just of reality TV but of the emergent television culture that it represents. In addition to helping students, scholars, and viewers understand the reality TV phenomenon, we hope that the collection will stimulate further attention to the "remaking" of television culture that it has brought about.

NOTES

1. Bill Carter, "Reality TV Alters the Way TV Does Business," *New York Times*, 25 January 2003, A1.

2. Lynn Elber, "ABC Defends Increased Use of Reality TV," *Associated Press*, 15 January 2003.

3. Stella Bruzzi, *New Documentary: A Critical Introduction* (New York: Routledge, 2000), 255–59.

4. John Corner, "Performing the Real: Documentary Diversions," *Television and New Media* 2.3 (August 2002), 255–69.

5. Quoted in *Reality TV Magazine*, 13 September 2005, at www.realitytvmagazine.com.

6. Dean E. Murphy, "As Security Cameras Sprout, Someone's Always Watching," *New York Times*, 29 September 2002, A1.

7. Ibid.

8. For more on reality TV as social welfare, see Laurie Ouellette and James Hay, *Better Living through Reality TV: Television and Post-welfare Citizenship* (Malden, Mass.: Blackwell, 2008).

9. See Bertolt Brecht, *Brecht on Theatre*, ed. and trans. John Willett (New York: Hill and Wang, 1964), and Hans Magnus Enzensberger, "Constituents of a Theory of the Media," in *Video Culture*, ed. John Hanhardt (New York: Visual Studies Workshop Press, 1986), 96–123. For an overview of the history and goals of alternative television, see Dee Dee Halleck, "Towards a Popular Electronic Sphere, Or Options for Authentic Media Expression beyond *America's Funniest Home Videos*," in *A Tool, A Weapon, A Witness: The New Video News Crews*, ed. Mindy Faber (Chicago: Randolph Street Gallery, 1990), n.p.; Deirdre Boyle, "From Portapack to Camcorder: A Brief History of Guerrilla Television," *Journal of Film and*

Video 44.1–2 (1992), 67–79; William Boddy, "Alternative Television in the United States," *Screen* 31.1 (1991), 91–101; and Laurie Ouellette, "Will the Revolution Be Television? Camcorders, Activism and Alternative Television in the 1990s," in *Transmission: Toward a Post-Television Culture,* ed. Peter d"Agostino and David Tafler (Newbury Park: Sage, 1995), 165–87.

10. Sadie Benning is best known for her intimate autobiographical videos made with a Fisher-Price videocamera when she was a teenager in the 1990s. It was intensely personal when she addressed topics such as sexuality, abuse, homophobia, sexism, and racism.

Part I

Genre

"Stanley Milgram, Allen Funt, and Me"
Postwar Social Science and the
"First Wave" of Reality TV

Anna McCarthy

> I come more and more to think that TV's forte is as it
> plays on life and that . . . the make believe of drama
> strains the psychological and physical dimensions of the
> TV screen.
>
> —Charles Siepmann

Charles Siepmann, a professor of television studies at New York University, wrote the above note in response to a telecast of the Ford Foundation's prestigious arts and culture variety program *Omnibus* in 1954.[1] One of several in-house critics hired by *Omnibus*'s producer, Robert Saudek, Siepmann wrote weekly reviews of the 90-minute program for the entire 1954–55 season. The representation of "life" that drew his praise was a short, humorous hidden camera film called *Children of the U.N.* The film was shot at an international school in New York and featured interviews with and observational footage of children from around the world. One of several "candid films" made for the 1954–55 season of *Omnibus,* it was produced by Allen Funt, creator of the comedic hidden-camera program *Candid Camera* (1959–67).

Children of the U.N. was a timely social document. Airing on United Nations Day, it offered viewers, as *Omnibus* host Alistair Cooke noted, a glimpse of "a miniature international society . . . without protocol, and without taboos, but with a pride all its own." Funt's ability to communicate this idea of a microcosm of international relations was what stirred

Siepmann to state his preference for the aesthetics of actuality to those of drama on television.

This appreciative assessment is striking for several reasons. First, Siepmann seems at first to be an unlikely person to profess admiration for the work of Allen Funt. Siepmann was a TV blue blood. A former program director at the BBC, he was a staunch advocate of public service broadcasting—in fact, he was the primary author of the FCC's 1946 "Blue Book" outlining the public service responsibilities of U.S. broadcasters. In contrast, Funt is most often remembered as the lowbrow prankster *of Candid Camera* and its R-rated feature film spinoff, *What Do You Say to a Naked Lady.*

Second, the very fact that Funt's films appeared on *Omnibus* is itself notable. *Omnibus* was a program designed to appeal to "minority taste groups" with edifying presentations of learning and artistic genius. Even without the jokey sound effects that would later characterize Funt's candid camerawork, hidden camera films were a far cry from the typically didactic documentary fare the program offered, which ranged from recycled propaganda films for the U.S. Information Agency to industrial films to short human interest stories about people with unusual occupations, like tugboat captains.

Third, Siepmann's remarks on "TV's forte" are especially notable in light of prevailing definitions of "good television" at that time. This was a period when aesthetic ideals for television rested on the medium's ability to reproduce the conditions of live theater (the so-called Golden Age).

In 1954, before the quiz show scandals and the subsequent valuation of network documentary as the "oasis in the wasteland,"[2] it is striking to find a prominent advocate of high standards in television belittling "make believe" in favor of actuality programming. Siepmann's praise suggests that the reality genre's "first wave" might occupy a quite different relationship to the medium's aesthetic hierarchies than its current manifestations. Indeed, it implies that Funt, often hailed as reality TV's creative ancestor, belongs in the postwar pantheon of liberal-minded, aesthetically ambitious television pioneers such as Reginald Rose, Worthington Minor, Edward R. Murrow, and Robert Saudek.

If the hidden camera's view of social life provided Siepmann with an opportunity to articulate a realist ideal of television, it also provides a way of thinking about the cultural value, and social uses, of what might be called "reality television" before its (re)emergence in the 1990s. Reality television today is a cheap, endlessly recyclable, and licensable programming format, a product of the collapse of the three-network system and the rise of cable television and new networks like FOX.[3] But in the postwar period, Allen

Allen Funt (*right*) with Durwood Kirby on the set of *Candid Camera.*

Funt's covertly filmed records of real people in unusual situations were an esteemed form of culture. Even as critics condemned his work as an invasion of privacy, many agreed with sociologist David Riesman's assessment of Funt as the "second most ingenious sociologist in America" (after Paul Lazarsfeld).[4]

This assessment, widely cited in postwar analyses of Funt's work, suggest that the television programs and films that he made were, at least for some observers, a valuable and educational visual record, capable of providing a critical analysis of modern society within mass culture.[5]

The value of the hidden camera's social record for postwar observers lay in the way it could supplement liberal projects of reform and advocacy. Indeed, Funt's method was frequently cited or duplicated as a way of inculcating responsible forms of citizenship both domestically and internationally. The hidden camera could document the world of institutions, from the judiciary system to the mental hospital.[6] It could, moreover, present an image of planetary unity for Americans, an image that resonated strongly with centrist liberals of all political stripes in a period when U.S. foreign policy and international economic policy went global. And it could do so in ways that combined the powers of apparent "objectivity" with polemicism.

Thus, writing on Funt's *Children of the U.N.*, another of Saudek's hired reviewers, Ruth Sayers, commented on the "nice quiet vein of one-world propaganda running through it in an unobtrusive way."[7] The New York magazine *P.M.* had a similar view of Funt as a sociological spokesman for the liberal viewpoint, regularly reprinting transcripts from Funt's radio program *Candid Microphone* as illustrations of broader problems in U.S. society.[8] And Funt's status as privacy-busting truth teller led University of Chicago professor Richard Stern to immortalize him in the 1960 novel *Golk*, in which a morally ambiguous Funt-like figure uses his candid camera to expose corruption in the government. In these moments of engagement with Funt's work, the representation of real people through concealed observation on television is understood as working in the service of socially liberal models of culture.[9]

In what follows I situate this first wave of reality television in a broader context of popular and intellectual culture, examining the intersections between the realist capacity of the hidden camera as a potent tool for the production of social knowledge and the methods and techniques of social science. The kinds of social dramas that liberal media producers like Allen Funt played for laughs throughout the 1950s and 1960s were simultaneously raising deep moral questions for experimental social scientists like Yale's Stanley Milgram, the instigator of the ethically compromised obedience experiments. Milgram was only one of several social psychologists who turned to the work of Allen Funt as a template for their experimental situations and as a teaching tool in the classroom. Indeed, up to and including the broadcast of PBS's *An American Family*, a series Margaret Mead hailed as a social scientific breakthrough, reality television served as a place where popular culture and social science overlapped, via a realist ideal in which social norms, mechanisms of conformity, ritualized scripts, and modes of interaction were put on display.

It might be tempting to construct a narrative of decline in which this first wave of reality television, understood as unequivocally good, instructive, and socially progressive through its association with social science is replaced by the current wave of voyeuristic, theatrical, and exploitative formats and modes of address. But social scientists continue to serve as consultants in reality TV to this day, screening contestants for reality game shows like *Survivor* and *Big Brother* and helping to design situations and guidelines for interaction.

Similarly, reality TV producers then and now cross over into nonentertainment terrains of culture. Funt used his hidden camera skills to make industrial and training films for corporations in the 1950s and 1960s; *Survivor* producer Mark Burnett has a second career as a management consultant, serving as a motivational speaker in workshops designed to help brand managers and executives develop team-building skills to compete effectively in the corporate "jungle." In short, the stark differences in status and prestige accorded reality television in the 1950s and today should not obscure the fact that in both moments the genre occupies a privileged place in aesthetic discourses about the medium, and in each case it is a place where TV and social and applied psychology come together.

A preferable interpretation is to see each stage of reality TV's vision of social life as an expression of broader ideologies of citizenship. If, as Laurie Ouellette persuasively argues, reality genres today often serve a neoliberal cultural agenda that outsources the state's social functions (e.g., policing and social welfare) to popular media,[10] it is worth asking how the hidden camera's production of knowledge about ordinary people might have expressed models of civic responsibility and moral behavior in an earlier period. My reading of the close affinity between the first wave of reality TV and the scenarios played out in social psychology at that time proposes that both conform closely to a cold war elite understanding of the uses of visual culture.

For Allen Funt, Stanley Milgram, and others, covertly filmed behavior was a tool for teaching responsible citizenship on multiple scales, from the interpersonal to the institutional to the national. However, as will become evident, this thinking was beset by ongoing tensions between pedagogical presentation and sensational entertainment. As a visual document, the hidden camera's social scientific record seemed poised between fiction and reality; this equivocalism shaped popular and scholarly production, and reception, creating persistent dilemmas for those who would use it for broader purposes of social critique and knowledge production.

The Sociological Realism of Allen Funt

> The worst thing, and I see it over and over, is how easily people can be led by any kind of authority figure. . . .
> We need to develop ways to teach our children to resist unjust or ridiculous authority.
>
> —Allen Funt[11]

The emergence of deception and simulation as scientific tools—as means for exposing how real people really act—in both *Candid Camera* and the social psychology laboratory can be seen as part of two broader tendencies in art and science in the postwar decades. One was the development of realist aesthetic norms in postwar visual culture and their specific articulation in relation to television, a topic I sketch in this section as a context for understanding the way that tensions between science and art manifested themselves in the cultural phenomenon of *Candid Camera*.

The other, which I treat in the following section, is the rise of avant-garde thinking in areas of social and natural science dealing specifically with the unthinkable.[12] The latter concept, linked to horrific forms of state violence from the Holocaust to nuclear war, was the behavioral science preoccupation in which Milgram's horrific experiments at Yale emerged.

The aesthetic values attached to Funt's work on *Omnibus* are fully in step with a broader discourse of television realism in the postwar period, one that was actually, despite Siepmann's separation of the two, quite compatible with the Golden Age ideal of live drama. Hinging on the idea that TV could represent "ordinary" people better than any other medium, this discourse of social realism manifested in multiple sites, formats, and modes. Whereas today "real people" define the lowest of televisual forms, from the afternoon talk show to various reality genres, in the postwar period they defined what the medium could ideally accomplish.

This is evident in the neorealism-inspired social dramas written by playwrights like Paddy Chayefsky and the method-acting performance styles these dramas showcased. It is also an animating force in the work of Edward R. Murrow who, despite his enthronement in the pantheon of TV history for the low-rated though critically acclaimed *See It Now,* achieved most of his popular recognition in the early 1950s for the much more highly rated weekly program *Person to Person* (CBS). This show, which aired on Friday evenings, featured Murrow interviewing celebrities at home via live remote. Hailed for its ability to show the real person behind the celebrity, *Person to Person* can be thought of as the unacknowledged precursor of "celebrity at home" reality programs like *Cribs* (MTV) and *The Osbournes* (MTV).

Thus, although he disparaged drama, Siepmann's comments on the hidden-camera film's ability to record social life and, by extension, to represent people as they actually *are* should be interpreted as an expression of the postwar realist sensibility towards which all television—both fictional and nonfictional, should strive.

Underlying this realist sensibility is an aesthetic ideal in which the theatrical and the everyday converge, although how that convergence might be accomplished was not always clear. The difficulty of balancing the two is evident in Siepmann's comments on a second Funt film for *Omnibus, Jury Duty*, in which the hidden camera investigated the social world of the judiciary system. This film dwelled at length on the arguments ordinary people made in order to get out of jury duty, and it showed viewers the difficulties faced by judges and other legal workers trying to select jurors. Siepmann's comments were generally positive. He commended Funt's efforts at depicting reality and, in particular, of exposing the hypocrisy of the judiciary system: "We mouth devotion to democracy and fairly run when called on to enact it."[13]

Like Siepmann, Ruth Sayers also praised this film: "Allen Funt's ability to give us a look-in on the real thing was never more effectively used. This slice of Americana had its connection with every viewer—and a moral to boot—which added depth to the very considerable interest of the feature." Sayers's assessment of the film emphasized "the *honesty* of the piece—the obvious fact that it was not being done for television but that we were being allowed to spy on some actual occurrences."[14]

For Siepmann, however, this honesty was insufficiently compelling, and he criticized the film's visual flaws and lack of editing: "The realism had interest but it lacked art." In the end, real people's appearances on television needed to be shepherded by the hand of the artist. Siepmann unfavorably compared Funt to Murrow, who managed to do a "skilled and remorseless job of refining out the dross."[15]

The difficulty that the candid film faced on television, in other words, was its tendency to lapse into an overly sociological, noninterventionist mode of representation. In fact, this was Funt's ideal for what *Candid Camera* could achieve. His own evaluation of his work tended to bemoan the necessity for deception and manipulation that made the program more suitable for prime-time TV. If left to his own devices, he would have spent his time producing an unadulterated record of the social—indeed, his aesthetic preferences leaned toward a nascent form of cinema verité.

In his 1952 book *Eavesdropper at Large*, Funt noted that "the reflection of life through a camera lens without interpretation, without individual expression, is something less than real art, say some critics." Countering with the idea that the selection of material itself constitutes a form of art, Funt proposed that "both sides of this argument can be applied to a comparison of creative drama and real life drama. . . . Whether or not candid speech is artistic, I confess it has great appeal to me."[16] The appeal, for Funt, was the way that "real-life drama" revealed the ever-changing scenery and natural resources of the human mind."[17] What he wanted to show the public was "'pure' situations, where the subjects are relatively unprovoked . . . or on 'mood spots' (a father telling his child a bedtime story, children playing with a kitten)."[18]

Funt thus saw himself as both an aesthetic pioneer in the realm of minimalist realism and a social scientist. In both capacities he had lofty goals for the social impact of the hidden camera. Indeed, he thought of this impact in therapeutic terms. In a 1976 interview he told social psychologist Philip Zimbardo, "I wish I could use *Candid Camera*'s humanness and non-threatening approach to help parents, teachers, or salespeople reexamine what they are doing to learn from their mistakes."[19]

This sense of the camera as a social tool led Funt into consulting work for psychologists in the 1950s, when *Candid Camera* was only sporadically on the air. Noting this sideline, a *New Yorker* profile went on to describe other projects that Funt hoped might have a social impact: "One of his proudest experiments was a hidden camera study of disturbed children under clinical observation. A cherished objective of his was, and still is, a full-length 'Candid' film depicting the working day of an average twentieth century American. . . . Another was somehow to employ his camera with the educational aim of breaking down harmful national stereotypes."[20] In these aspirations for his candid camerawork, Funt expressed an ideal of the hidden camera as a tool for advocacy social science; if it was art, it was art with a larger, liberal-reformist social purpose.

This advocacy orientation makes the uses of Funt's films on *Omnibus* seem less incongruous, for *Omnibus* was itself founded on an instrumental model of culture, one in which ideals of informed, responsible citizenship were fully active.[21] *Omnibus* viewers were understood to be interested in bettering themselves through exposure to American and foreign forms of high culture, educational and didactic presentations of national and world history, and work being done on the frontiers of science. This construction of the audience and the programming decisions that emerged from it reflected the broader cultural mission of the Ford Foundation in the postwar period, when it expanded from its original role as a local philanthropical concern in Michigan and became the largest foundation in the world. In the first decade or so of its operations, the foundation obeyed the dictates of its 1949 mission document, the so-called Gaither Report, which specified a very particular, highly instrumentalist understanding of the purpose of funding cultural programs.

For example, a discussion of the need for liberal education to "train youth for better citizenship" includes among the tools for attaining "the balance necessary to live integrated and purposeful lives" the goal of assisting individuals "to acquire tastes for literature, music, and the arts."[22] *Omnibus* and the Television-Radio Workshop that produced it represented one such method of assistance. As the 1952 press materials for the program's inauguration explained, the Workshop was established "as the first major implementation of a mandate of the [Ford Foundation] trustees that 'the Foundation will support activities directed toward the effective use of mass media for non-academic education and for better utilization of leisure time for all age groups.'"[23] Culture, from the perspective of the Ford Foundation, was all about producing an American populace capable of stepping up to the challenge of citizenship in an internationalist United States.

Funt's use of the hidden camera to expose the mechanisms, behaviors, and rituals of everyday interaction was fully in step with the ways in which *Omnibus* presented high culture to its imagined audience of aspirants. Both hinged on the mode of address Neil Harris calls "the operational aesthetic."[24] Like the displays of P. T. Barnum, in whose work Harris identifies the formation of the operational aesthetic's simultaneously didactic and sensationalist appeals to its viewer, *Candid Camera* and *Omnibus* sought to both educate and entertain. *Omnibus* translated classics of Western art, literature, and learning into a commercially sponsorable and popularly palatable form; Saudek worked hard to make the arcane accessible to a mass audience.

Funt similarly endeavored to show how ordinary social situations work and (à la Barnum) how hoaxes are staged, without diminishing the powers of technological surveillance and deception in the process. The operational aesthetic was thus integral to the representation of social reality and the promotion of citizenship ideals via artistic representation and via a popular social science interested in norms of behavior and the extent to which individuals will work to maintain them.

If both *Omnibus* and the candid film were poised between theatricality and pedagogy as modes of address, the history of Funt's transition to prime time suggests that the wider circulation of his work required the subordination of the pedagogy to the theater. *Candid Camera* entered CBS's prime-time lineup in the 1960s, airing on Sunday evening immediately before another sociological TV classic, *What's My Line*. But the network insisted that the show have a more "show biz" host. It hired Arthur Godfrey as the front person communicating with the audience and relegated Funt to the role of onscreen prankster.

Another significant theatricalization occurred when the show entered prime time. In the 1962–63 season, Funt hired dramatist and *Omnibus* veteran William Saroyan, possibly at the instigation of *Candid Camera*'s producer Bob Banner, who had worked as a director on *Omnibus*. Named "writer in residence," Saroyan was hired to create sketches for actors to perform; Funt would then try to duplicate the social situations Saroyan created in his interactions with people on the street. Saroyan's remarks on the show indicate the affinities between hidden camerawork and naturalistic television theater: "It shows people who don't know they're being watched. And that's the essence of drama, isn't it?" The point of using both modes of presentation, according to *Newsweek*, was "to compare fiction and reality."[25]

The idea of comparing reality and fiction strengthened the show's reliance on the operational aesthetic. It engaged the spectator on the level of both *spectacle*—showing real people in unusual situations—and pedagogy, thereby inviting viewers to contrast drama and real life, presumably as a way of understanding the extent to which codes of fiction depart from the social world they represent.

As a form of popular social science, blending educational and entertaining elements, *Candid Camera* quickly attracted the attention of social scientists themselves. The points of institutional, biographical, and intellectual contact between social scientists and Allen Funt are numerous. James Maas of Cornell University's psychology department persuaded Funt, an alumnus, to donate film segments from *Candid Camera* to the university, for distribution to psychology departments across the country. Maas was the first of several social scientists to publish essays on the value of *Candid Camera* as an educational tool for social psychology.

Two other prominent—if ethically compromised—social scientists also expressed their admiration for Funt as an amateur experimentalist. In the 1970s, Stanley Milgram coauthored an essay on *Candid Camera* as a form of social science with one of his graduate students.[26] And Philip Zimbardo, the psychologist who created a mock prison using Stanford University students as guards and prisoners, was particularly close to Funt, collaborating with him on a series of classroom films called *Discovering*

Psychology. For Zimbardo there was a concise patrilineal explanation for the intellectual affinity between *Candid Camera* and experimental social science. Noting that Funt was an undergraduate research assistant for social psychologist Kurt Lewin's famous experiments on mother-infant interactions, Zimbardo described Lewin as "the intellectual grandfather of Stanley Milgram, Allen Funt, [and] me."[27]

As suggested in the next section, the continuities between Funt's social scientific vision and that of men like Milgram and Zimbardo goes beyond their genealogical connection to Kurt Lewin. Rather, these men shared a sense of theatricality, simulation, and dissimulation as necessary tools for understanding the complex dimensions of human behavior in modern society. Each saw techniques of deception as components of empirical investigation, and each articulated a working model of realist representation as the foundation for such investigations.

But what were the broader circumstances that made it possible for intellectuals engaged in politically motivated, if ethically unconscionable, empirical research to locate the imaginative horizons of their work in the world of popular entertainment? One suggestive coincidence offers a way into the answer to this question. Both Allen Funt and Stanley Milgram received money from the Ford Foundation in 1955. Funt's check was payment for his *Omnibus* films; Milgram's was a stipend. Like many graduate students in psychology in this period, Milgram was the recipient of one of the fellowships created by the foundation to strengthen the behavioral sciences in the 1950s.

Milgram went to Harvard to study conformity with Solomon Asch. Under Asch's guidance, he instigated the first of the many experimental practical jokes through which he would investigate social norms: a comparative study of conformity mechanisms in the United States, Norway, and France. Milgram staged an experimental group situation in which he led unwitting subjects to agree with the statements of others in the group even though they were obviously incorrect.

This was the kind of situation that Funt would dramatize many times over in his candid camerawork. In the TV version, for example, he posed as a public opinion researcher and solicited emphatic opinions on a non-existent TV program called *Space Doctor* from people on the street. In *What Do You Say to a Naked Lady,* his hidden camera filmed a roomful of men, all but one of them hired as plants, waiting for a job interview. When the plants started taking off their clothes, the "mark," bewildered but resigned, removed his, too. This was the kind of observational revelation that Milgram particularly admired. In the 1970s, when choosing *Candid Camera* films from the Cornell catalogue in preparation for his article on the program's social scientific value, Milgram selected the *Space Doctor* segment for further analysis.[28]

Social scientists' infatuation with *Candid Camera* must be understood in the context of the behavioral sciences in the postwar period. These years saw the emergence of a liberal social science in which the predictability of human behavior was a matter of heavily funded research, as well as popular ethical discourse. It was a moment in which role-playing and deception seemed utterly necessary as research techniques and methods. Alongside mainstream approaches to social psychological problems, like attitude change, the Ford Foundation was placing a great deal of money into the emerging field of "systems research" in the behavioral sciences.

As a model of totality, systems research was thoroughly compatible with cold war scientific programs, especially those involved in the global threat posed by nuclear war. It was thus integral to the social and natural science projects funded by the defense department, as Sharon Ghamari-Tabrizi shows in her fascinating study of the culture of war gaming at the RAND Corporation during this period. As she notes, this was a moment in which civilian defense intellectuals like Herman Kahn, in many ways the avant-garde of the behavioral and physical sciences, began to use simulation as a problem-solving tool. Simulation, in the kinds of projects undertaken at the RAND Corporation, was not just a technique for modeling ideas but was a means for producing new knowledge. Anti-empirical skills like "intuition, insight, discretion, and artistry" were essential, given that there was no empirical way to test the validity of the "data" produced in simulated exercises of thermonuclear war.[29] Because of the need to be able to organize and depend on the actions of the citizenry if the bomb were to be dropped, behavior prediction and control was important for this culture of civilian war modelers.

At the same time that men like Kahn were bringing games and simulations to the Defense Department, liberal intellectuals like Milgram set a different agenda for behavioral research through simulation. The legacy of the Holocaust, coupled with McCarthyism's effects on political culture and the recent exposure of Stalinist atrocities, created a need to understand how ordinary people could commit unconscionable and frequently horrific acts as part of the bureaucratized hierarchies of the state. For Milgram, deceptive games were a necessary tool for probing the dynamics of human behavior in situations of perceived social threat.

As discussed, ordinary people were crucial to Funt's work, as they allowed him to position his films as a documentary corollary to the socially realist drama of the Golden Age and as part of the entertaining pedagogy of the operational aesthetic. For Milgram, similarly, the behaviors of what Funt called "the average man in a crisis"[30] was central to his research program. Only by using the most "ordinary" of subjects could he understand the social processes of obedience that enable the perpetration of large-scale atrocities. It was the very ordinariness of Milgram's subjects that demonstrated to the citizens of an era haunted by authoritarianism's effects that there is no such thing as an authoritarian personality. Rather, in situations where individuals believe they have no power, Milgram concluded, most people are capable of committing acts that are unthinkable to them under ordinary circumstances.

It was not possible to re-create the Holocaust in the laboratory in order to study the social relations that allowed it to continue and grow, but it was possible, through simulation, to re-create situations in which these relations could be studied. As the next section proposes, the methodology of *Candid Camera,* taken to an unethical extreme, helped define the structure of Milgram's simulated interaction between the state and its citizens.

Candid Compliance: Milgram's Experimental Film

> Whether all this points to significant social science or
> merely good theater is an open question.
> —Stanley Milgram, notes on the *Obedience* experiments, 1962[31]

As the above quotation illustrates, the same tensions between pedagogy and sensationalism that marked Funt's work were present in Milgram's, too. Much as Funt found himself wondering whether *Candid Camera* could really be considered art, Milgram found himself wondering whether his experiments could legitimately be called science.

These experiments, which are considered one of the most notorious experiments in the history of social psychology, were devised to test how far people would go in obeying orders. They were indeed highly theatrical. Using actors, props, a script, and an artificial laboratory setting, Milgram deceived human subjects into believing that they were administering punitive electric shocks to other participants, ostensibly as part of a Yale University experiment on the role of pain in the learning process.

But although he used the term "theater," the kind of deception that Milgram carried out was more directly reminiscent of Funt's popular sociology. Like *Candid Camera*, the deception rested on a misleading scenario. And like many segments of the highly popular program, it was structured as a macabre practical joke.

To create the impression that subjects were participating in an experiment on learning, Milgram hired an actor to play the part of a scientist in a white coat. A second actor played the part of another subject, the "learner." The subjects, the so-called naive participants who came to Milgram's lab, were asked to administer a memorization test to the learner. When the learner gave the wrong answer, the subject was instructed to correct the learner and reinforce the point by pressing a lever on a formidable-looking technical apparatus that would, they were told, deliver an electric shock. The shock levels increased as the experiment wore on, as did the frequency of wrong answers. Eventually, the subjects heard the learner register vocal protest and injury with every shock (his cries of pain were recorded on tape and played back to minimize the impact of performance variables on the experiment). At this point, thinking that they were causing harm, most subjects refused to participate further in the "experiment." But once the "experimenter" pressured them to continue, almost two-thirds of the subjects did so. Although it caused them obvious distress, they administered increasingly higher shocks as the learner's cries grew louder, and even after the learner fell completely silent.

The theatrical nature of this research situation fascinated Milgram. The experiments, he felt, derived their "drawing power" from their "artistic, non-scientific component."[32] Indeed, this sense of theatricality was so strong that he made a documentary about them, using hidden-camera footage. *Obedience* (1965), an audiovisual mainstay of the psychology classroom, was the first of six films he would make before his death at the age of 51. In fact, he took classes in film production in the 1970s and eventually included the title "filmmaker" in his professional biography.[33]

While conceiving of *Obedience*, Milgram must have recognized the ethical problems attendant on the visual experience of the experiments in action, which after all involved seeing people in obvious psychological distress complying unwillingly with orders to hurt another person. This may explain why his 1962 speculations on the question of art versus science concluded with a musing that reflects both his anticipation of the experiment's notoriety and a sense of himself as a historical figure—a misunderstood genius: "It is possible that the kind of understanding of man

I seek is an amalgam of science and art. It is sure to be rejected by the scientists as well as the artists, but for me it carries significance."[34]

In making the film, Milgram sought to synthesize and manage the theatrical and the pedagogical, the art and the science, perhaps in order to cement his place in the pantheon of genius. In the end, he merely mapped the two tendencies on the soundtrack and the image, respectively. He recorded an extensive voice-over commentary that outlined the experiments and their social and moral significance for the viewer, but he also hired a Harvard University graduate with strong aspirations in the area of narrative filmmaking to select and edit the footage. This assistant, Christopher Johnson, viewed all the raw footage and gave Milgram his handwritten notes on the performances of the various subjects. Essentially, he treated the hidden-camera film as a screen test and saw himself as "casting" the film. Johnson's notes focused exclusively on the theatricality of the interactions and performances on screen. One man, for example, is characterized as "reeking of obedience . . . cringing look." Johnson noted details like a subject's "nervous smile" or the "learner's" gaffes ("he doesn't yell right").[35]

Watching the film, it is hard not to think of *Candid Camera* as its closest intertext. Although Milgram's personal papers, housed in Yale University's Sterling Library, are voluminous and complete, they do not contain any direct evidence that Milgram modeled the experiment, and the film based on it, on Funt's work. However, they offer plenty of direct material in which to read the points of commonality between the two men's projects. The overlap between the obedience experiments and *Candid Camera* extends beyond their structural similarity—the fact that both created situations in which unwitting individuals are observed responding to, and performing within, unusual or extreme social situations—and even their dependence on ordinary people.

Perhaps the most obvious parallel is the way that *Obedience* is structured. This is the fact that both end with a moment of unmasking—a return to "normalcy" that Funt called "the reveal" and which he communicated to his subjects with the trademark phrase, "Smile, you're on *Candid Camera!*" Milgram integrated a similar, though obviously less jocular, moment of revelation into the end of the experiment. Once the subject either refused to participate any further or, in the case of the majority, continued to administer electrical shocks to the "learner" up to the highest level, Milgram would enter the room. Much like a bearded, academic-looking version of Funt, he informed the subject that the situation was contrived and that the electric shocks were simulated. A "debriefing" followed, in which subjects discussed their responses to the situation with Milgram. Finally, to dispel any residual misunderstanding, the putative "victim" joined Milgram and the subject and confirmed that he was an actor and that he had not received any shocks.

In the film, the reveal is not a moment of levity, although the film's subjects nevertheless uncannily replicate the reactions of the subjects recorded by Funt's camera. As Funt noted in his autobiography, "marks" tended to conceal their surprise when informed that they have been filmed. Milgram's on-camera participants adopted a similarly guarded nonchalance, merely nodding or saying "oh" when informed of the real experiment in which they had participated. In the script of the film, Milgram asks one man, on camera, whether he objected to the hidden-camera film being shown to other psychologists and students. The man defers at first, and it seems likely that *Candid Camera* is on his mind when he asks whether "my face is nationwide or something." When reassured that this will not be the case, he agrees.[36]

The common structure of the reveal is an important element of the experiment's pedagogical program. As Funt pointed out, the reveal is itself a form of social pressure, as it asks the victim to accept his or her deception and be a "good sport."[37] The reveal also exploits the conventions of the operational aesthetic—unmasking the hoax is a way of affirming the fact that it was mounted not out of cruelty or sadism but in the interest of knowledge.

The similarities between Funt's reveal and the experimental debriefing were not lost on Milgram, although he seems to have been unable to reconcile himself to the parallel. A decade after he completed the film, Milgram coauthored an essay on *Candid Camera* with John Sabini, who had studied under Milgram at the City University of New York's Graduate Center and was then a professor at the University of Pennsylvania. In his hurriedly penned notes for this project, Sabini recorded extended observations on the social scientific function of Funt's reveal as "formally analogous to the experimental debriefing."[38] Nevertheless, despite the fact that Sabini spent some time articulating this point, it may have resonated a little too strongly with Milgram, given the criticisms of his work's ethical implications in human subjects research. The point did not appear in the final essay.[39]

For Milgram, to compare *Obedience* and *Candid Camera* would be to expose the possibility that something entertaining existed in the horrifying image of coercion and cruelty. Still, in his notes on the experiment, Milgram spent as much time thinking about their staging and dramatic effects as he did about their broader moral and scientific implications. These notes show that Milgram clearly relished planning the mise-en-scène details of the situation he was setting up. This relish is apparent in the great attention he lavished on the design of the simulated shock generator, making several detailed drawings of it—at least four—in the experimental setting.

More disturbingly, Milgram's desire for verisimilitude meant that he spent significant time wondering how to produce a convincing audio impression of physical pain for the experiment. In April 1961, he wrote a note to himself considering the possibility of contacting two other psychologists who were using real electrical shocks in their work on "traumatic avoidance conditioning" to see if it would be possible to borrow "good recordings of a persons [*sic*] vocal response to high level electric shock."[40] Even more horrifyingly, he considered producing a test of the experiment using *actual* victims and real electrical current. His interest in doing this was expressed in purely clinical terms: "This might be quite interesting in seeing how persons actually react as victims."[41]

This is also why Milgram might have avoided the comparison between his own work and Funt's in his 1979 essay coauthored with Sabini; it suggested that the experiments could easily be interpreted as a sick joke. Like a cruel prank, the experiments relied on Milgram's emotional distance from the struggles of his subjects in the laboratory. This sense of detachment was something Milgram noticed in himself and in the others who viewed the experiment in action. In particular, he was very curious about the ways that the experiment, when viewed, produced laughter—often hysterical laughter—among those who viewed it.[42] But although this would have been an obvious point to bring up in his essay on *Candid Camera*, the comparison between Funt's audience reactions and Milgram's is significantly absent from the piece.

Despite what seems to be a clear attempt to "de-sensationalize" *Obedience* by avoiding comparisons with *Candid Camera*, media producers were immediately drawn to the former's sensationalist representation of real people. After he completed *Obedience*, Milgram found himself negotiating repeatedly with TV corporations interested in broadcasting his film. In 1969, several producers from Canada contacted him for this purpose, citing its ethical relevance to the emerging evidence of U.S. military atrocities in Vietnam. Milgram at first denied these requests because showing them on English-language stations would have violated the privacy of his subjects.

But as time went on, he was more and more liberal in granting rights to the film and in abetting the sensationalization of his work. He did not hesitate to grant permission to use the film to television producers in Italy and Germany in the 1960s and, according to Sabini, he allowed *60 Minutes* to air the film in the 1970s. In this broadcast, apparently the first in the United States, Milgram insisted that only the compliant subject segments be shown. This was because those in which subjects defied the orders showed how easy it would have been to disobey—a revelation that Milgram felt would have been psychologically damaging and socially stigmatizing for those subjects who complied.[43]

Of course, these compliance segments are also the most suspenseful and sensationalist elements of the film. Milgram's evident willingness to exploit the theatricality of his work is evident in the fact that in the same period, he served as a consultant for the 1975 CBS TV movie based on the experiments. Called *The Tenth Level*, it starred William Shatner as Milgram and interspersed the story of Milgram's experiments with a romantic subplot. The week it aired, *TV Guide* featured an article by Milgram, explaining his thinking and the broader ethical and moral implications of the work.[44]

The media afterlife of the obedience experiments in the 1970s suggests that Stanley Milgram should join Funt as ancestral figure in the genealogy of reality television. Indeed, Milgram's work seems closer to the contemporary hidden-camera genres than Funt's. In popularizing his experiments on TV, Milgram might have seen himself as a crusader, educating the populace about the microlevel operations of totalitarianism, but these broadcasts exhibited a cruel and exploitative disregard for those unwitting subjects he deceived and covertly filmed. Moreover, the extreme nature of the *Obedience* situation, quite different from the routine institutional worlds that Funt placed under the microscope in films like *Jury Duty*, makes them far closer to contemporary reality programs than Funt's observational realism.

But Milgram merely extended the theatrical and sensational tendencies that were present in Funt's work, too. Potentially, all observational footage of ordinary people can be appropriated within other genres and modes of address. The PBS program *An American Family*—surely the type of purely observational, nondeceptive documentary that Funt valued most—may have been conceived within the postwar liberal project of displaying the everyday lives of ordinary citizens, but this did not prevent critics from seeing it as a "soap opera."

Social Scientific Theater Today

The shift toward the criminalizing and conservative visions of law and order that defined the rise of reality television at the end of the 1990s is not so much the triumph of the sensational over the pedagogical as it is the transformation of the political imaginary underlying the depiction of ordinary citizens on television.

Just as electoral politics and dramatic TV programming took a "right turn" in this period, so did the citizenly uses of the real-life dramas of the hidden camera. It is a testimony to the changing cultural role of experimental social psychology that Zimbardo, once regularly quoted as a consultant in prison reform because of his notorious and ethically compromised Stanford prison experiment, is now far more likely to appear in print as a commentator on, and even as a consultant to, new reality TV programs.

An August 2000 *New York Times,* article titled "Hey, What if Contestants Give Each Other Shocks?" compares social psychology to reality TV, although it stressed that—unlike reality television producers—Milgram, Zimbardo, and others "had noble aspirations."[45] This recognition of the obedience experiments as reality television's ancestors would surely have pleased Milgram, who told a researcher in 1974 that he was blessed with something he called "prescient ability" and claimed that many of his randomly jotted, undeveloped ideas regularly showed up in the work of others decades later.[46]

Indeed, his sick jokes live on in today's reality TV generation, where pranksters portray average citizens as mooks and buffoons, and critics bemoan the fact that people respond with homemade pratfall videotapes of their own. Tom Green, Johnny Knoxville, and the creators of *The Man Show,* who once used a hidden camera to capture mensroom visitors fishing a $20 bill out of a loaded toilet, might want to add Milgram's name to the credits.

NOTES

I am grateful to Susan Murray, Laurie Ouellette, Sharon Ghamari-Tabrizi, Torey Liepa, Meghan Sutherland, and the staff of the Wesleyan Cinema Archives and Yale University's Sterling Memorial Library for their help in the research and writing of this essay.

    1. Wesleyan Cinema Archives Omnibus Collection (henceforth WCA–OC), series 4, box 18, folder 801.

2. This was the title of a *Commonweal* article (6 October 1961, 30) on *Walk in My Shoes,* Bell and Howell's 1961 ABC documentary on black life in the United States.

3. See Chad Raphael, chapter 6 in this volume.

4. For example, J. M. Flagler, "Student of the Spontaneous," *New Yorker,* 10 December 1960, 59–72.

5. David Riesman (with Nathan Glazer and Reuel Denney), *The Lonely Crowd: A Study of the Changing American Character* (New Haven, Conn.: Yale University Press, 1950).

6. The film about mental hospitals was *Out of Darkness,* a CBS documentary that aired 18 March 1956.

7. WCA–OC, series 4, box 18, folder 798.

8. Flagler, "Student of the Spontaneous," 84.

9. On the broader cultural implications of technological observation in relation to *Candid Camera,* see Andrew Ross, *No Respect: Intellectuals and Popular Culture* (New York: Routledge, 1989), 105–7.

10. See Laurie Ouellette, chapter 11 in this volume.

11. Quoted in Philip Zimbardo, "Laugh Where We Must, Be Candid Where We Can," *Psychology Today* 119 (June 1985), 47.

12. Sharon Ghamari-Tabrizi, "Simulating the Unthinkable," *Social Studies of Science* (April 2000), 163–223.

13. WCA–OC, series 4, box 18, folder 801.

14. Ibid., folder 798.

15. Ibid., folder 801.

16. Allen Funt, *Eavesdropper at Large* (New York: Vanguard, 1952), 128.

17. Flagler, "Student of the Spontaneous," 59–60.

18. Ibid., 64.

19. Quoted in Zimbardo, "Laugh Where We Must," 47.

20. Flagler, "Student of the Spontaneous," 82.

21. Saudek notes, WCA–OC, series 1, box A.

22. Ford Foundation, *Report of the Study for the Ford Foundation on Policy and Programs* (Detroit, 1949), 40.

23. WCA–OC, series 1, box A.

24. Neil Harris, *Humbug: The Art of P. T. Barnum* (Boston: Little, Brown, 1973), chapter 3.

25. "Time of His Life," *Newsweek,* 10 September 1962, 94.

26. Stanley Milgram and John Sabini, "Candid Camera," *Society* 16 (1979), 72–75.

27. Philip G. Zimbardo, Christina Maslach, and Craig Haney. "Reflections on the Stanford Prison Experiment: Genesis, Transformations, Consequences," in *Obedience to Authority: Current Perspectives on the Milgram Paradigm,* ed. Thomas Blass (Mahwah, N.J.: Lawrence Erlbaum Associates, 2000), 197–98.

28. Cornell University Catalog of *Candid Camera* Films. Milgram's annotated copy is in the Stanley Milgram Papers, Sterling Memorial Library, Yale University (hereafter MP), box 66, folder 208.

29. Sharon Ghamari-Tabrizi, *The Worlds of Herman Kahn: The Intuitive Science of Thermonuclear War* (Cambridge: Harvard University Press, 2005).

30. Funt, *Eavesdropper at Large,* 29.

31. MP, box 46, folder 164.

32. Ibid.

33. Thomas Blass, personal communication.

34. MP, box 46, folder 164.

35. Ibid., box 76, folder 440.

36. Ibid.,folder 439.

37. Quoted in Zimbardo, "Laugh Where We Must," 47.

38. MP, box 66, folder 209.

39. John Sabini, phone interview with the author, 29 October 2002.

40. MP, box 46, folder 165.

41. Ibid.

42. Ibid., folder 163. For a fascinating discussion of inappropriate humor in the postwar scientific avant-garde, see Ghamari-Tabrizi's work.

43. Sabini, phone interview.

44. "Obedience to Authority," *TV Guide,* 21 August 1976, 24.

45. Erica Goode, "Hey, What if Contestants Give Each Other Shocks?" *New York Times,* 27 August 2000, 3.

46. Carol Tavris, "Man of a Thousand Ideas," *Psychology Today* (1979), 74.

2

|||||||||||||||||||||||||||||||||||||||||||||||||||||

Performing the Real
Documentary Diversions

John Corner

Where do we locate *Big Brother,* and the shift in the relationship between television and everyday life that it signals, within the generic system of the medium? This generic system is not, as we know, a neat and stable set of discrete categories of work. It is a changing and increasingly hybridized set of practices, forms, and functions, one in which both cultural and commodity values lie most often in the right blend of the familiar and the new, of fulfilled expectation and shock.

We might place *Big Brother* within the history of the game show—this would certainly be true to some of its ingredients and part of its appeal. Location with the history of the talk show, particularly in its newer variants of revelation and confrontation, would be instructive, too. At times, the tones and values of a "Jerry Springer experience" are closely shadowed. We might see it as an experiment in a kind of drama—a less direct connection perhaps, but questions of theatricality and the performance aesthetic nevertheless hold the possibility of illuminating some of its shape and impact.

However, "documentary" is the category that seems most obvious to start with and work from. This, despite the clear disjunction between the terms of the series and those even of most other types of "reality TV" variant on the observational documentary model, let alone those of the more established, mainstream formats. For it is clear that right at the heart of the series is the idea of observing what is a mode of "real" behavior. Such observation finds its grounding reference, and a large part of its interest and pleasure, in the real characteristics of real people, even if the material and temporal conditions for that behavior have been entirely constructed by television itself. *Big Brother* comprehensively and openly gives up on the kinds of "field naturalism" that have driven the documentary tradition into so many contradictions and conundrums for near on 80 years, most especially in its various modes of observational filming (e.g., cinema verité, direct cinema, and the various bastardized "fly-on-the-wall" recipes of television). Instead, *Big Brother* operates its claims to the real within a fully managed artificiality, in which almost everything that might be deemed to be true about what people do and say is necessarily and obviously predicated on the larger contrivance of their being in front of the camera in the first place. Documentary has a lengthy and various history of concern for the historical and social world, the imaging of which in terms of followable and significant action (even for the duration of a scene) continues to pose considerable problems of accessibility and scopic coherence, despite new technology.

Alongside this concern with the outer world, an interest in inner stories has developed, too, particularly in the last decade of work on television. The development of inner stories often requires extensive use of interview and sometimes of part-dramatization to get the personal and the microsocial fully realized on the screen. The inner story (for example, about the road accident, about the crime, about the illness) has tended in some treatments to be pulled rather sharply away from its broader social conditions and contingencies. The documentary foreground has frequently become a highly defined narrative of localized feelings and experiences presented against what is often a merely sketchy if not entirely token background of social setting.

Clearly, both the changing formats of the talk show and the soap opera have mapped out in advance some elements of the "structure of feeling" (Raymond Williams's phrase is entirely appropriate to the affective emphasis) toward which a new documentary energy has been drawn. An adjustment in, as it were, the "focal length" of documentary has been required, together with a changed tonality of the documentary voice (quite literally, in the case of the registers required of commentary in routing us through inner stories with optimum satisfaction). The viewing invitation slides from the dynamics of understanding to the involving, but at the same time more passive, transaction of vicarious witness and empathy.

Big Brother in a sense takes the next logical step in this process and dispenses with the difficulties of extracting the personal from the social (e.g., all those problems about authenticity in docusoap, all that debate about "directorial intervention") by building its own social precisely for the purpose of revealing the personal. This social is comprehensively available to television; it has indeed been built for the daily delivery of behavior to camera.

Strictly speaking, then, the circumstances are not so much those of observation as those of display; living space is also performance space. The availability is both tightly spatial and urgently temporal, clearly. But it is also, in its scopic comprehensiveness, emotional. "Outside" and "inside," objectification and subjectification, empathy and detachment, fondness and dislike—these are positional variables on a spectatorial grid across which rapid switching can occur. The interplay between observed action, the "cameos" of to-camera participant testimony, and the framing of voiced-over commentary is the required communicational mix for delivering this form of viewing experience. The use of the Internet to extend further the public existence and availability of the event, to create optional and selective viewing opportunities "beyond the edges" of the television text itself, enhances the sense of a concurrent, live, and open narrative (perhaps previously most marked in sports coverage). It also provides another resource in exercising spectator control (voting participants off the show). Whereas George Orwell's *Big Brother* used surveillance to inhibit the terms of normal living in private space, TV's *Big Brother* promotes abnormal terms of living within surveillance space. Whatever the more serious justifications for this that may be advanced in self-justification (for a popular "experiment" in modern human interaction, a few hired psychologists always need to be on hand), the clear purpose of the whole microsocial event is to deliver fun.

Yet to say this does not amount to claiming that *Big Brother* is trying (and failing) to be a "proper documentary." That would be a wildly inaccurate misreading of its design and success, as well as begging big questions about what precisely constitutes the "proper." It is simply to suggest that in coming to terms with how the series works, we need to see how its practices, forms, and functions are placed within what I am calling the "postdocumentary" culture of television. We also need to note how, within that culture, the legacy of documentary is still at work, albeit in partial and revised form.

In this article, I develop some points about postdocumentary television as one way, among others, of approaching the new and entertaining forms of tele-factuality that will directly concern most other contributors to this volume. At stages, I will review and reconsider some of the elements of documentarism in its more established forms in order to plot more clearly the nature of current shifts.

We can start by reviewing the idea of "documentary" itself. As I suggest above, this might now be an unhelpful category with which to assess the changes occurring in factual television and particularly unhelpful in thinking about the new links between popular knowledge and audiovisual experience. The problem is that too many assumptions and, I think, too many idealizations have now gathered around the notions of the "social" and the "public," which the term mobilizes. Paradoxically, for us to understand much of the current change in television's factual output, the term needs pressing back toward the broader category of "documentation" from which it initially sprang (most explicitly, for Britain, in John Grierson's written advocacy of a documentary cinema during the early 1930s[1]). In doing this, we are not only going from narrowness to breadth, we are being descriptive rather than evaluative. We are trying to relocate the rich, generically ambitious (in some versions, rather preposterous) idea of documentary within the bewildering range of practices now available for depicting the real on screen, including the screen of the computer. *Big Brother* is just one particular, highly successful, formula within this range.

I have noted in recent writing[2] that the term "documentary" is always much safer when used as an adjective rather than as a noun, although its noun usage is, of course, a form of abbreviation, championed by the cinema pioneers and established through sheer familiarity. To ask "Is this a documentary project?" is more useful than to ask "Is this film a documentary?" with its inflection toward firm definitional criteria and the sense of something being more object than practice. This is particularly true of documentary work within television, and my feeling is that in the next few years it will become more obviously so. Documentary within cinema (in many countries now a marginal form, where it exists at all) still has the strong contrast with its dominant Other—feature film—against which it can be simply defined as "nonfiction." Television nonfiction describes half the schedule, and so the question of generic identifiers becomes immediately more troublesome. Before I address directly the question of change, and the sorts of change, like that indicated by *Big Brother,* which seem to warrant my postdocumentary label, I want to say a few things about documentary functions.

Documentary Functions

The functions of documentary work have been at least as important in its history and generic identity as its forms. Both function and form have an unstable, historically contingent character, but there has been enough broad continuity across national histories of media development for us to talk about a documentary tradition. One might introduce a third element here—production practices. Specific production practices, forms, and functions all work to hold together (or not) the documentary identity at different times and places. Briefly put, they concern how a film or program was made (according to what recipes, methods, and ethics), how it looks and sounds, and what job it was designed to do: what kind of impact and use-value it was to have for audiences. Only in relation to at least one of these features, and probably by reference to more than one, will we identify something as documentary work, thus placing it at the intersection point of a number of lines on which can be plotted matters of degree rather than of categoric kind. These lines lead to and from other things, including news, advertising, and drama, as well as a whole range of presenter-led television (e.g., cooking, travel, motoring, sport) and, of course more recently, the various possible formats and settings for location "games," tests, and challenges.

It seems to me that there are three classic functions to which documentary exposition, testimony, and observation have variously been harnessed.

1. *The Project of Democratic Civics.* Documentary is regarded here as providing publicity and propaganda for dominant versions of citizenship. This is documentary cinema in its classic, modernist-realist phase, funded (directly or indirectly) by official bodies. In Great Britain, it is certainly this function that Grierson saw the documentary as primarily fulfilling in the 1920s and 1930s. Not surprisingly, extensive and "heavy" use of commentary is a defining feature. It should also be noted that a directly affective, as well as a cognitive, impact is often sought, an intention for which the use of music and a range of rhetorical tropes, visual and verbal, gives support. The protocols of informational rationalism that frequently govern broadcast journalism do not hold sway across documentary discourse in this mode, given its function as a form of promotionalism, indeed often a form of national advertising.

2. *Documentary as Journalistic Inquiry and Exposition.* This is essentially the documentary as reporting, possibly the most extensive use of documentary methods on television (at least, until very recently). Through in-camera presentation, or commentary voice-over, and perhaps with interviews interspersing either or both, the documentary work grounds itself not in an idea of "publicity" but in an idea of "reportage," which importantly includes an experience of looking at kinds of visual evidence, an experience of witness (see John Ellis's *Seeing Things: Television in the Age of Uncertainty* [2000] on the importance of this notion).

3. *Documentary as Radical Interrogation and Alternative Perspective.* This is documentary as developed initially within the independent cinema movements that have maintained a presence in some national audiovisual cultures (the work of Bill Nichols is the major text for U.S. developments and an essential reference for all writing on this topic[3]). The authorial position is not "official," nor does it claim journalistic warrant. Implicitly, sometimes explicitly, the documentary discourse attempts a criticism and a correction of other accounts in circulation. Some public broadcast systems have tried to develop work of a parallel kind (Channel 4 in Great Britain would be a good example). A wide range of styles has been deployed, including techniques of disruption and distancing, taking their cue from nonrealist cinema but also including direct-cinema styles of observationalism, modes of dramatization, and kinds of personal testimony extending well beyond both the duration and format of the conventional interview. The anthropological levels of scrutiny offered by some projects in observational and oral history television could be included here.

This typology leaves out many important variants that have flourished within different national television systems, but I believe it has a certain rough adequacy (in *The Art of Record* I explore examples across all three categories over a 60-year period[4]). It is worth noting that, by design, all of the functions listed tend to produce work that is quite low in commodity character. Use value is stronger than exchange value (leaving aside for the moment the question of how the audience realizes this use value).

To these three functions, there has been added, by a process of steady development (involving one or two periods of faster change), a fourth function to which I have already alluded in my opening comments. This started within the established documentary parameters but is now evolving beyond them by a process both of "longitudinal" subgeneric developments and intensive cross-fertilization with other formats.

> 4. *Documentary as Diversion.* At one time, this was most often manifest in the occasional "lightness" (of topic and/or treatment) shown by many television documentary series as part of their mix. In many countries, it has become a new documentary imperative for the production of "popular factual entertainment." Performing this function, documentary is a vehicle variously for the high-intensity incident (the reconstructed accident, the police raid), for anecdotal knowledge (gossipy first-person accounts), and for snoopy sociability (as an amused bystander to the mixture of mess and routine in other people's working lives). Propagandist, expositional, or analytic goals are exchanged for modes of intensive or relaxed diversion—the primary viewing activity is on looking and overhearing, perhaps aligned to events by intermittent commentary. In seeking its new pact with the popular, documentary-as-diversion has tended to shadow previously established fictional formats. So the early reality TV shows, focusing on the work of police and emergency services, learned a lot from the style of dramatic action narratives.[5] "Docusoaps" have clearly learned a lot from the more relaxed rhythms of the soap opera and a good bit, too, from the newer styles of talk show.[6] We are, of course, presently seeing a whole range of documentary-style projects emerge that have made strong and successful connections with the idea of the "game" (one often also cast as an "experiment," with location spaces—interior or exterior—as "laboratory").

Clearly, *Big Brother's* preplanned group surveillance within a "game frame" that permits a measure of viewer intervention through the regular voting-off of participants, is the outstanding example of this. Other instances would include the BBC's rather more ambitiously anthropological *Castaways,* with an entire small community assembled on a remote Scottish island for the purposes of a social and psychological scrutiny by television, a scrutiny at once both informative and entertaining. Channel 4's *The 1900 House* and then *The 1940s House* worked with the idea of taking a family back to the conditions of previous periods for a sustained experiment in domestic living. They combined observationalism, participant direct address, and commentary to develop family narrative, historical exposition, and elements of the game-show challenge with great success.

Within the basic framework of taking a number of people to a comprehensively tele-available location for some form of "experiment in living," clearly quite a wide range of options present themselves. Most examples use a constrained time frame to provide a structure and an urgency of plot to the narrative. The more obvious titles (e.g., *Shipwrecked, Survivor*) have been quite quickly gone through. Social cohesion, personality, and capacity to perform tasks can variously be emphasized within combinations of the instructive and the entertaining. The "self" can be put on display in various modes of affection, solidarity, insincerity, confrontation, and downright aggression (two-phased onscreen captions before an advertising break in one episode of *Big Brother* are more generally revealing of its dynamics—"ALLIANCES . . . and ALLEGATIONS").

Participant self-reflection and commentary can deepen the plots thrown up by interaction. Self-knowledge can strengthen viewer empathy, while "self-ignorance" (along with its partner, overconfidence) holds, as ever, its classic potential for comic effect. A good deal of embarrassment and humiliation is assured, with the "outrageous" always there as an engaging possibility within the pressures and play of relationships—a moment of personal confrontation or the transgression of group or game "rules." The mutually modifying interplay of relationships and identities delivers the crucial open plot of the program's narrative.

One might use the term "selving" to describe the central process whereby "true selves" are seen to emerge (and develop) from underneath and, indeed, through, the "performed selves" projected for us, as a consequence of the applied pressures of objective circumstance and group dynamics. A certain amount of the humdrum and the routine may be a necessary element in giving this selving process, this unwitting disclosure of personal core, its measure of plausibility, aligning it with the mundane rhythms and naturalistic portrayals of docusoap, soap opera itself, and, at times, the registers of game-show participation. Karen Lury gives a very useful account of some of the paradoxes and tensions of "ordinary performance" that this type of portrayal encourages from its participants.[7] She also emphasizes how crucial these are in regulating the viewing experience as a kind of para-social encounter in which, as it were, the risks of "being and seeming" taken by others are part of the pleasure.

Here, the relative failure on British television of *Survivor* (ITV 2001) is interesting. This format replaced an enforced domesticity with the exoticism of group life on a desert island setting. Its viewing figures were only one-half those expected, and the show had to be radically rescheduled

within a week or so of opening. One of its problems may well have followed from the way in which its emphatic, indeed almost camp, exoticism (a sub-Malinowski stress on tribes, gods, and the mythic force of
the natural elements) pulled away from viewer fascination with the more
familiar dimensions of "living together" that characterize *Big Brother*.

I would not want to underestimate the real degree of innovative adaptation and creativity that has gone into these developments. Questions of
scopic appeal, forms of talk, and narrative system have been vigorously
readdressed in all but the most dull and imitative of formats. The organization of an observed spectacle that is both personal (sustained by forms
of personal talk, as well as by personal depiction) and social (sustained
by interaction, at least some of which needs to be confrontational enough
to provide the appropriate intensity) requires a high level of prior stage
management. This is such as to defy most previous protocols of documentarism, with their various anxious (and sometimes concealed) play-
offs between authenticity and artifice.

In documentary as diversion, by contrast with the previous three functions, we have forms that are very high in exchange value, strategically designed for their competitive strength in the television marketplace. They
are far less clear in their use value (although this cannot be dismissed
merely because it does not seem to conform to traditional knowledge criteria). It is important to see the newer forms of documentary as having an
identity quite distinct from that provided by the longstanding requirement
for documentary to do some entertaining to gain and keep a popular audience. Their identity is also different from those many other forms of
presenter-based factual formats (including, importantly, travel programs
and the more adventurous types of cooking and motoring series), which,
as I noted earlier, have an established link with selected elements of documentary portrayal.

Television documentary producers have often produced work that entertains, sometimes in surprising and subversive ways, sometimes with
populist calculation. However, when a piece of work in documentary
format is entirely designed in relation to its capacity to deliver entertainment, quite radical changes occur, both to the forms of representation and
to viewing relations.

Elements of a Postdocumentary Context?

There has, then, been a decisive shift toward diversion. This has not had the effect of completely displacing "serious" output, but it has certainly had the effect of reworking the identity of this output, both within television's generic system and within the pattern of viewing habits and expectations. In what ways might this constitute a postdocumentary setting?

First, and most obviously, because audiovisual documentation, under the drive of diversion, has become too extensive and varied to allow documentary what one might see as its minimum sufficient level of generic identity. There has been a quite radical dispersal of documentary energies across the schedules. As a category of work, documentary has required certain things to be assumed, taken as given (it is, indeed, a question-begging category and always has been). Looking and sounding different from other kinds of program helped this process along, supporting what we might call "documentary authority." Extensive borrowing of the "documentary look" by other kinds of program, and extensive borrowing of nondocumentary kinds of look (the dramatic look, the look of advertising, the look of the pop video) by documentary, have complicated the rules for recognizing a documentary. They have thereby contributed to a weakening of documentary status.

Second, as I noted earlier, a performative, playful element has developed strongly within new kinds of factual production. This is evident not only in documentary styling (including the much wider scope given to musical accompaniment) but also in such features as the degree of self-consciousness now often displayed by the participants in observational sequences. This self-display is no longer viewable as an attempt to feign natural behavior but is taken as a performative opportunity in its own right. As such, it constitutes a staple element of docusoap in contrast with the self-restrained naturalism of demeanor, speech, and behavior in classic observationalism. Such naturalism, often highly implausible when subject to close analysis, was nevertheless considered as one founding marker of documentary integrity.

Within the calculatedly nonnatural setting of *Big Brother*, performance is freed from even the minimal requirement made of "lead players" in docusoap to project their personality outward to the viewer from a context of circumstantial clutter and action. The "house" is a predefined stage precisely for personality to be competitively displayed (the intimate to-camera testimony of the video room being one privileged moment) and for its "ordinary" participants to enter the celebrity system of popular culture with minimal transitional difficulty (we know them as performers already), if only for a brief period. As so often in contemporary circuits of fame, intensity is in inverse proportion to duration!

Gossip pleasures abound as surmise and rumor join the data generated by the spectacle itself to provide a thick judgmental and speculative discourse around participants' motives, actions, and likely future behavior. In the first British series, the activities of "Naughty Nick" in covertly attempting to manipulate voting, his subsequent admonishment by the rest of the group after the discovery of his tactics, and then his ousting from the house by the program managers, constitute a paradigm case. Even the most optimistic producer could not have imagined such a wonderful enhancement to the developing story. In the second British series (2001), the central portrayal of house events is set within a thick and extensive context of chat show interview and speculation together with phone-in assessments—a self-generating gossip machine.

I noted earlier how the new levels of representational play and reflexivity will undoubtedly have an impact on the conventional rhetorics of documentary seriousness, requiring in some cases quite radical adjustments and accommodations to be made. Documentary is no longer classifiable as a "discourse of sobriety," to use Bill Nichols's much-cited phrase.[8] It has become suffused with a new "lightness of being," and it will need care and creativity to get the mix right in specific projects for specific audiences. This aesthetic instability, and the reorientations around tone and content, also bears witness to a degree of instability in the factual programming market, an uncertainty and a risk about who wants to watch what and why.

As yet, it is hard to gauge the implications of the new playfulness for documentary credibility. Newspaper stories about the forms of representational fraud in the newer formats have combined with the brazenly performative nature of much on-screen action in a way that must have raised popular audience awareness of just how constructed audiovisual documentation can be. But this also appears to have gone along with, if anything, an increased viewing enthusiasm. It is clear that in the "diverting" mode, belief in the veracity of what you are watching is not a prerequisite to engagement and pleasure. Indeed, quite the reverse rule would seem to apply. What also seems clear is that the generous license accorded to the more diverting modes cannot, as yet, be simply transferred across to more serious kinds of documentary claims-making. In the notable British case of Carlton Television's *The Connection,* a documentary purporting to show the activities of a Colombian drug cartel, there was widespread and deep public disquiet when revelations of "staging" and falsification appeared in newspapers.[9] Only research on viewing groups will enable us to understand what new blurrings, and what new differentiations, now inform the interpretative frameworks used by different segments of the audience. However, it is hard to see how any form of television documentary program can remain completely unaffected by the new ecology of the factual.

Third, and related to these questions about style and performance, the broader range of cognitive and affective investments that people make in audiovisual documentation is likely to have undergone a shift, even if, again, only audience research (now very much required in this area) can establish its scale. The "back story" to this shift involves changes in the nature of public and private life over the last two decades and the complex ways in which both the contours of social knowledge and emotional experience have been reconfigured. Such processes have strongly national dimensions, of course, but at their broadest, they involve the way in which selfhood is set within culture and culture is set within a particular political and economic order. The terms of "seeing others" and "seeing things" on the screen today are very different from those of the defining moments of documentary history, those moments when an expository realism seemed to resonate at least partially with a public, democratic rhetoric of reform and progress. These stealthier and more long-term changes are ones to which the newer forms of factual programming, with their emphasis on microsocial narrative and their forms of play around the self observed and the self-in-performance, seem to have brought an accelerated momentum.

"Documentary" is a category that has very largely been defined and applied in relation to a sense of public values, and, of course, there has been considerable variety in just how such values have been thought about and positioned in national life. Ideas have been framed by a range of authoritarian, liberal, and radical perspectives. In many countries, however, I think there is a quiet but deepening crisis over the very idea of "the public." This has something to do with changing terms of citizenship and a move away from the once-established (whether coercive or voluntary) forms of solidarity. It has very much to do with the changing character of the national and international economy and the increasing emphasis on market systems, market values, and the dynamics of consumption, which has generated a version of "the popular" grounded in consumption that is often in direct tension with notions of "the public." Throughout the twentieth century, these two terms have displayed a developing history of tension, often overlaid by an assumed synonymity. They now offer increasingly disconnected versions of the self in society and present to many social democratic projects profound challenges of reconfiguration and reframing within different areas of social and economic policy. In a number of countries, television's role as agency, both of public knowledge and of popular entertainment, has led to an awkward straddling across a dual value system, and a dual set of criteria, often for many years. Indeed, several debates in television studies have their origins in this duality, sometimes unrecognized, with the one side frequently perceived only in the terms of the other, either in advocacy or in critique.

In fact, within the contemporary crisis around public values, broadcast documentary is more vulnerable than news programming, since it is premised on a deeper and a broader engagement with perceptions of social community—its varieties, rhythms, problems, and tensions: the interplay of the specific with the general. Documentary has assumed and fostered rhetorics of belonging and involvement, albeit with elements of the manipulative, the socially exclusive, or the sentimental, that are now increasingly difficult to sustain, even in revised form. A mood at once both more cynical and more comic, a mood in which versions of performance cut through questions of sincerity and authenticity, has started to change television's terms of secondary seeing. Within this new affective order, this emerging "structure of feeling," a busy dialectic of attraction and dislike provides the mainspring of the entertainment. The very volatility of the feelings here allows for a viewing combination in which what are, for nonfictional formats, quite unparalleled modes of "getting close" become mixed with a remarkably cold, objectifying distance.

Popular Factual Entertainment and the Survival of Documentary

I have described a situation in which subjective factors to do with audience expectations, social affiliation, and modes of cognition and affect combine with the objective factors of a multichannel and intensively commercialized television industry. Only a more systematic attempt to measure what is going on in the schedules under different program categories, as well as sustained inquiry into viewer choice, expectation, and judgment, can allow us to be confident about the scale and direction of change. The combination of factors presents a challenge to the documentary project, at both the infrastructural and cultural levels. Its funding base is threatened by the intensified commodity status of all programs in the television marketplace. Meanwhile, the aesthetic, political, and cultural coordinates that helped hold it together have both reduced in strength and shifted apart.

I would not expect the production of serious documentary simply to disappear in these circumstances. As I indicated at the start of this article, my use of the idea of "postdocumentary culture" is not meant to signal that documentary is now finished but to signal the scale of its relocation as a set of practices, forms, and functions. Some established strands of practice will undoubtedly continue across the disjunctions I have discussed. They will win viewers and deserve critical support. But they will do this in what, for many national television systems, will be a radically changed setting for audiovisual production and consumption. To the extent it wishes to enjoy a popular reach, the future documentary project in television will need strategically to reconfigure itself within the new economic and cultural contexts.

I am aware that much discussion of the threat to documentary carries the ring, if not the explicit claim, of a protectionism, one that is finally aesthetically and socially conservative. The contrary option, welcoming the brave new populist-realisms for their decentering, postmodern energies and thereby downplaying the consequences of their market rationale and their commodity cynicism, looks as crass as ever, although doubtless some commentators will continue to sound that note. It is not surprising that, in this situation, a degree of ambivalence is often a defining feature of academic commentary, as the diverse commercial and sociocultural dimensions of the "popular" seem to resist neat separation. Kees Brants and Jay Blumler provide together a useful exchange on the broader but related question of evaluating "infotainment."[10]

Moreover, the question of precisely how far, and at what rate, new forms of programming are driving out the more established modes of practice and function is not yet properly answered. In a recent survey, Brian Winston suggested that the success of popular factual entertainment in the schedules, far from exerting a directly displacing effect, may have been, for the time being at least, "the price of survival" of other, more serious fare.[11] Whatever the pattern finally to emerge, producers with a commitment to the popular audience that goes beyond profitability but that can nevertheless also generate profits will clearly be an important factor in documentary's survival.

Documentary, in all its complexity as an indicator, points essentially to a project of political and cultural modernism, predicated on quite specific contexts of mediation and of public and private experience. Its characteristic modes have shown an expositional and analytic dynamic together with a real ethnographic zeal in the portrayal of different forms of living. At the same time, authoritarian and patrician tones have frequently become woven into its textures. In many countries, documentary has bestowed a mixed representational legacy—of investigative, exploratory energy and of epistemic and aesthetic containment. It has served to open up and also to close down. Neither postmodern skepticism nor the techniques of digital manipulation present documentary with its biggest future challenge. This will undoubtedly come from the requirement to reorient and refashion itself in an audiovisual culture where the dynamics of diversion and the aesthetics of performance dominate a greatly expanded range of popular images of the real.

Big Brother's distinctive mixture of surveillance and display, placing the viewing audience as both voyeurs and talent-show judges, has certainly been an important moment in the emergence of reality television from its documentary origins. Reality television has worked cleverly with its ingredients, some of which have been drawn from other formats while others have been quite new. In taking a popular audience beyond the confines of the broadcast text into the continuity of an online narrative, reality television will also prove to have been significant. In assessing it, we should neither simplify nor forget the relationship between its representational system and its commodity functions. By "performing the real" with such strategic zeal, framing its participants both as game players and as television "actors," reality television has helped mark a shift in the nature of television as a medium for documentation. Perhaps it marks a shift, too, in the nature of that broader sphere, a sphere where vectors of both structure and agency combine to produce experience, that John Hartley has suggestively dubbed "popular reality."[12]

Afterword

This chapter, originally published in 2002, was developed from papers I had given in 2000 and 2001. The first paper was presented at a seminar in Florence organized as part of the European Science Foundation (ESF) project titled "Changing Media/Changing Europe." Those attending were invited to overview their areas of specialist interest, reflecting on current and imminent change in media structures and provision. It seemed to me to be useful to take the opportunity to reflect on some of the shifts in the area of documentary television, particularly those shifts that had established themselves more clearly since the publication of my book, *The Art of Record,* only four years earlier. A subsequent invitation by the University of Bergen to talk at a seminar organized to examine current issues in documentary helped develop these reflections further. The presence of Ib Bonderbjerg, John Ellis, and Brian Winston at this event provided me with the stimulation of their own papers on current trends, as well as their views on mine. A written working paper arising out of the Florence and Bergen seminars was placed on the ESF project website under the title "Documentary in a Post-Documentary Culture?"

It was at the Bergen event that I first introduced the notion of a post-documentary culture into my account. As my notes for this talk indicate, I commented how anyone seeking to make further use of the term "post" as a prefix probably deserved to be shot but that, notwithstanding this, there was perhaps some advantage to be had in the sharper, dramatic focus given to questions of generic transformation by at least posing them for debate in such a way. My usage was thus partly tongue-in-cheek, and it was received by the Bergen gathering very much in the spirit of a touch of humor put to the service of exploring change, although my particular reading of the nature and scale of the shifts was debated with a full sense of the seriousness of the principal issues and a sharp awareness of other ways of looking at things.

A year later, in autumn 2001, the opportunity to write something for *Television and New Media* allowed me to develop and refine the working paper further, partly in response to comment, and to bring in the media phenomenon of *Big Brother* as another significant point of reference from which to take stock of the intergeneric dynamics modifying and expanding the ways in which television "claimed the real," to use Brian Winston's resonant phrase. Although *Big Brother* represented a development of a very different kind from earlier modes of "reality television" (the question of how to place these different strands of development both in relation to each other and to the category of "documentary" remains an active one), its mixture of open artifice and observational intensity, the core recipe for a brash reconfiguration of television–real world relations, was rightly seen as significant by most writers on the medium, whatever their specialist interests.

The article as published in 2002 has received a good deal of citation and comment. Its formulations have often been taken up positively (occasionally with an assertive confidence that exceeds my own) but also questioned and directly challenged. My general position has been subject to a certain misreading on occasion, for which I take some of the responsibility, although the urge to simplify a view in the interests of strengthening a criticism of it is a widespread and pretty harmless academic practice and attempts to preclude it (e.g., by careful qualification of all points made) are often ineffective.

Insofar as a retrospective account can be useful, I think the emphasis is best placed on my assessment of how the core ideas of the piece stand up in light of the attention they have received from a range of scholars.

The main focus of the article is the way in which the rise of reality formats on television, and their success with popular audiences, might figure within a broad and historical reading of the documentary project and its likely future. What kinds of relation of continuity and difference with earlier work could be identified? What did the new approaches of "popular factual entertainment" mean for the more established practices and terms of mediated engagement with "reality"? Was something entirely different happening, or was there, beyond the novelty, a clear set of connections with what had gone before? It seemed to me that in order to answer these questions some close attention to the way the new programs worked, and what it felt like to watch them, was necessary. I was not interested in simply delivering yet another denunciation. I wanted to ask some questions to which I did not know the answers.

What I could have brought out more sharply was my sense that it was in its *purposes* rather than in methods, forms, or specific content (even though purpose impacts powerfully on all of these) that much of the new work opened up the greatest gap in relation to established documentary practice. While an extremely wide range of styles, moods, and specific intentions, including aesthetic innovation and humor, were to be found in this practice, the arrival of work specifically designed to entertain and divert, crafting actuality materials expressly to this end, took us, it seemed to me, in new directions. To use Raymond Williams's suggestive phrase, the "structure of feeling," the cultural coordinates on which the documentary project had sustained itself across its variety and historical development (sometimes generating a mythic dimension to its self-description and sense of continuity), was in transition. Again to borrow from Williams, there was a strong sense of "emergent" elements (cultural but also strongly economic) being played off against the "dominant" and the "residual." This could be seen as part of "generic renewal" (some writers saw it this way), but even though renewal might be part of it, "generic dispersal" seemed also to be at work. This weakening of the documentary imperative, in part a weakening of documentary authority within a broader undercutting of documentary seriousness, was not all loss by any means (a judgment that I think still makes my commentary different from many other overviews, even if it also contributes to some moments of ambivalence).

By working with a contrasting duality of reference in the phrase "documentary in a postdocumentary culture," I meant to signal a sense of a growing misalignment and tension between established identifiers and a changing audiovisual culture, between continuities of practice and radical disjunctions of context. What I did not want to do was suggest that documentary was now somehow "finished" as a form, although a few people took my comments, despite the duality noted above, as declaring such a definitive closure and then (rightly) moved to champion its continued existence. Just *how* continuity would be achieved, in what adaptive relationship with the new dynamics of the audiovisual economy and the culture of popular viewing, was a matter of speculation in the paper, not of any firm verdict. Of course, the arrival of reality television produced sharply conflicting judgments as to its impact, leading some writers to talk of the "death" of documentary and others to celebrate its "renaissance," often with the same work cited by way of example. When some of those who had talked of death decided later to revise their judgments in light of the success of feature documentary in the cinema, there was even a "resurrectionist" position on offer!

I placed a good deal of emphasis on performance as a significant factor of change, a term which clearly related directly to several levels of the *Big Brother* project but which had also been identified by a number of writers as a dimension of a much broader range of new work. For instance, Bill Nichols, although writing one of the most coruscating critical accounts of reality television had, during the same period, introduced "the performative" as the latest in his much-cited and regularly revised range of documentary modes, following after the "reflexive" and describing work using an expanded expressive range, as well as showing deepened self-awareness.[13] However, I was talking of "performance" mostly in terms of the organization and mode of display of observed behavior rather than the openly subjective and affective expressivities of a kind of documentary authorship. For me, such "performance of the real" was questionable, its self-conscious and often mannered display to camera an element of the "commodity real" within the new framework of "reality-as-entertainment."

For others however, the break with observational naturalism seemed wholly positive. Stella Bruzzi has recently observed how "acknowledgement of and interplay with the camera" is now part of documentary's engagement "with its own constructedness," a welcome shift in the approach of producers, bringing with it a new critical awareness in audiences.[14] I am not so sure how well this applies to the kind of "diversions" with which I was principally concerned.[15]

For a start, much reality television, including a range of natural-location formats but also built-location shows like *Big Brother*, mix moments of self-conscious and playful artifice with moments of intensive commitment to the truthfulness of their images, the "reality claims" of which at least equal the much-discussed "ideology of transparency" of classic observational work. That the introduction of stronger and more overt forms of performance in reality formats involves a new reflectiveness on the part of program makers concerning the status of televisual representation or a new refusal on the part of audiences to accord reality status to what they see on television seems to me to be doubtful.

Bruzzi queries the assumptions behind the very idea of my use of the phrase "performing the real," suggesting that I "still hold on to the idea that 'living' and 'performance' are two entirely separate states."[16] In a phrasing that risks a degree of banality, she notes how what emerges from the new work is a sense that "performance is an integral part of living." But the kinds of self-conscious behavioral performance involved in being a voluntary provider of front-of-camera action in a reality show (and performance requirements do vary radically across formats) cannot simply be *equated* with those levels of routinized performance involved in everyday social and occupational relations (and so well analyzed by Erving Goffman). To fail to differentiate here is to produce a blurring just where there should be a sense of specificity, even if we should be alert to the continuities, too.

Since the publication of my piece, the newer forms of factual television as well as continuity and innovation in documentary modes have become the subject of acute critical attention and dispute. Certainly in Great Britain, the play-off between the "civic" or "public" dimension to factual programming and the "commodity" dimension has become more fraught as television's broader economies of production and consumption have undergone substantial revision. If finding a popular audience for se-rious, thoughtful, inspiring, and sometime discomforting encounters with reality is one of the core commitments of the documentary project, then how will the present condition of the audiovisual economy and the per-formance requirements now becoming installed in its stylings of actuality affect this commitment? It may well provide the stimulus for innovation and an expanded sense of creative options. But it will certainly also pres-ent it with further strong, displacing, and reconfiguring challenges to both principles and practices, to the kind of social meanings that recorded im-ages can carry and the social uses to which they can be put within the changing dynamics and circuits of popular knowledge. Trying to make the best sense of these transformations will continue to give international media scholars one of their most significant and lively topics of inquiry.

NOTES

1. Forsyth Hardy, ed. *Grierson on Documentary* (London: Faber, 1979).

2. John Corner, "What Can We Say about Documentary? *Media, Culture and Society* 22.5 (1986), 681–88.

3. Bill Nichols, *Representing Reality* (Bloomington: Indiana University Press, 1991).

4. John Corner, *The Art of Record* (Manchester, NY: Manchester University Press, 1996).

5. Ib Bondebjerg, "Public Discourse/Private Fascination: Hybridization in 'True Life Story' Genres," *Media, Culture and Society* 18.1 (1996), 27–45, and Richard Kilborn, "How Real Can You Get? Recent Developments in Reality Television," *European Journal of Communication* 9.4 (1994), 421–39.

6. For a critical review in the context of broader intergeneric shifts, see John Dovey, *Freakshow: First Person Media and Factual Television* (London: Pluto, 2000).

7. Karen Lury, "Television Performance: Being, Acting and 'Corpsing,'" *New Formations* 27 (Winter 1995–96), 114–27.

8. Nichols, *Representing Reality.*

9. For details of this instance, see Brian Winston, *Lies, Damned Lies and Docu-mentary* (London: British Film Institute, 2000).

10. Kess Brants, "Who's Afraid of Infotainment?" *European Journal of Commu-nication* 13.3 (1998), 315–35; and Jay G. Blumler, "Political Communication Systems All Change: A Response to Kees Brants," *European Journal of Communication* 14.2 (1999), 241–49.

11. Winston, *Lies, Damned Lies.*

12. John Hartley, *Popular Reality* (London: Arnold, 1996).

13. Bill Nichols, *Blurred Boundaries: Questions of Meaning in Contemporary Culture* (Bloomington: Indiana University Press, 1994).

14. Stella Bruzzi, *New Documentary: A Critical Introduction* (New York: Routledge, 2000), 252.

15. For a sustained account of the idea of the performative in relation to new documentary and reality modes, taking issue with Bruzzi's earlier arguments, see Rune Gade and Anne Jerslev, eds., *Performative Realism* (Copenhagen: Museum Tusculanum Press, 2005).

16. Bruzzi, *New Documentary*, 151.

3

||||||||||||||||||||||||||||||||||||||||||||||||||||||||||

"I Think We Need a New Name for It"
The Meeting of Documentary and Reality TV

Susan Murray

Shooting with handheld cameras, a film crew follows the everyday happenings and interpersonal relationships of an upper-middle-class California family for seven months. Television viewers have a "fly-on-the wall"
perspective as they engage in heated political debates at the dinner table,
frequent neighborhood dinner parties, struggle with internal and external conflicts, take vacations, work, and attend high school. Viewers are
also privy to the breakdown of the parent's marriage and the details of
one son's openly gay lifestyle in New York City. All of this is tied together
through interweaving multiple plot lines, presented without voice-over
narration or interviews, and edited in serial form.

Based on this brief description of the premise and style, are we able
to identify whether this nonfiction series was a documentary or a reality
television program? Would it help us to know that it was funded by and
shown on public television or that it was made by two well-respected, independent filmmakers and produced by someone whose past works had
focused on the fine arts? What if we also discovered that it was simultaneously criticized for exploitation and sensationalism? Or that it was marketed as a "starkly intimate portrait of one family struggling to survive a
private civil war" in newspaper ads?[1]

Producer Craig Gilbert described the above nonfiction program, *An
American Family,* as a "real-life soap opera" in regard to its narrative
structure but crafted it using many of the stylistic techniques of the direct cinema movement.[2] By the time it aired in 1972, the program's resulting generic hybridity and instability so befuddled critics that they ended
up comparing it to everything from home movies to situation comedies.[3]

Such confusion over how to place the series led anthropologist Margaret Mead to remark to *TV Guide*, "I do not think that *American Family* should be called a documentary. I think we need a new name for it, a name that would contrast it not only with fiction, but with what we have been exposed to up until now on TV."[4] Thirty years later, the program's generic status remains liminal as it is now alternately discussed as an observational documentary and an early form of reality television. The struggle to define exactly what *An American Family* was bespeaks much of what is at stake in our current generic placement of texts into the categories of documentary and reality television.

While some nonfiction television texts fit squarely within the generally agreed-on borders of either documentary or reality television, many others seem to defy easy classification. In a recent essay on *Big Brother* and tele-reality, John Corner argues that the "extensive borrowing of the 'documentary look' by other kinds of programs, and extensive borrowing of non-documentary kinds of look by documentary, have complicated the rules for recognizing a documentary."[5] For this and other reasons, Corner wonders whether we are entering a postdocumentary cultural moment.

In this chapter, I am not interested in redefining, reclaiming, or reasserting the documentary genre—or in predicting its demise. Instead, I explore how a network's brand image and marketing and positioning of particular programs work in conjunction with our critical judgments, expectations, and knowledge of previous documentary and reality forms, to help us as viewers and critics decide what is "reality TV" and what is a "proper" documentary. In this way, I'm engaging in the type of analysis that Jason Mittell calls for, which at its base, conceives of television genres as discursive practices. As Mittell argues, "[the] goal in analyzing generic discourses is not to arrive at the 'proper' definition, interpretation, or evaluation of a genre, but to explore the material ways in which genres are culturally defined, interpreted, and evaluated."[6]

Traditional analyses of the documentary form have focused on the textual elements that distinguish it from other forms of nonfiction film and video. While there is no doubt that such elements do work to define the genre, the goal of this chapter is to examine the ways in which certain extratextual factors can impel the viewer to see a nonfiction television text as either documentary or reality television, sometimes even despite its textual characteristics. This type of discursive generic analysis helps us understand what reality television is, since it reveals many of the assumptions that surround the generic category, as well as the cultural role assigned to it, particularly in relation to that of documentary.

Genre, "Social Weight," and the Observational Mode

To begin a discussion of the reality television genre, it is important to first recognize that there are many different formats—most of which are generic hybrids themselves—that fall within this category. Some of these formats are more readily differentiated from documentary than others. Gamedocs (such as *Survivor*), for example, embody only a few aesthetic or textual characteristics of the documentary and seem more closely aligned with game shows.

The types of reality programs that share the most textual and aesthetic characteristics with documentaries tend to focus on the everyday lives of their subjects in somewhat "natural" settings without a game setup, use cinema verité techniques, and do not contain flagrantly commercial elements such as product placement or the promise of prizes. One such type is the docusoap, which Stella Bruzzi has identified as a legacy of direct cinema (also called observational or cinema verité).[7] She points out that British nonfiction programs such as *Vets in Practice* and *Driving School* (American equivalents include *The Real World* [MTV] and *American High* [FOX/PBS]) combine many of the textual and aesthetics characteristics of direct cinema (handheld camerawork, synch sound, focus on everyday activities) with the overt structuring devices of soap operas (short narrative sequences, intercuts of multiple plot lines, mini cliff-hangers, use of a musical soundtrack, and a focus on character personality).[8]

Yet there are programs that have been classified rather definitively by critics as documentaries that look—in terms of their aesthetics and narrative structure—quite similar to the docusoaps mentioned above. In the United States, the public television series *An American Love Story* (which chronicled a year in the life of an interracial family in Queens, New York) and *A Farmer's Wife* (which centered on a Midwest farming family's economic and domestic struggles), for example, followed the *American Family* model quite closely, yet they were never considered to be reality television. Therefore, there must be characteristics beyond narrative form and aesthetic qualities that help critics and viewers define such programs.

Indeed, much of our evaluative process is based in the belief that documentaries should be educational or informative, authentic, ethical, socially engaged, independently produced, and serve the public interest, while reality television programs are commercial, sensational, popular, entertaining, and potentially exploitative or manipulative.[9] These somewhat subjective assumptions work to construct a dialectical relationship between documentary and reality television, even as they have many similar characteristics. Documentary is seen as a valid and productive social and artistic endeavor, while reality television is often vilified or dismissed. Consequently, generic placement becomes a way in which to gauge a program's cultural value and import through discursive means.

Documentary has traditionally been assumed to be rather high-minded and, if not fully educational, than at least informative. Mobilizing a "discourse of sobriety" documentaries reference established traditions of ethical and political mandates for their own form.[10] Although observational documentaries tend to focus on the mundane, the everyday, the personal—and as a result, can appear just as obsessed with the intimate as reality TV—they are seen by many viewers and critics as doing this for the greater good of the subject, the viewer, and the society at large.[11] Bruzzi contends that the most important distinction between observational projects and docusoaps is the "social weight" of their content—specifically, the latter's focus on entertainment rather than the exploration of cultural and political issues.[12]

This is familiar logic and has been borne out throughout the history of television as documentaries have often been produced and aired to compensate for the "sins" of commercial television. For instance, in response to the quiz show scandals in the late 1950s and growing criticism of the networks for their failure to serve the public, networks commissioned more documentaries to recoup their public image, appease critics, and win back the trust of the viewing audience.[13] Largely because of this rhetorical and social positioning, documentary producers are often the recipients of government and private funding, and their resulting work is commonly shown on PBS—which maintains a mandate to provide its viewers "programs that the present system, by its incompleteness, denies [them]."[14] Documentaries are therefore *believed* to play a central cultural role in representing minority viewpoints and having serious historical or social significance (although this has been troubled during different historical moments, such as the "culture wars" of the 1980s).

Yet "social weight" is an interesting and potentially contentious distinction here, since claims of social relevance are often made by the creators of docusoaps as well. As Jon Kraszewski's research has shown, *The Real*

World, for example, often highlights the ways in which it consistently deals with issues of race and sexuality.[15] Social weight is not something that can be empirically measured, nor is it necessarily an inherent textual characteristic. Rather, it is a rhetorical stance that can be mobilized in an effort to endorse or authenticate a particular television text and to attract an audience who cherishes liberal notions of social responsibility or public service. Even if it is possible to measure social import/impact in some way, it is still important to ask whether "entertainment" and "social weight" really exist as mutually exclusive terms, since, as I detail later in this chapter, programs such as *American High* and *America Undercover* are presented as both sensational and educational.

To court a particular type of audience identification and set of expectations, television networks can take a program that has somewhat liminal textual generic identifiers and sell it as either a documentary or a reality program by packaging it in such a way to appear either more educational/informative or more entertaining/sensational, or, in some cases, both. In this way, the networks are working with the audience's prior experience and expectations of each form and then highlighting certain aspects of the text to ensure that it is read (and therefore classified) in a particular way. As Bill Nichols points out, "The distinguishing mark of documentary may be less intrinsic to the text than a function of the assumptions and expectations brought to the process of viewing the text."[16] Although Nichols is talking primarily about the ways in which the audience experiences with prior documentaries informs their encounters with future examples of the genre, I would also add that the site of exhibition (and the discourses that construct it) plays a vital role in the audience's process of generic classification and their assignment of social weight to a particular text.

In the following section, I focus on two programs, *America Undercover* (HBO) and *American High* (FOX/PBS), that serve as productive examples of the ways in which the context of reception of a program can be manipulated to encourage a viewer to understand the meaning of the text through a particular generic lens. If a viewer reads the text though the lens of "documentary," for example, they will be more likely to read it as socially engaged, informative, authentic, and artistic. In the following examples, I explore the ways that FOX, the U.S. public television channel PBS, and the premiere cable channel HBO mobilized their different brand images along with publicity and marketing tools to push viewers to see programs carrying signifiers of both documentary and reality television as simply one or the other. In these instances, genre turns on the industrial management of extratextual discourses. Through these examples, we'll see that these strategies do not always work out as planned, since the tensions that exist in the bifurcation of the two generic categories can, at times, be difficult to contain.

American High *and* America Undercover: *Packaging Documentary/Reality Television*

American High was sold as a reality program on FOX and, a year later, as a documentary series on PBS. Obviously, these two networks have disparate brand images, financing structures, and target audiences and therefore had different interests to serve. Executives at both networks believed they could alter the reception context of *American High* to suit their particular needs.

The production context of the series reveals direct links to documentary practice. Director R. J. Cutler, a renowned documentarian who received an Academy Award nomination for *The War Room* (1993), shot 2,000 hours of film tracking the lives of 14 seniors in a suburban Chicago area high school. He also arranged for the students involved in the show to take a video diary class, the results of which were edited together with the verité-style footage to create the final product. Cutler claimed to use *An American Family* as his model, yet he also told reporters at the time of the program's premiere that he was influenced as well by the fictional teen drama *My So-Called Life,* thereby underscoring the hybrid nature of his series.[17] He appeared to avoid using the term "documentary" to describe the project in interviews and press conferences, but also he refused to overtly align it with reality television. In a chat room interview, Cutler told fans that shows like *Big Brother* and *Taxicab Confessions* "are not real the way our show is. . . . Our show is a drama series with real characters and real stories that continue over the course of a year."[18]

In contrast, FOX was eager to label *American High* a reality program as executives were hoping that it would be FOX's answer to CBS's recent success with *Survivor* and *Big Brother.* Aired on the network late in the summer of 2000, the show was scheduled against *Big Brother* and was expected to win over the youth demographic with its combination of reality and teen drama. At a press conference before the show's premiere, a cast member played up the program's competition with other reality series:

"This is our real life. We're living in our real houses, and we get cameras where we get to talk about what we're really feeling. Compared with *Real World* and *Survivor,* I think we are the closest you can get to reality."[19] FOX entertainment president Gail Berman used the series' documentary heritage to make a similar assertion: "This is the real *Real World.* No False Settings, no contrived situations. This is a type of reality programming that can be enlightening as well as entertaining."[20] Despite such allusions to enlightenment, FOX hyped *American High* with its usual antiestablishment style, creating bumpers that declared (over a hard rock sound track), "What you're about to see will get you hooked! Real Kids! Real Families! Real Life! . . . Find out what its like to be young in America. The bold new summer series—American High!" Such promotions played up the series' sensational aspects and reality television conventions in order better suit the network's brand identity.

Since its inception, FOX has crafted itself as an antiestablishment provider of innovative and often controversial, youth-directed programming. As such, it was one of the first networks to experiment with prime-time reality formats in the mid-1990s. Under the leadership of Mike Darnell, FOX's alternative programming unit succeeded in attracting large numbers of young male viewers with reality specials such as *When Good Pets Go Bad, World's Scariest Police Chases,* and *Alien Autopsy,* which were derided by critics as "gross-out shockumentaries and socially unredeeming freak shows."[21] In February 2000, the network was forced to reign in Darnell's programming style as a result of the backlash that resulted from the airing of *Who Wants to Marry a Multi-Millionaire.* Although highly rated, the special—a bridal/beauty pageant culminating in an on-air wedding— was lambasted by the press and scared off advertisers after the bridegroom's background and financial standing was put into question.

Coming in the wake of that scandal, *American High* allowed FOX to retain its reputation for groundbreaking and risky programming while providing an opportunity to clean up their public image. It was a balancing act meant to redefine reality television for FOX, while not straying too far from viewer expectations. Even though it did receive much critical acclaim at the time of its premiere, FOX dropped *American High* from its lineup after only four episodes. Although network heads simply cited low ratings as the reason for their rather hasty decision, it appears that this series' particular blend of formats and aesthetics did not ultimately square with the average FOX viewer's vision of what reality television was supposed to provide. By the time *American High* aired on public television almost a year later, the series had been repackaged in a strikingly different manner.

Pat Mitchell, a former CNN producer, was hired in 2000 as president and chief executive officer of PBS after the channel's prime-time ratings hit a historic low and its average viewer age had reached a high at 56.[22] As part of a larger effort to attract younger viewers, Mitchell acquired *American High* in 2001, touting it as a hip but ultimately educational documentary series from an acclaimed independent filmmaker. Just like the executives at FOX, Mitchell tried to use *American High* to renegotiate her organization's brand identity. Yet, in contrast to FOX's marketing strategy, she downplayed the "boldness" of the program's more controversial elements—such as its use of explicit language, frank discussions of sex and sexuality, and intense family conflicts—and emphasized its "authentic" and informative representation of the adolescent experience.

In other words, in an effort to temper the negative connotations that accompany the reality television label, Mitchell worked strenuously to assert the program's ties to the values and traditions of both PBS and the documentary project. She was also aware that a program harboring similarities with network reality programs would help draw younger viewers, particularly when such a show centered on teen life.

At this point, PBS had already experienced success with one reality program, *1900 House,* which placed a family in a demodernized London townhouse in order to experience middle-class life as it was in 1900. This series, however, was produced with the average PBS viewer in mind and therefore eschewed commercialism, had historical reference, and represented an idyllic vision of family togetherness. *American High* did not contain any such features, but nevertheless had the potential to resonant with the PBS audience through its references to documentary traditions.

By engaging in a two-pronged campaign, using both conventional PBS marketing methods and overtly commercial strategies, it would seem that Mitchell hoped to appeal to new and old viewers alike. She convinced Coca-Cola to sponsor the series and entered into promotional deals with MTV (which cosponsored a contest in which the winners would appear on *Total Request Live* with the *American High* cast) and *Teen People* to cohost dances at high schools where clips of the program would be shown on dance floor Jumbotrons.[23]

In addition, ads for the series (shots of individual cast members in their bedrooms or school hallways, accompanied by copy such as "No actors. No scripts. Just life.") were placed on the teen websites alloy.com, launch.

com, and bolt.com. In an attempt to balance the PBS mandate with her aggressive marketing, Mitchell also used the PBS.org *American High* website to situate the program as an educational and therapeutic documentary tool for families and teachers.

Besides the message boards, chat rooms, production stills, cast biographies, and streaming videos that make up most television program webpages, the *American High* site contained a Teachers' Lounge and Parents' Guide. The Teachers' Lounge used the tools of media literacy to instruct teachers how to teach students to make their own videos of their high school experience, as well as to explore "the legal and ethical aspects of reality TV." (It is interesting to note that the only time the term "reality genre" is mentioned in this campaign is when it is directed toward the teens, and then only in terms of its ethical ramifications.) The downloadable 25-page Parents' Guide, which consistently described the series as a documentary, begins with a letter from Pat Mitchell:

> [*American High*] is not just a remarkable window into the lives of teens, but also a frank, gripping and often poignant depiction of the teens' parents and the daunting challenges they're facing in raising teens. As a mother of a teenager now, and having raised another, I immediately felt a sense of gratitude for what I learned from watching *American High*. The father of one of the teens in the series told the press, "watching the series is like the anthropology of our family. It made us look at issues in a completely new light—one that probably saved our relationship with our son." We at PBS believe this series can be meaningful for you, as well. And, to deepen your viewing experience, we have created this *American High* Parent's Guide. With insights from parenting experts and psychologists, the Guide uses the real life stories from *American High* as catalysts to help you better understand the world through your teenager's eyes. Plus, the Guide provides a wealth of ideas to support you in what is arguably the most difficult relationship on earth: parent and teen.[24]

For parents and teachers, the series was constructed as what Mitchell calls "an observational documentary in the tradition of PBS,"[25] or, as the parent in the preceding quote describes it, an anthropological project, that was made to be viewed and processed within an institutional—either school or family—context so that the more sensational or explicit aspects of the program could be "properly" narrativized as socially relevant issues. The idea was to attract teens to PBS by making the series appear entertaining, while simultaneously appeasing its core audience—many of whom would be parents or grandparents—by wrapping it in the discourse of education.

The strategy failed on both fronts. Although the program did attract a significant number of young viewers, it was not as popular as PBS executives had initially hoped. And, perhaps even more important, *American High* offended and alienated the sensibilities of the network's older viewers with its frank themes and explicit language, forcing Mitchell to admit that, by choosing to air the series, PBS had "built an audience and then let them down."[26] It would seem that a specific set of expectations for and understanding of the form and function of documentary were so formed in the minds of the core PBS audience that Mitchell's attempt to refashion them through extratextual means did not take. It is also possible that PBS viewers may not only be sensitive to sensational and sexual content but also reject programs that could be seen as too commercial in regard to content or marketing.

While PBS viewers may have a difficult time accepting strategies that work to redefine social relevance and public service outside the conventional liberal model, HBO viewers seem to be more willing to ascribe social weight to programs that are both sensational and commercial. This may have to do with the history of HBO's nonfiction programming division, which grew largely in response to PBS's content limitations. The early- and mid-1990s saw a significant shift in the market for television documentaries, since the culture wars over arts funding and increasing competition from cable outlets left PBS (the primary outlet for television docs up until that point) in a state of crisis.

Due to the close scrutiny the network was receiving, it became increasingly difficult for them not only to fund documentaries but also to air work that was explicit or controversial. And it is exactly this type of content that HBO excelled at. The very nature of HBO's premium channel payment structure allows the network to escape the cultural vilification and calls for censorship that plague broadcast and some basic cable stations. This, coupled with an audience that wishes to see itself as more capable, responsible, and mature than the average television viewer, creates an ideal setting for the presentation of "tasteful" but possibly lurid nonfiction programming.

Since the 1990s, HBO has aggressively marketed itself as a quality network for the (paying) television connoisseur. Through its original programming, such as *The Sopranos, Six Feet Under,* and *Sex in the City,* the cable network has refashioned liberal notions of "quality" television to include "adult" content. Consequently, viewers come to programs such as the nonfiction anthology series *America Undercover* with the expectation that what they are about to see is above and beyond the usual network fare.

Shelia Nevins admits that early in her career as HBO's head of adult documentary and family programming she saw documentaries primarily as cheap time-fillers, but now she considers them an essential marker of prestige for the company. Certainly Nevins has deliberately cultivated this prestige, as she has spent years showcasing the work of renowned established talent, such as Albert Maysles, Jon Alpert, Barbara Kopple, Lee Grant, and Alan and Susan Raymond (*An American Family*), as well as supporting up-and-coming independent filmmakers. The resulting critical praise and industry accolades that her programs have acquired over the years have helped HBO in its effort to brand itself as *the* quality cable network.

Yet Nevins is also responsible for such series as *Real Sex, G-String Divas, Autopsy, Cathouse,* and *Taxicab Confessions,* which have come under some scrutiny from critics for their sensational subject matter. These programs share a number of aesthetic characteristics with the networks' more serious fare, are often shot or directed by independent documentarians, and are packaged alongside more traditional documentaries as a part of HBO's "investigative" *America Undercover* series. Although Nevins packaged many of her documentary programs under the *America Undercover* heading for 19 years, in 2002 the program was moved into one of HBO's prime program slots. Showing at 10:00 PM eastern standard time on Sunday nights in the spring and summer that year, the program followed *Six Feet Under* and *The Sopranos,* which gave the show not only increased visibility but also a higher level of prestige. The network has invested more in its promotion of the show, even taking out two-page, full-color ads in highbrow venues such as the *New Yorker.*

America Undercover is marketed in such as way as to intentionally blur the boundaries between reality and documentary. Alternating between works that engage in the "discourse of sobriety"[27] covering topics such as labor struggles, racial profiling, terrorism, and the death penalty and the regular round of sex-based programming, *America Undercover* straddles traditional formats and viewing positions. As Nevins herself states, she and her staff "try to balance programs that nudge the world and programs that are more titillating and fanciful" in order to temper or contain the

America Undercover's ad in a spring 2002 issue of the *New Yorker* reveals the way that HBO highlights the sensational in the series even as it tries to appeal to a so-called quality audience.

reception of its risqué episodes and to help sensationalize more staid subject matter.[28] It is important to note, however, that the narration and editing of *Real Sex* works to position the series as investigative and somewhat cerebral explorations of the sexual underground rather than straightforward pornography or erotica. In other words, the episodes employ the discourse of traditional documentary to mitigate or justify their more voyeuristic tendencies. The show also enables viewers to feel better about their engagement with text as they can more easily read it as an educational text if they wish.

Outlining the way in which she negotiates the often-conflicting desires of her audience, Nevins told the *Los Angeles Times* that "if you could see it on A&E, if an advertiser would sponsor it, then I don't want to put it on HBO, because people are paying to see something a little spicier. But if it's ugly like *Playboy*, if it's lowbrow sexuality, then it's not what I like to call 'erotic eros.' I don't want it."[29] Nevins also has asserted that the unifying element of the nonfiction programs that air on *America Undercover* is their ability to fully represent "the real." She told *Reelscreen* in 1998:

The concept of our unexpurgated [programs] began to mean a certain kind of license to push reality to where it would naturally go without any censorship. There was no need to curtail what was happening. That's when reality began to be as interesting to me as theater, because it meant people could realize their stories to their full extent and where they could take them, whether the stories were happy or sad or violent or tragic or sexual.[30]

Nevins is making a claim here for all her nonfiction programming, equating lack of mediation or censorship from higher authorities with the ability of these programs to move beyond realism into the area of unfiltered reality. In doing this, she is touching on arguments given by both reality television and documentary producers and marketers. However, texts that are placed in the documentary genre tend to make an additional claim—that of social and historical relevance, or, in the language of television, public service. Nevins is trying to shift the discourse to incorporate her presentation of sexual and other such controversial content as a public service in itself.[31] Or at least she is alleging that sensational/sexual and educational/informational contents are not mutually exclusive.

In Nevin's explication of her tactics and reasoning, it becomes clear why the documentary label is so important in this context. If her programming was classified simply as reality television, it is possible that programs such as *Real Sex* would be evacuated of any sense of social weight. As it stands, *America Undercover* is able to mix content and form because it is wrapped in a redefined discourse of public service or education. Consequently, viewers of the program exist in a context of reception that tells them that "documentary," as defined by HBO, can both educate and titillate.

With *America Undercover,* HBO was able to do what FOX and PBS could not: successfully incorporate popular pleasure into a discourse of quality. Nevins and her team reworked the discourse around their program not only to suit their network's brand image but also to redefine the terms on which it was understood and classified. Certainly *America Undercover's* anthology format contributed to the success of their strategy, but it was also a result of an audience who, through their prior experience with HBO and their conception of themselves as a unique and select audience, were willing to accept a dismantling of the bifurcations that separated traditional definitions of documentary and reality television.

Some of this willingness can be attributed to HBO's championing of the First Amendment, which Nevins says provided "[HBO] with a comfort zone. If you had a Richard Pryor special, you could do a show called *Eros America;* if you showed an [unedited] R-rated movie, you could push your exposure of a crack house to the full extent of what was going on inside. It was the mandate of the network, because that's what people were paying for."[32]

With *American High,* both PBS and FOX had difficulty balancing their audiences' notions of quality with mainstream tastes and pleasures. FOX has cultivated a core constituency of viewers for its nonfiction programming who have little interest in texts that profess social significance and instead find delight in the outrageous, the lowbrow, and the sensational. The meanings that accompany the documentary are contrary to what they hope to get out of FOX's reality lineup. *American High,* while sold as reality television, still bears many of the marks of documentary conventions and therefore held little interest for FOX viewers. In contrast, PBS has constituted an audience for documentaries who imagines itself as above the machinations of commercial or mass entertainment.[33] Their pleasure is contingent on a text's perceived social weight or historical relevance, and, as a consequence, they seem to prefer more conventional documentaries such as those produced by Ken Burns. They may resist nonfiction programming that is "tainted" by the popular or is marked by a relationship to the commercial.

The generic instability of *American High* and *America Undercover* demonstrates just how difficult it is to define documentary and reality television (or any television genre, for that matter) outside of reception and industrial contexts. As I have shown, it is possible for networks to frame a generically unstable program as a documentary or reality program in order to activate the perceived values and implications that surround these categories. Yet the success of such rhetorical framing is contingent on an audience's preconceived ideas about the functions of that genre. A viewer may accept that a program is a documentary if a network proclaims it as such, but that doesn't guarantee that the text will meet their needs and expectations. If a program is ultimately unable to provide them with the knowledge and pleasures they have come to expect from documentaries, they may simply choose to stop watching it. To put it another way, textual signifiers commingle with present and past extratextual generic discourses to generate spectator positioning.

American High and *American Undercover* also remind us that the often tenacious assumptions that structure our prior knowledge of nonfiction television genres do not only inform our ability to classify a new program but also subjectively assign it a particular level of social value and artistic validity. This is because, as Mittell argues, genres are malleable, historically situated, cultural categories and, as such, "evolve out of the specific cultural practices of industries and audiences."[34] The distinctions we make between forms of nonfiction television are not based on empirical evidence but are largely contained in the evaluative connotations that insist on separating information from entertainment, liberalism from sensationalism, and public service from commercialism. When it comes to reality-documentary hybrids, we may not, as Margaret Mead suggests, "need a new name for it." Instead, we might just need to look at why it's so important for us to label it at all.

NOTES

1. Jeffrey Ruoff, *An American Family: A Televised Life* (Minneapolis: University of Minnesota Press, 2002), 101.

2. Ibid., 23.

3. Ibid., 108.

4. Ibid., xxv.

5. John Corner, "Performing the Real: Documentary Diversions," *Television and New Media* 3.3 (2003), 255–70.

6. Jason Mittell, "A Cultural Approach to Television Genre Theory," *Cinema Journal* 40.3 (2001), 9.

7. Stella Bruzzi, *New Documentary: A Critical Introduction* (New York: Routledge, 2000), 89.

8. Programs such as *Cops* (syndicated) and *Maternity Ward* (TLC) are episodic in structure rather than serial, but they are otherwise stylistically related to the docusoap.

9. Some network executives fear the documentary label will turn off mainstream viewers because they don't tend to associate the genre with pleasure. When asked why networks shy away from the term "documentary," ABC News Senior Vice President Phyllis McGrady answered: "When you think documentary, you think black-and-white, old, and boring. People are just afraid of the word. We did let it get a little fuddy-duddy." Quoted in Gary Levin, "None Dare Call It a Documentary," *USA Today*, 18 June 2002, 3D.

10. The term "discourse of sobriety" comes from Bill Nichols, *Representing Reality: Images and Concepts in Documentary* (Bloomington: Indiana University Press, 1991), 3–4.

11. Corner argues that the "discourse of sobriety" is no longer relevant in television's postdocumentary context as most documentaries are now infused with a "lightness of being." Corner, "Performing the Real," 264.

12. Bruzzi, *New Documentary,* 78–79.

13. For more on this, see Michael Curtin, *Redeeming the Wasteland: Television Documentary and Cold War Politics* (New Brunswick, N.J.: Rutgers University Press, 1995).

14. Carnegie Commission on Educational Television, *Public Television: A Program for Action* (New York: Bantam, 1967).

15. See Jon Kraszewski, chapter 10 in this volume.

16. Nichols, *Representing Reality,* 24.

17. Mark Jurkowitz, "'High' Time at PBS," *Boston Globe,* 4 April 2001, C10, at http://www.pbs.org/americanhigh/behind/index.html.

18. From a chat room transcript found at http://www.pbs.org/americanhigh/behind/index.html.

19. Quoted in David Zurawik, "This Is as Good as It Gets: School Series Really Is Reality TV," *Baltimore Sun,* 2 August 2000, 1E.

20. Quoted in David Zurawik, "A Silver Lining in the Reality Cloud," *Baltimore Sun,* 23 July 2000, 5F.

21. Alex Kuczynkski and Bill Carter, "Point Man for Perversity; 'World's Scariest Programmer,' Starring Mike Darnell as Himself," *New York Times,* 25 February 2000, C1.

22. By end of 2001, PBS was being viewed by 1.7 percent of U.S. homes. Elizabeth Jensen, "A Network's Mastery Has Gone to Pieces, " *Los Angeles Times,* 12 May 2002, A1.

23. Kay McFadden, "Kid You Not: PBS Going after Adolescent Viewers." *Seattle Times,* 31 March 2001, C1.

24. Parent's Guide, at www.pbs.org/americanhigh.

25. Quoted in David Bauder, "Finding an Audience for a Worthy Documentary," *Associated Press,* 24 April 2001.

26. Elizabeth Jensen, "A Network's Mastery Has Gone to Pieces," *Los Angeles Times,* 12 May 2002, A1.

27. "'Undercover' Wins Spotlight," *Boston Globe,* 9 March 2001, C4.

28. Ibid.

29. Quoted in Paul Lieberman, "Confessions of an HBO Original," *Los Angeles Times,* 28 May 2000, C3.

30. Quoted in Ed Kirchdoerffer, "Flash, Cash and the Ratings Dash: HBO's Shelia Nevins," *ReelScreen,* 1 September 1998, 33.

31. Brian Winston decries this sort of thinking, since he considers this willingness to investigate sexuality and nudity—which he calls "docu-glitz"—cable's "unpublic service" contribution to the documentary form." Quoted in Nichols, *Representing Reality,* 48.

32. Quoted in Kirchendoerffer, "Flash, Cash and the Ratings Dash," 33.

33. The history of the public television audience and how it has been constructed by PBS is a long and complicated one. It is described in detail in Laurie Ouellette, *Viewers Like Us: How Public TV Failed the People* (New York: Columbia University Press, 2002).

34. Mittell, "Cultural Approach," 10.

Teaching Us to Fake It

The Ritualized Norms of Television's "Reality" Games

Nick Couldry

Whatever its contribution to the overblown claims of semiotics as a general "science" of language, Roland Barthes's analysis of "myth"[1] and its connection to ideology remains useful as a specific tool to understand particular types of media language such as advertising and also, I suggest, that most striking recent phenomenon, "reality television." Myth itself, Ernesto Laclau has argued, is increasingly a requirement of contemporary societies whose divisions and dislocations multiply.[2] If this is correct, reality TV's mythical claim to represent an increasingly complex social space, for example in the largely entertainment mode of the gamedoc or reality game show, may have significance far beyond the analysis of television genre. I will make this argument more precise by considering reality TV's ritual dimensions and their link to certain media-centric norms of social behavior.

The idea underlying reality TV is hardly new. Here is the television anchorman who commented on the 1969 Apollo moon touchdown speaking three decades ago: "[Television's] real value is to make people participants in ongoing experiences. Real life is vastly more exciting than synthetic life, and this is real-life drama with audience participation."[3] This idea—and the associated claim of television to present "real life"—does not disappear in the era of television "plenty"[4] but instead comes under increasing pressure to take new forms. The subgenre of "gamedocs," on which I concentrate here, is a later adaptation to those pressures, succeeding an early wave of "docusoaps" and TV verité in the mid-1990s[5] and a subsequent crisis of many docusoaps' documentary authority because of scandals about fake productions[6] for example, over Carlton TV's documentary *The Connection* (1999), which supposedly uncovered an operation for smuggling drugs from Colombia but was alleged by the London *Guardian* to have faked various scenes.

If the gamedoc signifies a shift to a "postdocumentary" television culture,[7] the result is not an abandonment of reality claims but their transformation. As John Corner puts it, discussing the first British series of *Big Brother*: "*Big Brother* operates its claims to the real within a fully managed artificiality, in which almost everything that might be deemed to be true about what people do and say is necessarily and obviously predicated on the larger contrivance of them being there in front of the camera in the first place."[8]

My interest here is less in the gamedoc as generic form (excellently discussed by Corner) but in the wider social process that gamedocs constitute. At stake in these often much-hyped programs is a whole way of reformulating the media's (not just television's) deep-seated claim to present social reality, to be the "frame" through which we access the reality that matters to us as social beings.[9] In the gamedoc, this claim involves the promotion of specific norms of behavior to which those who court popularity by living in these shows' constructed spaces must conform.

To get analytic purchase on this complex process, the term "myth" by itself is too blunt. Instead, we need the more precise notions of "ritual" and "ritualization" that can link television form to wider issues of authority and governmentality.[10] As Gareth Palmer notes, most contemporary self-performance can be interpreted in the light of Michel Foucault's theory of governmentality, whereby power is reproduced through norms not just of control but also of expression and self-definition. But I want to push further than Palmer does the implications of the fact that in gamedocs "what develop[s is] not so much a self [as] a *media self*."[11]

What is this media self? What is its social status, and what are its social consequences? To link gamedocs to "governmentality" is not enough since all contemporary social space is in this sense "governed" by norms that regulate what is acceptable, meaningful, and pleasurable and what is not. We need also to ask: Are gamedocs such as *Big Brother*[12] spaces for reflecting on governmentality shared by performers and audiences alike; or are they spaces for audiences to reflect on governmentality by watching others (the performers) being "governed"; or, finally, are they a process whereby both performers and audiences are in effect governed through the unreflexive naturalization of particular behavioral norms?

The Ritual Space of the Reality Gameshow

What might we mean by the "ritual" properties of television forms such as the gamedoc?[13]

Ritual Action and Media Form

First, it is important to emphasize that by "ritual" I mean more than habitual actions. While much of gamedocs *does* consist of "rituals" in this common use of the term (as people get up, eat, wash up, chat, and sleep for the cameras), this use adds nothing to the idea of "habit." Instead, I am interested in the two more-substantive, anthropological senses of "ritual": (a) as formalized action and (b) as action (often, but not necessarily, formalized) associated with certain transcendent values.

Sense (a) captures how certain action-patterns are not only repeated but organized in a form or shape that has a meaning over and above any meaning of the actions taken by themselves. So putting a ring on a finger in the context of a wedding signifies the act of marriage, and putting a wafer in a mouth, again in a very specific context and not elsewhere, signifies the act of Holy Communion. The leading theorist of ritual, the late Roy Rappaport, defined ritual as "the performance of more or less invariant sequences of formal acts and utterances *not entirely encoded* by the performers";[14] ritual action, in other words, is always more than it seems. In sense (b) of the term "ritual," less emphasis is placed on the formality of actions and more on the kinds of values with which those actions are associated. In a line of argument that goes back to the great French sociologist Émile Durkheim's *Elementary Forms of Religious Life*,[15] many have seen in ritual action an affirmation of the values underlying the social bond itself, which is more important than its exact formal properties.

When I talk of "media rituals," I am combining aspects of these two senses. From the formal analysis of ritual (sense [a]), I am taking the idea that rituals can reproduce the building blocks of belief without involving any explicit content that is believed. Far from every ritual expressing a hidden essence in which the performers explicitly believe, rituals by their repetitive form reproduce categories and patterns of thought in a way that *bypasses* explicit belief. On the contrary, then, if made explicit, many of the ideas apparently expressed by ritual might be rejected or at least called into question; it is their *ritualized* form that enables them to be successfully reproduced without being exposed to questions about their "content." This is useful in understanding how ritual works in relation to media, where, quite clearly, there is no explicit credo of shared beliefs about media that everyone accepts.

From the "transcendent" account of ritual (sense [b]), I am taking the idea that there is an essential link between ritual and certain social values or at least certain very large *claims* about the social. As I have argued elsewhere, there is a striking similarity between the socially oriented values (our sense of what binds us as members of a society) that underlie Durkheim's sociology of religion and the types of claims that media, even now, implicitly make about their power to represent "the social."[16]

Media rituals are actions that reproduce the myth that the media are our privileged access point to social reality, but they work through the boundaries and category distinctions around which media rituals are organized, not through articulated beliefs. Let us adopt the following working definition: media rituals are formalized actions organized around key media-related categories and boundaries whose performances suggest a connection with wider, media-related values.[17]

What aspects of the gamedoc process would count as media rituals on this definition? One example would be the "ceremony" developed in the British version of *Big Brother* on each night when a housemate is evicted. Once the result of the week's popular vote has been announced to the housemates by live link from the *Big Brother* studio, the evictee is given one hour exactly to get his or her baggage ready. With one minute to go, the lead presenter, Davina McColl, walks live from the studio across the barrier to the house. The door to the house is opened, and the evictee emerges, clutching belongings, usually to the cheers of their supporters in the crowd outside. From the house door, McColl leads the evictee, as they take in the adulation of the crowd, back to the studio for a live interview, where they are asked to reflect on their time in the house.

This weekly pattern has been repeated in each British *Big Brother* series until the series' final week when the final housemate leaves the house as winner. In its regularity we have a clever simulation of other forms of television ceremonial. But it is not the formalization that I have most in mind in calling this a media ritual; rather, it is the way the whole sequence is based around a fundamental boundary between "ordinary person" and "media person"—in other words, around the media-value celebrity.[18] As a basic point of *Big Brother* is to enact a transition for each housemate from ordinary person to media person, the eviction ceremony is designed to make that transition seem natural (natural as television event, that is).

The "celebrification process"[19] in *Big Brother* is obvious to everyone, both performers and viewers, even though it is far from transparent in its details and exclusions.[20] But its significance goes wider, since underlying the idea that the housemates become celebrities is another more basic media value: that being in the *Big Brother* house is somehow *more significant* than being outside the house. In other words, mediated reality is somehow "higher" than, or more significant than, nonmediated reality—which, as I have argued elsewhere,[21] is the value that underlies the legitimation of media institutions' general concentration of symbolic power.

BB3's winner, Kate Lawler, in her reactions in her final hour in the house, vividly enacted the boundary and hierarchy between media and nonmedia "worlds." She cried and seemed overawed by the transition from the apparently private but of course intensely mediated world of the *Big Brother* house to the explicitly mediated world outside with its cheering crowds and press flash bulbs. When McColl came to interview her *inside* the house (on the series' final night, the winner gets to be interviewed inside the house, where only he or she has earned the right to stay), Kate had difficulty speaking. She acted starstruck in front of Davina (who in Great Britain is a minor celebrity in her own right, because of *Big Brother*). Davina turned back to her the standard phrase used by fans on meeting their idol: "No, it's me who can't believe I'm sitting here with *you*" (BB3, 26 July 2002).

Acting "Up" for the Cameras

At this point, I shift the focus to the related concept of "ritualization." For it is in the dynamic relationship between the ritual high points of, say, *Big Brother* and the wider process of ritualizing the often banal actions in the *Big Brother* house that we find the best entry point to the social, not merely textual, process that gamedocs constitute.

Media rituals cannot, any more than rituals in general, be studied in isolation from the larger hinterland of ritualization: that is, the whole gamut of patterns of action, thought, and speech that generate the categories and boundaries on which media rituals are based. It is this hinterland of everyday action that makes the special case of media rituals possible.

As anthropologist Catherine Bell argues in her study of religious ritual, ritualization organizes our movements around space, helps us experience constructed features of the environment as real, and thereby reproduces the symbolic authority at stake in the categorizations on which ritual draws.[22] The background ritualizations that underlie media rituals work in a similar way, through the organization of all sorts of actions around key media-related categories ("media person/ thing/ place/ world," "liveness," "reality").[23]

Ritualization is our way of tracing how rituals connect to power; for media rituals, the link in question is to the increasing organization of social life around media centers. Drawing again on Bell, we must study how:

> the orchestrated construction of power and authority in ritual . . . engage[s] the social body in the objectification of oppositions and the deployment of schemes that effectively reproduce the divisions of the social order. In this objectification lie the resonance of ritual and the consequences of compliance.[24]

In principle, this could lead us from the celebrification rituals of *Big Brother* to the mass of actions whereby all of us contribute to celebrity culture (buying celebrity magazines, for example). But with gamedocs, there is also a tighter link between ritual and ritualization: What are the nine weeks in the *Big Brother* house if not a space of ritualization, where housemates' banal everyday routines are tested for their appropriateness to a mediated space?

If rituals are naturalized, stable forms for reproducing power relations, ritualization is the much wider process through which the categories underlying those power relations *become* naturalized in action, thought, and words. The raw material of ritualization is much more liable to be destabilized by doubt, reflexivity, and correction. The action in the BB3 house reflected similar instabilities, as various housemates thought about leaving the house voluntarily (see below). A particular focus in BB3 was the housemates' mutual accusations of performing to the cameras and the anxious denials that resulted. It could be argued, of course, that all this was part of BB3's developing plot and entertainment value, but we see below how, on the contrary, this issue opened up conflicts among housemates, and between housemates and the show's producers, about the norms of behavior in the house, conflicts that could not be contained within BB3 as a "game."

Gamedocs and Real "Experience"

One of the words most frequently used by BB3 contestants was "experience": they wanted to make the most of the "*Big Brother* experience," they were asked how their "experience" in the house had gone when they left, and so on. Although hardly a simple word to disentangle, "experience" connotes something both significant and real, and usually something *more* significant and real than the everyday run of things. But since the conditions of the *Big Brother* house made it exceptional from the start, there was always a tension: Was the *Big Brother* experience significant because it was exceptional, or was it significant because, however exceptional it seemed, it showed something important about the underlying continuities of human nature? Such ambiguities are the very stuff of myth in Barthes's sense.[25]

However ambiguous the claims of *Big Brother* and other gamedocs to represent "reality," without *some* such claim, their status—as shows that make celebrities out of real "ordinary people"—collapses. Every gamedoc has a specific myth about how it represents the social world. A number of British shows rely on the myth that, in the face of extreme physical challenges, especially those requiring team collaboration (however artificially constructed), an important aspect of human "reality" is shown. This is the myth underlying *Survivor* (Carlton TV, 2000), an international format less successful than *Big Brother* in Great Britain, perhaps because it is less obviously aimed at a stereotypical "young" audience (having some middle-aged contestants and much less emphasis on celebrity and sex), although arguably the almost comic exoticism of *Survivor*'s British version (with its tribal gatherings and the like) undermines its wider reality claim in any case.[26]

In *Castaway 2000* (BBC1, 2000), a failed variant on the *Survivor* theme produced for the millennial year, 35 people were put onto Taransay, a deserted island just off the coast of the Hebridean island of Harris, to see how they would survive for one year. Taransay, in fact, is in full view of one of the most beautiful beaches in Scotland (I know because I holiday on Harris myself), so its claim to present a controlled experiment in genuine isolation was strained from the outset. The program's mythical intent was clear from its opening voice-over:

Castaway 2000 is a unique experiment to discover what happens when a group representative of British society today is stranded away from modern life. On the deserted Scottish island of Taransay, they'll have a year to decide how to run the community, devise new ways of living together, and reflect on what aspects of life are really important in the 21st century.[27]

Other recent experiments have sought to mine the old myth of "human nature" even further. *The Experiment* (BBC2, 2002; with a subsequent U.S. version) offered a reworking by two psychologists of the well-known U.S. 1970s "Prisoner" experiment, which had pitted two selected groups against each other, one in the role of "guards" and the other in the role of "prisoners," in order to test how far the former exploited their artificial authority over the latter. Here the program relied both on the myth of objectivity built into psychological experimentation and the additional myth that cameras changed nothing significant about the "experiment."

The BBC has now produced a further variation on *Castaway* and *Survivor*, sending a group of selected teenagers to the Borneo jungle. *Serious Jungle* has not been broadcast as I write,[28] but from the producers' comments, it is the youth (and supposed innocence?) of the contestants that underwrites its claim to truth, refracted through the fictional model of *Lord of the Flies:* "*Serious Jungle* has a serious point to it, and because it is focused on children, the viewers will see very clear and honest reactions to their experiences."[29] At the same time, the organizer of the teenagers' trip showed a touching faith in the quality of the experiences they would undergo, mixing the myth of television's superior "reality" with the older myth of the encounter with "nature":

> For the first time these children will be forging relationships that are no longer about what music they like or what trainers they wear. They will change so much during these few weeks that going home to their old friends could be quite difficult for them.[30]

In spite of the implied distinction from the youth culture represented by *Big Brother* here, nowhere is the underlying myth of gamedocs challenged: that there is plausibility in reading human "reality" into what transpires in a space made and monitored "for television."

The particular success in Great Britain of *Big Brother* may derive, in part, from its clever mix of mythical authorities: the suggestion of scientific experiment is there (with "top psychologists" even being given their own show on each Sunday night of BB3), along with the validating myths of celebrity and popular "interactivity." "Popular participation" is itself, of course, a useful myth; viewers of *Big Brother*, after all, have no control over its format, the initial choice of participants, the instructions or rules given to participants, the principles of editing, or, indeed, how the "popular vote" is interpreted to contestants and audience.

None of these contradictions should surprise us. For it is precisely in the oscillation between contingent detail and some broader mythical value that, for anthropologist Maurice Bloch, echoing Barthes, the power of ritual lies.[31] In Bloch's analysis of Madagascan rituals, the broader value is that of "ancient history" lost in the mists of time; in contemporary societies, no one believes in history in that sense, but the myths of human nature, science, and what Marc Auge has called "the ideology of the present"[32] are powerful substitutes.

The Norms of Reality Performance

There is another myth reproduced through the gamedoc form and its apparently innocent rituals of television celebrity. I say "myth," but it is more like a half-statement that works largely by *not* being articulated, hence its affinity to ritual. This is the idea that surveillance is a natural mode through which to observe the social world. Few, perhaps, would subscribe explicitly to the will to "omniperception" (as the leading sociologist of surveillance puts it)[33] implied here, but by constant media repetition it risks rigidifying into a myth that is fully integrated into our everyday expectations of the social.

The Pleasures of Surveillance

What are we to make of the idea that, to find out about an aspect of social reality, it is natural to set up an "experimental situation" (with or without the endorsement of qualified psychologists), watch what happens when people are either not yet aware of the presence of cameras or are presumed to have forgotten it, and treat the result as "reality"? You might think it hypocritical for a sociologist, like myself, who regularly interviews and observes others, to protest so much. But there is an obvious difference between the gamedoc and the normal context for sociological and psychological research: confidentiality.

Remember that *The Experiment* was in part designed by two psychologists as a hybrid of entertainment form and experimental situation.[34] Never in the recent history of the social and psychological sciences have studies been conducted for a simultaneous *public* audience, unless we return to Jean-Martin Charcot's public demonstrations in the 1870s with hysterics at the Paris Salpètriere, recalling the long history of public operations on the living and the dead that preceded him. Yet even in that early modern history of public experiment, there is no parallel for experimental subjects being watched in permanently retrievable form by an audience of millions.

The emerging model of surveillance and governance, and the rejuvenated "experimental science" that is parasitic on them, is disturbing. Its implications go wider than the popular legitimation of everyday surveillance, important as that is.[35] For surveillance-entertainment (a cumbersome, but equally accurate, name for the gamedoc) has implications for everyday social relations that surveillance focused on criminal activity does not. While the saturation of public space with closed-circuit TV (CCTV) is, of course, a matter of concern, the issue is more its effects on the quality of everyone's experience of public space rather than the effects on how people might perform in front of the visible and invisible cameras. And this is precisely why the performances in front of surveillance cameras, by New York art campaigners The Surveillance Camera Players, are striking, as ways of denaturalizing a dimension of public life that we screen out of our consciousness entirely. But in surveillance-entertainment, the impacts on "performance" are surely the *key* issue, since its underlying premise is that we can expect *any* everyday activity legitimately to be put under surveillance and monitored for a huge unknown audience.

It is remarkable how easy it is to hide this disturbing idea beneath the cloak of ritual. In a six-part series introduced by Britain's Channel 4 in 2002 called *Make My Day,* the *Big Brother* format was turned adeptly into a pure entertainment package. The idea of the program was a simple, if alarming, extension of the *Candid Camera* format: friends or family nominate someone to the producers to be put under secret surveillance for a day to test their reactions to five challenges; if all are passed, the unwitting contestant wins £5,000 and retrospectively the "benefit" of having "starred" for national television "in her very own game show" (as one episode put it). The "challenges" are simple tests of the subject's ability to act as a person with a "normal" sexual appetite and a "natural" interest in celebrity. Will this young woman let into her house a half-naked man

The Surveillance Camera Players, New York art campaigners, perform in front of surveillance cameras—in this case, by holding up a sign. Photo courtesy of Bill Brown.

(recruited to match her tastes in men) needing to make an urgent phone call? Yes!—move to stage two. Will the same young woman allow herself to be distracted from getting to work when a member of her favorite pop band approaches her in the street, pretending to be lost and needing help to find his way? Yes!—move to stage three, and so on.

This series attracted little attention, and the predictability of its challenges was surely a weakness. What is interesting, however, is how the unwitting contestants reacted at the end of the day, when its strange events were explained to them by the well-known British celebrity and show narrator, Sara Cox.[36] What we saw on the program—and, of course, we have no way of knowing how far this was rehearsed or edited—is the contestant delighted, even awestruck, at the revelation, clutching her face, crying out "Oh, my God!" and the like. Any later reflections by the contestant on having in effect consented to being submitted to 12 hours of secret filming for national television (including an opening scene in their bedroom) were left to our speculation.

My point is not to moralize about this particular series but to offer it as an example of how easily consent to the process of surveillance before a national audience (even if quite counterintuitive) can be made to seem natural, given the right ritual context. Here are Sara Cox's explanatory words to one contestant:

> Hello [NAME], it's Sara Cox here. You must be thinking you have had the strangest day of your life. Well it's all because of Channel 4's *Make My Day*. We have been secretly filming you using hidden cameras all day long and we reckon its about time you got out from under your mother's feet so as a big thank you we would love to give you a deposit on your first flat. . . . I really hope we've made your day.

The program is useful because it is so artless. Here we see quite directly how two positive behavioral norms (one automatically positive—obtaining your own independent place to live and the other increasingly constructed as positive in contemporary British culture: showing an interest in celebrity) are combined to make the program's whole sequence of events seem natural and legitimate. (It must also have helped the producers that the "contestant" was living with her mother, who presumably gave legal consent to the presence of cameras in her daughter's bedroom.)

Underwriting those norms here is the principle that "media experience" (discovering that the contestant's meetings with celebrities were not just accidental but "real," that is, planned specifically by the media for her) automatically trumps "ordinary experience," including any questionable ethical dimensions it may have. This is a social "magic" (in Marcel Mauss's sense): a transformative "principle that eludes examination" which nonetheless we must try to unravel.[37]

The Real (Mediated) Me

BB3 differed from previous British series of *Big Brother* in its emerging divide between those housemates who were clearly unhappy with the expected norms for behavior in the house and those who broadly accepted those norms. Even among the latter were a number who were unhappy at times, including the eventual finalists ("[*Big Brother* voice] How are you feeling, Alex? [Alex] Um . . . institutionalised").[38] Of the former, two left voluntarily and another (Sandy, who happened to be the only housemate without fashionable "young" looks) remained quiet and isolated for a few weeks before being voted out (as the *Big Brother* voice-over noted on one occasion: "Sandy was the first to go to bed," cut to Sandy reading a book in bed).[39]

An interesting case was Tim, the only obviously upper-class house-mate, a later replacement in the house who never settled. He was not so much withdrawn, like Sandy, as openly complaining about the "tasks" given to the housemates and the way others played up to the cameras. His complaints (in the program's famous Diary Room) were portrayed by the producers, through editing and commentary, as that of a moaner, who, conveniently, was also discovered to be physically vain when his black hair dye started to show and he was caught on camera shaving his chest in the apparent privacy of his bed.

There was no particular drama to his eviction (on 19 July 2002), since he had made it clear on camera that he was "desperate" to leave the house. The eviction was presented in a hostile manner by McColl before the vote result: "The whole house thinks Tim's going to be out and to be honest the whole of the nation thinks Tim's going to be out." Tim emerged from the house to boos and hisses from the waiting crowd. His live interview was more dramatic; criticized by Davina for his whining and unwillingness to play the *Big Brother* game, he responded that he had thought the set tasks "could have been a bit more mature." He was challenged to defend his charge that other housemates were playing up to the cameras:

Davina: On a number of occasions you talked about performing, other people performing, what did you mean by that?

Tim: The whole time I was in there I was very much myself. I don't think my whole personality came out, because there wasn't much to stimulate a lot of it . . . but there were a lot of people in there who I'm convinced are not like that in their normal life . . .

Davina: [interrupting] Like who?

Tim: [continues over Davina] and when I spoke to them one to one and you found out more about them as a person, that's the side I re-ally liked, but they never showed enough of that. As soon as a cam-era came in or they felt they were being watched, they were up and [mimes clapping to music] singing and dancing and sure the public obviously like it because they get really into it but . . .

Davina: [interrupts again] But it's not that it's that, I think that generally some of them are quite up, positive people. [cheering in background from crowd to whom the conversation is being relayed outside on large screens] If you can't perform, physically you can't do it, not for 7 or 8 weeks, you can't do it.

Tim: No, there were times when they didn't and they dipped, and that's the times you saw them when they weren't acting.

Davina: OK, Tim . . . let's move on to something a bit more positive.[40]

There is an unresolvable conflict here between two norms of how to behave in the house: first, to give the public what they are assumed to want ("singing and dancing" [Tim], or being "up, positive people" [Davina]) and, second, the unobjectionable but also vague norm of "being yourself." If as a housemate you find the second norm is incompatible with the first, what are you to do?

Many housemates betrayed anxiety about whether they had been "themselves," for example Jonny (the eventual runner-up) who asked Jade why his housemates had put him up for eviction more than once and was told it was because "you've studied it, you know what the people on the outside would like."[41] He vehemently denied this, but in his eviction interview on the series' final night (26 July 2002), he failed to resolve the contradiction. When asked by Davina "Who's the real you?," the melancholy loner smoking by the pool or the comic performer, he responded immediately:

Jonny: The real me's the stupid, idiotic clown, but it takes a lot to get us down to the serious quiet Jonny, but it worked in there.

Davina: It stripped you down, did it?

Jonny: Yes.

But he admitted at another point: "I don't care what anybody says, you're always aware of the cameras and on the other end of them cameras is your family and your friends who you love."

Or take Sophie, a late arrival who appeared unhappy during much of her time in the house but who (like Jonny) was treated favorably in the shows' comments on her performance. Here is an exchange from her eviction interview (28 June 2002), where Davina asks a standard question, drawing on the idea of "media experience" being better (or "bigger") than ordinary experience.[42] Sophie's answer is ambiguous:

Davina: What's it like in that house? . . . I mean it's like a pressure cooker . . .

Sophie: It is.

Davina: Everything's big, feelings are felt stronger, what was it like for you?

Sophie: Um, I felt. . . . It's very . . . false in a way. . . . I mean, everyone in the house, . . . they've not got a mask on but . . .

Here contemporary media's wide-ranging myth that cameras tell us more about underlying reality because they magnify feelings that are presumed already to exist is directly contradicted.

These contradictions matter, because they cannot, in principle, be resolved. They are contradictions within the myth that *Big Brother* produces to legitimate itself: on the one hand, it claims to show us the human reality that must "come out" when ordinary people live for a long time under the cameras; on the other hand, it polices any differences of interpretation about what that "reality" should be, ruling out any behavior excluded by the production choices it makes and ruling in the "positive" selves that it presumes the public wants to see and the contestants want to display. Once contestants start to doubt the latter reality, as in BB3, there is nowhere for the producers to turn but ritual: either rituals of vilification as turned on Tim, who posed the most direct threat to the show's norms, or rituals of incorporation, affirming the show's status by including successful housemates into the club of celebrity. Here are Davina's final words on the last night:

Kate entered the house unknown and now she's taking her first innocent steps into a world of unseen wealth and privilege, . . . offers of casual sex, fame beyond her dreams, and general admiration. . . . I hope you've enjoyed this as much as I have. This has been *Big Brother* 2002. Thank you for watching. Good bye.

The producers could afford some irony here, of course, in the show's final moments, but not, as we have seen, when the show's myth was directly challenged.[43]

Toward an Ethics of Reality TV

Where has this brief skeptical tour of the British gamedoc brought us? Clearly, the gamedoc is a generic adaptation of considerable robustness (after all, it no longer carries the docusoap's hostage to fortune, the residual claim to documentary authority), and, in the case of the British version of *Big Brother*, great resourcefulness and commercial promise: BB3 was widely reported as having "rescued" Channel 4 in the 2002 season.[44]

The underlying argument in this chapter, however, is that our analysis cannot rest with observations on the adaptability of television genres. For *Big Brother* and all gamedocs are *social* processes that take real individuals and submit them to surveillance, analysis, and selective display as a means to entertainment and enhanced audience participation. It is this social process, not the program's textual properties, that should be our main focus, and I offer some concepts (myth, ritual, and ritualization) to help us grasp its real and ideological dimensions.

There is, of course, one further stage to which the argument needs to be taken, and that is ethics. What are the ethics of surveillance-entertainment? Or, perhaps as the first question: Where should we stand to get an adequate perspective on the possible ethical dimensions of the social process that gamedocs constitute, both by themselves and in their interface with the rest of social life? Finding that perspective is not easy. Part of the fascination of that oxymoron, reality television, is its ambiguity, which in the case of *Big Brother* rests on another: between the expressive, almost obsessively self-reflexive individualization that it displays for us ("saturated individualism," as Michel Maffesoli has called it)[45] and the barely accountable "exemplary center"[46] that underwrites (or seeks to underwrite) the plausibility and legitimacy of that display.

By "exemplary center," I mean the mythical "social center"[47] that media institutions, even as they face unprecedented pressures from the dispersal of media production and consumption, attempt to project: the apparently naturally existing social "world" to which television likes to claim it gives us access. The point is not that we can do without media or that media are exactly the same as other unaccountable forms of governmental or corporate power, but that we cannot avoid at some point turning to ethical critique if we are to address how media are transforming, and being transformed by, the social space in which, like it or not, we have to live. This chapter, I hope, has provided some useful starting points for that wider debate.

NOTES

1. Roland Barthes, *Mythologies* (London: Paladin, 1972).

2. Ernesto Laclau, *New Reflections on the Revolution of Our Time* (London: Verso, 1990), 67.

3. Quoted in Carolyn Marvin, *Blood Sacrifice and the Nation* (Cambridge: Cambridge University Press, 1999), 159.

4. John Ellis, *Seeing Things: Television in the Age of Uncertainty* (London: IB Tauris, 2000).

5. Ib Bondjeberg, "Public Discourse / Private Fascination," *Media Culture and Society* 18 (1996), 27–45; Richard Kilborn, "'How Real Can You Get?' Recent Developments in 'Reality' Television," *European Journal of Communication* 13.2 (1994), 201–18.

6. Caroline Dover, "British Documentary Television Production: Tradition, Change and 'Crisis' within a Practitioner Community," Ph.D. diss., University of London, 2001.

7. John Corner, "Performing the Real: Documentary Diversions," *Television and New Media* 3.3 (2002), 255–70.

8. Ibid., 256.

9. Nick Couldry, *The Place of Media Power: Pilgrims and Witnesses of Media Power* (London: Routledge, 2000). See also Roger Silverstone, "Television Myth and Culture," in *Media Myths and Narratives*, ed. J. Carey (Newbury Park, Calif.: Sage, 1988).

10. Nick Couldry, *Media Rituals: A Critical Approach* (London: Routledge, 2002); and Gareth Palmer, "*Big Brother*: An Experiment in Governance," *Television and New Media* 3.3 (2002), 311–22.

11. Palmer, "*Big Brother*," 305–6; emphasis added.

12. *Big Brother*, third series, which I'll call "BB3" (May–July 2002), is my main example.

13. The term "ritual" is a difficult one, and there is no space here to explain in detail its history or my specific use of the term "media rituals" (but see Couldry, *Media Rituals*).

14. Roy Rappaport, *Ritual and Religion in the Making of Humanity* (Cambridge: Cambridge University Press, 1999), 24; emphasis added.

15. Émile Durkheim, *The Elementary Forms of Religious Life*, trans. Karen Fields (1912; reprint, Glencoe, Ill.: Free Press, 1995).

16. Couldry, *Media Rituals*.

17. For further background, see ibid., chapters 1–3.

18. Nick Couldry, "Playing for Celebrity: *Big Brother* as Ritual Event," *Television and New Media* 3.3 (2002), 289.

19. For this term, see Chris Rojek, *Celebrity* (London: Reaktion Books, 2001), 186–87.

20. Couldry "Playing for Celebrity."

21. Couldry, *Place of Media Power,* chapter 3.

22. Catherine Bell, *Ritual Theory, Ritual Practice* (New York: Oxford University Press, 1992).

23. On these categories, see Couldry, *Media Rituals.*

24. Bell, *Ritual Theory,* 215

25. Barthes, *Mythologies.*

26. Interestingly, the *Survivor* prize money is £1 million, compared with *Big Brother*'s £70,000 which is surprising until you realize that the more successful *Big Brother* contestants have in the past picked up promotional deals, hosted television shows, or issued pop singles.

27. *Castaway 2000,* 25 January 2000.

28. For more, see the *Serious Jungle* website, at www.bbc.co.uk/talent/jungle.

29. Marshall Corwin, producer, quoted in *Observer* (London), 31 March 2002, 15.

30. Alex Patterson, quoted in ibid.

31. Maurice Bloch, *Ritual, History and Power* (London: Athlone, 1989), 130.

32. Mark Auge, "Le Stade de l'écran," *Le Monde Diplomatique,* June 2001, 24.

33. David Lyon, *Surveillance Society: Monitoring Everyday Life* (Milton Keynes, Buckingham [England]: Open University Press, 2001), 124–25.

34. Steve Reicher and Alex Haslam, quoted in *Guardian* (London), 3 May 2002, 7.

35. For more, see Mark Andrejevic, "Little Brother Is Watching: The Webcam Subculture and the Digital Enclosure," in *Media/Space,* ed. Nick Couldry and A. McCarthy (London: Routledge, 2004); Couldry, *Media Rituals,* chapter 6; and Palmer, "*Big Brother.*"

36. Cox is host DJ of Radio 1's high-profile early morning show.

37. Quoted in Pierre Bourdieu, *The State Nobility* (Cambridge: Polity, 1996), 7.

38. BB3, 17 July 2002.

39. Ibid., 29 May 2002.

40. This and later passages are my transcription.

41. BB3, 28 June 2002.

42. See also Couldry, *Place of Media Power,* 113, cf. 47–48.

43. Such irony is often misinterpreted as skepticism or distance, when, in fact, its effect is just the opposite. Slavoj Zizek, *The Sublime Object of Ideology* (London: Verso, 1989), 32–33; see also Couldry, *Place of Media Power,* 45.

44. For example, *Guardian* (London), 27 July 2002, 7.

45. Michel Maffesoli, *The Time of the Tribes* (London: Sage, 1996), 64.

46. Clifford Geertz, *Negara: The Theatre State in Nineteenth-Century Bali* (Princeton, N.J.: Princeton University Press, 1980), 13.

47. See also Couldry, *Media Rituals,* chapter 3.

||||||||||||||||||||||||||||||||||||||||||||||||||||||

Extraordinarily Ordinary
The Osbournes as "An American Family"

Derek Kompare

On March 5, 2002, on MTV, a voice-over invited us to "meet the perfect American family." A teenage girl is seen throwing a ball at her brother's crotch; their mother tells the camera she's not Mother Theresa, and then tells her children to "shut the fuck up and go to bed." We see the son making annoying noises and the daughter dismissing other people's opinions about her hair. Finally, we're introduced to the dad, who screams "rock and roll!" at the camera and is shown in a quick montage of behavior: gyrating onstage, getting out of airplanes, watching TV, walking the dog. The opening sequence ends with a shirtless dad telling his family "I love you all . . . I love you more than life itself . . . but you're all fucking mad!"

Welcome to the Osbourne family, the "perfect American family" of MTV's *The Osbournes*. Dad (Ozzy) is a veteran heavy metal rocker in rehabilitation for years of excess; mom (Sharon) is his longtime wife/manager and unyielding household authority; son (Jack) is an "oddball" at school and plays with knives; daughter (Kelly) throws fits, teases her colorful hair, and strategizes about staying out past curfew without getting caught. Even in an age of constant media hype, the enormous notoriety of *The Osbournes* in the spring of 2002 was surprising. By its fifth episode, it was MTV's all-time highest-rated regular series, regularly capturing more than 6 million viewers numbers that the long-running reality pioneer *The Real World* had never attained. Moreover, the Osbournes' fame spread well beyond MTV, as the series and family were the subjects of numerous articles, analyses, and interviews in the media throughout the spring of 2002.[1]

While such coverage is not unprecedented for television families, it had been almost 30 years since a television series centering on an *actual*

The unconventional Osbourne family star in the first reality sitcom.

family garnered this much attention in the mainstream media. The 1973 PBS documentary series *An American Family* featured the Loud family of Santa Barbara, California, who were subject to similar media and viewer interest as nearly a year of their lives unfolded in 13 television episodes. Like the Osbournes, the Louds were featured on magazine covers and talk shows, quoted in reviews, and satirized in cartoons. As the title of their series indicated, they became an emblem for the "American family" of the early 1970s.

Both *An American Family* and *The Osbournes* were media phenomena. That is, they were idiosyncratic texts that commanded a sudden, high degree of attention during their initial runs, prompting discussions about family and television throughout the media and society. However, although markedly "different" from regular television fare, both series still had to engage with established normative codes of genre and family in order to succeed. The operation of these normative codes reveals how much power they still hold and how they are shrewdly used by newer techniques and approaches as a foundation of meanings from which to construct new texts. In tracing these familiar codes in these otherwise unique texts, we can understand how the categories of the "ordinary" and the "extraordinary" are deployed in the pursuit of textual coherence and cultural significance.

While *An American Family* and *The Osbournes* are similar in many respects, they also have significant differences. Foremost among these is the fact that the scandalous reaction to *An American Family* in 1973 did not materialize in regard to *The Osbournes* in 2002. In the early 1970s, *An American Family* was regarded primarily as a manipulative sociological experiment in perpetual surveillance. The Louds themselves were generally seen by critics either as ciphers (i.e., symbols of the fallout of the 1960s) or, conversely, as victims of unscrupulous producers.[2] By contrast, in the media-saturated early 2000s, *The Osbournes* was hailed as a pinnacle of innovative television comedy, and the Osbourne family was celebrated for their hip parenting and let-it-all-hang-out media savvy.[3]

The shifting mores of American family life may explain part of this perception, but the changing parameters of media representation constitute a more decisive factor. That is, the question of how to represent a "real family" on television is answered quite differently in the 2000s than it was in the 1970s, as the normative boundaries of television programming—particularly concerning the representation of "actualities": actual people and events—have changed considerably in the intervening years.

The very concept of a "real television family" points squarely to questions of *genre* and *family*. Each category establishes limits within which programs, and depictions in general, must adhere to, or at least acknowledge, in order to succeed. Both *An American Family* and *The Osbournes* were conspicuously situated on the boundary between actuality and fiction, drawing established generic codes of reality from the former and narrative and characterization from the latter. Each was widely touted as being the "first" of its particular hybrid genre: the "documentary soap opera" in the case of *An American Family* and the "reality sitcom" for *The Osbournes*.[4] In both instances, a joint claim to "reality" and narration is made, promising both an explicit and engrossing experience.

Both series also claimed to represent "the family." The family has arguably been the primary normative concept governing human interaction since the beginning of recorded history, and its media representations have always been a matter of contention.[5] This has particularly been the case on television, perhaps the media form most suited to promoting and representing familial experience, due to its domestic nature. Regardless of whether they are fictional or real, television families are sites of cultural anxieties, where the work of social cohesion is ritually enacted.[6]

Despite differences between the series, and in the families themselves, the Louds and Osbournes both performed the role of "family" on the national stage of television. It is important to note, however, that while the Louds achieved fame by becoming a television family, the Osbournes had already gained some celebrity, via patriarch Ozzy's notorious career as a heavy metal performer.[7]

Ozzy Osbourne is colloquially known as "the prince of darkness" for his theatrical performances—conveying standard heavy metal themes of gothic horror and, on occasion, biting the heads off of live animals—and lifestyle, which has included the requisite rock star litany of outrageous behavior and substance abuse. His famous physical and emotional excesses formed the basis for the representation of his family on television. Unlike the Louds, who were meant to represent an "every family" whose surface contentment hides emotional distance, the Osbournes were promoted as a specific "*anti*-family" whose visible eccentricities hid a reservoir of intimacy and affection. In keeping with codes of turn-of-the-century reality television, which center on the display of ignominious bodies, the Osbournes themselves literally embody this dichotomy of "ordinary" and "extraordinary" codes.

In this essay, I explore how normative discourses of television genre and family shaped both *An American Family* and *The Osbournes*. I first trace how the terms "genre" and "family" are linked through television and how each has been used to shape the medium's normative codes. Next, I explore the representation of actuality on television and describe how codes of "documentary" have largely ceded to "reality" via a concentration on what I call "ignominious bodies." Then, I focus more directly on *The Osbournes* itself, where these normative categories of genre and family are enacted largely through the Osbournes' bodies. In the end, the success of *The Osbournes* indicates how contemporary reality television, no matter how innovative, relies on established normative discourses.

Genre and Family

Both *The Osbournes* and *An American Family* were premised on an awareness of the categories of genre and family. That is, their representations of "real" families were informed by established television and cinematic genres and a self-conscious sense of normative family life. Genre and family are normative concepts that describe limited categories: a text or social grouping is only considered as an example of a particular genre or family if it meets certain expectations. While these expectations change over time and circumstances, the normative structure itself is constant.

For example, while there may be new or alternative conceptions of family (involving extended kinship, single parents, relationships of choice, etc.), these are still separated from groupings that are somehow "*not* family." Similarly, creators, users, and critics construct discursive boundaries between certain cultural artifacts organizing them into genres. While an artifact may represent multiple genres, it must also *not* represent others, otherwise the distinctions are meaningless.

Thus, the terms "genre" and "family," while ultimately arbitrary, remain important across time, regardless of what they may describe in specific instances. Rick Altman refers to this temporal function of genre as "pseudo-memorial": "When trying to bring together spectators who actually share less and less, what better meeting place than the common past provided by genre itself?"[8] That is, genre itself functions largely as a space of continuity, where particular texts are placed in a common history. The category of "family" has functioned in a similar manner, persisting for millennia, despite frequent social challenges. The two terms come together in media representation, where representations of "family" must adhere to particular generic codes. In turn, this genre of "family" circulates normative representations—that is, models—for real individuals and families to identify with and (ostensibly) emulate.

This process has been fundamental to television, where ideals of both genre and family have systematically organized representations, programs, and audiences for decades. Television genres delimit narrative and representational parameters, facilitating audience (including advertiser) expectations. Television programs have adhered to these boundaries throughout the history of the medium, with few exceptions.[9] Similarly, an entrenched conception of the nuclear family continues to structure television's representational, generic, and financial economy: characters and situations are generally rendered in familial terms; channels, times, and programs are geared toward particular members of the family; and individuals and subgroups within the family are sought by advertisers as potential consumers. There are family channels, family programs, and family hours; soap opera families, sitcom families, and even TV news families. As Ella Taylor remarked in her introduction to *Prime Time Families,* "[television] is watched by a vast number of people in their homes; its advertising is geared to both the parts and the whole of the family unit; its images, in both news and entertainment, are stamped with the familial."[10]

Thus, genre and family are not mere descriptive concepts; they have a normative function and are conceived and applied as social ideals on television and in other forms of media. While the question of whether they actually function as social ideals remains one of intense scrutiny, the *presumption* that they do governs most of the expectations of the medium. Television representations have always had to hold close to these established parameters in order to maintain these expectations.

The normative parameters of genre and family affected the conception, production, promotion, and reception of both *An American Family* and *The Osbournes.* Although both series dealt with real families, they had to engage with the dominant conceptions of genre and family to make the broadcast schedule, let alone reach an audience. However, there have been few available models for representing "real" families on television. Daytime talk shows and prime-time newsmagazines have regularly focused on the travails of families for almost two decades, but the families on these programs have functioned as ciphers for the voyeuristic and therapeutic purposes of these genres. The polarized thematic range of these programs, tending toward the "tragic" in prime time (e.g., diseased or injured family members) and the "excessive" in daytime (e.g., cheating spouses), has exacerbated this anonymity. In addition, these are only "one-off" families, forgotten as soon as the program has ended.[11]

In the 29 years between *An American Family* and *The Osbournes,* only a handful of prime-time documentary series—most on PBS—have explored the idea of family on a more extended basis. Although these programs all examined multiple families, thus diluting the effect of following one family for a sustained period, they still broadened the repertoire of representational codes for the "family" genre on television, and certainly informed the style of *The Osbournes.*[12]

Regardless, in the dominant discourses of television, fictional families like the Cleavers (*Leave It to Beaver*), Bradys (*The Brady Bunch*), Huxtables (*The Cosby Show*), and Simpsons (*The Simpsons*) have defined the "television family." The normative television family is thus a fully *scripted* set of generic expectations. While these expectations have shaped fictional representations, they have also had an effect on representations of actual families.[13] However, when the families in question are real, an additional set of normative expectations, based on the representation of actual people and events, also shapes the text and its reception.

"Documentary" and "Reality"

In *An American Family* and *The Osbournes,* discourses of genre and family are complicated by the fact that each series purports to capture not *normality*—the purview of fictional TV families—but *reality*—life as it "is." Over the past century, documentary has been the dominant cinematic genre of reality or, more accurately, of "actuality": people, objects, and events from real life not as it should be, but, ostensibly, how it is.[14]

As John Corner has recently argued, however, documentary is now "unhelpful" in accounting for the style and sociological impact of contemporary reality television. "Documentary" carries "too many assumptions . . . and idealizations," according to Corner, and he suggests a return to an older concept: "documentation."[15] A broader practice, documentation entails the cataloguing of documents—that is, productions of coded reality, such as performances, writings, and recordings—and not necessarily an explicit rhetoric. While documentary has traditionally claimed to produce truth(s) about its subjects, documentation instead displays examples of actuality; the former functions explicitly as an *argument,* the latter primarily as an *exhibition.*[16]

Documentation also allows for broader uses of cinematic actuality. Corner observes that whereas traditional documentary has followed the modernist truth-seeking functions of civic publicity, journalistic inquiry, and alternative exploration, it has historically not given much consideration for what he calls "diversion": the use of actuality for the production of entertainment rather than the pursuit of truth.[17] But because the familiar codes of actuality from documentary film and television are now not only normative but clichéd—"reality should look and sound like *this*"—they are regularly enlisted in support of entertainment rather than for the more austere practices of edification that the word "documentary" typically conjures up. Accordingly, "documentary," in quotation marks, has become another style to emulate, rather than simply a set of practices between producer and subject. Actualities are now regularly used in the "realist" genres of comedy, drama, and melodrama; have been used to bolster more "fantastic" genres like science fiction and horror; and are essential to pornography.

A new term is therefore needed to distinguish the documentaries of the past from the broader uses of actualities today. The contemporary term, appropriately enough, is "reality." As a major weapon in the pursuit of audience share, the current explosion of "reality television" *depicts,* rather than *explains,* placing a premium on diversion over education. It dwells on the spectacle of the world for its own sake, or in the service of narrative, rather than as proof of an extracinematic truth. Still, this does not necessarily negate the value of any particular reality text or of the endeavor of documentary in the traditional sense. I do not wish to revive the hoary argument that pits entertainment against education, as if the terms are mutually exclusive. Instead, I agree with Corner, who suggests that "documentary will need strategically to redevelop itself within the new economic and cultural contexts for engaging the popular audience, with an acknowledgement of the pattern of tastes that are newly established."[18]

Although Corner is concerned with this transformation in television (from "documentary" to "reality"), which commenced in the late 1980s in conjunction with the shifting economics and technologies of media, the same generic issue also applied to *An American Family,* produced years earlier. As Jeffrey Ruoff contends in his retrospective of the series, the narrative structure, cinematic style, and promotional strategy of *An American Family* indicate how the documentary ideals of the filmmakers—and, to an extent, even of the Louds themselves—were adjusted throughout the project to more closely adhere to the generic standards of television *drama,* and more specifically soap opera, rather than documentary.[19] For example, the opening sequence of the series ended with the title literally exploding, suggesting at the very beginning that the titular family was going to go through traumatic, maybe even fatal, events during the series.[20]

Fictional and nonfictional codes were blurred in both *An American Family* and *The Osbournes* because of similar concerns about genre and audience expectations. Both series contained as many generic elements from classical Hollywood as from classical documentary: the construction of real people as identifiable characters; the sequencing of events into clear, causal narratives; and the use of visual and aural "stings" to punctuate actions and dialogue. They each had a narrow range of codes to draw from, as expectations were limited on one side by fictional television families and on the other by the established genres of "documentary" and "reality," respectively.

While *An American Family* initially signaled a defiance of these limits, striking out against conventional fictional depictions of family life, it ultimately foundered, imploding under the weight of expectations (and even accusations), and achieving a kind of infamy in television history. Conversely, *The Osbournes* (as of this writing in 2008) succeeded in an environment in which "reality entertainment" thrives. The primary reason for its success is its embrace of the normative expectations of genre and family—the opposite of the strategy attempted by *An American Family*—and the primary vehicles for its expression are the bodies of the Osbournes themselves.

The Display of Ignominious Bodies

With an explicit goal of diversion, the reality television of the 1990s and 2000s has used actualities differently than the documentary television of the 1960s and 1970s did. Whereas *An American Family* proceeded from a concern with the "hidden truth" of its subjects, and attempted to reveal the "extraordinary" tensions beneath a veneer of "ordinariness," *The Osbournes* playfully depicted the very ordinariness of its otherwise extraordinary subjects. *An American Family* juxtaposes an archetypal family (e.g., the middle-class dream of a comfortable southern California lifestyle) with representations of "deviant" behavior (e.g., son Lance's homosexuality, the divorce) in pursuit of melodrama; *The Osbournes* contrasts a backdrop of "deviant" behavior (e.g., cursing, ostentation) with displays of archetypal familial bonding (e.g, Ozzy's surprise birthday party) in the service of comedy.

As Ruoff describes, the point of *An American Family* was to peek behind the screen of conformity to get at "the truth" of the typical American family.[21] Producer Craig Gilbert wanted to examine how family life had changed in the 1960s. His background in news production and observational documentary technique, particularly the style of Drew Associates, furnished a sociological dimension to the project that led to its financing and distribution by PBS.[22] Despite the ostensible pursuit of the "truth," however, the producers stacked the deck in their choice of the Loud family of Santa Barbara, California, as "an American family." According to Ruoff, Gilbert deliberately sought a family that resembled the normative ideal as presented in 1950s and 1960s sitcoms like *Father Knows Best* and *The Donna Reed Show*.[23]

Similarly, the chosen family's class status, southern California location, and simmering discontent were all inspired from preconceived ideals drawn largely from fiction.[24] Thus, to a great degree, the Louds were mere players in a preconceived scenario. Despite the project's documentary pedigree, the calculated casting and use of the Louds is similar to current practices in reality television. The major difference today is that, with a premium placed on entertainment, the reality genre has shifted even more toward self-conscious performance (i.e., exhibition) rather than the revelation of "natural behavior."

The prevailing purpose of reality television today, particularly on MTV, is to revel in public displays of ignominy, where actualities are used precisely for their violations of generic norms. Ignominy entails public shame or humiliation, and though this applies to the subjects of these programs, I believe it applies more directly to the genre and its viewers. That is, viewers should perceive these generic violations; a reaction of "you can't do that on television" is the goal of producers and participants.[25] Participants in these programs are regularly shown in various states of ignominy: exhausted, enraged, depressed, careless, undressed, asleep, inebriated, and sick.

Indeed, MTV series like *The Real World, Road Rules,* and *Jackass* are premised on directly placing their subjects in potentially humiliating or even physically dangerous situations.[26] "Reality" in each series is conveyed as a series of explicit encounters between people, or between people and circumstances, generating an engrossing spectacle of actions and reactions. Importantly, while the people and events in these programs need to be demonstrably "real"—not acting—to satisfy generic requirements, they are cast and planned as carefully as in any fiction: the effect of the actualities is amplified if the subjects are more "telegenic": that is, closer to normative codes of televisual appearance and behavior.[27] Both the casting and the limited scope of events allow for what might be called "maximum control of conditions of spontaneity": narrowing the likely range of actions to those with the greatest visual or narrative impact.

At the time of its original broadcast, the "invasion" of the private realm of the Loud family home in *An American Family* was perceived as scandalous. Indeed, the presumed manipulation of the family by the producers became the most contentious issue of public discussion, even more than the depicted actions of the family members themselves. By the time *The Osbournes* was produced, there was little left of the private realm that had not been made public, in a wide variety of media forms. The thrill and ignominy of reality TV is based on the notion that while privacy is still the "norm," it can pleasurably be violated by voyeurism and exhibitionism, as people clamor to see and show "it all."

This is a major shift in the representation of reality from the era of *An American Family*. While the Louds' typicality—though not their onscreen behavior—was, to a significant extent, a setup, it was at least *presented* as a genuine encounter with a real family. Conversely, no 2000s reality program makes a similar claim, as they are premised more on what Joel Black calls "reality effects" than on exploration of a "deeper" truth.[28] Media representation per se has become the "truth" of contemporary genres of actuality, and ignominy is the most efficient means to attain it. It is significant to note that while the observational technique of *An American Family* was the subject of scorn and ridicule throughout the 1970s, it has since become a standard style of reality television and, in the form of Internet webcams and titillating videos like the *Backyard Wrestling* and *Girls Gone Wild* series, throughout society.[29]

Accordingly, just as the crew of *An American Family* was largely drawn from and shaped by the cutting-edge documentaries of their time, *The Osbournes'* production crew worked on the most prominent reality television programs of the late 1990s and early 2000s, including *Big Brother, Survivor,* and *The Chris Rock Show.* Their professional experiences include not only the production of reality television—and the now-codified ignominious bodies—but also the more specific use of the codes of reality for comedy.[30]

"The First Reality Sitcom"

The normative range of television content has expanded in recent years, as long-standing broadcast taboos against coarse language, nudity, violence, and bodily functions have been eroded in the pursuit of young, affluent audiences. This process has been accelerated by the enormous critical and popular successes of pay-cable programs like HBO's *Sex and the City* and *The Sopranos,* which have flouted old content limits.[31]

While this trend has fueled the creation of new genres (including reality television itself), it has more profoundly affected established genres, which have had to adjust their traditional content with these broader limits in mind. Over the past decade, "old" genres have adapted to these demands and have shifted the level of their content while maintaining their basic generic codes. Accordingly, *The Osbournes,* in all its excessive glory, was more a *generic* product of its times than *An American Family* was of its.

The Osbournes was conceived with these new limits in mind, coupled with MTV's simultaneous necessity for innovation. MTV has gone from strength to strength since the late 1990s by keeping its series fresh, over-playing an idea in the short term rather than extending it into the future.

The network requires programming that appeals to the current exhibitionist sensibility, but it also takes a new approach or, in the case of their most successful programs, provides a new take on an old approach. Accordingly, a "real" situation comedy about an aging rocker and his unruly family seemed a likely fit for their needs.

The Osbourne family first appeared in a popular 2000 segment of *Cribs,* a series that features celebrities showing off their homes. The segment augured the potential of an extended visit to the Osbourne mansion, which the family was willing to accommodate in exchange for the publicity they might accrue if the series were successful. As recorded in late 2001, audio and video material culled from over a dozen cameras and microphones merged the now-familiar "roving" observational technique pioneered on *An American Family* with a bank of stationary surveillance equipment located throughout the house.[32]

With a wide selection of material at their disposal, and a relatively lengthy postproduction period (by reality television standards), the producers were able to structure the episodes using familiar generic codes: problems are introduced, conflicts play out, and the end of the episode reaches a mild resolution. Accordingly, MTV explicitly promoted *The Osbournes* as a sitcom. Programming chief Brian Graden appeared on *CNN Live Today* on the date of the premiere and claimed the series to be "the world's first reality sitcom because, like a sitcom, you have outrageous characters, very, very funny moments, and . . . the love between the cast members nonetheless."[33] Thus, both genre and family—via the sitcom— were identified up front as the key attributes of the new series.

The "hook" of *The Osbournes* is the fact that, despite their apparent excesses of wealth and behavior, the family somehow still functions as a normative, loving unit. The primary generic marker of both excess and normativity on *The Osbournes* is the family's conspicuous, unrepentant physicality. As explicitly documented in the series, the Osbournes—including their many pets—hug, kiss, wrestle, eat, drink, scratch, fart, burp, piss, and shit. They ruminate about vaginas, scrotums, and breasts and deal with dog turds left on the carpet. They reveal their bodies in various states of dress and decorum. They yell at their neighbors, shout at each other, and, most famously, say "fuck" more often than Tony Soprano. Theirs is a world of explicit bodily sights, sounds, smells, and sensations.

Though we are shown the Osbournes in this explicit, "real" detail, the series still functions predominantly as a "family sitcom," drawing heavily from well-worn generic codes. The Osbournes are self-consciously represented in the vein of the Cleavers of *Leave It To Beaver,* the Bradys of *The Brady Bunch,* and the Nelsons of *The Adventures of Ozzie and Harriet.*[34] Their house is a divided space of public and private areas, presented as in any family sitcom. The problems encountered—difficult neighbors, unruly pets, physical ailments, and an unwanted house guest—are clichéd sitcom staples and are conveyed in the standard stasis-disruption-resolution-stasis structure of TV narrative. Goofy musical bumpers even bridge scenes, as in any sitcom.

The series' opening sequence reproduces the archetypal family sitcom opening, as seen in the series listed above. An establishing shot of the family's Beverly Hills mansion leads to a series of tracking shots throughout the house, which reveals the Osbourne mansion to be both ostentatious and comfortably domestic, as recognizable domestic spaces (kitchen, living room, bedroom, backyard) open up to the camera. A series of framed family photos slides past, indicating a family history and reiterating normative expectations of the genre. Similarly, each family member is introduced in turn, with an animated freeze-frame and their name in a "space age" font reminiscent of 1950s advertising.

The poses of the family members in this sequence establish their personas as both typical *and* unique, engaged in quirky, yet recognizably "normal" behavior: mom Sharon is shown seated with her hands to her head, as if exasperated yet again; son Jack wears combat fatigues, a helmet, and knife, suggesting the "weird" brother; daughter Kelly pokes her head out of a closet door and sticks out her tongue, all teenage sass; and finally, dad Ozzy himself is introduced, shown taunting one of the family's many dogs with a "barking dog" toy, every bit the "madman" of his heavy metal persona. The sequence ends with a quick dolly up to the family posed on their front step and looking into the camera, as the title *The Osbournes* slides in. The theme song which runs under this sequence—a swing version of Ozzy's signature hit, "Crazy Train" (1980), sung by former 1950s pop star and Osbourne neighbor, Pat Boone—underscores this mix of the clichéd codes of family sitcom and heavy metal chaos.

Despite these conspicuous sitcom trappings, the Osbournes of 2002 are not quite the Nelsons of 1959; this gap is precisely the point of the series. Although prior sitcoms have played with the idea of "family normality," the relaxing content limits and ascendancy of reality television have enabled further exploration (and exploitation) of aesthetic and social norms.[35] As conveyed through the bodies and behaviors of its principles, *The Osbournes* stretches the familiar sitcom representational codes to their limits, while still remaining within recognizable normative constructions of dad, mom, son, and daughter.

In this case, dad is a veteran rock star notorious for his long hair, theatrical persona, and substance abuse. Ozzy's 50-something body displays the legacy of his life, as he shuffles around the house shirtless, bearing a tattooed, middle-aged paunch and with an uncontrollable tremor in his hands—a visible reminder of his excessive past.[36] Jack is overweight, wears trendy black-frame glasses, and sports several piercings and a modified mohawk haircut. Kelly wears an explosive mix of thrift-store and haute couture, regularly changes the color of her unruly hair, and periodically unleashes her rage on her brother. Sharon appears to be a normative suburban mom, with short, stylish hair, sweats, and running shoes. However, her behavior reveals that she is the de facto ringleader of the household, taking charge of most situations, her sharp, profanity-laced voice cutting through the noise. She is also arguably the most ignominious member of the family, as she burps, farts, handles her breasts, and, in one of the series' most infamous moments, apparently urinates in a houseguest's illicit bottle of whiskey.[37] The fact that the mom is in many ways the most excessive member of a family full of excessive characters indicates how shrewdly the series (and family) exploits normative expectations.

Ozzy's already-established celebrity as a heavy metal legend formed the rationale for the show and certainly ensured media attention. Yet the point of *The Osbournes* is to distinguish the "real" Ozzy (and his family) from that already established celebrity. To this end, the series pushes Ozzy's star persona to the background. While he is frequently seen in typical tour settings (buses, hotel rooms, dressing rooms, etc.) as well as at home, his actual performances are only glimpsed. Instead, we are constantly shown a "backstage" Ozzy, one closer to the established codes of sitcom representation: a wealthy, somewhat addled, middle-aged dad who just happens to be a rock star. As the series' biggest star, and least normative body, Ozzy is most often the subject of comic sequences, as he struggles with new technology (a state-of-the-art home theater system), animals (the unruly Osbourne pets), and the rest of the family (trying to restore order during an argument), all the while mumbling and stuttering in a near-incomprehensible Birmingham brogue and enduring the bodily tremors associated with his rehabilitation treatments.

Significantly, unlike every other member of the family, Ozzy's body is not just on display (as it has been for nearly 30 years); it is quite literally out of control, bearing the visible signs of a lifetime of substance abuse.

While Ozzy's body, the very medium of his notoriety and the family fortune, is often the subject of easy laughs, it is also a symbol of decay, a rather helpless condition of ignominy, as opposed to the exuberant exhibitionism of younger reality show subjects. These scenes are among the most ambivalent of the series, pushing the codes of the so-called reality sitcom near the outer limits of the representation of ignominious bodies. But Ozzy's body still remains just inside the generic sitcom requirements that dictate that dad must be somewhat eccentric and befuddled.[38] Those limits, and perhaps the entire *Osbournes* endeavor, were tested even more in the second season, as Sharon, who was diagnosed with colon cancer in July 2002 (and had several inches of her colon surgically removed), underwent cancer treatments.[39]

Conclusion:
"We Argue, but at the End of the Day, We Love Each Other"

The Louds' and Osbournes' family lives were further reproduced through press articles and interviews, appearances on radio and television talk shows, and, particularly in the case of the Osbournes, merchandising.[40] While space does not permit a more detailed investigation into each series' reception, it is clear that in expanding beyond their series, both families solidified their iconic status as archetypical American families for their respective eras.

Even though the genre is "reality," and the actions of the subjects are real, the production and promotion of reality television programs ensures that its subjects function in the end as *characters:* attractive constructions of personality. Such normative expectations hit the Osbournes to a degree the Louds never had to endure. The family has had to deal with constant crowds outside of its Beverly Hills home and insatiable public curiosity about (among other things) Ozzy's past substance abuse and violence toward Sharon; Jack's dangerous dive off a Santa Monica pier; and Kelly's weight.[41] In addition, the protracted and secretive negotiations with MTV for the second season of the series indicated how this family's reality became very big business: the Osbournes reportedly collected $20 million for the second season, in addition to licensing fees and outright ownership of the series and concept.

Significantly, the television version of the Osbournes is one member smaller than the actual family, as Ozzy and Sharon's eldest daughter

Aimee declined to participate, citing a desire to maintain her privacy. While this action may reveal a rift within the actual family, it also indicates how the normative codes of genre and family can still be considered too restrictive.[42] Her decision to forego appearing in a reality television series is certainly uncharacteristic of our times. The genre continues to expand, and has no lack of potential ignominious bodies. The success of *The Osbournes* has even inspired the development of other "celebrity reality" series, as similar projects featuring celebrities like P. Diddy, Anna Nicole Smith, and Jessica Simpson and Nick Lachey were produced, or at least considered.

While *An American Family* and *The Osbournes* are certainly unique television series, they both had to function under particular normative categories of genre and family in order to be comprehensible, let alone successful. The fact that they functioned in radically different ways indicates how the content of these terms—in particular, the effective meaning of television "reality"—has shifted considerably over three decades. Thus, the key question for reality television, now and for the foreseeable future, is not *whether* its reality is produced but *how* it is articulated with existing codes and expectations.

NOTES

1. In the space of one month alone, they were on the covers of *Entertainment Weekly, Interview, Rolling Stone,* and *Time.*

2. The relative novelty and reputation of the Public Broadcasting Service (PBS), the network that aired *An American Family,* also contributed to these reactions, as the new service was created (and perceived) in part to be a challenging alternative to the commercial imperatives of the established networks and stations.

3. For example, Michael J. Bradley, "Put 'em on the Couch," *Rolling Stone* 895 (9 May 2002), 36; Paul Farhi, "Make Room for Ozzy: 'The Osbournes' Recalls TV's Uncomplicated, Unpierced Past," *Washington Post,* 16 April 2002, C1; and Melanie McFarland, "Ozzy Knows Best?," *Seattle Times,* 22 April 2002, E1.

4. Jeffrey Ruoff, *An American Family: A Televised Life* (Minneapolis: University of Minnesota, 2002), 23, 102; Brian Graden, interview by Leon Harris, *CNN Live Today,* CNN, 5 March 2002. Alessandra Stanley of the *New York Times* also referred to *The Osbournes* as the first "docu-sitcom"; Alessandra Stanley, "No Rest for Family Values on Black Sabbath," *New York Times,* 2 April 2002, E1.

5. Stephanie Coontz, *The Way We Never Were* (New York: Basic Books, 1992); Ella Taylor, *Prime Time Families* (Berkeley: University of California, 1989).

6. Whether the family is or even should be the fundamental unit of social cohesion is certainly debatable, but I argue that the important point is that it is *treated as such* in virtually every society on the planet. Government policies, temporal and spatial organization, and commercial imperatives all center on conceptions of the family. The media's role in this is to circulate representations of families—most normative, some (i.e., "dysfunctional" families) not—in order to facilitate this system.

7. Osbourne was the lead singer of heavy metal pioneers Black Sabbath in the 1970s and became a superstar with a string of best-selling solo recordings in the early 1980s. During the 1990s, he parlayed his earlier successes into the annual Ozzfest tour, which linked his celebrity to younger, similar artists.

8. Rick Altman, *Film/Genre* (London: British Film Institute, 1999), 190.

9. As John Thornton Caldwell points out, despite periodic innovations in content, the situation comedy is, stylistically, arguably the most stable genre in American television, remaining largely the same across several decades. John Thornton Caldwell, *Televisuality: Style and Crisis in American Television* (New Brunswick, N.J.: Rutgers University Press, 1995), 5.

10. Taylor, *Prime Time Families*, 1.

11. On occasion, some of these programs have had "where are they now" segments that update the stories of particular families that have been presented on the show, but these are most often as brief and functional as the earlier segment.

12. A significant variation on this approach has been the *Survivor*-like genre of isolation and survival, in which groups (including nuclear families) are followed as they adapt to an uncomfortable environment without the luxuries of twenty-first century life, as in series like *Frontier House, 1900 House,* and in the U.K. *Castaway*. While these series have a more earnest educational purpose than most reality series (e.g., in their display of long-outmoded homemaking skills), they also explore family relationships across the period of the show, which generally lasts for months, or even, in the case of *Castaway,* an entire year. In the case of *Frontier House,* one married couple even endured a Loud-like emotional and, eventually, legal separation by the end of the series.

13. Indeed, as Coontz observes in *The Way We Never Were,* representations of the archetypal "fifties" television family have even informed American social policies, despite their disconnection from actual, lived family life (even in the 1950s).

14. Indeed, documentary's generic opposite is ostensibly fiction; hence the use of the broad term "nonfiction" as a synonym.

15. John Corner, "Documentary Values," in *Realism and "Reality" in Film and Media,* ed. Anne Jerslev (Copenhagen: Museum Tusculanum Press, 2002), 145–46.

16. Granted, the lines between documentary and documentation are blurry. Joseph Wiseman's often-ambiguous films certainly *feel* more like an exhibition than an argument. Still, Wiseman's methodical technique and choice of subjects

suggests an activist engagement with his material that exceeds the requirements of documentation.

17. Corner, "Documentary Values," 147–49.

18. Ibid., 153.

19. Ruoff, *An American Family,* 53–68, 109–11.

20. Ibid., 48–49.

21. Ibid., 11–15.

22. Gilbert's main collaborators, Alan and Susan Raymond, were also enthusiastic practitioners of the observational style and shot the entirety of the footage. A team of experienced news documentary editors, led by David Hanser, edited the series.

23. Ruoff , *An American Family,* 17.

24. Gilbert was particularly inspired by the detective fiction of Ross MacDonald, which portrayed the materially comfortable and morally bankrupt lives of the Santa Barbara upper crust. MacDonald was even personally consulted to help locate a suitable family in the area. Ruoff, *An American Family,* 17–18.

25. For example, the *Naked News* website and television series features attractive male and female newscasters who strip while they're reading the news, thus violating the boundary between professional television journalism and pornography, producing the shock of ignominy. An early, long-running Nickelodeon series was actually titled *You Can't Do That on Television;* its trademark action was to "slime" its subjects with a load of green goo dropped from above, thus humiliating them. Interestingly, yesterday's Nickelodeon viewers (born between the mid-1970s and mid-1980s) are precisely today's reality television target audience.

26. Other prominent reality series, such as *Survivor, The Amazing Race, Fear Factor, Dog Eat Dog,* and *American Idol,* function in a similar manner.

27. A list of "telegenic" qualities would include physical attractiveness, gregariousness, intelligibility, and physical activity; in other words, attributes that translate most easily to the medium's visual vocabulary, time limits, and perceived audiences.

28. Joel Black, *The Reality Effect: Film Culture and the Graphic Imperative* (New York: Routledge 2002), 15–20.

29. The entire endeavor of producing a film about a "real family" was mercilessly satirized in Albert Brooks's 1979 film *Real Life* and in a 1980 episode of the situation comedy *WKRP in Cincinnati* titled "Real Families."

30. *Osbournes* crew members worked widely on programs such as *Survivor: Africa* (sound supervisor Jenny Green), *Big Brother 2* (editor Matthew Gossin), and *Bands on the Run* (director Brendon Carter), and also in the "comedy reality" subgenre: executive producer Jeff Stilson was a producer on both *The Chris Rock Show* and *The Daily Show* and a writer on Michael Moore's *TV Nation.*

31. Cable programming is not subject to the same legal content restrictions that over-the-air broadcasters must abide by. Language barriers, in particular, are

falling in basic cable and have increasingly been broken on broadcast television in recent years. For example, the FX original series *The Shield* regularly features once-taboo expletives; the Comedy Central series *South Park* had its animated characters say "shit" over 130 times in one episode; and a May 2002 episode of NBC's highly rated medical drama *ER* had the dying Mark Greene yell the familiar expletive.

32. Only the master bedroom and bathrooms were declared "off-limits" to surveillance. In addition, the now-standard use of video, rather than film, ensures that virtually everything that occurs in the house *will* be recorded and thus made available to structure episodes.

33. Graden interview, *CNN Live Today.* Note that the Osbournes are here "cast members" rather than "family members."

34. Ozzie Nelson and Ozzy Osbourne obviously share first names, but that is only the most superficial comparison. Both families were actual families, their real personas sharing the same names and personalities as their TV counterparts. Both families were actively engaged in show business. While both families also had ultimate control over their television representations, the Nelsons' series was carefully scripted and produced; *The Adventures of Ozzie and Harriet* (1952–66) is perhaps the only series in television history in which the entire regular cast play themselves as scripted characters.

35. The "fantastic" family sitcoms of the mid-1960s, such as *The Addams Family, Bewitched,* and *The Munsters* are indirect influences on *The Osbournes.* Indeed, in an *Entertainment Weekly* article covering the success of his series, Ozzy implicitly compared his family with the fictional TV monster family: "My one regret is that we used our real house. I mean, the Munsters didn't use their real house!" Quoted in Nancy Miller, "American Goth," *Entertainment Weekly,* 19 April 2002, 22. For an examination of these 1960s sitcoms in their original context, see Lynn Spigel, *Welcome to the Dreamhouse: Popular Media and Postwar Suburbs* (Durham, N.C.: Duke University Press, 2001), 107–40.

36. For the sake of clarity, I refer to the Osbourne family members by their first names only for the remainder of the article.

37. A scene in which Sharon stuck her hand down her pants, rubbed her vagina, and chased Kelly around the room was cut from an episode, though the two are shown talking about the incident immediately afterward; Kelly is disgusted, while Sharon is amused.

38. Ozzy's befuddlement is reminiscent in particular of earlier sitcom dads Tim Taylor (*Home Improvement*), Cliff Huxtable (*The Cosby Show*), Howard Cunningham (*Happy Days*), George Jetson (*The Jetsons*), and Danny Williams (*Make Room for Daddy*).

39. However, even this frontier is not unheard-of for MTV, as the network covered gross-out comedian Tom Green's surgery and recovery from testicular cancer in 1999.

40. The title of this section is taken from Sharon Osbourne, quoted in David Bauder, "Ozzie and Harriet It Isn't," *Associated Press*, 5 March 2002. While a few books were published by and about the Louds in the early 1970s, the Osbournes have been featured on a wider array of products, including a CD soundtrack of the series, a DVD set of the first season, and even a collection of back-to-school supplies.

41. Although she has become a new icon of independent-minded teenage girl-dom, Kelly has had to deal with public comments about her body. While her body is healthy and normal for her age and height, it does not meet the current stick-thin ideal as presented in most mainstream media. As is usually the case, real women are forced to bear the brunt of normative media codes. See Miller, "American Goth."

42. Given her famous father and industry connections, it is just as likely that she wishes to pursue other normative codes of celebrity than would be available were she to become a television *Osbourne*.

Part II

||||||||||||||||||||||||||||||||||||||||||||||||||||||||||

Industry

The Political Economic Origins of Reali-TV

Chad Raphael

From the sea change in American television in the 1980s emerged a pro-gramming trend variously described as "infotainment," "reality-based television," "tabloid TV," "crime-time television," "trash TV," and "on-scene shows." The welter of terms created by television critics to describe these new programs masked their underlying connection as a response to eco-nomic restructuring within the industry. In this essay I offer a rough cat-egorization of these programs, sketch the industrial context from which they emerged, and point to the economic problems they were meant to solve. I focus mostly on the distinctive conditions of prime-time series, putting aside made-for-TV docudramas and entire cable channels (such as Court TV) that may have similar production practices and genres.

Although my focus here is on political economy, rather than on textual or audience issues, I do not want to imply that these programs' cultural significance can be reduced to their relations of production and distri-bution. Yet without understanding the political and economic forces that drove the spread of this genre, textual and audience studies may risk rei-fying it as an expression of audience demand; or of their creators; or of a cultural, discursive, or ontological shift unrelated to the needs of those who run the television industry. If this genre exhibits a kind of textual excess, its emergence reflects a relative scarcity of resources for television production.

Among the swirl of neologisms, my preferred term for these programs is "Reali-TV," which points to the inseparability of the television indus-try's economic needs and how this genre represents reality.[1] This term stresses television's particular reasons for embracing reality shows, as op-posed to claims about the spread of infotainment across the media. At the same time, this designation illuminates connections between seemingly different television programs (such as crime-time, tabloid TV, and on-scene shows) and avoids the high cultural bias implicit in the notion of trash TV. The term indicates not only how these programs make distinctive claims to represent the real but also their common impact on the realities of power and economic relations in the industry. Reali-TV, then, is an umbrella term for a number of programming trends that have rapidly expanded since the late 1980s across all hours of network schedules, first-run syndication, and cable.

Production practices common to most of these programs include extensive use of "actuality" footage of their subjects, whether these are police staking out a drug den or mom and dad yukking it up in front of the camcorder; reenactments of events, performed by professional actors, or by the people who experienced them, or a mix of both; a tendency to avoid the studio in favor of on-scene shooting, sometimes at the same place where the events they represent occurred; mixing footage shot by unpaid amateur videographers with that of professionals; appealing to the conventions of "liveness," and "immediacy" through on-location interviews, subjective camera work, and synchronized sound; and appropriating traditional conventions of news coverage, such as the use of anchors or hosts, remote reporting, and the pretense to "spontaneity." Studio-centered formats, principally game shows and confessional talk programming, are the obvious exceptions to these common practices.

These production techniques are combined differently in numerous Reali-TV formats, which can be distinguished according to how much each relies on nontraditional labor (for story development, writing, performing, and camerawork) and production inputs (such as sets, props, and costumes.) Some formats continue to depend mainly on professional labor and traditional inputs. The network newsmagazines—whose ranks have swollen in the past few years with the introduction of *48 Hours* and *Street Stories* (CBS), *Primetime Live* (ABC), *Dateline NBC,* and others—are still entirely professionally produced and employ the same mix of studio and location footage as the evening news. The same is true of tabloid TV shows (such as the syndicated *A Current Affair* or *Entertainment Tonight*), despite their unique representational strategies.

Several other Reali-TV formats use hybrid production techniques. Hidden-video programs (such as *Totally Hidden Video*), which enjoyed a minor resurgence in the early 1990s, rely on professional camera crews and actors maneuvering nonprofessional performers into embarrassing or humorous situations. So do experiment-based programs that place and observe nonactors in contrived living arrangements (*The Real World*) and increasingly add the element of competition for money and prizes (as in *Survivor* and *Fear Factor*). Crime-time and emergency response programs (*Rescue 911, America's Most Wanted, Unsolved Mysteries,* and the many imitators these shows have spawned on cable and first-run syndication) are shot and edited by professionals and introduced by a regular host. Yet they also may employ some amateur footage of disasters, as well as non-professional performers enacting their own rescues or crime experiences. These programs also take advantage of props, sets, and costumes provided by law enforcement authorities, corrections institutions, parole boards, and emergency medical crews. Clip shows (such as *The World's Wildest Police Videos* and other "World's Best/Worst/Most" programs) similarly mix amateur and professional video. Finally, home video programs (such as *America's Funniest Home Videos*) rely entirely on amateur footage that is professionally edited. This format depends most heavily on nontraditional inputs and labor, not only for "scripting," performing, and shooting the hijinks but also to do the work of studio audiences (who vote for the funniest video, for example). Before discussing how these techniques have lowered production costs, we need to examine the larger economic picture from whence they sprang.

Decline of the Networks: Webs Wane as Competition Climbs

As a fiscal strategy, Reali-TV emerged in the late 1980s in response to the economic restructuring of U.S. television. Much of the restructuring story has been told by scholars and in the trade press: how the number of video distribution channels expanded rapidly, with the growth of cable, VCRs, the FOX network, and local independent stations; how the television audience was increasingly fragmented; how advertising revenues now had to be spread among a larger pool of distributors; and how this dilution of advertising spending created pressure on broadcasters and cablecasters to cut per-program production costs.[2] Less cited causes for production budget cuts included the high levels of corporate debt incurred by the big three networks after each was sold in the mid-1980s and advertiser-driven changes in audience-measurement techniques designed to identify specific market segments (the most notorious of these was the People-Meter, which yielded dramatically lower ratings for the networks).[3]

By the late 1980s, then, the economic picture of American television had become decidedly more crowded. If the networks remained in the foreground as the major economic force in the industry, the purveyors of cable, VCRs, and first-run syndication winked and beckoned viewers in the background. Advertisers and audience-measurement services busily tried to record who was watching what, how much attention they paid to the commercial breaks, and whether they were buying any of it. But to understand how Reali-TV emerged as a cost-cutting solution in this new economic environment of the late 1980s, we need to examine how increased competition in the distribution of television programming affected the sphere of production.

The Squeeze on Production: Ouch! Webs and Suppliers Feel the Pinch

As television distributors fought over smaller advertising shares and shouldered more debt, program producers (network production arms, major Hollywood studios, and the few small independent production companies) all faced rapidly rising costs in the 1980s. For prime-time producers, the average cost of an hour drama soared to over $1 million per episode by the end of the decade, and costs were increasing by roughly 8 to 10 percent a year.[4] Prices were driven up primarily by "above the line" costs such as talent, direction, scriptwriting, music composition, computer animation, and location costs.[5] The star system for above-the-line labor became especially pronounced, as network programmers, agent-packagers, and production companies responded to the greater risks of capital involved in the creation of new shows by increasingly demanding names associated with a prior record of success. Greater demand for stars created an artificial labor shortage and inflated salaries for the lucky few.

These rising costs were accompanied by smaller per-show revenues, creating a squeeze on production companies' earnings from both sides of the ledger. Producers now had to accept smaller license fees for their programs than they had commanded from the networks before the new era of competition. The threatened networks were scaling back outlays, and cable network distributors and syndicators also lacked deep pockets for program purchases. In addition, changes in federal tax laws eliminated producers' investment tax credits, which often meant the difference between earning a profit and taking a loss on a program. Before the 1986 restructuring of federal tax laws, producers were able to deduct 6.7 percent of the cost of their productions from their federal tax bills. By the mid-1980s, caught between rising costs and lower network license fees, most producers could no longer make back their investments in first-run network showings. By 1986, producers were losing up to $100,000 per episode for half-hour shows and $200,000 to $300,000 for hour dramas.[6] Producers now were forced to deficit-finance their programs and cross their fingers in hopes the show would survive three network seasons, providing enough episodes for domestic and foreign syndication and a chance to recoup their initial investments.

Producers to Labor: Drop Dead

Feeling the squeeze on profits, production companies and the networks initiated a series of cost-cutting strategies that translated into an attack on labor, mainly on below-the-line workers such as technicians, engineers, and extras.[7] The first move was a wave of staff cutbacks at studios and network news departments. In the mid-1980s, FOX cut 20 percent of its studio staff, Capital Cities/ABC cut 10 percent of its staff, and CBS cut 30 percent of its administrative staff and 10 percent of its news division. NBC resisted a 17-week strike by the National Association of Broadcast Employees and Technicians (NABET) in 1987, shedding 200 union jobs. By 1992, NBC had eliminated 30 percent of its news division through lay-offs and bureau closings. Even network standards and practices departments, the much-derided self-censors of the broadcasting industry, faced the budget-cutting ax.

The second part of the cost-cutting strategy involved bypassing union labor, spurring an unprecedented wave of strikes by above-line and below-line labor unions and craft guilds. In the 1980s and early 1990s, the NABET, the Directors Guild, the American Federation of Musicians (AFM), the Screen Extras Guild (SEG), and the American Federation of Radio and Television Artists (AFTRA) all struck, while the Screen Actors Guild (SAG) struck twice and the Writers Guild three times. Above-the-line workers especially sought more residuals for the use of programs on new media and overseas. Lower-paid labor, such as members of the SEG, took a more defensive stand commensurate with their weaker bargaining power. The SEG strike ended with union members accepting a 25 percent wage cut, changes in overtime schedules, and the acceptance of producers' prerogative to hire more nonunion labor (the extras' bargaining position was hurt by SAG's refusal to merge with the less-powerful union or even to support its position in contract negotiations).

This increase in labor unrest was both a response to and a motivating force in attempts to break the power of the unions. As a result, producers exacerbated the long-term split in the Hollywood labor market between core workers (such as the successful SAG members who enjoy higher pay and more job security and who share management tasks and interests) and periphery workers (such as the SEG members, who have little job security, work part-time schedules, and endure far lower wages).[8]

Producers also responded to union demands by using nonunion Hollywood labor and shifting production to regions where cheaper labor was available, such as Canada and the "right-to-work" states of the U.S. South. These tactics cut across entertainment and news program production. Disney and MCA led the industry shift toward building studio complexes in Florida. The loss of the investment tax credit, which was only applicable to programs produced in the United States, helped spur a shift of production to Canada, where lower costs and more pliable unions could save $200,000 to $300,000 an episode for dramatic series.[9] In news programming, CNN and FOX led the way in producing with lower-paid, nonunion labor and by breaking down job classifications. Their "success" was increasingly imitated by the traditional networks. One former CBS executive noted that the lesson of CNN was "Break the unions!"[10] NBC appears to have the learned the lesson quickest, developing a 24-hour affiliate news service based in Charlotte, North Carolina, staffed with nonunion labor. Some FOX affiliates experimented with subcontracting their entire evening newscasts.

Survivor Economics: Reali-TV Fits the Bill

Reali-TV shows gained currency in this environment of relative financial scarcity and labor unrest of the late 1980s. Economically, the genre fit the needs of producers and distributors alike for cheaper programming. These programs largely did away with higher-priced stars and union talent. In the early days, the only "name" actors on these shows were briefly seen as hosts.

More recently, a subgenre has developed that trots out minor celebrities and has-beens that come cheap to endure humiliating tests of their mettle, fighting each other in *Celebrity Boxing* or plunging themselves in vermin in *Celebrity Fear Factor.* In the crime-time/emergency shows, roles in reenactments of crimes and rescues have been filled by unknown actors and, sometimes, by the people on which the stories were based. In programs such as *Cops,* segments followed law enforcement officials in the course of their work, eschewing reenactments and the need for actors entirely. The home video and hidden-video programs likewise avoided professional union talent, as have more recent experiment-based shows. In bypassing more-expensive performers, program producers also escaped the grips of the Hollywood agents, who had come to occupy the role of program developers and packagers in the early 1980s, and who exacted considerable fees for their services.[11]

Producers of Reali-TV, particularly of the crime-time/emergency shows and home and hidden-video programs, led a wider industry move toward using nonunion, freelance production crews. The Arthur Co. offers a good example. In 1987 it lost the rights to produce the network prime-time drama *Airwolf,* after battling with the Writers Guild over cable royalties, then turned to producing low-budget, nonunion programs for syndication and basic cable. In 1991 Arthur Co. returned to prime time with *FBI: The Untold Stories,* a Reali-TV reprise of the bureau's long-running romance with the tube. Similarly, FOX's *America's Most Wanted,* one of the trendsetters of Reali-TV when it premiered in 1987, used different freelance crews for each segment. Even some newsmagazines, such as *CBS Street Stories,* turned to freelance camera crews and news producers. The home video programs relied on amateur camcorder enthusiasts and freelance professionals. Reali-TV producers also partook of the move to cheaper labor regions. Grosso-Jacobson Entertainment, a prolific creator of crime-time shows (including *Top Cops, True Blue,* and *Secret Service*), shot its patriotic paeans to America's law enforcers in Toronto.[12]

The genre has also been an integral part of network strategies to control labor unrest. The 1988 Writers' Strike, a 22-week affair that delayed the opening of the fall season, proved crucial to the rise of Reali-TV. Existing Reali-TV shows were largely unaffected by the strike, as they already relied very little on writers. In addition, the delay of the season gave producers and programmers the impetus to develop future shows that did not depend on writing talent. Tabloid TV pioneer Peter Brennan (of *Hard Copy*), when asked whether he was concerned about a potential SAG strike in 1992, shrugged off the threat: "Remember the Writers Guild strike in '88? . . . That was the year that gave rise to reality TV."[13]

The second wave of Reali-TV programming, ushered in by the ratings success of the game show *Who Wants to Be a Millionaire* in 1999 and *Survivor* in 2000, came amid threatened walkouts by writers and actors. The networks ordered more Reali-TV series in part to prepare for potential strikes and not simply because they could be produced without union employees. Reality series can be developed more quickly than fictional programs partly because they do not rely on lining up talent and writers. Newsmagazines can be expanded relatively easily to fill additional hours on the network schedule because news workers are typically affiliated with different unions than other television talent. "There is a quick turnaround time with reality," noted CBS President Leslie Moonves in detailing his network's plans for a possible writers' strike in 2001.[14]

Reali-TV programs also cut costs by wholeheartedly embracing low-end production values. Direct cinema techniques such as handheld cameras and the use of available lighting made shows without reenactments (such as *Cops* and the network newsmagazines) particularly cheap. Programs that employed reenacted material (such as *Rescue 911* and *Unsolved Mysteries*) often avoided traditionally painstaking lighting and makeup to approximate the "real" look of direct cinema footage and its relatively low production costs. Although reenactments required some expenses for on-location shooting, going on-scene was often less costly than renting studio space. In addition, crime-time and emergency shows minimized costs of sets, props, and costumes by convincing the agencies they profile to donate police cars, equipment, and even uniforms for the production crew, so they could pass for police at crime scenes.[15] Finally, research and logistical costs for most categories of Reali-TV shows are tempered by the information subsidies traditionally extended to the news and entertainment media by public relations operatives hoping to plant favorable stories about their corporate and government clients.[16]

As a result of their shoestring production budgets, prime-time Reali-TV shows cut production costs dramatically and recouped their makers' investments from network license fees alone. With rare exceptions, Reali-TV was the only category of prime-time programming that was not deficit-financed in the early 1990s (table 6.1 lists production costs for a representative season). In the same year, one-hour dramas and 30-minute sitcoms often lost $100,000 to $300,000 an episode. At a time when dramas routinely cost over $1 million per episode, and half-hour sitcoms cost $500,000 to $600,000 apiece, Reali-TV programs offered considerable savings in production costs, sometimes

TABLE 6.1

Prime-Time Reali-TV Programs at the Start of the 1991–1992 Season

Program	Network	Minutes	Producers	Deficit	License Fee per Episode
America's Funniest Home Videos	ABC	30	ABC/Vin di Bona	$0	$375,000
America's Funniest People	ABC	30	ABC/Vin di Bona	$0	$300,000
American Detective	ABC	30	ABC/Orion TV/ Paul Stojanovich	$0	$450,000
FBI: The Untold Series	ABC	60	The Arthur Company	$25,000	$450, 000
Primetime Live	ABC	60	ABC News	$0	$500,000
20/20	ABC	60	ABC News	$0	$500,000
48 Hours	CBS	60	CBS News	$0	$500,000
Rescue 911	CBS	30	CBS/Arnold Shapiro	$0	$650,000
60 Minutes	CBS	60	CBS News	$0	$600,000
Top Cops	CBS	60	CBS News	$0	$650,000
Exposé	NBC	30	NBC News	$0	$300,000
Real Life with Jane Pauley	NBC	30	NBC News	$0	$300,000
Unsolved Mysteries	NBC	60	Cosgrove-Meurer	$0	$800,000
America's Most Wanted	Fox	60	STF Productions	$0	$500,000
Cops	Fox	30	Barbour-Langley/ Fox TV Stations	$0	$325,000
Cops II	Fox	30	Barbour-Langley/ Fox TV Stations	$0	$325,000
Totally New Totally Hidden Video	Fox	30	STF Productions	$0	$500,000

Source: Variety, 26 August 1991, 48–54.

over 50 percent compared with fictional programming.[17] Reali-TV also enjoyed success in the low-fee first-run syndication and made-for-cable fields.

Deregulation: Reali-TV Right for Finsyn, Public Service Fights

A changing regulatory climate also contributed to the economic advantages of Reali-TV. In 1970, amid concerns about network power over production companies, the FCC barred the networks from owning a financial interest in, and retaining syndication rights to, most prime-time entertain-ment programming (daytime shows, sports, and news were not affected). The financial and syndication, or "finsyn," rules also limited the number of hours of prime-time shows the network could produce. A 1980 consent decree in an antitrust case further limited network prime-time entertain-ment production to 2.5 hours per week for several years.

When the FCC enacted the finsyn rules, its stated goals were to en-courage local programming and small independent producers. The FCC hoped that if network production were reined in, other producers might create more innovative, diverse programming. But the small independents did not flourish, as the large capital investments and risks required of pro-gram producers meant that Hollywood studios with substantial financing still controlled the field. As with the small independents in the film indus-try, television's smaller production houses depended on winning network contracts for their programming before they could secure bank financ-ing to make it.[18] Independents did not exercise much financial or creative power over the development of new programming, especially when com-pared with the major studios or the top agent-packagers. In many ways, the same relations held in first-run syndication and the made-for-cable markets. Here, the small independents were often financed by large mul-tisystem operators (such as AOL-Time Warner) and the dominant distri-bution companies (including those run by major studios) in exchange for syndication rights.

Throughout the 1980s, the networks challenged the finsyn rules, argu-ing that they were no longer in a position to dominate program distri-bution as they had before the spread of cable and VCRs, and that they needed to be allowed to compete internationally in the global television market. In April 1991, the FCC allowed the networks to finance and syn-dicate their own in-house or coproduced programs and to negotiate for the rights to some outside-produced shows. Hollywood studios and inde-pendent producers exhausted a long series of appeals, and the finsyn rules were repealed in 1995.

Although FOX has was exempt from the finsyn rules and always pro-duced the bulk of its programming in-house, the three major networks may very well have anticipated the repeal of these restrictions and posi-tioned themselves to syndicate Reali-TV programming domestically and abroad.[19] From the start, one of the striking characteristics of prime-time Reali-TV programs was that so many of them are network productions or coproductions (see table 6.1). This was true not only of the network newsmagazines, which are produced by their news divisions, but also of crime-time/emergency response and the home video shows. As producers and coproducers of the shows, networks could retain the rights to distribute them under the new rules.

Reali-TV has also played a role in the redefinition of public service programming. In the Reagan-Bush climate of lax regulation, programmers did not need to fear FCC scrutiny of the violence and sexual content of Reali-TV, avoiding the costs of in-house standards and practices departments' close screening of these programs, along with the potential legal costs of defending them before the FCC.

In addition, many Reali-TV producers recast broadcasters' "public service" and "educational" responsibilities to champion the civic value of their programs. Producers ignored traditional definitions of serving the public interest, which focused more on the discussion of public affairs, coverage of local issues, and developing children's intellectual or emotional abilities. Instead, the creators of crime-time programs in particular touted their public contribution as prompting citizens to help law enforcement officers track down their quarry. The executive producer of *America's Most Wanted* opined to the *FBI Law Enforcement Bulletin*: "I believe we are witnessing the birth of a new era in citizen involvement. *America's Most Wanted* has organized some 22 million viewers into the first nationwide neighborhood watch association."[20] In this vision of public service, surveillance and voyeurism replace debate over public affairs, an oxymoronic "nationwide neighborhood watch association" offers a false sense of localism, and education is reduced to instructing viewers about how to avoid becoming a crime victim.

The more recent crop of Reali-TV game shows and survival contests make far less pretense to public service, except for the network newsmagazines. These programs still purport to offer investigative reporting even as they abandon the kinds of subjects most in need of journalistic scrutiny. A recent study of four network newsmagazines found that over one-half of all stories focused on lifestyle, human interest, and celebrity news. Just 8 percent of reports were about politics, economics, social welfare and education.[21] As the newsmagazines began to compete with fictional and tabloid television programs, such as *Entertainment Tonight* or *Inside Edition,* all increasingly focused on the same topics. By 1997, there was little difference in story selection between the tabloid programs and the network newsmagazines, according to one television monitoring company. The runaway story of the year for both was Princess Diana's death.[22]

International Distribution: The Other Real World

Producers and network investors have also been attracted to Reali-TV because of its ability to sell abroad. Because prime-time Reali-TV earns back its production costs with the first U.S. network showing, any further syndication represents pure profit. American Reali-TV has been sold overseas using two methods. Some shows are licensed outright to foreign broadcasters, the way most U.S. programming traditionally has been marketed. Episodes of the top-rated network crime-time/emergency programs *Unsolved Mysteries* and *Rescue 911* have been sold abroad in this manner. One international program distributor claims that "the easiest and most profitable thing for a distributor to do with reality shows is to license them as they are. Prices can even approach what distributors get for action-adventure hours in some territories."[23] By 1991, *Rescue 911* could be seen in Germany, Denmark, and Sweden; *Unsolved Mysteries* was available in Canada, Spain, France, and Japan.

Many more shows have been formatted because of their topical or local nature, however. This method involves selling or licensing the program's concept for local production with local subjects. American program footage may be sold as well to supplement the local version. "In syndication," notes one executive producer, "shows tend to be more topical and current . . . but they have to be more timeless for that backend revenue"[24] As Asu Aksoy and Kevin Robins note, the challenge for contemporary media distributors "is to transcend vestigial national difference and to create standardized global markets, whilst remaining sensitive to the peculiarities of local markets and differentiated consumer segments."[25]

Reali-TV has participated in this "glocalization" strategy. Fremantle, a distributor of game shows and *Candid Camera,* provides a good example of how formatting works. Fremantle's chief executive officer maintains that the company "operates in foreign markets like McDonald's does. . . . There are Fremantle subsidiaries in some countries; in others there are franchise-holders who produce their own local versions of the original product."[26]

Home-video and hidden-video shows tend to be formatted rather than licensed, allowing foreign broadcasters to insert their own clips into the programs. Crime-time shows have also been formatted. The Swedes developed a version of *Cops,* and *America's Most Wanted* was transformed into the short-lived *Australia's Most Wanted.* Tabloid TV programs and newsmagazines are especially likely to be formatted or customized because the appeal of their stories and journalists tends to be culturally specific. Newsmagazines, such as *60 Minutes,* often export stories after stripping them of their original graphics, voice-overs, journalists, and hosts so that local journalists can tailor the stories and insert themselves into them.[27]

Reali-TV's growth abroad, especially in Europe, was aided by the widespread movement to privatize and deregulate broadcasting. As one distributor put it in the early 1990s:

> With some exceptions, public service broadcasters have always kept a tight lid on the definition of reality. . . . The taste [for Reali-TV] has been stimulated abroad by increased commercialism, but reality shows haven't yet taken hold *en masse.* . . . But because foreign broadcasters are tight for money, the attraction of reality will no doubt be considerable.[28]

Although both private and public broadcasters have purchased Reali-TV, the genre's growth was especially symptomatic of the need for European public broadcasters to operate according to the logic of private channels, as competition for audiences and funding mounted.[29]

In addition, the explosion of distribution channels in the 1980s was not only an American phenomenon but a global one. Thus, some of the same cost pressures encountered by U.S. producers were being felt abroad. To better adapt to an unevenly globalizing television market, some Reali-TV has been conceived for international audiences first. Time Warner/HBO's *World Entertainment Report,* for example, was prelicensed across Europe, Australia, and Japan. The program had a modular format that broadcasters could recompose to fit their needs, inserting local entertainment coverage if desired.

The international spread of Reali-TV cannot be explained as the result of American product innovation because many European and Japanese programs predated their American counterparts. The top-rated American tabloid in the late 1980s and early 1990s, *A Current Affair,* was developed in Australia. *Crimewatch UK,* which reconstructs crimes and asks for viewers' assistance, preceded *America's Most Wanted* and *Unsolved Mysteries,* as did a similar Dutch program.

These transborder flows suggest that programs that appear to be products of rapid American innovation when glimpsed from the national perspective were actually the result of an increased international circulation, and recirculation, of products through globalized media markets. For example, the widely formatted *America's Funniest Home Videos* was itself inspired by segments of the Japanese variety show *Fun Television with Kato-chan and Ken-chan,* which broadcast humorous videos sent in by viewers. King World's early 1990s revival of *Candid Camera* for foreign and domestic syndication, an attempt to capitalize on the success of *America's Funniest Home Videos,* similarly indicated that there was as much recycling of program formats as rapid innovation at work in the growth of Reali-TV. Mark Burnett, a former parachutist for the British Army and the creator of *Survivor,* based the program on Swedish and Dutch models.[30]

If U.S. television has always mixed the shock of the new with the familiarity of the formulaic, Reali-TV's rise suggested that American producers looked further abroad for "new" ideas, then repackaged them for domestic and international audiences. To the extent that the spread of the genre represented a "victory" for U.S.-based media producers, it was largely a triumph of packaging and marketing.

What Price Reality?

American television underwent a dramatic restructuring in the 1980s, largely precipitated by changing patterns of distribution with the spread of cable and VCRs. Audiences fragmented as these new forces challenged the networks' oligopolistic control over the distribution of television programming. Producers faced smaller license and syndication fees from an expanded customer base, which now included not only the networks but also local independent stations, cable networks and superstations, and first-run distributors. Confronted with rapidly rising above-the-line production costs, producers took it out on below-the-line labor and sought cheaper forms of programming. Reali-TV fit the bill.

In the early years, networks stepped in to produce examples of this programming that were permissible according to the FCC (news magazines for the big three, and all forms for FOX) and coproduced the kinds they were not allowed to own and syndicate under the finsyn rules until the rules were repealed. Reali-TV made a splash in Europe and Japan in the late 1980s and early 1990s as well, but many American programs of this kind that were licensed and formatted abroad drew on foreign models in the first place. This suggests that if American television turned to Reali-TV to solve its particular economic crisis, the industry both borrowed and exported abroad to do so, touching off a recirculation of products among global media corporations.

But Reali-TV has not always solved the economic problems it was meant to address. The genre declined for several years in the mid-1990s for several reasons. First, Reali-TV was not always successful in off-network syndication markets, as the genre's topicality and timeliness made it less attractive to audiences the second time around. *Unsolved Mysteries,* a top ratings winner in prime time, was one of the first such programs to be offered for syndication. Although it was sold to broadcast stations in reedited and often updated episodes, it was a financial disappointment to its producers before it found a home on the Lifetime channel, a cable network that could settle for smaller audiences. Similarly, reruns of the first season of *Survivor* did not attract strong viewership. "Reality shows have a short shelf life," one programmer noted; "they just don't seem to sell well in syndication."[31]

Under the old finsyn rules, when the networks could not take an ownership interest in most prime-time programs, executives did not have to worry about whether programs were attractive for syndication. Today, the networks produce and own most of their prime-time schedules, sharing the rewards but also the risks of investing in new shows. Thus far, the rewards have been few, as no network has produced a hit series that has sold well in syndication, although that is likely to change soon as the current crop of hit programs reach maturity.

Second, the genre's excesses drove away some advertisers that do not want to be associated with its tawdry image and generally lower-income audiences.[32] There have been public embarrassments, most notoriously FOX's *Who Wants to Marry a Multi-Millionaire,* in which a man picked his bride from the 50 women who auditioned on television for the job. FOX had to cancel the rebroadcast after news reports aired allegations of abuse by the groom's former girlfriend, raised questions about whether he was indeed a multimillionaire, and exposed the bride's claims to be a Persian Gulf War veteran as misleading. The on-air wedding was quickly annulled. Even more scandalous from advertisers' point of view, much Reali-TV has failed to attract affluent 18 to 35 year olds, appealing more to preteens, seniors, and low-income viewers. This is especially true of the tabloid programs, crime-time, and emergency programs. There are exceptions that draw more upscale viewers, such as *Survivor,* or young consumers, such as *The Real World,* but the genre's demographics have sometimes forced the networks to sell advertising time on Reali-TV shows at a discount compared with other programs with similar ratings and shares.[33]

Finally, a small legal backlash raised costs to some producers and limited their access to some of the most sensational types of footage.[34] Programs that rely on producers' ability to ride along with police or emergency workers and follow them into homes and ambulances have provoked a rash of suits for invasion of privacy. In 1999, the Supreme Court ruled that it was a violation of Fourth Amendment protections against unreasonable searches for media personnel to enter a home on the authorities' coattails unless aiding in executing a warrant. This is unlikely to curb ride-alongs but should discourage media entries into suspects' homes without permission.

Some producers may be affected by antipaparazzi laws that sprang up in the wake of Princess Diana's death in a high-speed car accident while fleeing photographers. California's law, for example, criminalizes the use of visually or aurally enhancing technology to capture sound and video in private places that would otherwise be inaccessible. The newsmagazines– indeed, any show that relies on personnel going undercover or using deception to get information–must take stock of the unsettled state of law in this area.

Many journalists were chilled by a 1997 jury award of $5.5 million to supermarket giant Food Lion in its lawsuit against an ABC *Primetime Live* undercover report that portrayed unsafe food handling and labor conditions at the chain. An appeals court later reduced the damages to $2 but upheld convictions of ABC on two counts. The networks' journalists, who got jobs at several Food Lion stores so they could gather hidden-camera footage behind the scenes, were found guilty of trespass and breach of loyalty (the latter charge was for gathering hidden-camera footage for the network while being paid by Food Lion as its employees). The case is one of several that have cast doubt on some uses of deception and hidden cameras.

Nonetheless, Reali-TV is still with us and is not likely to go away. Television broadcasters now must compete with cable channels by airing new series all year round. The return of labor-management strife in Hollywood, including the 2007–2008 Writers Guild of America strike, has recently sparked a resurgence of reality programming. As long as the networks' desperately need to fill the hours around expensive dramas and sitcoms with cheaper programming, to offer new fare throughout the year, to sell in international markets, and to control labor, they will provide us with their peculiar brand of reality.

NOTES

1. The earliest use of this term I have encountered is in Ed Siegel, "It's Not Fiction, It's Not News. It's *Not* Reality. It's Reali-TV," *Boston Globe*, 26 May 1991, A1.

2. For example, Ken Auletta, *Three Blind Mice: How the TV Networks Lost Their Way* (New York: Random House, 1991).

3. John Downing, "The Political Economy of U.S. Television," *Monthly Review* 42 (1990), 30–41.

4. Harold L. Vogel, *Entertainment Industry Economics: A Guide for Financial Analysis,* 2nd ed. (Cambridge: Cambridge University Press, 1990), 171.

5. Patricia Bauer, "Production Scene: Hollywood's New Low-End Market," *Channels* 6 (1986), 14.

6. Ibid.

7. The discussion of staff cutbacks and strikes at the networks draws on Downing, "Political Economy of U.S. Television," 37–38, and J. Max Robins, "Hired Guns Take over Local News," *Variety,* 24 September 1990, 21.

8. On core and periphery labor forces in the Hollywood entertainment industry, see Susan Christopherson and Michael Storper, "The Effects of Flexible Specialization on Industrial Politics and the Labor Market: The Motion Picture Industry," *Industrial and Labor Relations Review* 42 (1989), 331–47.

9. Bauer, "Production Scene," 14.

10. Quoted in Downing, "Political Economy of U.S. Television," 39.

11. On the role of agent-packagers, see Todd Gitlin, *Inside Prime Time* (New York: Pantheon, 1983), 143–57.

12. On the Arthur Co., see Bauer, "Production Scene," 14. On *America's Most Wanted,* see Daniel R. White, "America's Most Wanted," *ABA Journal,* October 1989, 94. On *Street Stories,* see J. Max Robins, "Producers for Hire," *Variety,* 24 February 1992, 81.

13. Quoted in Robins, "Producers for Hire," 81.

14. Quoted in Paula Bernstein, "CBS Set for Strikes with News, Reality," *Variety,* 16 March 2001, 1; see also Josef Adalian and Michael Schneider, "FOX Strike Protection: Reality," *Variety,* 11 August 2000, 5.

15. Scott A. Nelson, "Crime-Time Television," *FBI Law Enforcement Bulletin,* August 1989, 5.

16. On the role of information subsidies in news selection, see Oscar H. Gandy Jr., "Information in Health: Subsidised News," *Media, Culture and Society* 2 (1980), 103–15.

17. Economic data in this paragraph are from "1991–1992 Primetime at a Glance," *Variety,* 26 August 1991, 48–54.

18. On the constraints faced by "independent" film producers, see Asu Aksoy and Kevin Robins, "Hollywood for the 21st Century: Global Competition for Critical Mass in Image Markets,"*Cambridge Journal of Economics* 16 (1992), 1–22.

On the similar financial dependence of small television producers, see Vogel, *Entertainment Industry Economics,* 117; Gitlin, *Inside Prime Time,* 136.

19. The finsyn rules were not applied to FOX as the FCC did not define it as a network because it distributed fewer than 15 hours a week of programming.

20. Quoted in Nelson, "Crime-Time Television," 8.

21. Committee of Concerned Journalists, *Changing Definitions of News,* April 1998, at http://www.journalism.org/ccj/resources/chdefonews.html. See also Bill Kovach and Tom Rosenstiel, "Are Watchdogs an Endangered Species?" *Columbia Journalism Review,* May–June 2001, at http://www.cjr.org/year/01/3/rosenstiel.asp.

22. Aaron Barnhart, "Lawrence Company Has Its Finger on the Pulse of TV Topics," *Kansas City Star,* 10 January 1998, E4.

23. Quoted in Elizabeth Guider, "Yanks Deal for Real," *Variety,* 3 June 1991, 35.

24. Quoted in James McBride, "'On-Scene' Shows Flood Airwaves," *Variety,* 3 June 1991, 32.

25. Aksoy and Robins, "Hollywood for the Twenty-First Century," 18.

26. Quoted in Guider, "Yanks Deal for Real," 1.

27. Clay Calvert, *Voyeur Nation: Media, Privacy, and Peering in Modern Culture* (Boulder, Colo.: Westview, 2000), 102.

28. Quoted in Guider, "Yanks Deal for Real," 75.

29. Graham Murdock, "Television and Citizenship: In Defence of Public Broadcasting," in *Consumption, Identity, and Style,* ed. Alan Tomlinson (New York: Routledge, 1990), 77–101; Paddy Scannell, "Public Service Broadcasting: The History of a Concept," in *Understanding Television,* ed. Andrew Goodwin and Gary Whannel (New York: Routledge, 1990), 11–29.

30. Edward D. Miller, "Fantasies of Reality: Surviving Reality-Based Programming," *Social Policy* 31 (2000), 10.

31. Quoted in John Dempsey, "Hot Genre Gluts TV Market," *Variety,* 3 June 1991, 32.

32. Michael Schneider, "True Believers: Nets Reap Ratings from Reality Shows," *Variety,* 12 November 1999, 1.

33. Steve Coe, "Reality 1994: 'The Reality Is That [Some Network] Reality Bites,'" *Broadcasting and Cable,* 9 May 1994, 30.

34. The discussion in this paragraph is based on Calvert, *Voyeur Nation,* 133–206.

Television 2.0

The Business of American Television in Transition

Ted Magder

Not so long ago, the prime-time television universe in America had a fixed point of reference. It was Thursday night, the night coveted by advertisers trying to reach audiences before the weekend, a night dominated throughout the 1990s by NBC's formidable lineup of programming, self-lovingly dubbed "Must See TV." In its final iteration, which began with *Friends* at 8:00 PM and ended at 11:00 PM when *ER* was over, NBC's Must See TV embodied the classic elements of American network television: to capture and hold a large audience over the course of an entire evening with a mix of situation comedies and one-hour dramas. For roughly 15 years—with programs such as *Cheers, Seinfeld, Hill Street Blues,* and *The Cosby Show*— NBC reigned supreme atop the network heap. That reign came to an end in 2003. Must See TV now serves as a nostalgic reminder of better times, not just for NBC but for the business of television in general.

During the second month of the 2006 fall television season, the then-head of NBC Universal's TV division, Jeff Zucker, summoned the press to announce a major shake-up in his business plan. Now floundering near the bottom of the network race for audiences, NBC's operating earnings had fallen for each of the preceding three quarters, and its parent company, General Electric, was getting restless. Predictably, Zucker began by cutting costs, outlining reductions of $750 million in administrative and operating expenses and eliminating roughly 750 jobs, about 5 percent of NBC's workforce.

What came next was more of a surprise: Zucker announced that NBC would substantially reduce its commitment to scripted programs, such as one-hour dramas and situation comedies; instead, the first hour of prime time each evening would normally be devoted to reality TV, game shows, and other types of format programming. Zucker even had a name for his strategy. With a nod to the surging popularity of social networking websites and to Google's $1.65 billon purchase of YouTube that same month, he called it "NBCU 2.0." "We have to recognize," Zucker was reported as saying, "that the changes of the next five years will dwarf the changes of the last 50."[1]

The other major networks, ABC, CBS, and FOX, had already made similar moves, though without the same public fanfare.[2] Now, across the board, dramatic programming is no longer the sine qua non of prime-time programming. Of course, there have been instances in the past when game shows, variety programming, and newsmagazines have occupied prime-time slots. But since the summer of *Survivor* and *Big Brother* in 2000, reality TV, or what is also referred to as "unscripted" programming, has become a television staple in the most coveted time slots. What some perceived as a fad has become the norm. At the time of Zucker's announcement, unscripted programs accounted for 15 hours of prime-time programs a week; by comparison, the number of prime-time hours devoted to sitcoms was roughly 10 hours a week, down from 20 hours a week in 2004[3] Whatever its cultural and social resonance, reality programming is now firmly entrenched in the business model of American television, yet another sign that the enterprise of television faces an uncertain future.

In general terms, this uncertainty has to do with the shift from an analog to a digital environment for the production and distribution of the content we associated with television. Technological innovations have overturned television's linear and monologic universe: a single screen where content was centrally scheduled to play out sequentially over the minutes and hours of the day and where audience attention was sold to advertisers.[4] The television industry now confronts an array of new devices for the delivery and storage of programming (from digital video recorders attached to conventional TVs to iPods, computers, and mobile phones) and new, more-sophisticated techniques for measuring audience attention and behavior.

Of course, the appliance known as television is still a fixture in American households, and it remains the destination of choice for more advertising dollars than any other medium. But television's central position in the media environment and the dominance of the major networks, unchallenged for almost 50 years, now seem less certain. This article focuses primarily on how reality TV, and format television more generally, both illustrate and influence the alterations under way to the business land-scape of American television.

Reality TV Comes to America

In the grand American tradition of network TV, the summer season has always been an afterthought—a time for reruns, old movies, cheap alter-native programs, some pilots, and an out-of-favor, made-for-TV movie. But the summer of 2000 was the summer of reality TV, *Survivor,* and, to a lesser extent, *Big Brother.* In a desperate attempt to boost its ratings among younger viewers, the CBS network tried its luck with two formats showing great promise in Europe. *Survivor* caught everyone's attention, building over its 8-week run to become every programmer's dream—a "watercooler" must-see-at-least-once kind of show. Over 50 million peo-ple tuned in for the final episode.

Given its success, no one was surprised that CBS ordered a second in-stallment of *Survivor* to begin January 2001. It was the choice of time slots that raised eyebrows: *Survivor II: Australian Outback* was scheduled for 8:00 PM on Thursday nights, right opposite *Friends,* the anchor comedy in NBC's Must See TV lineup. A lot of revenue was a stake. According to *Advertising Age,* of the five most expensive 30-second commercial slots during the 2000–2001 season, four were on Thursday nights during shows aired by NBC: *ER* at $620,000 for a 30-second slot; *Friends* at $540,000; *Will and Grace* at $480,000; and *Just Shoot Me* at $465,000.[5] Eager to protect its golden goose, NBC took some inventive steps to thwart the *Survivor* challenge: it ran extralong episodes of *Friends* until 8:40, and it ran highlight reels from *Saturday Night Live.* But *Survivor II* could not be beaten back. By the end of the 2001 season, CBS had doubled its Thurs-day-night audience, from 10 to 20.5 million, and most of the new viewers were in the coveted 18–49-year-old age bracket.[6] The two networks were now nip and tuck in a battle for Thursday-night supremacy.

Audience figures tell only half the tale. To understand the impact of *Survivor,* and reality TV more generally, one has to look at both sides of the balance sheet for television programming. While audience figures re-veal much about revenues, they reveal nothing about production costs. And by 2001, NBC's Thursday-night lineup came with an exceedingly high price tag: each episode of *Friends* cost $5.5 million, making it the most expensive half hour of network television; NBC shelled out $13 million more for *ER,* making it television's most expensive hour-long drama.

The lofty price tags for *Friends* and *ER* are representative of the business model that has driven network TV since the 1960s. Broadcasters do not necessarily own the programs they air but license them from other firms. In the case of *Friends* and *ER,* NBC paid a fee to Warner Bros. Television, the shows' producer and owner, for the right to air each show twice over the course of a season and to control all advertising placed around them.[7] When hit shows outlast their initial contract, the price per episode usually goes up.

Take *Friends,* for example. In 1994, the six principal actors agreed to five-year contracts at $22,500 each per episode. At each renewal of the contract for *Friends,* the cast negotiated as a group, with threats to move on and pursue other projects. In 1999, each of the six actors was paid $125,000 an episode; the following two seasons, each received $750,000 an episode. For the 2002 season—the final year for the show—each cast member earned $1 million an episode, with each episode budgeted at $7.5 million.[8]

Though *Friends* (and *ER*) are extreme examples of escalating production costs, they reflect a general trend. Traditional scripted drama on TV is expensive (and becomes even more expensive over time), in large measure because of the high costs of getting and keeping the above-the-line talent (actors, writers, directors).

Survivor, in contrast, represents an entirely different business model. The most obvious difference is that for *Survivor,* and shows of its ilk, the on-screen "talent" is dirt-cheap. But *Survivor* broke the mold in other ways as well. Instead of handing its producer, Mark Burnett, a license fee to deliver the show, CBS agreed to share *Survivor*'s advertising revenue and asked him to help presell the sponsorship.[9] Burnett secured eight sponsors before the first day of principal photography, selling most of the 30-second spots around the show as well as prominent brand placements in the show itself. These eight advertisers, including Anheuser-Busch, General Motors, Visa, Frito-Lay, Reebok, and Target, paid roughly $4 million each for a combination of commercial time, product placement in the show, and a website link.[10]

For the next few versions of *Survivor,* advertisers shelled out close to $12 million each before the show went on air. With presold sponsorships covering the costs of production and 30-second spots running just ahead of *ER* (*Survivor: Africa* topped *ER* with the most expensive 30-second spot during the 2001–2002 season, at $445,000 to *ER*'s $425,000), *Survivor* was proving lucrative.[11]

The managers and executives who run America's networks were paying close attention. *Survivor* became the tipping point—not only for its content and the genre it represents but also for the business model it offered. NBC struck a deal with Mark Burnett for a show called *Destination Mir,* an astronaut-training competition with the winner taking a trip (a real one) aboard a Soyuz rocket to the Mir space station. General Electric, NBC's owner and a major aerospace contractor, agreed to provide $40 million to fund the project. The other networks moved quickly into the genre as well, with shows like *The Bachelor* and *The Mole* on ABC and *American Idol* on FOX.

By 2002, the prime-time schedule included eight hours of "unscripted" reality programming. And there was more to come: by 2005, with new shows like *The Apprentice* (NBC), *Wife Swap, Trading Spouses,* and *Extreme Makeover: Home Edition* (ABC), almost 20 percent of prime-time program hours consisted of reality programming.[12] Unlike traditional scripted programs, most of which are cancelled before they return a profit, almost every new reality show found an audience and made ends meet. NBC's *Destination Mir* was one of the few exceptions to the early charm of reality programming: the space station fell out of orbit, spreading its debris over the South Pacific ocean about 3,000 miles east of where the second installment of *Survivor: the Australian Outback,* was taking place.

The Business of TV in America

The business of television begins with a simple observation: people like to watch. Since the late 1960s, at any particular hour of the day or night, the number of people watching TV has been a stable, predictable number. TV takes up almost 50 percent of the time Americans spend with media products and cultural events; on average, each American household watches just over 1,600 hours of TV a year.[13] On any given day, an audience is out there, predictably flipping through channels and looking for something to watch. The challenge for television's managers and programmers is to grab the attention of viewers and hold on to them for as long as possible.

That attention is sold to advertisers. And until the late 1980s, the dominance of an advertiser-funded model made the U.S. system unique.

Elsewhere, public or state-sponsored television was a core feature of television systems, either as a monopoly or a privileged institution in a carefully regulated system of public and private broadcasters. Now, throughout most of the world, TV relies heavily on the buying and selling of audiences. Even so, the American TV system stands out, primarily because of the scale of the money involved. All told, with just over 100 million households, U.S. TV advertising expenditures amounted to a little more than $60 billion in 2002. For the following twelve countries combined— Australia, Canada, France, Germany, Italy, Japan, Mexico, the Netherlands, Spain, Sweden, Switzerland, and the United Kingdom—with more than double the number of households, total advertising expenditures amounted to $53 billion.[14] To say the least, the U.S. TV market is awash with advertising revenue, which goes a long way to explaining how the system works.[15]

It is sometimes said that TV, as a business, does what any business tries to do: give customers what they want or need at an agreeable price, and, over time, develop a stable and trustworthy commercial relationship. But, in the case of television, the customer is really the advertiser, not the viewer. What TV in America does—and does rather well on the face of it—is triangulate between the wants and needs of advertisers and the wants and needs of viewers. Advertisers pay for the attention of viewers, but not every viewer is valued equally. Preference is given to those viewers who have a decent supply of cash (or credit), those with a willingness to spend, and especially those who are young enough to develop long-term brand loyalty. In the language of television, advertisers pay more for younger adult viewers, typically defined as 18 to 34 year olds. Few people in the industry trust the validity and reliability of the underlying mathematics of television advertising, but this lack of faith matters less than one might think. The blunt language of age demographics and ratings and shares (which at best tell you what channel a TV is tuned to but precious little about the attention or interest of viewers) is the currency of the television business.[16] It is simple and easy to follow. Those who pay the bills have accepted its imperfections for a long time.

Given these fundamentals on the revenue side, it is wrong to say that TV in America gives people what they most want to watch or that TV responds primarily to the interests and needs of viewers. Instead, in light of the household habit of TV viewing and the interests of advertisers, TV executives try to produce or schedule shows that are only marginally better than other offerings available at the same time. The goal of American

TABLE 7.1

Average Cost of Original Programming: Estimates, U.S. Market, 2005

Genre	Cost per Episode
Prime-time drama (1 hour)	$3.0 million
Situation comedy (30 minutes)	$1.5 million
Reality TV (1 hour)	$700,000–$1.25 million
Game show (1 hour)	$300,000
Daytime soap opera / Telenovela	$200,000

Sources: Figures are best estimates based on various trade journals and financial reports.

Note: Production costs for reality TV programming vary considerably, as illustrated above.

TV is to give people programming that they are willing to watch or, at the very least, programming from which they will not turn away. From time to time, hits emerge and certain programs develop loyal followings. But the day-to-day business of TV doesn't run on hits and loyalty. It runs on habit.

The effect of television's dependence on advertising with respect to programming and scheduling has to be considered in relation to the process by which television content is produced. As Grant Tinker, who piloted NBC's emergence as a network power in the mid-1980s, once said: "Television would be wonderful if it were only on Wednesday nights."[17] Tinker was referring specifically to the problem of creativity: there are only so many good writers, actors, and other talented people to go around, while the medium of TV requires thousands of hours of new programs each year. The talent problem is real enough. But the economics of television are burdened by a peculiar problem, one that characterizes the creative industries as a whole: close to 100 percent of the costs are incurred making the first copy of a finished TV program. In the case of prime-time dramatic programming, original episodes now cost over $2.5 million an hour. (Table 7.1 shows the average costs of original programming.)

Once a program is finished, the cost of making extra copies and distributing them is virtually zero. Because most TV programming is serialized, first-copy costs are incurred for a number of episodes in advance (the creativity deficit would be that much greater if TV consisted mostly of one-time programs). And until the program airs, it is virtually impossible to predict its success—sunk costs are high, and so is the risk of failure.[18]

Richard Caves refers to this problem as the "nobody knows" principle.[19] American TV runs on it.

To deal with the nobody knows principle, U.S. network television has followed a few programming axioms for most of its history. First, deliver audiences in a "buying mood" to advertisers; viewers need to be tuned in but not unduly upset or disturbed by the program's content. Second, stick to established program genres and avoid challenging the genre expectations of viewers. Third, recycle and copy successful shows: on television, imitation is the sincerest form of flattery.

Hit shows beget spin-offs or siblings; the *Law and Order* franchise, which includes the original show, as well as *Law and Order: Special Victims Unit* and *Law and Order: Criminal Intent,* is one example. Other examples include ABC's development of *The Bachelorette* after the success of *The Bachelor* and NBC's *The Apprentice* (with Donald Trump) spawning *The Apprentice: Martha Stewart.* Hit shows also beget copycats, shows that attempt to replicate the successful formula with slight modification. The success of ABC's *Who Wants to Be a Millionaire* led to a revival of game shows on prime-time television, with copycat shows like *Greed* (FOX) and *Twenty-One* (NBC).[20]

The game trend continues: *Deal or No Deal* was a staple of NBC's 2006 prime-time schedule. In each of these examples, the goal is the same: to reduce creative uncertainty by using a template that has proven successful. The last axiom is the most important: every programming trend runs its course and programmers must constantly scan the horizon for the next sure thing.

As program production costs escalated by as much as 30 percent over the course of the 1990s, TV programmers developed other techniques to raise revenues and reduce costs. On the revenue side, the average number of prime-time ads jumped from 6 minutes an hour in 1986 to nearly 11 minutes an hour by the mid-1990s; in 2005, that number reached roughly 17 minutes an hour (the networks air even more commercials per hour during the other dayparts: 18 minutes during early morning, 19 minutes during late night, and 21 minutes during daytime).[21]

To protect against the price inflation exhibited by *Friends* and *ER,* the standard contracts for dramatic shows have been lengthened to six or more years. In addition, the networks increasingly turned to cheaper "alternative" programming in prime time and reduced the number of hours committed to original drama. In the late 1990s, prime-time news-magazines, such as NBC's *Dateline* and CBS's *48 Hours,* took advantage of overheads already committed to news divisions to produce an hour of television at a fraction the cost of fictional programming. Game shows also fall into the category of alternative programming.

In an effort to reduce the burden (and risk) of creating new programming, the networks have aired shows more than once over the course of the same week, often on an affiliated cable channel, a strategy that has come to be known as "repurposing" and "multiplexing." These days, the major networks are even more likely to concentrate their programming and scheduling around their hit shows: by 2005, the *Law and Order* franchise made up close to 30 percent of NBC's prime-time schedule, while the *CSI* franchise accounted for slightly less of CBS's schedule, roughly 25 percent.[22] In each case, the goal was the same: reduce the costs and risks of producing original content, while giving audiences what they are willing to watch.

Reality TV, Formats, and the New Business of Television

European Producers and the Lure of Formats

The emergence of reality TV is most certainly part of the general effort to reduce production costs and financial risk. But it is more than that. Reality TV illustrates four significant changes to the production side of TV: the growing enthusiasm for prepackaged formats as a basis for program production; the emergence of product placement, or brand integration, as a source of revenue to program producers; the increasing tendency to use TV programs as the springboard for a multimedia exploitation of the creative property; and the growing strength of European program suppliers in the American (and international) television market.

No two companies better illustrate this last trend than Endemol, which is headquartered just outside of Amsterdam, and FremantleMedia, based in London. Endemol continues to build on its pioneering success with *Big Brother*, which debuted on Dutch television in 1999.[23] At any one time, Endemol has as many as 300 formats in production around the world, including such titles as *Fear Factor, Big Diet, Extreme Makeover: Home Edition, 1 vs. 100*, and *Deal or No Deal*; its corporate holdings and affiliates now span over 20 countries, including France, the United Kingdom, Germany, Portugal, the United States, Brazil, India, Russia, Mexico, South Africa, and Australia. FremantleMedia's international success has much to do with the acquisition of companies such as KingWorld, a giant in the

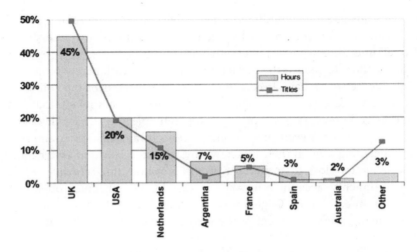

Figure 7.1. TV exports in the international marketplace: percentage share of scheduled imported format time and number of titles by exporters to the market, 2003. *Source:* Television Research Partnership, "Rights of Passage: British Television in the Global Market," *UK Trade and Investment,* February 2005, p. 17, figure 10.

business of game shows (*The Price Is Right, Wheel of Fortune*), and the *Idol* franchise (known as *Pop Idol* in the U.K., where it started, and *American Idol* in the United States, with local versions of the format in more than 30 other countries).

The success of European producers is a noteworthy feature of reality TV and, more generally, of the worldwide market for format television. According to one recent report, while U.S. productions account for roughly 70 percent of the export market for finished made-for-TV programs (such as situation comedies and one-hour dramas), U.K. exporters account for almost one-half of the international market for TV formats, to be followed, in turn, by U.S. and Dutch companies, at 20 percent and 15 percent, respectively (figure 7.1).[24]

Sometimes referred to as "unfinished programming," formats make good business sense for a company like Endemol, based as it is in a small national and linguistic market. Producers of formats hope to generate a modest profit in a number of linguistic and cultural markets rather than the super profits that emerge from a finished program that might become an international hit. By 2006, Endemol had sold the *Big Brother* format in more than 20 different countries. Where national markets may be too small (in economic terms), it has also produced regional versions of the show: in *Big Brother Africa* (2003), for example, the contestants came from Angola, Botswana, Ghana, Kenya, Malawi, Namibia, Nigeria, South Africa, Tanzania, Uganda, Zambia, and Zimbabwe.

A good format like *Big Brother* is a template providing detailed production and marketing guidelines that can be tailored to each locale.[25] Peter Bazalgette, chairman of Endemol UK and a founding producer of *Big Brother*, has noted that "formats are simply concentrated ideas with rules. The key to most of these things is to have the kind of idea that works for everyone."[26] Everyone, in this case, means different audiences in different markets. Brian Briggs, an international line producer at Endemol, put it this way: "The reason why Endemol is so successful is that we take a format that works in one country, strip everything cultural off of it, export it to a new country and then, over time, add cultural aspects of that country to it."[27]

The fundamentals differ little from market to market. Endemol supplies a "playbook" (or guidelines) and "coach" (or producer), who consults with the local producer on the adaptation of the show's fundamental elements. In the case of *Big Brother*, those elements include no communication with the outside world, the weekly competitions and eliminations of contestants, and, most important, the round-the-clock use of cameras that monitor the contestants' activity.[28] When things work well, a format becomes an international brand with distinctive, and carefully modulated, local variations—a classic formula tweaked to suit local tastes.

Whether the broadcaster is FOX Television in the United States or Rajawali Citra Televisi Indonesia, both of which hold the license to broadcast *Idol* in their respective national territories, the purchase of a format offers some advantages. Most obviously, formats greatly reduce the financial risks associated with the nobody knows principle of traditional, finished programming. Instead, the format producer has already assumed most of the creative risks and the associated expense of creating a generic first copy, as well as considerable experience honing its programming to meet varying audience and broadcaster expectations in different markets. Recalling an old industry axiom that four out of five original programs fail, Ben Silverman, who brokered the deals for *Big Brother* and *The Weakest Link*, notes that three out of four shows based on a proven format succeed, having stayed on the air through at least two "seasons."[29]

Not surprisingly, formats have been used more frequently outside the United States, where, generally, commercial broadcasters cannot afford the trial-and-error approach that has been the hallmark of developing hit shows in the United States.[30] And, since most broadcasters in countries other than the United States are required by law to produce a certain amount of domestic or national content, formats offer one more advantage: because the finished program is produced by a local crew and consists of a local cast, format programming typically qualifies as a domestic production.

Follow the Money: Before and Beyond the Box

Reality shows demonstrate the viability of three business strategies that together may fundamentally alter the logic of TV production (Figure 7.2). First, almost every show in the genre demonstrates the growing importance of product placement or brand integration. Money from sponsors for TV production was common in the early days of American television: as the names suggest, shows like *Texaco Star Theatre*, *The Colgate Comedy Hour*, and *The Goodyear Television Playhouse* were under the sponsor's thumb. Between 1951 and 1955, *I Love Lucy*, the most popular show on U.S. television, was sponsored exclusively by Philip Morris cigarettes, with a variety of ad campaigns built around the show's stars, Lucille Ball and Desi Arnaz.[31]

But American TV moved away from this model of funding in the 1960s. Advertisers bought time from the networks but no longer played a direct role in the production phase of programming. Even as Hollywood discovered the advantages of product placement as a way of offsetting rising movie costs in the 1990s, TV generally steered clear of product placement.[32] *Survivor*'s $12 million placement deals opened the gates. So, too, did the brief but spectacular success of *Who Wants to Be a Millionaire* in which the host, Regis Philbin, would ask AT&T to provide the "phone-a-friend" lifeline. The pace has quickened in the past five years. Nielsen Media Research recorded more than 100,000 placements on American television in 2006, with reality shows leading the way: *American Idol* had almost double the number of placements that appeared on *The Amazing Race* and *Extreme Makeover: Home Edition* (table 7.2).

In terms of money changing hands, TV product placements are now double those in filmed entertainment and more than 30 times higher than those in other media such as video games and magazines.[33] Paid placements on television are also growing more rapidly than placements in other media. According to TNS Media Intelligence, more than 10 percent of all

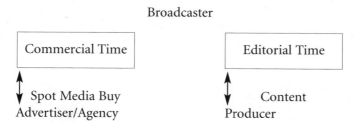

TRADITIONAL TV MODEL

Broadcaster

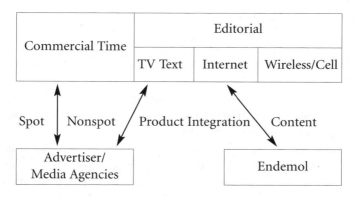

MULTIMEDIA/ADVERTISER INTEGRATED MODEL

Broadcaster

Figure. 7.2. A new model for content delivery and financing. Adapted from a presentation by Michiel Dieperink, executive director for advertising-funded programming. Endemol International, June 2002, Aalsmeer.

television programming now contains some brand reference. As shown in Tables 7.3 and 7.4, in a few cases, the number of minutes devoted to branded appearances outstrips the time given over to commercial messages. The price range for placements is considerable: while some placements on *The Apprentice* go for about $1 million, a regional ice-cream manufacturer paid just $14,000 to the show's producers (and handed over its factory for a half day of shooting); Coca-Cola, AT&T, and Ford pay about $50 million for a combination of placements and ad time on *American Idol*.[34]

TABLE 7.2

Top Ten U.S. Television Programs by Product Placement, 2005

Program	Network	Occurrence (no. of placements per year)
1. American Idol	Fox	4,086
2. The Amazing Race	CBS	2,790
3. Extreme Makeover Home Edition	ABC	2,701
4. The Biggest Loser	NBC	2,405
5. America's Next Top Model	CW	2,309
6. Hell's Kitchen	Fox	1,909
7. The Apprentice	NBC	1,831
8. The King of Queens	CBS	1,742
8. Rock Stars: Supernova	CBS	1,609
10. Big Brother	CBS	1,591

Source: Nielsen Media Research.
Note: Of the top ten, only The King of Queens is a scripted program.

Over time, product placement may come to be regarded as a modest example of the shifting relationship between producers, advertisers, and distributors. Branded content, where advertisers retain creative control over the content, is a more radical step away from the traditional business model of television, though it, too, has its antecedents in television history. Proctor and Gamble, the company that might be said to have started branded content with the soap opera *Guiding Light,* and the company that routinely spends more money on advertising than any other, has renewed its interest in program production. In 2006, for example, the cable channel TLC started broadcasting Proctor and Gamble's *Home Made Simple* based on home-making tips that are also on the company's website.[35] In February 2006, beer manufacturer Anheuser-Busch shifted an estimated 10 percent of its advertising budget, roughly $60 million, to launch BUD. TV, an Internet venture featuring original content destined for seven separate "channels."[36]

The economic value of product placement on American television is still a small fraction of the nearly $70 billion to be spent on conventional television advertising in 2007. And brand integration is still a sideline business. But together they represent one of the tactical responses to the growth of personal video recorders that have made time-shifting and ad-skipping more commonplace. Across the media landscape, audiences and advertisers seem locked in a war of position and attention; content producers and distributors in all media must adjust their business strategies as a result. As more and more people have access to personal video recorders, programming that is designed to be watched live becomes more attractive to advertisers; and here competitive reality programs that feature lots of losers and (an eventual) winner, like *American Idol, The Apprentice,* and *America's Next Top Model,* offer roughly the same benefits as sports programming: committed viewers want to watch these programs at their scheduled time. More and more, liveness is a premium.

TABLE 7.3

Brand Time versus Commercial Time: U.S. Television, 2005, 4th Quarter

Schedule Time	Branded Appearances (minutes per hour)	Commercial Messages (minutes per hour)
Network prime time overall	4:24	17:35
Prime-time reality shows	11:05	17:04
Prime-time scripted shows	3:07	17:41
Late night (after 11 PM)	11:06	20:33

Source: Magna Global (2006), "Product Integration News," March. Data are for the fourth quarter of 2005 only.

TABLE 7.4

Top Shows: Brand Time versus Ad Time, 2005, 4th Quarter

Reality Shows	Branded Appearances (minutes per hour)	Commercial Messages (minutes per hour)
The Apprentice: Martha Stewart	33:51	16:32
Biggest Loser	23:08	16:14
The Apprentice	21:15	16:55
Amazing Race	19:40	16:14
Fear Factor	17:11	16:46

Source: Magna Global (2006), "Product Integration News," March. Data are for the fourth quarter of 2005 only.

A second strategy in the search for new revenue is the expansion of mer-chandise tie-ins.[37] These, too, have been around since the beginning of televi-sion—*Hopalong Cassidy* gun-and-holster sets and the music of *The Monkees*, for example—but the phenomenon has picked up steam, especially in con-nection with reality shows and their affiliated websites. There are now well over 150 *Survivor*-themed products that are available in the United States, everything from CDs and bug spray to board games and bandanas. Fans can also play a *Survivor* trivia challenge online.[38] In Australia, Energizer Max batteries were sold with a sticker carrying a code that when entered into the *Big Brother* website allowed viewers to watch up to 10 audition videos; in the United States, *Fear Factor* has teamed with ice-cream manufacturer Baskin-Robbins and in 2005 licensed its name to the first reality TV–inspired theme park attraction, Fear Factor Live, at Universal Studios Florida.[39]

Not surprisingly, the trend continues with the *Idol* franchise, which has generated sales of close to 20 million CDs and roughly 2 million concert tickets. The *Idol* name has been slapped on close to 50 products and ser-vices, including key chains, t-shirts, food items, card games, and a kara-oke home version, with sales of over $50 million in the first four seasons.[40] And while Coke, Ford, and AT&T remain *Idol*'s principal on-air sponsors, the show now has six off-air partners as well; for the 2007 season, Nestle, for example, expected to produce 70 million "official" *Idol* candy bars, with one lucky chocolate lover winning a trip to the finale.[41]

The third strategy in search of new revenue streams is easily the most revolutionary: it extends the "program" beyond the confines of the box in the living room and encourages audiences to pay to participate in the show's dramatic arc or to use other media to stay in touch with the show. *Big Brother* led the way and its producer, Endemol, remains at the fore-front of something now referred to as "Participation TV." In the summer of 2001, the Real Network/CBS webcast of *Big Brother 2* drew just more than 50,000 monthly subscribers, who paid fees ranging between $9.95 and $19.95 to receive round-the-clock video feeds of the program. With $15.00 as an average purchase, the webcasts generated around $850,000—not a huge sum in the scheme of things.[42]

In general, this subscription model has been replaced by a more mo-ment-to-moment approach to interactive engagement—SMS (short mes-sage service) and online voting, for example, have both proven to be more lucrative. In the U.K., where *Big Brother* captured up to 35 percent of the television audience in the summer of 2002, some 3.5 million viewers (a little more than 50 percent of the average audience) voted on the eviction of Adele Roberts.[43] They paid 25 pence each to do so, which translates into £875,000, more than the cost of producing the episode and considerably more than the £40,000 paid for a 30-second slot during eviction night.[44] As the head of interactive media at Endemol UK put it at the time: "We're creating this virtuous circle that excites the interactive audience about what's going on in the house, drives them toward the TV program, the TV program will drive them to the internet, the internet to the other ways they can get information, and the other ways back to the TV."[45]

In 2002, this multiplatform strategy might have seemed a bit dreamy; it is now very much a routine element in the business plan for much of the content that premieres on television and has a second life on the Internet and mobile phones. In its 2005 U.S. incarnation, *American Idol* recorded a whopping 500 million votes, with 63 million votes recorded for the finale alone. Those who voted by mobile phone paid a 99 cent fee. Those who voted via the *Idol* website saw a great deal of advertising. As of summer 2006, viewers of NBC's *Deal or No Deal*, produced by Endemol, were encouraged to play along at home by going online or using SMS on their mobile phones to play "The Lucky Case Game." At the end of each night's broadcast, the host announces four grand prizewinners of $10,000—one winner for each of the continental U.S. time zones. Endemol reports that its various participation TV platforms combined with its traditional platforms, such as *Big Brother*, received a total of 300 million calls and SMS in 2005.[46]

Premium-rate SMS and "red-button" voting using the television remote control is also on the rise. In the U.K., a wave of low budget, simple-minded game shows—with names like *Jackpot TV, Get Lucky*, and *Gala Games*—involve no on-screen contestants. Viewers at home play along using their remote or mobile phones. At present, these programs represent television's wild west; game producers have been accused of manipulating and falsifying votes, and a newly formed regulatory agency, ICSTIS, the Independent Committee for the Supervision of Standards of Telephone Information Services, is undertaking an investigation.[47]

On the Air, Online, and On-the-Go

Whatever reality TV's specific appeal to audiences, television's movers and shakers see it as an effective business strategy in a time of turbulence: reality programming attracts younger viewers, lowers production costs, and offers opportunities for audience engagement across a variety of platforms.

Reality TV has become an established genre of television at precisely the moment that television's future is a little less certain.

Over the next few years, those uncertainties will likely multiply. Two trends stand out: first, it will become easier for audiences to personalize their use of programming, via digital video recorders attached to television screens, or access via computers (the second screen) and other mobile players, such as iPods and mobile phones (the third screen). Increasingly, as Jeff Zucker has remarked, the networks will have to figure out how to reach audiences "on the air, online and on-the-go."[48] And they've started to. In October 2005, ABC was the first network to makes its programming available on iTunes and, in May 2006, it became the first to build a website offering free, ad-supported video streaming of some of its prime-time programming. By late 2006, all the major broadcast networks and many cable networks had placed their programming on iTunes and introduced streaming video on their own websites.[49]

Needless to say, the box in the living room is not about to become obsolete, if only because that's where the majority of the advertising dollars (and the majority of viewers) can still be found. But here, too, uncertainty is the order of the day. Digital platforms make it possible to measure and monitor the attention and activity of audiences with a precision that is minute-to-minute, even second-to-second. But as these new numbers begins to accumulate, they destabilize the fundamental business transaction that drives commercial television: the manner and rate at which audience attention is sold to advertisers. Last May, for example, at an annual event in television's business cycle known as the up-front market, where the networks preview their fall schedules and sell a good percentage of the ad time for the upcoming season, negotiations stalled over how to account for the audiences using digital video recorders. As of January 2006, Nielsen had been publishing three time-based ratings: live, live plus same day, and live plus seven day.

Tellingly, though DVR households comprise under 20 percent of the total, their influence on program ratings can be considerable: for example, among viewers aged 24 to 52, the live plus seven-day rating for *CSI* is double the live-only rating.[50] The networks wanted to charge advertisers an additional fee for the DVR audience. The advertisers wanted to know whether DVR users were watching the ads at all. For a few weeks, no money changed hands.

Soon enough, even the dispute over DVR ratings may seem quaint. The science of measuring audiences—what the Nielsen Company refers to as Anytime/Anywhere Media Measurement (A2/M2)—has reached the point where it is now possible to offer data on audience attention during ad breaks. In other words, the business model of television can now be based on who is watching the ads versus who is watching the programs. The 2008 television season will be the first to conduct business using commercial ratings. Television 2.0 may be on its way.

NOTES

My thanks to Joanna Keller and Lauren Hughes for providing research support.

1. Quoted in David Teather, "Television: NBC to Leave Blood on the Studio Floor," *Guardian* (London), 20 October 2006, 35. See also Brooks Barnes, "Reality TV: NBC Universal to Slash Costs in News, Prime-Time Programs; Unit Aims to Cut $750 Million It Confronts New Media; More Spending on Internet; Heir Apparent Makes a Move," *Wall Street Journal,* 19 October 2006, A1. Four months later, in February 2007, Jeff Zucker was promoted to president and chief executive officer of NBC Universal.

2. For a good overview of recent changes to network television, see Bill Carter, *Desperate Networks* (New York: Doubleday, 2006). For an excellent overview of the economics of the entertainment industries, including television, see Harold Vogel, *Entertainment Industry Economics: A Guide for Financial Analysts,* 7th ed. (New York: Cambridge University Press, 2007). For periodic assessments of industry trends, see Standard and Poor's, *Industry Surveys: Broadcasting, Cable and Satellite,* various years.

3. Richard Verrier, "No Time for Making New 'Friends' at NBC: Sitcom Writers Lament the Industry's Changes as the Network Plans to Devote 8 P.M. to Reality and Game Shows," *Los Angeles Times,* 7 November 2006, C1.

4. This article focuses on the television industry in the United States where the basic business model has always involved the sale of audiences to advertisers. Elsewhere, for much of its history, television programs were financed by the public purse but with much the same temporal experience.

5. Stuart Elliott, "TV Networks Wonder How Much Lower Prices for Commercial Time Could Go," *New York Times,* 25 September 2001, C1, C16 (chart).

6. Bill Carter, "Thanks to 'Survivor,' CBS Gains on Thursday," *New York Times,* 3 May 2001, C1; Bill Carter, "Successes of Reality TV Put Networks in 'Survivor' Mode," *New York Times,* 3 February 2001, C1.

7. Michael Freeman, "TV in Transition: Forging a Model for Profitability, Repurposing the First Step toward Fiscal Viability," *Electronic Media,* 28 January 2002, 1. See also Vogel, *Entertainment Industry Economics,* chapters 7–8.

8. Joe Flint, "NBC Finalizes Deal to Keep 'Friends' for Final Season: Cast Will Get Raise," *Wall Street Journal Online,* 28 February 2002. In 2002, Warner Bros.

made 22 episodes and received $6 million in license fees from NBC. License fees typically cover about 80 percent of a show's production costs, and the producer picks up the rest of the tab. Because it owns the show, Warner Bros. reaps all the income from international sales and the market for reruns in the United States, which is typically referred to as the "syndication market." It has been estimated that *Friends* may generate more than $1 billion in revenue for Warner Bros. in all the various syndication markets. See also Bill Carter, "'Friends' Deal Will Pay Each of Its 6 Stars $22 Million," *New York Times,* 12 February 2002, C1.

9. The story of Burnett and his negotiations with CBS is told at length in Bill Carter, "Survival of the Pushiest," *New York Times Magazine,* 28 January 2001, and Carter, *Desperate Networks,* especially chapter 4. Mark Burnett has also produced *The Apprentice* and *The Contender* and coproduced *On The Lot* with Stephen Spielberg, which aired in spring 2007 on the FOX network.

10. Michael McCarthy, "Sponsors Line up for 'Survivor' Sequel," *USA Today,* 8 October 2000, 1B. See also Michael McCarthy, "Ads Are Here, There, Everywhere: Agencies Seek Creative Ways to Expand Product Placement," *USA Today,* 19 June 2001, 1B; and Michael McCarthy, "Surviving Sponsors," *Broadcasting and Cable,* 9 September 2002, at www.tvinsite.com.

11. *Survivor* has become a fixture on U.S. network television, routinely landing a place among the year's top ten shows by audience ratings. The fourteenth installment, *Survivor: Fiji,* aired during the 2007 season.

12. Steven Sternberg, "Program Type Trends," *Magna Global,* 3 March 2005.

13. CBS Office of Economic Analysis, Wilkofsky Gruen Associates, table 1.2, in Vogel, *Entertainment Industry Economics,* 9.

14. In 2005, total TV advertising dollars spent per household in the United States amounted to $494. That year, the comparable figure in the United Kingdom was $256; in Germany it was $143. Universal McCann, Zenith Optimeedia, industry estimates, table 7.2, in Vogel, *Entertainment Industry Economics,* 277. Between 1996 and 2002, advertising expenditures on television grew at a faster rate in the United States than in Europe, despite the expansion of European private broadcasting.

15. With the advent of cable, two new revenue streams emerged: cable TV channels, such as Discovery Channel and MTV, are paid a fee by cable companies, such as Time Warner Cable and Comcast, to be part of the package of channels offered to cable subscribers. The cable fee, which runs from a few pennies to a few dollars a month per subscriber, is in addition to revenue from advertising. Premium cable services, such as HBO, derive the lion's share of their income from monthly subscription fees paid directly by viewers, with additional income from program rentals to foreign distributors and DVD sales. HBO does not interrupt the flow of its programs with advertising. In 2006, HBO earned an estimated $3.5 billion. Though known for its original dramatic programming, such as *The Sopranos,* HBO's schedule consists primarily of feature-length films, rounded out with

sports and a mix of documentaries and talk shows. Like others, HBO has dabbled in unscripted programming with shows such as *Project Greenlight*.

16. Erik Larson, "Watching Americans Watch TV," *Atlantic Monthly,* March 1992, 66–80; and Philip Napoli, *Audience Economics: Media Institutions and the Audience Marketplace* (New York: Columbia University Press, 2003).

17. Quoted in Todd Gitlin, *Inside Prime Time* (New York: Pantheon, 1983), 82.

18. Program producers try to reduce the risk of failure by pretesting pilot episodes and monitoring audience reaction, but the history of American TV is riddled with so many examples of hits that tested poorly (like *All in the Family* in the 1970s) and duds that tested well that TV veterans rarely regard audience testing as definitive. Ibid, chapter 2. See also Joyce Nelson, *The Perfect-Machine: TV in the Nuclear Age* (Toronto: Between the Lines, 1987), especially chapter 6.

19. Richard Caves, *Creative Industries: Contracts between Art and Commerce* (Cambridge: Harvard University Press, 2000), especially chapter 1. For an excellent overview of the financial and economic dimensions of the media industry, see Vogel, *Entertainment Industry Economics*. See also David Hesmondhalgh, *The Cultural Industries* (London: Sage, 2002); Colin Hoskins, Stuart McFadyen, and Adam Finn, *Media Economics: Applying Economics to New and Traditional Media* (London: Sage, 2004); and Gillian Doyle, *Understanding Media Economics* (London: Sage, 2002).

20. Bernard Weinraub, "Sudden Explosion of Game Shows Threatens the Old TV Staples," *New York Times,* 9 February 2000, E1.

21. Standard and Poor's, *Industry Survey: Broadcasting, Cable and Satellite,* 14 December 2006, 16.

22. Steven Sternberg, "Programming Insights: Program Type Trends," *Magna Global,* 3 March 2005.

23. Endemol was established in 1994 through a merger of two Dutch companies bearing the names of their principal owners, Joop van den Ende and John de Mol. I have benefited from visits to Endemol's studio in Aalsmeer, Netherlands, in June 2001 and June 2002. See also Albert Moran, *Copycat TV: Globalisation, Program Formats and Cultural Identity* (Luton, U.K.: University of Luton Press, 1998), 33–37; and "The Reality after the Show," *Economist,* 14 September 2002, 65.

24. Television Research Partnership, Tim Colwell, and David Price, *Rights of Passage: British Television in the Global Market* (London: UK Trade and Investment, 2005). See also Des Freedman, "Who Wants to Be a Millionaire? The Politics of Television Exports," *Information, Communication and Society* 6.1 (2003), 24–41.

25. Moran, *Copycat TV,* especially chapter 2. John De Mol's original concept, called *The Golden Cage,* was to enclose participants in a dome for a year. Concluding that the idea was too expensive and risky, he shortened the duration to 80 days, changed the dome to a prefabricated house, and added a competitive element—each week a contestant is removed from the house. Peter Thal Larsen, "Father of Big Brother," *Financial Times,* 12 August 2000, 9.

26. Quoted in Michael Collins, "Who Owns Our Lives? Copyrights and Wrongs: In the Global TV Market, Great Ideas Are the Key," *Observer* (London), 22 April 2001, 17.

27. Brian Briggs, interview by author, Endemol, Aalsmeer, Netherlands, 19 June 2001.

28. In the case of *Who Wants to Be a Millionaire*, U.K.-based Celador Productions requires that the lighting, set, and sound be identical around the world. Charles Goldsmith, "American Agent Strikes Gold with British TV Programs," *Wall Street Journal*, 18 May 2001, B1.

29. Silverman's remarks are borne out. Of the first five Endemol formats introduced into the U.S. market, only one, *Chains of Love*, did not get renewed. The show also tanked in Australia. Silverman is now cochairman of NBC Entertainment and NBC Universal Television Studios. Ibid. See also Michael Wolff, "The Missing Link," *New York Magazine*, 4 June 2001.

30. Format TV did not begin with reality TV. In the international TV market, the most common format genre is the game show. The two most successful companies in this area are FremantleMedia and King World.

31. For example, Erik Barnouw, *The Sponsor: Notes on a Modern Potentate* (Oxford: Oxford University Press, 1978).

32. On product placement in Hollywood, see Mark Crispin Miller, "Hollywood: The Ad," *Atlantic Monthly*, April 1990, 41; and Janet Wasko, *Hollywood in the Information Age: Beyond the Silver Screen* (Austin: University of Texas Press, 1994), chapter 8.

33. PQ Media, "Executive Summary," *Global Product Placement Forecast 2006* (Stamford, CT: PQ Media, 2006), 11–13. Though the phenomenon is worldwide, product placement in the United States far outstrips other markets, accounting for $4.48 billion out of a total of just under $6.0 billion. Brazil and Australia are the next largest markets for paid placements with $285 million and $104 million, respectively. Primarily on the strength of its film industry, France ranks fourth at nearly $57 million. The pace of television product placement will likely pick up more steam in 2008 when the directive is lifted from the European Union Television without Frontiers, which currently prohibits paid product placements on European programs.

34. Brooks Barnes, "Air Power: Low-Budget Reality-TV Shows Have Given Small Businesses a Shot at the Once Unreachable—Prime Time," *Wall Street Journal*, 25 September 2006, R9.

35. Louise Story, "Brands Produce Their Own Shows," *New York Times*, 10 November 2006. See also Stephanie Thompson and David Goetzl, "P&G Melds Product into Entertainment," *AdAge.com*, 8 July 2002, at www.adage.com/news.cms?newsld=35332.

36. Lorne Manly, "Brew Tube," *New York Times Magazine*, 4 February 2007, 51; and Brad Berens, "Anheuser-Busch Speaks! Execs Talk Bud.TV," 12 September

2006, at www.imediaconnection.com. Yet another telling example of the blurring lines between advertising and programming is ABC's announcement that it would produce a pilot for a 30-minute situation comedy featuring the caveman characters starring in a recent set of Geico insurance ads. Michael Schneider, "Comedy Pilot Based on Geico Ads," *Variety*, 2 March 2007.

37. Bob Tedeschi, "Television Networks Sell Tie-Ins on the Web," *New York Times*, 7 June 1999, C4.

38. Michael McCarthy, "Major Marketing Deals for 'Survivor' Win CBS' Vote," *USA Today*, 21 February 2001, 1B; and Bill Carter, "New Reality Show to Place Ads between the Ads," *New York Times*, 30 April 2001, A1; and Michael McCarthy, "Ads Show up in Unexpected Places: Line between Reality, Marketing Gets Fuzzy," *USA Today*, 23 March 2001, 1B.

39. Orietta Guerrera, "How a Series Was Sold to Saturation." *Sunday Age* (Melbourne), 21 April 2002, 7; and Paige Albiniak, "The Selling of Prime Time," *Broadcasting and Cable*, 16 September 2002, at www.tvinsite.com.

40. Dale Peck, "Production Values," *Atlantic Monthly*, November 2006, 110–17; and Brian Garrity, "The 'American' Way," *Billboard*, 20 January 2007, 21.

41. Gail Schiller, "Six Off-Net Partners Bask in 'Idol' Glow," *Hollywood Reporter*, January 2007.

42. In Sweden, the summer 2002 version of *Big Brother* featured live streaming to mobile phones. Josef Adalian, "Webcasting of 'Big Bro 2" Shows Net Can Be Profitable," *Variety*, 27 September 2001, 5. See also Jeremy Head, "Technical Advances Are Turning Big Brother into a Big Money-Spinner," *Irish Times*, 24 May 2002, 59; and Jason Deans, "A Date with Davina: As Big Brother Fever Gripped the Nation, Viewers Flocked to Its Website," *Guardian* (London), 21 May 2001, 60.

43. Leo Hickman, "Big Brother, Where Art Thou?" *Guardian* (London), 10 July 2002, 4; and Raymond Snoddy, "Big Brother Means Big Bucks for Channel 4," *Times* (London), 15 June 2002.

44. "Four Corners: Reality Check," transcript of program broadcast on the Australian Broadcast Corporation, 30 July 2001, at www.abc.net.au/4corners/stories/s335957.htm.

45. Chris Short, quoted in Head, "Technical Advances Are Turning Big Brother into a Big Money-Spinner," 59.

46. VeriSign, " VeriSign Powers Interactive Campaigns for Top NBC Shows," Press Release, 13 September 2006, at http://www.verisign.com/verisign-inc/news-and-events/news-archive/us-news-2006/page_039253.html.

47. Stephen Armstrong, "The Game Show Goes On," *New Statesman*, 29 January 2007, 42. The money is rolling in: ITV recently reported that it receives about 6,000 calls a minute at a rate of 75 pence, roughly £270,000 for the hour.

48. Jacques Steinberg, "Digital Media Brings Profits (and Tensions) to TV Studios," *New York Times*, 14 May 2006.

49. Standard and Poor's, *Industry Survey: Broadcasting, Cable and Satellite,* 14 December 2006, 2

50. In 2006, the live-only rating for *Gray's Anatomy was* 7.2, while the live-plus-seven-day rating was 18.2. David Poltrack, "Why TV Needs Commercial Ratings—Now," *Advertising Age,* 13 November 2006, 22.

||||||||||||||||||||||||||||||||||||||||||||||||||||||

Hoaxing the "Real"
On the Metanarrative of Reality Television

Alison Hearn

Schoolteacher Randi Coy deliberately deceives her family, convincing them that she is engaged to marry a stranger that she has met on a "reality show"; she doesn't know that her big, fat, obnoxious fiance, Steve, is an actor, hired to make her the butt of the joke. Ana, a 20-something woman from Georgia, weeps in front of the camera as she expresses how much she wants to win a job as Andy Dick's personal assistant; she is oblivious to the fact that she is an unpaid participant in Andy Dick's elaborate parody of all reality shows. Exhausted and emotional after days locked inside a mansion on what he thinks is a reality program called "The Lap of Luxury," law school dropout Matt Kennedy Gould breaks down after his good friend Earl is voted out; he is not aware that his "good friend" is actually an actor hired to deceive him, as are all the other contestants on the show.

Hoax reality shows, such as *My Big Fat Obnoxious Fiance*, *The Assistant*, and *The Joe Schmo Show*, feature unwitting contestants who believe they are participating in a reality show but are actually subject to an extended practical joke, which makes fun of their desire to be on TV and features their ongoing humiliation.[1] Through a detailed examination of the first of these shows to emerge, *The Joe Schmo Show*, in this chapter I delineate a metanarrative line that, arguably, runs through all of reality programming. Beyond the lessons about love or adventure, the transformation of the home or body, or the survival of deprivation or fear, reality television programs are, for the most part, stories *about* television itself—its modes of production, its commercial and promotional logic, its specific privations and rigor, and its mechanisms for celebrity-making and work.

Promotional Prime Time

A number of key factors set the stage for the emergence of hoax reality shows. Changes in the industrial structure, business practices, and modes of production of television programming, such as those outlined by Chad Raphael and Ted Magder in essays in this volume, play a big role.[2] The broader context for the emergence of these changes, however, is the rise and consolidation of what critic Andrew Wernick has called our "promotional culture."[3]

Promotionalism has been on the rise in the West since the beginning of the mass production of goods, as it addressed the need to advertise and market those goods to consumers. Locating the first successful branding exercises in the development of the distinct style of Wedgewood pottery in the mid-1700s, Wernick traces the way in which industrially produced goods came to serve, simultaneously, as useful commodities and as advertisements for their corporate brand. He notes how "the substance, shape, and ornamentation of Wedgewood's plates and vases were continuous with how they were promoted." In this early moment of industrial capitalism, then, we see the rise of "market-oriented design," whereby "production and promotion [were] integrally co-joined."[4]

There can be no doubt that promotionalism is now a dominant cultural condition. Our clothes, our cars, our homes—even our own senses of self—are intricately bound up with the logic and meanings of corporate brands and promotional messages. But how is a promotional message distinct from any other form of communication? Wernick argues that it is a "complex of significations which at once represents (moves in place of), advocates (moves on behalf of) and anticipates (moves ahead of) the circulating entity . . . to which it refers." Promotion entails a rearrangement of the relation between sign and referent. The sign comes to displace the material object to which it refers and, in this way, acquires a kind of agency: "In this integrated system of production/promotion, the commodity and its double—the commodity sign and the promotional sign—are deployed together in a mutually referring and self-confirming way." At some point along the line, goods come to be designed less for their direct usefulness and more for the meanings and myths they are able to mobilize and represent. A promotional message, then, "is a mode of communication, a species of rhetoric. It is defined not by what it says but by what it does"; it works to perpetually persuade.[5]

In this era of post-Fordist capitalism, goods, corporations, and people are all implicated in the processes of promotion and branding. We see the rise of branded goods, branded corporations, branded politicians and political parties, branded nations and cultural events, even branded individuals (say, Oprah™, Tiger™, Michael Jordan™). In order to succeed in a promotional culture, at some level, we all must generate our own rhetorically persuasive meanings and become "commodity signs," which "function in circulation both as an object(s)-to-be-sold and as the bearer(s) of a promotional message."[6] The overall effect of these communicative processes of promotion, Wernick argues, is a kind of "instrumentalization" of culture, whereby our values and commonly used symbols are colonized by the market and put to work to *sell*.

Without a doubt, reality television programming is at the forefront of this culture of promotion. As Magder points out, the business practices of the television industry have recently changed in profound ways; deregulation has allowed networks to become producers and producers to directly solicit corporate sponsors and advertisers for their shows. This has resulted in what is now being called "branded entertainment" or "advertainment." The quintessence of Wernick's commodity sign, advertainment is "programming designed to sell as it entertains."[7] Sponsors buy the rights to product integration in the show itself, in addition to spot ads around the show.

While many note that direct corporate sponsorship is a reversion to older forms of commercial television funding, where a corporation sponsors the entire run of a series, what differentiates the current sponsorship model from the one used in the early days of television is the degree to which sponsoring products and services are deeply embedded in the narratives of the shows themselves. Products and brands become central characters in the stories and it's impossible to tell where the advertising ends and the entertainment begins. On *The Apprentice,* contestants are asked to create an ad for Crest toothpaste. On *Survivor,* starving contestants endure intense competition for one mouth-watering package of Doritos or some Mountain Dew. The friendly folks on *Extreme Makeover Home Edition* take shopping trips to Home Depot or Sears, whose "real" employees often play a part in the makeover.[8]

In the finale of season 3 of *American Idol,* the two remaining contestants dance into the TV studio on either side of a Ford car—Fantasia, Diana, and the car, all under the heading: "America's Idols." Here the elision between person and thing is startlingly clear; all three are competing for a market share, all of them the quintessence of the logic of promotion and the commodity sign.[9] In addition to blatant product placement and show sponsorships, show formats themselves are now notable "brands." The *Idol* and *Big Brother* franchises are for sale in media markets all over the globe.

Many in the industry now openly acknowledge that television content should first and foremost function as a clearinghouse for products and services and as a source of diverse revenue streams beyond the shows themselves. As Mark Burnett himself has stated:

> *Survivor* is as much a marketing vehicle as it is a television show. My shows create an interest, and people will look at them, but the endgame here is selling products in stores—a car, deodorant, running shoes. It's the future of television.[10]

Product integration fees for television programming grew 84 percent in 2004, amounting to $522 million in revenue for broadcasters, networks, and cable channels. Plans are in the works to retrofit older TV series with product placement.[11] The growing trend in advertainment indicates the degree to which television's cultural function has been subordinated to its commercial and promotional function; perhaps more important, it marks the overt mythologizing of promotion itself.

As reality television becomes a marketing vehicle for various corporate brands, the stories it tells inevitably reflect those same processes of marketing and selling. Shows like *American Idol* and *America's Next Top Model* explicitly narrate the hard work involved in becoming a celebrity brand, while makeover shows like *I Want a Famous Face* and *Extreme Makeover* tell stories about the construction of a rhetorically persuasive body according to the dictates of celebrity culture.[12]

In addition, reality shows formally enact the processes of commodification and promotion, not only marketing goods but also, through their specific labor practices, marketing people, by providing the means by which contestants can become saleable image commodities—or branded selves.[13] Omarosa, Trista and Ryan, and Rob and Amber are perhaps the most famous examples of this branding process; they began as "real," unknown people, and, through the course of the show, they "became" famous. Arguably much of the pleasure in reality programming for viewers is in watching contestants move through the star-making machinery of television and come out the other end as freshly minted celebrity brands.

So, in an attempt to extend its economic viability, the television industry began to market *itself* in earnest; as it sells access to its own modes of production to people on the "outside" in order to cut its labor costs, it narrates and mythologizes its own production processes. In this way, we can see reality television programming as the "promotional supplement" of broadcast television in general.[14] Transforming the television commodity as it doubles and extends it, reality television programming simultaneously narrates, produces, and markets the practices of televisual commodification and, indeed, of promotion itself. In the conclusion of his study, Wernick argues that a promotional culture is "radically deficient in good faith."[15] There is no more salient example of this deficiency than the hoax reality TV show.

Savvy Joe

As the generic conventions of reality television programming have become more established and increasingly reflect their material conditions of production, which emphasize the selling of people and products, we have seen the simultaneous growth of what Todd Gitlin and Mark Andrejevic have called a "savvy" consciousness on the part of viewers.

Gitlin examines the rise of metanews coverage, which reports on the manipulative elements of the news itself, and, in so doing, produces viewers who are simultaneously flattered by this knowing mode of address and assured that, as viewers, "they remain sovereign." Hailed by the television industry as "hip" enough to understand the constructedness of television's "realism," savvy viewers are postmodern viewers; they embrace their interpellation by the industry as consumers of crass and base pop culture, and "take a certain pleasure in that identification." In exchange for feeling on the "inside" of the production process, empowered and knowledgeable, savvy viewers align their interests with those of the program producers and the television industry and construe their knowledgeable spectatorship as a kind of meaningful participation.[16] The disturbing result, Andrejevic argues, is that "viewers . . . adopt the same low estimate of themselves that they attribute to producers."[17]

In order to cater to the increasingly savvy viewer, the industry deploys more and more sophisticated forms of audience participation and other kinds of "behind the scenes" formats that appear to provide access to the "real" inside of the industry. In the spate of DVD extras, and "the making of" programs, we can see the industry deploying "the promise of demystification . . . as a marketing strategy."[18] And, as it provides heavily stylized and constructed versions of itself for popular consumption, the television industry invites the viewer to become a participant in the process, to literally *become* a media spectacle. We might see all of reality television as employed in this purpose, promoting "being on TV" as a realistic and potentially lucrative goal for the average "joe." The savvy viewers' simultaneous intellectual acceptance of commercial television's instrumental logic and emotional investment in the values of television's image economy make them ideal marks for the hoax reality show.

Big, Fat, Obnoxious Hoax Shows

The general proliferation of reality programming, its growing role as branded entertainment, and the increase in savvy viewers who revel in stories about the internal workings of the industry produced ripe conditions for shows that claim to hoax "reality." Indeed, it did not take long for parodic versions of reality television shows to appear on the dial. *The Joe Schmo Show* was the first of these programs. Originally produced in 2003, it has been followed by a second version of itself, as well as by similar shows, including *The Assistant, My Big Fat Obnoxious Fiance, My Big Fat Obnoxious Boss,* and *SuperStar USA,* to name only a few.[19]

All of these programs use well-established reality show conventions as their backdrop, but each adds a parodic spin. *The Assistant* parodies tropes from other reality programs, such as *Survivor, The Apprentice,* and *American Idol,* in each of its elimination rounds. In addition, Andy Dick self-consciously narrates, and often complains about, the process of making the show. A featured tag line of the program is a shot of Dick, running from the cameras, screaming; "this reality show is ruining my life!" *My Big Fat Obnoxious Fiance* draws on tropes from *The Bachelorette* but pairs a beautiful woman with an uncouth, overweight klutz. The mansion is extravagant, but the fiance is always breaking things; the outings to spas or yachts are inevitably disrupted by the klutz's inappropriate behavior; the show's logo features a red rose surrounded by bloodstains.

These reality show conventions provide a context for the main event—the extended duping of unwitting, "real" contestants, drawing on the tradition of the hoax show genre, pioneered by *Candid Camera.*[20] While the narrative of deception is not overtly foregrounded on *The Assistant,* the contestants are subjected to over-the-top challenges and demands by Dick, such as being forced to sleep in a garage and be awakened by a fire alarm, to break up Dick and his girlfriend, or to procure him a star on the Hollywood walk of fame. Much of the narrative pleasure comes from witnessing the clueless contestants' naive investment in Dick's parodic treatment of life in "Hollyweird."

My Big Fat Obnoxious Fiance makes the story of the deception of Randi Coy its central focus. Much of the program involves the juxtaposition of Randi's confessions about her frustrations and concerns about Steve with the actor Steve's confessions about his (and the producers') plans to keep Randi on the verge of an emotional breakdown. The narrative tension is derived from watching Randi as she is forced to lie, repeatedly, to her family about her intentions to marry Steve. The family is visibly shaken and upset, and in a moment of narrative rupture, appear on the verge of rejecting their savvy status, insisting: "There are certain things you do in the privacy of the family."[21]

All hoax shows feature the contestants' continuing humiliation within reality show conceits and, in the end, work to palliate the contestant's exploitation with greater-than-expected cash and prizes. A closer examination of the first of these shows, *The Joe Schmo Show*, however, reveals that these shows do a specific kind of cultural work that moves them well beyond the label of hoax or parody; they are promotional instruments for the values and dictates of the broadcast television industry in general.

Joe Schmo in "The Lap of Luxury"

The Joe Schmo Show is produced by "SPIKETV: The Network for Men." Owned by VIACOM, SPIKE targets the lucrative demographic of young men between the ages of 18 and 34. The show tells a story of a "real" person, a young 20-something Matt Kennedy Gould, who is brought onto a fake reality show titled "The Lap of Luxury." On this fake show, everyone is an actor except Matt. The premise of the fake show is that contestants are confined to an extravagant mansion and must endure grueling competitions and intense psychodrama in order to "outdo, outshine, and outperform" their opponents. The grand prize is $100,000. *The Joe Schmo Show* narrates Matt's experience as he participates in what he believes to be a "real" reality show, as well as the trials and tribulations of the actors, producers, and writers as they try to keep Matt from catching on. The central narrative tension derives from whether the practical joke will succeed; whether Matt will go the full nine episodes without figuring out that he is being duped.

The Joe Schmo Show features unwitting contestants who believe they are participating in a reality show but are actually subject to an extended practical joke.

Matt proves to be a stand-up guy who tells the truth, cares for and often defends the other characters, and expresses more concern for "having the experience" than actually winning. In episode three, Matt experiences a crisis when his good friend "Earl the vet" gets voted off. Matt breaks down crying and wonders aloud why he has come on the program, and, as Matt is having his breakdown, the cast and crew are shown behind the scenes worrying about him. Some of the female actresses are crying, moved by Matt's emotion. The actors and producers anxiously wonder whether they can go on with the joke and question whether hurting Matt's feelings is actually worth it to them. After several scenes of apparent soul-searching on the part of the show's producers, the decision is made to continue.

When Matt is asked to eat dog feces as a part of a competition, he refuses and is provided a chance to speak to one of the show's producers. An actor is in place to take on the role. The fake producer suggests that, instead of Matt eating the poop, he convince the two remaining female contestants to either kiss or go topless. Matt agrees and returns to the fake contestants, stating: "Obviously the whole reason for our being here goes way beyond the nine of us having a good time. They want ratings." When one of the contestant actresses protests, saying she thinks it's sleazy, Matt responds, "Welcome to television."[22]

In the last episode, Matt is still questioning why he decided to come on the show and states that he just wants the ordeal to be over, insisting that, "they're not getting anymore good television out of us."[23] The story of the actors and producers is underlined as they worry about how Matt will take the impending reveal.

During the "fake" finale, the grand prize is awarded to one of the actor/contestants. After this, "Ralph the host" is contacted by the fake producers and announces that someone is "not who they say they are." One by one, the actors reveal that they are actors. During this process, Matt Gould becomes increasingly worried and agitated, finally exclaiming, with a phrase that has since become the tagline for the series, "*What is going on?!*" Ralph the host pulls Matt to the center of the frame and exclaims, "The only real thing on this reality show is you!" He explains that "hundreds of people had worked for over a year" to bring the show together and that they had done it all *for* Matt. "The Lap of Luxury" is an elaborate cover story, providing the means for Matt to star in his very own show. Thanks to the producers, cast, and crew, Matt has gone from "being the nice guy next door to America's hottest new star." Ralph proceeds to give Matt all the prizes, along with a check for $100,000. Matt is overwhelmed, weeping, sweating, alternatively grateful and confused, as he is introduced to the "real" actors, producers, and director.[24]

Parsing Joe

The diegesis of *Joe Schmo* is comprised of the highly artificial and clichéd elements of reality television: a luxurious mansion, complete with pool and Jacuzzi; free-flowing food and drink; ridiculous competitions, such as "Hands on the High-Class Hooker" and "Sumo Slam," during which one of the contestants "wins" a prize or immunity from eviction; and a formal eviction ceremony, complete with secret parchment ballots and the hyperdramatic smashing of the plate into the fire when a contestant is evicted. The show is also populated by stock reality show contestants: "the vet," "the buddy," "the schemer," "the asshole," "the gay guy," "the virgin," and "the rich bitch." The diegesis also includes the world around the show: the cramped showbiz trailers in which the actors receive their daily notes, the control room in which the directors and writers monitor Matt's every move on 26 surveillance cameras, and the secret room in the mansion where the actors go to give their confessional interviews. The show segments are always introduced by a screen split four ways, illustrating the different worlds of the show: Gould's, the actors', and the behind-the-scenes producers, director, and crew.

The discourse of the show remains relatively seamless, even as it straddles the two worlds of the fake show and the real show. Ralph Garman is both the narrator of the show and the host of the fake show. He gives confessional camera interviews as himself, discussing his experiences duping Matt and playing his role as the smarmy host. He also provides the voice-overs for show, introducing the ruse at the beginning of every episode and giving occasional updates about the decisions of the producers and directors. Ralph speaks using a collective "we," conceptually binding together all the workers on the show, except Gould, and stands in for the implied narrator of the series, the industry people at SPIKE Network.

The actors are represented both as their characters and as themselves. Most of the time, we see them playing their characters with and against Gould, but the episodes are also interspersed with scenes of the actors "confessing" in traditional reality show style to an implied narratee—SPIKE's demographic of 18–35-year-old males. In these sessions, the actors discuss Matt's behavior, the demands of playing their parts, and their fears about the continuing deception. The producers and director are depicted giving notes and doing their jobs, but they are never interviewed directly during the show itself.

The general aesthetic and discursive style of the show is uniform and tends to mimic standard reality show techniques. The camerawork is at times documentary style and at others more traditionally dramatic. The same kind of music is used to signal high tension on the fake show as is used when there might be tension or worry behind the scenes. Drumbeats, heartbeats, and *Survivor*-style Australian didgeridoo music are used throughout, as are soaring sentimental strings whenever there are moving moments within the fake show and during the testimonials of the actors or crew. The confessional camera, the de rigueur element of reality shows, is utilized freely, as is fast-paced editing. (Before the finale of the show, when the reveal is about to take place, the audience sees the mansion, control room, and various members of the production crew shot through a blurred and topsy-turvy camera, overcoded with screechy violins and scary music, illustrating the nerves and concern on the part of everyone involved in the project.)

While the show is marketed as satire, it stops short of parodying the distinct signifying practices of the reality show genre itself, employing them all to tell the "real" story of this elaborate practical joke. Much of the show content, while ridiculous, plays on well-entrenched reality show clichés, but audience members are still invited to invest in the gaming aspect of the show. Even though we know the competitions and evictions are all rigged, we are never told who will win or be evicted beforehand. The clips at the beginning of every episode, which show the director giving the actors their notes, reveal very little actual information about the storyline or the production process. These scenes situate the story from the point of view of the actors, writers, and director; we are clearly seeing *their* story. In this way, *Joe Schmo* is a reality show about making a reality show.

Hoaxing the "Real": What Is Going On?

In *Joe Schmo*, the highly artificial premise and diegetic universe characteristic of standard reality shows becomes the narrative ground, and Andrejevic's savvy viewer—the average "joe" who wants to be on TV and to endorse the values and dictates of the industry, becomes figural. The dramatic content of *Joe Schmo* does not come from games or competition, or even from social conflict, but from watching Gould participate in what everyone else knows is an illusion, from witnessing his attenuated duping, and from the struggle by the actors and producers to make sure that the deception is not revealed. Audience pleasure derives from witnessing Matt's eventual "capture" inside a cultural logic he wishes to be a part of but cannot, ultimately, control.

Through its representational practices, *Joe Schmo* also asks for viewers' emotional investment in a story about how to succeed on the terrain of

TV production, about what kinds of characters "work" on television. As the show focuses on the actors' struggle to stay in character; on the hard work of the director, writers, and producers; and on Matt's embodiment of the ultimate TV nice-guy, it succeeds in narrativizing the difficult kinds of facework and persona construction required by the industry. While traditional reality shows tell the story of real events inside artificial formats, *Joe Schmo* mythologizes the real story behind the construction of the artifice and highlights the laborious and painstaking processes involved.

In this way, *Joe Schmo* is not a satire of reality television but, rather, a story about the challenges of reality television production. In the sympathetic telling of the difficulties of maintaining the hoax and the show's narrative emphasis on the caring and humane people behind Matt's duping, any truly satirical or subversive potential in the content is clawed back. In effect, the show is a narrative that naturalizes, excuses, and promotes the spectacularizing work of the television industry. This is most pointedly illustrated at the climax, when the "truth" is revealed to Gould. Gould is immediately bought off with the prize money as the host repeatedly states that the whole ruse has been for Gould's *good*. So, even as the producers have purposefully humiliated Gould, they contain any fallout by figuring the humiliation as a gift; a potent metaphor, some might argue, for the general conditions of life under spectacular consumer capital and its promotional culture.

Matt Kennedy Gould embodies the classic savvy viewer, but the fact that he has been turned into Joe Schmo without his knowledge reveals that he is clearly not quite savvy enough. The moral or ideological message of *The Joe Schmo Show*, and indeed of all hoax reality shows, is simple: you can be as savvy as you want, you can align your interests with those of the industry and submit to its determinations, but be careful what you wish for. In the end, you are still on the outside of the "real" machinations of the industry, you can still be figured as the butt of its practical jokes.

In effect, these shows give the lie to the claim that reality television is democratizing the industry by bringing real people into the fold. While the free labor of participants is necessary, these shows work to maintain the exclusivity of the industry and suggest that access to it may rest not on talent but on tolerance for humiliation. Hoax shows work to draw a line in the sand between those on the inside and those of the outside, serving to remystify the industry even as they claim to demystify it.

The Reality of Promotional Television

As reality television is increasingly overdetermined by the logic of marketing and promotion, its central job remains to promote itself: its narratives, its values, its representational strategies, and its corporate structure. Hoax reality shows appear to serve an explicit purpose within the genre and to do a specific kind of cultural work. Through the strategy of ridicule, these shows reinscribe the industry's image economy, which is predicated on exclusivity, and, in this way, they help to ensure a steady supply of free labor.

Programs like *The Assistant, My Big Fat Obnoxious Fiance,* and *The Joe Schmo Show* are not simple practical jokes or parodies of other well-established genres. They are stories about their own making—simultaneously producing themselves while narrating and mythologizing the processes of that production. By drawing our attention to the television studio as the current site of cultural competence and success, these shows clearly express the metanarrative of all reality programs: television's modes of production and promotional values constitute the only "reality" that matters.

NOTES

1. C. Cowan and J. M. Michenaud (producers), *My Big Fat Obnoxious Fiance* (Los Angeles: FOX Broadcasting Network), first aired 2004; A. Cohen, A. Dick, C. Tapper, and J. Vernetti (producers), *The Assistant* (Los Angeles: Music Television), first aired 2004; and A. Ross, D. Stanley, P. Wernick, R. Reese, and S. Stone (producers), *The Joe Schmo Show* (Los Angeles: SPIKE Television), first aired 2003.

2. Ted Magder, "The End of TV 101," and Chad Raphael, "The Political Economic Origins of Reali-TV," both in Susan Murray and Laurie Ouelette (eds.), *Reality TV: Remaking Television Culture* (New York: New York University Press, 2004).

3. Andrew Wernick, *Promotional Culture: Advertising, Ideology and Symbolic Expression* (London: Sage, 1991).

4. Ibid., 15.

5. Ibid.,182, 16, 184.

6. Ibid.,16.

7. June Deery, "Reality TV as Advertainment," *Popular Communication* 2.1 (2004), 1.

8. A. Burman, D. Trump, and M. Burnett (producers), *The Apprentice* (Los Angeles: National Broadcasting Corporation), first aired 2004; M. Burnett (producer), *Survivor* (Los Angeles: Columbia Broadcasting System), first aired 2000; C. Armstrong, D. Cramsey, and T. Forman (producers), *Extreme Makeover: Home Edition* (Los Angeles: American Broadcasting Corporation), first aired 2004.

9. C. Frot-Coutaz, K. Warwick, N. Lithgoe, S. Fuller (Producers), *American Idol*, Los Angeles: FOX Broadcasting Network, First aired 2002.

10. Mark Burnett, "What I Have Learned," *Esquire*136.1 (July 2001), at http://www.esquire.com/features/learned/010701_mwi_burnett.html (accessed December 2005).

11. Gail Schiller, "Product Placement in TV, Films, Soar, Study Finds," *Reuters Online* (30 March 2005), at http://www.reuters.com/newsArticle.jhtml?type=industryNews&storyID=8031889 (accessed 15 April 2005).

12. K. Mok and T. Banks (producers), *America's Next Top Model* (Los Angeles: United Paramount Network), first aired 2003; D. Sirulnick and L. Lazin, *I Want a Famous Face* (Los Angeles: Music Television), first aired 2004; ABC 2002.

13. Alison Hearn, "'John, a 20-year-old Boston Native with a Great Sense of Humor': On the Spectacularization of the 'Self' and the Incorporation of Identity in the Age of Reality Television," *International Journal of Media and Cultural Politics* 2.2 (2006), 131–47.

14. Wernick, *Promotional Culture*, 190.

15. Ibid.,193.

16. Todd Gitlin, quoted in Mark Andrejevic, *Reality TV: The Work of Being Watched* (New York: Rowan and Littlefield, 2004), 133; Andrejevic, *Reality TV*, 136.

17. Ibid.,134.

18. Ibid.,132.

19. C. Cowan and J. M. Michenaud (producers), *My Big Fat Obnoxious Boss* (Los Angeles: FOX Broadcasting), first aired 2004; and Mike Fleiss (producer), *Super-Star USA* (Los Angeles: Warner Borthers Television Network), first aired 2004.

20. A. Funt (producer), *Candid Camera* (Los Angeles: American Broadcasting Corporation), first aired 1948.

21. *My Big, Fat, Obnoxious Fiance*, episode 5.

22. *Joe Schmo*, episode 7.

23. Ibid., episode 9.

24. Ibid.

II

Global TV Realities

International Markets, Geopolitics, and the Transcultural Contexts of Reality TV

John McMurria

In January 2007, U.K. broadcaster Channel 4 and global TV format producer Endemol placed 10 international celebrities in a confined space equipped with 37 cameras for the most recent installment of *Celebrity Big Brother,* including Bollywood star Shilpa Shetty, Jackson Five member Jermaine Jackson, Hollywood actor Dirk Benedict of *A-Team* fame, former Miss Great Britain Danielle Lloyd, former S Club 7 band member Jo O'Meara, and *Big Brother* veteran turned celebrity Jade Goody. A series of racially charged events ensued. Goody's mother asked Shetty if she lived in a "house or shack" and referred to her as "the Indian." Goody's boyfriend allegedly referred to Shetty as a "bloody Paki bitch," and Lloyd, O'Meara and Goody clashed with Shetty over house decorum.

Britain's telecom regulator Ofcom received a record 38,000 complaints, and a poll indicated that most viewers thought Channel 4 orchestrated these clashes to gain ratings. London Mayor Ken Livingstone told the BBC, "The fact that Channel 4 bosses edited the program and maximized the racism, I think shows they were just using racism as a way of getting more profits." A Channel 4 spokesperson said it was "unquestionably a good thing that the program has raised these issues and provoked such a debate." The event spiked ratings, but a major advertiser withdrew sponsorship and Channel 4 closed the street outside the studio where protesters gathered.[1]

Protesters also gathered in city streets in India. The Indian Ministry of External Affairs filed a formal complaint, while the British Chancellor, who was in India at the time, announced, amid burning effigies of the show's organizers, "I want Britain to be seen as a country of fairness and tolerance, and anything that detracts from that I condemn."[2] Members of the British Parliament and House of Commons condemned the remarks as racist and blamed Channel 4 for instigating them, while Prime Minster Tony Blair condemned "racism in any form." The British Education Secretary responded that "the current debate over *Big Brother* has highlighted the need to make sure our schools focus on the core British values of justice and tolerance" and recommended that compulsory citizenship lessons examine the idea of "Britishness."[3]

The incident also evoked class conflicts as commentators referred to Shetty as the beautiful "classy" film star to Goody's street-talking "white trash."[4] One editorial stressed that Shetty's "poster-girl example of the virtuous woman" did not represent the "post-*Sex and the City* generation" of South Asian women.[5] In the end, Goody, her mother, and the other cast members were evicted, leaving Shetty the winner.

U.K. *Celebrity Big Brother,* one of 36 local versions of the format around the world, exposes the global realities of unscripted entertainment television. Joseph Straubhaar describes global TV as an economic and cultural process of *asymmetrical interdependence* across global, regional, national, and local contexts.[6] *Big Brother* characterizes this as a complex interplay between transnational industry conglomeration, exemplified by Endemol, the most prolific producer of global TV formats, and the national structures of television regulation and culture that find the British broadcaster Channel 4 implicated in a public debate over British identity.

The postcolonial dynamics reveal the asymmetry of this interdependence as global format profits accrue to European conglomerates while Eurocentric racial hierarchies persist. As commodity forms in an increasingly deregulated and market-driven television industry, reality TV formats such as *Big Brother* reduce risk through localizing proven commercial hits across regions and minimizing costs through casting cheap labor in the form of D-list celebrities or "ordinary" folk. As cultural forms, they engage with transnational popular culture (American music and TV from the 1970s and 1980s, Bollywood film and U.K. tabloid personalities) in unscripted ways that in this case publicly exposed hidden layers of everyday racism—as Goody put it, "things that I may not think are racist can actually be racist."[7]

To assess the global realities of unscripted television's multiple scales of economic and cultural consequence, as evidenced in the case of *Celebrity*

Big Brother, in this essay I consider the global economies of transnational television, the specific regional and national trends in reality TV, and the implications of reality TV's engagement with the urgent contemporary geopolitical context of the so-called war on terror. Informing the broader analysis of globalization is a four-dimensional process that Anthony Giddens calls the "globalizing of modernity." This includes a *world capitalist economy* that has anchored economic power in the industrialized and imperial first-world countries in western Europe, the United States, and Japan; an *international division of labor* through which first-world countries leverage this economic power over peripheral third-world and semiperipheral nations; a *nation-state* system that continues to influence economic and cultural authority; and a *world military order* defined by U.S. military aggression.[8]

Reality TV exemplifies the economic power and divisions of labor of a globalizing modernity as European-based television format conglomerates have developed programs for wealthy industrialized markets before reproducing them in peripheral secondary markets. However, reality TV developments in Asia, Africa, and Latin America reveal regional cultural contexts that exist in dynamic tension with this economic power as formatted reproductions have negotiated local culture, evaded copyright regimes, found uneven success, and disturbed authoritarian national politics and elite tastes. The case of reality TV and post-911 U.S. military aggression further suggests the importance of local context as reality TV formats in Iraq have challenged U.S. geopolitical militarism and western cultural imperialism, while a mostly patriotic U.S. reality TV has promoted military action.

TV Globalization

The economic, regulatory, and cultural dimensions of television in the 1950s and 1960s were largely national in scope. Whether advertising-sponsored commercial systems in the United States and Latin America; the publicly supported systems of most European countries, Japan, and India; or the government-controlled systems in the Soviet Union, China, and countries in Southeast Asia, the Middle East, and Africa—in all of these, most television systems comprised a small number of national networks programmed for a national citizenry.[9]

In the postwar period, the United States led world television exports, aided by Hollywood's established global dominance in film distribution.

U.S.-based transnational advertisers convened a World Congress on Commercial Television to spread the gospel of international commercial television. The U.S. networks set up international trade operations and invested in foreign television industries supported by State Department subsidies. The U.S. government facilitated the export of TV documentaries supporting U.S. imperialist aspirations during the height of the cold war. By the early 1960s, U.S. television producers made over $30 million in TV exports to over 40 nations, most of the revenues coming from Canada, the U.K., Australia, and Latin America.[10]

In the 1970s and 1980s, the United States remained the top TV exporter although regional television markets expanded within multilingual trading zones, including the European Union, and in peripheral geolinguistic regions that exported popular audiovisual forms, including Hong Kong TV and action films, Hindi film musicals, Egyptian melodramas, and Latin American telenovelas.[11] Attendance at international television trade shows grew rapidly.[12] In the 1980s, neoliberal political movements in Europe deregulated state monopoly and publicly supported television, which facilitated the growth of commercial broadcasting. A tripling of European advertising expenditures fueled this growth.[13] Advertising agencies merged to form global mega-agencies to coordinate promotional campaigns that spanned international television markets.[14]

In the late 1980s and 1990s, cable and satellite television increased the number of commercial channels in many regions. In 1989, western Europe aired 40 TV channels, but by 2002 offered 1,500, though 50 national terrestrial channels still attracted 75 percent of all viewers. U.S. TV comprised 70 to 90 percent of imported fiction in western Europe in 2002, but larger national markets increasingly displaced U.S. TV with locally produced programs in prime time.[15] U.S. transnationals, including Sony, responded by producing local-language TV programs.[16] In the mid 1990s, satellite television in India initially imported programs from the West but soon provided dozens of Hindi-language channels.[17] Still, in 2006, the annual worldwide trade in TV programming rights was valued at $10 billion, with the United States holding the largest share at 60 percent and the United Kingdom coming in second with 21 percent.[18] Television imports into the United States have been much less substantial beyond the Spanish-language networks, though foreign-language broadcasts have provided important sources of community building for Korean, Chinese, and Iranian diasporas in the country.[19]

Though national systems of television production remain central in most regions, with the United States profiting most from international program sales, in the 1990s four developments in transnational television production emerged. First, national governments formed international coproduction treaties to share creative and financial resources so that cooperative ventures would qualify for national subsidies and meet local quota requirements in participating countries. Regional multilateral coproduction treaties were written for Ibero-America, the Pacific Rim, and the European Union.[20]

Second, international program producers and syndicators established international distribution networks and relations with global advertisers to produce programs designed for transnational audiences. Specializing in hour-long action series, made-for-TV movies, children's programs, and nature spectaculars, companies such as Hallmark produced TV movie adaptations of classic literature such as *Arabian Nights* (2000). Saban profited globally from the kids' show *Power Rangers,* national broadcasters worldwide adapted local versions of *Sesame Street,* and the U.S.-based Discovery Network and the BBC coproduced *Walking with Dinosaurs* for global circulation.[21] The infrastructures and production protocols for Latin American telenovelas also were increasingly structured for transnational markets as Miami emerged as a pan-American locus for the Spanish-language TV industry.[22]

Third, large media conglomerates including Viacom, Newscorp, Disney, Time Warner, Sony, and Discovery created global TV networks with a mixture of U.S. and localized programming. For example, MTV and Discovery created localized channels in over 150 countries.[23] The U.K.-based Zonemedia developed a number of global channels, including the 24-hour unscripted entertainment channel Reality TV in 1999 (renamed Zone Reality in 2006). The channel programs five different schedules catered to regional markets with most programs coming from English-language territories.[24]

Fourth, and most critical to the proliferation of reality TV, the global TV formatting business grew rapidly in the 1990s as companies with bases in western Europe built vertically integrated transnational television companies with huge inventories of game shows and reality TV formats. These companies generate program ideas, sell concept rights, provide detailed production manuals, offer consultancy services, supply computer software, and create graphics and set designs to aid licensors in localizing formats. While Hollywood has dominated the export of more expensive audiovisual forms, including motion pictures, sitcoms, and TV dramas, these European-based companies pioneered the less costly reality TV formats to meet the more limited production budgets of smaller national markets. There are four times the number of companies specializing in TV formatting in western Europe than in the United States or Asia.[25]

One study found that the global format business was worth $2.4 billion in 2004, the number of format hours broadcast had increased by 22 percent since two years prior, the United States was the most valuable market for licensing formats followed by Germany and France, and the United Kingdom was the largest exporter of formats where 32 percent of all format hours originated. Game shows represented 50 percent of global format airtime, but reality TV formats created the most production value.[26]

Endemol, the largest reality TV format producer, was formed in 1994 from a merger of two Dutch-based TV producers; within two years, it had established offices in Germany, Portugal, Spain, and Belgium. In 2000, Endemol was acquired by the Spanish telecommunications conglomerate Telefónica and since has established base operations in 24 countries, including Mexico, Brazil, and Argentina, though the conglomerate profits most from the wealthy western European and U.S. markets. In 2003, Endemol produced over 400 different programs totaling 15,000 hours. Six of Endemols top ten formats were reality TV, including *Big Brother, Fear Factor, Extreme Makeover: Home Edition, Star Academy, The Farm,* and the talent show *Operación Triunfo.*

FremantleMedia, the second largest global format conglomerate, begun as the U.K.-based Pearson Television specializing in game shows and dramas, purchased Grundy World Wide in 1995, an Australian-based transnational specializing in game shows and soap operas, and acquired All American Television in 1997, a U.S. producer of game shows and made-for-TV movies. The RTL group, which owned 23 television channels across Europe and is itself owned by the German-based transnational media conglomerate Bertelsmann AG, purchased Pearson in 2000 and merged with Fremantle, a U.S. television distributor. FremantleMedia owns the *Pop Idol* format, which has aired in local versions in 35 territories, and lifestyle reality formats including *Farmer Wants a Wife, How Clean Is Your House?, Grand Designs,* and *Families Behaving Badly.*[27]

After a decade of rapid growth in formatting and costly legal battles over copyright infringement, the western European–based industry created the Format Registration and Protection Association (FRAPA) in

2000, a self-regulating organization to share business strategies and create a format registry for copyright protection. In its first six years, the organization was not effective at arbitrating copyright disputes because format producers had been reluctant to trust an unofficial forum outside legal arenas, despite the uncertainties that differing national copyright standards posed.

Formatting cases consider dramatic elements, game rules, original music, sound motifs, and overall aesthetic, but attempts to include the category of "formats" under copyright law have failed. Dutch courts are stricter than German courts about copyright-infringing elements in formats, while cases in the United Kingdom and the United States have been more unpredictable. For example, the U.K. company that owned *Survivor* sued Endemol, the creators of *Big Brother,* for copyright infringement in a Dutch court. The court found that while *Survivor* did indeed have a copyright claim to its unique combination of 12 elements, from the 24-hour video surveillance to contestants creating video diaries, the court found that *Big Brother* only *substantially* copied three elements, so the case was dismissed.[28]

Regional Developments in Reality TV

The emerging transnational dynamics in television, including the deregulation of national public service broadcasting, the proliferation of international cable/satellite commercial channels, the emergence of international coproductions, and the dominant economic position of European-based TV formatting conglomerates—all register in complex and uneven ways when considered within the contexts of cultural difference, moral convention, industry culture, and national politics across the regions of Asia, Africa, and Latin America.

In Japan, the second largest television market in the world where 95 percent of programming is domestically produced, producers created a local version of *Who Wants to Be a Millionaire* in 2000 and *Survivor* in 2002. Unlike the U.S. version of *Survivor* that foregrounds the plotting and gamesmanship of competing contestants, the Japanese version focused on the life story and inward emotional conflicts of each contestant as they developed friendships under difficult conditions. But the format's competitive individualistic components conflicted with the localized focus on the collectivist spirit of the emotional journeys and failed to engage large audiences. For similar cultural reasons, *Big Brother* has not reached Japanese TV screens because contestants must privilege individual goals of winning approval at the expense of others being voted out.

Japan has incorporated Anglicized characters in Japanese animation (*Astro Boy*) and video games (*Super Mario Brothers*) in part to facilitate export to a culturally insular West. More recently, Japan has exported reality TV formats that include *Takeshi Castle,* created in 1986, and *Funniest Home Movies* in 1987, both developed by the Tokyo Broadcasting System; the former included a U.S. version that added localized commentary and was renamed *Most Extreme Elimination Challenge.* Later, *Happy Family Plan*, involving a father mastering a task to perform in front of a studio audience, was exported to over 30 countries, and *Future Diary,* a dating show where contestants are told what to say and do, has sold in 16 countries. Also, Fuji TV's hybrid cooking show/arena sport *Iron Chief* has exported widely. Exports to the United States and Europe are most valuable as format prices are 10 to 40 times higher there than in regional Asian markets.[29]

Though postcolonial South Korea has effectively banned Japanese television imports, South Korean television producers have long adapted popular Japanese programs and genres, particularly games shows and science and nature infotainment. In 1997, South Korean producers made an unofficial adaptation of *Happy Family Plan* called *Special Task! Dad's Challenge.* The similar patriarchal family structures of the two nations made for a successful imitation, though the producers of *Happy Family Plan* forced the South Korean adaptation off the air two years later with a lawsuit threat.[30]

In Hong Kong, despite the introduction of the pan-Asian STAR satellite television that offers Hollywood film and TV in addition to other pan-Asian programming, most residents still watch the two free-to-air Cantonese-language channels that show popular local dramas, soap operas, and dubbed imports from Japan, Taiwan, and mainland China. In a ratings war in 2001 the two networks bought format rights to *Who Wants to Be a Millionaire* and *The Weakest Link* in addition to creating local quiz shows such as *Knowledge Is Power* and *Chinese Cultural Ambassador.* While these quiz shows tapped into sentiments that knowledge was an avenue for economic recovery following the Asian economic crises in the late 1990s, the format rights were expensive, and strict adaptation rules constricted the networks' temporal in-house production cultures. Also, Hong Kong's British colonial past and cosmopolitan port have facilitated hybrid identities and a recombinant culture of unofficial blending of international formats. For example, in 2002, one of the Hong Kong TV networks created *The Wild*, a hybrid between *Temptation Island* and *Survivor* where couples worked out relationship issues in a remote area of Queensland, Australia, and endured physical and mental challenges but without the overtly sexual connotations of the original shows to avoid strict censorship rules and comply with moral conventions.[31]

China's TV industry comprises the state-controlled China Central Television (CCTV), hundreds of fragmented provincial television stations, and regional cable and satellite systems. Most programming consists of socialist realist dramas; Royal Court costume dramas; and variety, game, and quiz shows that are often cloned across regional Chinese television stations. China has only recently entered the international format business in licensing *Happy Family Plan* from Japan in 2001 and *The Weakest Link* from the BBC in 2002. More ambitious was the 2002 unlicensed adaptation of *Survivor* called *Into Shangrila*, which included contestants from multiple provinces. The U.S.-educated Chinese producer organized a symposium with members of CCTV and the Chinese cultural ministry to sufficiently differentiate the Chinese version from the western format, including requiring contestants to cooperate rather than compete against each other.[32]

Chinese authorities have eagerly supported TV that promotes an entrepreneurial business ethic to fuel China's rapid economic growth, including *Wise Man Takes All* in 2005, which has contestants compete for startup capital for a new business.[33] A number of hit talent shows have aired in China since 2005, including Shanghai Media Group's *My Show* and the men-only *My Hero*, CCTV's *Dream China*, and Hunan Satellite TV's women-only *Super Girl*.[34] With viewer participation and contestants from throughout the country, talent shows such as *Super Girl* have challenged Asian pop gender norms, as one commentator said: "With their spiky short crops, androgynous dressing and tomboyish demeanor, champion Li and runner-up Zhou shatter the long-haired, Barbie-doll mould of countless female Mandarin pop stars." Another reported that a 15-year-old girl from Hunan province starved to death while slimming down for the next season's competition. Commentators from CCTV criticized the show as "vulgar, boorish and lacking in social responsibility," to which the show's producers responded by toning down the "outrageous" outfits and introducing patriotic folk songs.[35] While some hailed the viewer voting as a form of "grassroots democracy," reports that several families of the contestants bribed mobile phone companies for votes and producers leveraged the "brand" through merchandising reinforced the commercial aspirations of the show.[36]

Whether a perceived democratic threat or a challenge to cultural authority, in 2006, the State Administration of Radio, Film and Television enacted new rules to restrict the number of talent shows and ensure that they "be positive, healthy, cheerful and have a favorable influence on morality."[37] A similar government crackdown on popular real-life crime and supernatural reality TV programs in Indonesia ensued following vocal disgust from intellectuals and the political elite.[38]

Reality TV has targeted the Chinese diaspora, including *Quest USA* (*Da Tiao Zhan*), a Mandarin-language series hosted by the popular pan-Asian entertainer David Wu (Wu Da Wei), which followed four competing teams representing mainland China, the United States, Hong Kong, and Taiwan on a cross-country tour from Boston to Miami. The series aired on five local U.S. television stations, as mini episodes in subway terminals in major cities in China, on a Hong Kong satellite channel, and on the Internet Protocol TV network Jeboo in China.[39] Also, *Chinese Gongfu Star* held televised competitions in six cities in China and six western countries in search of a top gongfu master.[40]

In India, the state broadcaster Doordarshan monopolized television until deregulations in the mid-1990s authorized satellite TV. In 2000, the U.K.-originated Star TV aired the immensely successful *Kaun Banega Crorepati* (KBC), a local version of *Who Wants to Be a Millionaire,* hosted by the Bollywood film giant Amitabh Bachan. Three staff from the *Millionaire* format owners in the U.K. traveled to India to consult, while a team from KBC traveled to the United States to study the show there. Bachan's Hinglish phrase "lock it in" entered popular parlance.[41]

In 2006 Sony's satellite TV channel created a marginally successful Hindi version of Endemol's *Celebrity Big Brother* called *Bigg Boss.* Sony had difficulty recruiting Bollywood celebrities and settled for D-list film actors, models, and TV personalities but chose those who had relationship histories in hopes of sparking love interest in the house.[42] No cameras were installed in changing rooms and bathrooms to avoid depictions of nudity and sex. One commentator speculated that the show was only moderately successful because celebrity culture in India was less voyeuristically focused on illicit affairs and wayward acts than elsewhere.[43] Sony also aired *Fear Factor India,* which subjected celebrities to physical challenges and gross-out dares but failed to draw large audiences. However, Sony's dance competition

Jhalak Dikhla Jaa, Star One channel's celebrity dance show *Nach Baliye,* and Zee TV's music contest *Sa Re Ga Ma Pa* achieved high ratings. The Hindi-language MTV created *Roadies,* a local version of the U.S. *Road Rules* that involves teams competing during road trips.[44]

Reality TV has aired on satellite TV in Africa, including the continent-wide *Big Brother Africa* (2005) and *Idols West Africa* (2006), but the genre has proliferated in Nigeria where the "Nollywood" film and TV industry has prospered. Talent shows including *Guilder Ultimate Search* (2003) and *The Next Movie Star* (2005) and gamedocs such as *Big Brother Nigeria* (2006) and the tourism-promoting *Hidden Paradise* (2005) have attracted large audiences. Also, *Intern Reality TV* (2006) had teams compete for business careers that complimented "Project Nigeria," a new government initiative to re-brand the country as an entrepreneurial society.[45]

Across Latin America, reality TV has had only a marginal effect on prime-time schedules otherwise filled with local and transnational tele-novelas. Buena Vista International TV Latin America has made local versions of *Amazing Race* and *Extreme Makeover,* and the U.K.'s Channel 4 International sold a local format of *Supernanny* to a Brazilian terrestrial channel that won high ratings.[46] Local formats and imported reality TV shows are more prevalent on U.S.-backed cable and satellite channels. Discovery Networks and the BBC aired the English-language originals of *Wife Swap* and *While You Were Out* on their Latin American pay-TV channel People and Arts in 2004, and then commissioned Buenos Aires–based Promofilm to make the Spanish-language versions *Cambiemos esposas* and *Mientras no estabas* in 2005. Promofilm has also made Spanish-language versions of *Survivor* (*Expedición Robinson*) for a FOX-owned Latin American channel and *Temptation Island* for Telemundo in the United States.[47]

In 2002, Endemol formed a joint venture with a producer in Argentina to shoot Spanish-language reality TV and to use cheaper production crews to make versions of *Fear Factor* for Belgium, the United Kingdom, Mexico, Canada, and France.[48] Endemol also entered a join venture with Brazil's TV conglomerate Globo in 2001 to facilitate format exchanges.[49] Popular reality TV shows of Quinceañera, a celebration of a girl's fifteenth birthday as a rite of passage into womanhood, play on Telemundo and MTV Latin America.[50] In the summer of 2006, Sony aired *Latin American Idol* to its 12 million pay-TV subscribers in 24 countries throughout Latin America and the Caribbean. The Cuban, Mexican, and Puerto Rican judges scrutinized 10 finalists from five Latin American countries.[51] Just before airing, format owner FremantleMedia won a copyright suit against Peru's Panamerican Television for airing a similar unauthorized version called *Superstar*.[52]

Though these Latin American reality formats aspire for ratings and entertainment, they have also prompted public debates over national politics and culture. In the Chilean reality TV contest *Protagonists of Fame*, where contestants vie to become a *televovela* star, debate ensued as to whether a contestant who was the grandson of a Pinochet general who headed the infamous secret police should be allowed to remain on the show. In the wake of Argentina's economic collapse, contestants on *The People's Candidate* competed to represent a new political party. Contestants on Argentina's *Human Resources* competed for jobs.[53] In Guatemala where gang violence has escalated, local businesses and the U.S. Agency for International Development sponsored *Desafío 10,* a reality show that placed 10 former gang members in a house for two weeks to learn business skills.[54]

Reality TV and the Geopolitics of the "War on Terror"

The uneven globalizing of modernities in Asia, Africa, and Latin America across particular formations of capitalist markets, international divisions of labor, and national industry formations concentrated origination of reality TV in Japan, Nigeria, and U.S.-owned pan–Latin American Satellite channels. At the same time, reality TV throughout these regions asymmetrically transformed formats via local culture and custom, threatened authoritarian politics and taste, exploited peripheral labor, broadened gendered representations, engaged in political and cultural controversies, redefined postcolonial relations, and excited and bored viewers.

In addition to these regionally and nationally situated cultural and political contexts, reality TV has also engaged in another globalizing force, world militarism, defined at the dawning of the twenty-first century by an aggressive and preemptive U.S. "war on terror."

Hollywood has long worked closely with the Pentagon in shaping screen representations of the U.S. military.[55] These collaborations initiated reality TV shows in the pre-9/11 spring of 2001 when branches of the U.S. military sought new ways to bolster their image as polls showed waning public support for the military and Defense Secretary Donald Rumsfeld planned to radically restructure the armed forces.

The Marine Corps worked with FOX to produce the reality series *Boot Camp,* which followed 16 civilian contestants through basic training led by active-duty Marine sergeants.[56] FOX was looking to match the ratings success of its earlier reality hit *Temptation Island,* which tempted couples toward infidelity, but when several advertisers withdrew their sponsorship to distance their products from the show's "immoral" themes, FOX picked up *Boot Camp,* which advertisers embraced as "a little bit of Americana."[57] Blending Marine Corps basic training with the game components of *Survivor,* each week the contestants voted a fellow trainee out, and the ousted peer selected another to leave. The creators of *Survivor* and CBS sued FOX for copyright infringement, which the parties settled out of court. Marine Corps public relations officials and recruiters were happy with the strong ratings among their core 18–34-year-old recruiting demographic.[58]

Two other reality series promoted all four branches of the U.S. military. In March 2001, TBS debuted *War Games,* a two-hour reality special involving combat scenarios including Air Force dogfighting, "live fire" exercises, and Navy submarine warfare, which was particularly suspenseful since the Navy had accidentally sunk a Japanese submarine, killing nine, just a month before. Linking American masculinity to war as sport, the strong-jawed sportscaster and former football player Howie Long hosted the show, along with Anne Powell, daughter of Secretary of State Colin Powell.[59]

Similarly, Mark Burnett, creator of *Survivor,* produced *Combat Missions,* where teams from the Green Berets, Delta Force, Central Intelligence Agency special operations and a SWAT police force competed against an enemy "shadow squad." Shot for the USA Network before 9/11 at a mock military installation in the Mojave Desert and hosted by ex-Navy SEAL and *Survivor* contestant Rudy Boesch, *Combat Missions,* originally planned for the fall, was postponed until January 2002 after the United States began military operations in Afghanistan.[60]

From the producer of *American Gladiators* and with Hollywood special effects experts who worked on *Heartbreak Ridge* (pro war in Greneda), *Under Siege* (pro U.S. aggression in the Middle East) and *Pearl Harbor* (patriotic World War II), *Combat Missions* deployed true Hollywood patriotic flash.[61] However, the realities of real combat missions were starkly rendered when Scott Helvenston, a contestant on the Delta Force team, was killed in Fallujah on March 31, 2004—his charred body, along with three others, was hung from a bridge. The gruesome event prompted multiple U.S. sieges in Fallujah, which, in turn, fueled Iraqi insurgencies.[62]

The four men who died were not enlisted in the military but worked for the private company Blackwater USA, which provided diplomatic security under a $300 million State Department contract. With military and reserve troops stretched thin and the lure of better pay, some 20,000 private security forces have worked in Iraq outside the military chain of command and without coordinated intelligence information. The families of the four men sued Blackwater for sending them on a perilous mission without an armored vehicle, automatic weapons, or a map.[63] *Combat Missions* was not renewed for a second season. In 2007, the FBI found Blackwater employees guilty of killing 14 Iraqi civilians without cause.[64]

Following the U.S. invasion of Afghanistan, reality TV producers left the mock military installations for an actual combat zone. In 2002, Hollywood producer Jerry Bruckheimer (*Peal Harbor* [2001]; *Black Hawk Down* [2001]) collaborated with the Pentagon to follow the Special Forces in a planned 13-week reality series titled *Profiles from the Front Line* that premiered on ABC in February 2003. In support of U.S. actions, Bruckheimer said the Pentagon wants to "attract the best and the brightest to the military, so we don't want to make them look terrible."[65] Coexecutive producer Bert Van Munster, former producer of the reality TV shows *Cops* and *Amazing Race*, concurred, saying, "we're going to have a pro-military, pro-American stance. We're not going to criticize."[66]

Some critics found the Hollywood-style patriotism more of a "Pentagon infomercial," and others commented how American operatives repeatedly referred to their targets as "the bad guys" and treated the people of Afghanistan "as props in the background," mirroring similar strategies used in *Cops* that aligned viewers with the police officers against an impersonal, uncivilized "other."[67]

The ABC news department was reportedly unhappy about the entertainment division encroaching on their news turf. The director of the Joan Shorenstein Center on the Press, Politics and Public Policy at Harvard University concurred, saying, "I have a problem with the idea of confusing the entertainment side of ABC with something as serious as soldiers doing their job."[68] However, these rigid binaries between entertainment and serious news obfuscate our understanding of how reality TV formats might involve viewers in thinking more critically about the war. For example, in the first episode, an ex-Wall street broker in charge of a refueling station suspected all Afghanis of terrorism: "I don't feel funny searching through anybody's personal stuff because they wiped how many thousands of people's personal stuff at the World Trade Center."[69] Yet in a later episode the ex-broker softened his Manichean perspectives toward the Afghan people in his personal encounters, teaching local boys to play baseball, as perhaps did viewers who otherwise shared the broker's initial dehumanized perspectives. Also, with special access to the daily operations of under-cover operatives, *Profiles* provided coverage of military actions not seen on news coverage. As Van Munster put it, "*Profiles* was more critical than most of the networks. In one episode, a master sergeant got killed and we followed him from battlefield to the hospital to his coffin."[70]

However, as the Bush administration built its case to invade Iraq in March 2003, ABC had only aired a few episodes before taking the series off the air. These scenes of U.S. soldiers being killed in Afghanistan proved too controversial for the commercial imperatives of the network and its advertisers. Meanwhile, the military closely managed the "serious" news coverage of the war through "embedding" reporters in heavily armored vehicles from the perspective of endangered U.S. soldiers and feeding the press with the prowar "consensus" views of official sources.[71] The ABC entertainment division turned down Bruckheimer's offer to create an Iraq version of *Profiles*, so Van Munster filmed 60 hours of the Iraq war exclusively for the Pentagon.[72]

While reality TV in the United States predominately supported U.S. military aggression in the Middle East, though in a format that potentially offered more humanizing and graphic depictions than did news coverage, reality TV in Iraq engaged more broadly in the complexities and tragedies of the war-torn Middle East. Before the war, three Saddam Hussein–controlled TV channels aired in Iraq. Two years later, Iraqis could watch more than 30 channels in addition to dozens of satellite channels.[73] With theaters and cinemas closed, curfews enforced after dark and violence in the streets, the sale of TV sets soared as Iraqis increasingly turned to television for news, soap operas, comedies, talk shows, and reality TV.[74] Former Iraqi information minister Saad al-Bazzaz returned from exile in London soon after the U.S. invasion to launch the first privately financed Iraqi satellite network, Al-Sharqiya (The Eastern).[75] In four years, Al-Sharqiya became one of the most watched networks in Iraq by offering locally produced alternatives to foreign satellite channels such as Al-Jazeera and the U.S.-supported Al-Hurra and Al-Iraqiya.[76]

Al-Sharqiya aired the first Iraqi reality TV series in the spring of 2004 with *Labor Plus Materials,* which sent production crews to rebuild and refurnish houses that were damaged or destroyed by U.S. or insurgent attacks. In an opening voice-over that introduces "the stories of families forced to pay the bills of war" with "no shelter and no roof over their heads," and occasional shots of U.S. Humvees in the background, the series recounts Iraqis' daily struggles, anti-U.S. sentiments, and frustrations at an overstretched and unstable government. While counterinsurgencies escalated sectarianism, the third episode rebuilt a car bomb–damaged Christian church and home where a Kurd, an Arab Muslim, and an Arab Christian lived together.

Many on the TV crew were former employees of the Ministry of Information where all journalists and TV personnel worked under the Hussein regime—some expressed nostalgia for more stable working conditions.[77] The show built six homes in its first two years on the air, but in 2006 only built one due to rising sectarian fighting. The series producer voiced caution regarding these sectarian tensions: "When we rebuild a house of a Sunni, the show makes sure the next house to rebuild belongs to a Shia."[78]

Al-Sharqiya produced other reality series focused on helping struggling Iraqis, including *Ration Card,* which supplemented families on limited rations; *Blessed Wedding,* which awarded poor couples $6,000 for their nuptials; and *Clothes and Money* and *Supreme Knowledge,* both of which awarded provisions and cash prizes to citizens in need.[79] Al-Sharqiya reality genres also offer entertaining diversions for war-torn citizens. A hybrid of *Big Brother* and *Survivor* called *Beit Beut* ("Playing House"), named after a traditional childhood game, aired every night during the month of Ramadan in September 2006. A dozen contestants including Shiites, Kurds, Sunnis, and Christians from disparate regions lived together in a remodeled inn in the less-violent northern Iraq, where they formed teams and competed against each other. Each week viewers chose between two contestants nominated among the loosing team for removal from the house. Despite these competitions, the show steered clear of clashes of religion, regional identity, or politics; as a young Sunni contestant put it: "The show emphasizes this point to the Iraqis, that we are living together, we can live together, we don't care what is going on, what plans others may have for us, we are connected to each other." In deference to religious beliefs, the series shied away from romantic couplings and housed the men and women in segregated sleeping quarters.[80]

In 2006, Al-Sharqiya began *Saya Wa Surmaya* ("Fame or Fortune"), a reality series with different themes designed to help contestants "realize their dreams." One theme had contestants create a spoof news program similar to *The Daily Show* with Jon Stewart in the United States, while another offered interest-free loans to start a small business. The talent contest *Youth Project* infused a western format with Islamic mores by using Frank Sinatra's "My Way" as the series theme song but allowed only hand shakes between the male and female contestants to avoid the controversies of the imported Lebanese *Star Academy*, where impassioned fandom for a contestant heartthrob articulated the women's struggle for political and cultural rights in Kuwait, even as Saudi Arabia's Grand Mufti warned Muslims not to watch.[81] *Iraq Star*, a less-controversial talent show from rival satellite channel Al-Sumaria that launched from Lebanon in 2004 to create programming for a "unified Iraq," had contestants from different Iraqi provinces sing patriotic folk songs.[82] Despite these efforts to avoid sectarianism, seven Al-Sharqiya employees were killed in its first four years on the air, including comedian Walid Hassan, whose program *Caricature* mocked coalition forces and the Iraqi government.[83]

The Iraqi government-run local news channel Al-Iraqiya, founded by the U.S.-led Coalition Provisional Authority in 2003 with seed money from the Pentagon, created a reality series in 2005 that more directly confronted the escalating insurgencies. *Terrorism in the Grip of Justice* followed the elite Iraqi Wolf Brigade in their pursuit and interrogation of suspects. U.S. military officers in Iraq said the show prompted more Iraqis to come forth with intelligence information. However, the Iraqi Ministry of Human Rights faulted the show for violating prisoner rights. Sunnis blamed the show and the network run by the U.S.-backed Shiite-dominated government for inflaming sectarian tensions.[84] Though run by a supposedly independent board of governors, many criticized Al-Iraqiya for catering to Shiite interests.[85] After Al-Iraqiya news commentators criticized Al-Sharqiya for exaggerating Iraq's security problems, in December 2006, the U.S.-supported Iraqi government ordered the Al-Sharqiya station closed.[86]

U.S. diplomats concerned about the image of the United States in the Middle East turned to reality TV as a new weapon in public diplomacy. Richard Fairbanks, a Middle East peace negotiator during the Reagan administration, founded Layalina, a nonprofit organization to combat anti-American sentiments through producing television programs for Arabic-speaking audiences abroad. Its board of councilors included the Iraq Study Group cochairs James Baker III and Lee Hamilton, former president George H. W. Bush, and former secretaries of state Henry A. Kissinger, Zbigniew Brezezinski, and Lawrence S. Eagleburger.[87]

In 2006, the organization funded *On the Road in America,* a 12-part reality series following three university students from Egypt, Saudi Arabia, and Lebanon on a trip across the country. The series premiered in January 2007 on the Saudi Arabia–based pan-Arab satellite network MBC (Middle East Broadcasting Centre). Episodes included frank discussions of Middle

Eastern politics among Palestinian and Israeli students in Washington, D.C., a visit to the Mississippi Delta to meet Americans living in poverty, and a hike with "cowgirls" in Montana.

Despite its up-with-America tone, these frank exchanges provided diverse cross-cultural perspectives. However, as of May 2007, the producers had yet to find a U.S. distributor. Unlike Iraqi citizens who have access to the U.S.-backed Al-Arabyia and Al-Hurra satellite channels, in addition to CNN and FOX News, U.S. citizens have little chance to see Arab-produced reality TV and news.[88] A year after Al-Jazeera launched an international English-language 24-hour news channel in November 2006 with 60 global news bureaus, only two U.S. cable operators in Toledo, Ohio, and Burlington, Vermont, carried the network.[89]

In summary, reality TV in the United States exposed ongoing ties between the Pentagon, commercial television networks, and their cautionary blue chip advertisers that largely bolstered a consensus politics of U.S. military aggression, even as unscripted formats potentially offered more complex and unstructured portraits of war not found in fictional and "serious" news accounts. In Iraq, the U.S. invasion released television from Saddam Hussein's authoritarian control, opening the airwaves to new terrestrial and satellite channels that produced low-cost reality TV genres and an audiovisual space for diverse ethnic and religious groups to work together in displays of national unity.

Even as commercial channels did this to attract broad audiences, television personnel risked their lives doing so, and the United States attempted to shut down the popular Iraqi network Al-Sharqiya. Unlike in the United States, where the federal government and commercial TV distributors have blocked television from Iraq and the Middle East, U.S. commercial and Pentagon-backed English-language and Arabic-language networks have traveled more freely in Iraq.

Conclusion

As commodity forms designed for reproducibility by European format conglomerates within an increasingly deregulated and market-driven global television economy, reality TV propagates the international divisions of labor that have characterized the exploitative patterns of world capitalism. Regional contexts reveal uneven development, with reality TV originating in the larger television markets of Japan and Nigeria, and from

U.S.-owned pan–Latin American satellite channels. Reality TV engaged with the "war on terror," where national contexts largely determined geopolitical orientation, though Iraqi viewers had access to diverse international perspectives on television whereas U.S. viewers did not.

But the global TV realities examined here also reveal challenges to these legacies of a globalizing modernity. Hong Kong's transnational past established an ethics of cultural hybridity that undermined western legal regimes for copyrighting unscripted TV formats. Talent contests in China incited a form of citizen participation that threatened an authoritarian government. European-originated reality TV formats have had little influence on a Latin American audiovisual culture steeped in regional dramatic fiction, although original reality TV there has engaged with pressing social issues. Just as the surveillance themes of the Indian version of *Celebrity Big Brother* failed to engage viewers, the U.K. *Celebrity Big Brother* sparked a transnational debate about persistent postcolonial racial hierarchies. The Iraqi *Labor Plus Materials* did not signify western cultural imperialism as a remake of the U.S. *Extreme Makeover: Home Edition* but tapped into anti-U.S. imperialist sentiments.

Similar to the emergence of other popular cultural forms, including television itself, culture elites—whether those who pleaded for viewers and politicians to "ignore the antics of these TV idots" on U.K. *Celebrity Big Brother*, the Chinese Communist Party that rolled back "vulgar" talent contests, U.S. academics who defended the boundaries between entertainment reality TV and serious news, or Indonesian politicians who dismissed popular supernatural reality TV—expressed animosity toward this new television form.[90]

Within these more complex contextual global realities, unscripted entertainment represents neither a fundamental break from the forces of a globalizing modernity nor another western imperialist cultural form but, rather, a new development in global television worthy of serious attention, contestation, and study within particular localized contexts.

NOTES

I thank the following for their insights and expertise: Luisela Alvaray, Nitin Govil, Shawn Shimpach, Ting Wang, and Marion Wilson.

1. Aditi Khanna, "Big Fuss about *Big Brother*," *India Today* (New Delhi), 29 January 2007, 68; Jeevan Vasagar, "Majority Think C4 Should Have Stopped Big Brother Racism," *Guardian* (London), 20 January 2007, 1; Lachlan Carmichael,

"British TV Bosses on the Spot in Anglo-Indian Race Row," *Agence France Presse* (Paris), 21 January 2007; Tim Lott, "The Witches of Endemol," *Independent* (London), January 2007, 36.

2. Quoted in Bruce Loudon, "Brown in India as TV Fury Flares," *Australian* (Sydney), 19 January 2007, 8.

3. Quoted in Roy Bayliss, "Schools to Fight the Big Brother Bigots," *Sunday Mercury* (Birmingham), 21 January 2007, 10.

4. "Ridiculed in India, Shilpa Shetty Is the New Darling of UK South Asians," *Financial Express* (New Delhi), 21 January 2007.

5. Wersha Bharadwa, "I Feel for Shilpa, but She Doesn't Speak for British Indians Like Me," *Independent* (London), 21 January 2007, 36.

6. Joseph D. Straubhaar, *World Television: From Global to Local* (London: Sage, 2007).

7. Quoted in Carmichael, "British TV Bosses on the Spot."

8. Anthony Giddens, "The Globalizing of Modernity," in *Media in Global Context: A Reader*, ed. Annabelle Sreberny-Mohammadi, Dwayne Winseck, Jim McKenna, and Oliver Boyd-Barrett (London: Arnold, 1997), 19–26.

9. Anthony Smith and Richard Paterson, eds., *Television: An International History*, 2nd ed. (Oxford: Oxford University Press, 1998).

10. Kerry Segrave, *American Television Abroad: Hollywood's Attempt to Dominate World Television* (Jefferson, N.C.: McFarland, 1998), 3–36; Michael Curtin, *Redeeming the Wasteland: Television Documentary and Cold War Politics* (New Brunswick, N.J.: Rutgers University Press, 1995).

11. John Sinclair, Elizabeth Jacka, and Stuart Cunningham, eds., *New Patterns in Global Television: Peripheral Visions* (Oxford: Oxford University Press, 1996).

12. Timothy Havens, *Global Television Marketplace* (London: British Film Institute, 2006), 25.

13. Chris Barker, *Global Television: An Introduction* (Oxford: Blackwell, 1997), 155.

14. Edward S. Herman and Robert W. McChesney, *The Global Media: The New Missionaries of Corporate Capitalism* (London: Cassell, 1997), 58–59.

15. Petros Losifidis, Jeanette Steemers, and Mark Wheeler, *European Television Industries* (London: British Film Institute, 2005), 132–50. For TV imports into Europe, see http://www.obs.coe.int/about/oea/pr/pr_eurofiction_bis.html.

16. "Sony Pictures Unveils China Venture," *Asia Pulse* (Rhodes, NSW, Australia), 26 November 2004.

17. Daya Kishan Thussu, "Localizing the Global: Zee TV in India," in *Electronic Empires: Global Media and Local Resistance*, ed. Daya KishanThussu (London: Arnold, 1998), 273–94.

18. Peter Feuilherade, "Global TV Industry on a Roll," *BBC Monitoring International Reports*, 13 October 2006.

19. Hamid Naficy, *The Making of Exile Cultures: Iranian Television in Los Angeles* (Minneapolis: University of Minnesota Press, 1993).

20. Toby Miller, Nitin Govil, John McMurria, Richard Maxwell, and Ting Wang, *Global Hollywood* 2 (London: British Film Institute, 2005), 173–212.

21. John McMurria, "Long-Format TV: Globalization and Network Branding in a Multi-Channel Era," in *Quality Popular Television: Cult TV, the Industry and Fans*, ed. Mark Jancovich and James Lyons (London: British Film Institute, 2003), 65–87; Marsha Kinder, "Ranging with Power on the FOX Kids Network: Or, Where on Earth Is Children's Educational Television?," in *Kids Media Culture*, ed. Marsha Kinder (Durham, N.C.: Duke University Press, 1999), 177–203; Heather Hendershot, "*Sesame Street:* Cognition and Communications Imperialism," in *Kids Media Culture*, ed. Marsha Kinder (Durham, N.C.: Duke University Press, 1999), 139–76; Cynthia Chris, "Discovery's Wild Discovery: The Growth and Globalization of TV's Animal Genres," in *Cable Visions: Television beyond Broadcasting*, ed. Sarah Banet-Weiser, Cynthia Chris, and Anthony Freitas (New York: New York University Press, 2007), 137–57.

22. Daniel Mato, "Miami in the Transnationalization of the Telenovela Industry: On Territoriality and Globalization," *Journal of Latin American Cultural Studies* 11.2 (2002), 195–211.

23. John McMurria, "Global Channels," in *Contemporary World Television*, ed. John Sinclair (London: British Film Institute, 2004), 38–41.

24. Havens, *Global Television Marketplace*, 142–46; and see http://www.zonereality.tv/.

25. Albert Moran with Justin Malbon, *Understanding the Global TV Format* (Briston: Intellect, 2006), 85–100.

26. *The Global Trade in Television Formats*, at http://www.screendigest.com/reports/gttf05/readmore/view.html.

27. Moran with Malbon, *Understanding the Global TV Format*, 91–95; see also http://www.endemol.com/ and http://www.fremantlemedia.com/.

28. Moran with Malbon, *Understanding the Global TV Format*, 101–3, 111–42.

29. Koichi Iwabuchi, "Feeling Glocal: Japan in the Global Television Format Business," in *Television across Asia: Television Industries, Program Formats and Globalization*, ed. Albert Moran and Michael Keane (London: RoutledgeCurzon, 2004), 21–35.

30. Ibid., 31–33; Dong-Hoo Lee, "A Local Mode of Program Adaptation," in *Television across Asia: Television Industries, Program Formats and Globalization*, ed. Albert Moran and Michael Keane (London: RoutledgeCurzon, 2004), 37–53.

31. Anthony Fung, "Coping, Cloning and Copying: Hong Kong in the Global Television Format Business," in *Television across Asia: Television Industries, Program Formats and Globalization*, ed. Albert Moran and Michael Keane (London: RoutledgeCurzon, 2004), 74–87.

32. Michael Keane, "A Revolution in Television and a Great Leap Forward for Innovation? China in the Global Television Format Business," in *Television across Asia: Television Industries, Program Formats and Globalization*, ed. Albert Moran and Michael Keane (London: RoutledgeCurzon, 2004), 88–104.

33. "Chinese Reality TV Models Itself on Tycoon Trump's *Apprentice*," *Agence France Presse* (Paris), 17 August 2005.

34. Alice Yan, "China Hong Kong Daily Predicts Rise of Reality TV," *BBC Monitoring International Reports* (London), 22 December 2006.

35. "Country Gripped by Reality TV Show," *BBC Monitoring International Reports* (London), 30 August 2005.

36. John Hartley, "'Reality' and the Plebiscite," in *Politicotainment: Television's Take on the Real*, ed. Kristina Riegert (New York: Peter Lang, 2006); Clarissa Oon, "Reality Talent Shows All the Rage in China," *Straits Times* (Singapore), 7 October 2006; Clarissa Oon, "Networks, Sponsors and Telcos Laughing All the Way to the Bank," *Straits Times* (Singapore), 7 October 2006.

37. Quoted in Bill Savadove, "Brakes Put on TV Talent Programs," *South China Morning Post* (Hong Kong), 17 March 2006, 8.

38. Mark Hobart, "Entertaining Illusions: How Indonesia Élites Imagine Reality TV Affects the Masses," *Asian Journal of Communication* 16.4 (December 2006), 393–410.

39. See http://www.pacificepoch.com/newsstories/74522_0_5_0_M; and http://www.c21media.net/resources/detail.asp?area=74&article=29793.

40. Oon, "Networks, Sponsors."

41. Amos Owen Thomas and Keval J. Kumar, "Copied from Without and Cloned from Within: India in the Global Television Format Business," in *Television across Asia: Television Industries, Program Formats and Globalization*, ed. Albert Moran and Michael Keane (London: RoutledgeCurzon, 2004), 122–37.

42. "Someone Is Watching You," *Hindustan Times* (New Delhi), 9 December 2006.

43. "Reality Bites," *Hindustan Times* (New Delhi), 27 January 2007.

44. "Sony's *Big Boss* Raising Eyebrows," *Indo-Asian News Service* (New Delhi), 18 November 2006.

45. "Katung Wins *Big Brother Nigeria*," *Africa News*, 9 June 2006; *Intern Reality TV* Show Boosts 'Brand Nigeria,'" *Africa News* (Haarlem, Netherlands), 31 July 2006; "Just How Real?," *Africa News*, 8 February 2007; "*Big Brother Africa* Goes to Nigeria," *Africa News* (Haarlem, Netherlands), 10 December 2005.

46. Fernando Barbosa, "Latin America Gets Fired Up," *Television Business International* 6 (1 June 2006), 1.

47. "US Reality Skeins Find Latin Accent," *Daily Variety*, 1 August 2005, 48.

48. "Argentina Is "Fear" Friendly," *Daily Variety*, 7 October 2003, 6.

49. Moran with Malbon, *Understanding the Global TV Format*, 93–94.

50. Christina Hoag, "Quinceanera Parties a Reality TV Sensation," *Knight Ridder Tribune Business News*, 11 June 2006, 1.

51. Brian Byrnes, "Latin 'Idol' is Getting Its Big Break," *Hollywood Reporter*, 24 October 2006; Michael O'Boyle, "Latin 'Idol' Belts out Blow," *Daily Variety*, 11 July 2006, 26.

52. Ann Marie de la Fuente and Mary Sutte, "Fremantle Wins Suit," *Daily Variety*, 1 August 2006, 8.

53. See http://sfgate.com/cgi-bin/article.cgi?f=/c/a/2003/02/27/MN104981.DTL.

54. See   http://www.washingtonpost.com/wp-dyn/content/article/2006/02/23/AR2006022301252.html.

55. David L. Robb, *Operation Hollywood: How the Pentagon Shapes and Censors the Movies* (Ahmerst, N.Y.: Prometheus, 2004).

56. David Wood, "Operation Makeover," *New Orleans Times-Picayune*, 1 April 2001, 29.

57. Bill Carter, "Reality TV Goes Back to Basic," *New York Times*, 2 April 2001, C1.

58. Donna Petrozzello, "*Boot Camp* Suffers 21% Loss in Week 2," *New York Daily News*, 6 April 2001, 139; Michael Freeman, "Reality TV Lands in Courtroom," *Electronic Media*, 16 April 2001, 22.

59. Jennifer Harper, "*War Games* View with Reality Shows," *Washington Times*, 25 February 2001, A3.

60. Jim Forkan, "'Missions': Possible Hit for USA," *Multichannel News*, 17 December 2001, 14.

61. Mark A. Perigard, "'Missions' Accomplished: USA Reality Series Crowns a Champion Tonight," *Boston Herald*, 17 April 2002, Arts and Life 47.

62. Jeremy Scahill, "Bush's Mercenaries Thrive in Iraq," *Toronto Star*, 29 January 2007, A13.

63. Bill Lubinger, "Contractor Deaths Leave Families Asking Why," *Cleveland Plain Dealer*, 7 May 2006, A8.

64. David Johnston and John M. Broder, "FBI Says Guards Killed 14 Iraqis without Cause, *New York Times*, 14 November 2007.

65. Quoted in Xan Brooks, "That's Entertainment," *Guardian* (London), 22 May 2002, 14.

66. Quoted in James Hibberd, "Pushing the Reality Envelope," *Television Week*, 14 July 2003, 12.

67. Joy Press, "The Axers of Evil," *Village Voice*, 11 March 2003, 51; Robert Bianco, "*Profiles* Finds ABC AWOL from Reality," *USA Today*, 27 February 2003, 3D; Elayne Rapping, "Aliens, Nomads, Mad Dogs, and Road Warriors: The Changing Face of Criminal Violence on TV," in *Reality TV: Remaking Television Culture*, ed. Susan Murray and Laurie Ouellette (New York: New York University Press, 2004), 214–30.

68. Donna Petrozzello,"War on Terror, the TV Series," *New York Daily News*, 21 February 2002, 100.

69. Press, "Axers of Evil," 11.

70. Quoted in Hibberd, "Pushing the Reality Envelope."

71. Howard Tumber and Jerry Palmer, *Media at War: The Iraq Crisis* (London: Sage, 2004).

72. James Hibberd, George Rush, and Joanna Molloy, "Bruckheimer's Battle for Baghdad," *New York Daily News*, 26 March 2003, 34.

73. "Iraq Rechannels Its Battle Fatigue," *Daily Variety*, 24 October 2005, 4.

74. "TV Drama Popular in Iraq," *China Daily* (Beijing), 23 June 2005.

75. Yochi J. Dreazen, "Copying West, Iraqi TV Station Creates Hits," *Wall Street Journal*, 22 August 2005, B1.

76. Edward Wong, "In War's Chaos, Iraq Finds Inspiration for Reality TV," *New York Times*, 28 August 2005, 1.

77. Anne Barnard, "Reality TV Show, Iraqi Style, Fixes Houses, Lives," *Boston Globe*, 12 September 2004, A12.

78. Quoted in Sudarsan Raghavan, "In Iraq, Singing for a Chance of Hope and Glory," *Washington Post*, 2 September 2006, A1.

79. "Iraqi Reality TV Leads to Deadly Ambush," *UPI*, 27 January 2007.

80. Kim Murphy, "Reality TV Programs Show a Different Iraq," *Los Angeles Times*, 27 October 2006, A6.

81. Marwan Kraidy, "Reality Television and Politics in the Arab World (Preliminary Observations), *Transnational Broadcasting Studies* 2.1 (2006), 7–28; Rawya Rageh, "Iraqi Reality TV Show Defies Odds in This Violence Plagued Country," *Associated Press*, 8 August 2006; Elizabeth Davies, "Iraqis Opt for an Alternative Reality on Television," *Independent* (London), 28 October 2006, 36.

82. Raghaven, "Singing for a Chance of Hope and Glory"; see also http://www.alsumaria.tv/en/about_us.html.

83. Mazin Yahya, "Professor and Economist Who Helped the Poor Is Shot Dead in Baghdad," *Associated Press*, 24 January 2007; "Iraqi Reality TV Lead Dies," *UPI*, 27 January 2007.

84. Neil MacDonald, "Iraqi Reality TV Hit Takes Fear Factor to Another Level," *Christian Science Monitor*, 7 June 2005, 1.

85. Charles Levinson, "Iraq's 'PBS' Accused of Sectarian Slant," *Christian Science Monitor*, 10 January 2006, 6; Jim Krane, "US Funds Iraqi TV Network in Battle against 'Hostile' Arab News Stations," *Associated Press*, 29 November 2003.

86. Christopher Torchia, "Iraq Orders Shutdown of Baghdad Office of TV Station Accused of Inciting Hatred," *Associated Press*, 1 January 2007.

87. See http://www.layalina.tv/meet/.

88. Guy Dinmore, "Troubled TV Network Draws Fire," *Financial Times* (London), 7 November 2005, 8.

89. Mimi Turner, "Ál Jazeera English on Air," *Hollywood Reporter*, 16 November 2006; Roger Cohen, "Bring the Real World Home," *New York Times*, 12 November 2007.

90. "Ignore the Antics of These TV Idiots," *Plymouth* (Mass.) *Western Morning News*, 20 January 2007.

Part III

Culture and Power

III

Country Hicks and Urban Cliques
Mediating Race, Reality, and Liberalism on MTV's The Real World

Jon Kraszewski

Within the very first minutes of its series premiere, MTV's *The Real World* announced that race would be one of the show's most prominent cultural concerns. As its premise, the first season brought together seven strangers between the ages of 19 and 26 in a luxurious New York City loft for 13 weeks.[1] The show seemed to capture a real life portrayal of young adults living in the wake of the Rodney King trial and the riots in Los Angeles, both of which occurred just a few months before *The Real World's* May 1992 debut. As the roommates sat down for their first dinner, conflict erupted between three housemates: Heather, Kevin, and Julie. Heather and Kevin were two African Americans already living in New York City, Heather working as a professional rapper, Kevin a professional writer. Julie, still in a bit of a culture shock, had just moved to the city from Alabama. As Heather's beeper went off during dinner, Julie asked, "Do you sell drugs? Why do you have a beeper?"

Although the very title *The Real World* propounds that the show simply *presents* reality, we should interrogate such face-value claims and explore how this opening scene *mediates* race and reality itself. *The Real World* does not simply locate the reality of a racist statement and neutrally deliver it to an audience. Although not scripted, the show actively constructs what reality and racism are for its audience through a variety of production practices. For instance, the reality encountered on the show was partially created through the casting decisions of the producers, Mary-Ellis Bunim and Jonathan Murray, who chose these three individuals who might have potential

The friendship between Julie and Heather was constructed as a solution to the problem of rural white racism on *The Real World*, season 1.

conflicts over race. The reality was also shaped by the decisions made about where to film and what to film. The producers chose to set the show in New York City, which automatically put Julie in the position of outsider, and the directors chose to film the dinner in the first place. Thus, the producers selected potential elements of racial conflict and misunderstanding, setting up possible versions of reality for the show.

Editing also shaped the reality of the issue. The show produces millions of hours of footage that the producers, in the case of the New York season, cut into thirteen 22-minute episodes. Thus, numerous events took place when the roommates first moved into the loft, and the producers could have focused on any of them to start the show. Odds are that some of them raised different issues of racism. For instance, what if the show fixated on a racist statement from one of the white, liberal, and urban roommates? The very idea of racism and where it is located would be different.

Finally, the narrative structure of the series placed the event as a catalyst that brought Julie and Heather together, where they would eventually overcome this incident and become best friends. Thus, the show narratively constructs this opening event less as a quintessential moment of

American racism and more as a lesson of how people can overcome and discard their own racisms. Rather than assuming that this incident involving Julie, Heather, and Kevin displayed the reality of racism and race relations in the United States, it's better to ask why *The Real World* would use this event to mediate racism and reality to its audience.

In exploring this issue, it helps to conceive of a show like *The Real World* as, on some level, a media event. John Fiske defines this term as

> an indication that in a postmodern world we can no longer rely on a stable relationship or clear distinction between a "real" event and its mediated representation. Consequently, we can no longer work with the ideas that the "real" is more important, significant, or even "true" than the representation. A media event, then, is not a mere representation of what happened, but it has its own reality.[2]

In other words, media that attempts to document reality actually shapes it, filtering it through a variety of discourses and unequal fields of social power. But in using Fiske's concept of the media event, we should pay careful attention to key differences between Fiske's project and my own.

One is the nature of the event itself. Fiske analyzes events that happen once: the beating of Rodney King, the L.A. riots, and the O. J. Simpson trial. Part of Fiske's goal is to explore how these taped events are repeatable when various agents replay and alter them in legal and media institutions, recasting the tapes in new discourses and different fields of social power. *The Real World,* on the contrary, uses a different concept of time. A new episode airs during each week of a new season, and the producers create one or two new seasons each year, with a season lasting between three and six months. This brings with it different strategies for mediating reality, most notably the casting of roommates, the editing of the show, production decisions of what to film, and the organization of events into a serial narrative. We need to consider how these production decisions specific to a reality TV show construct cultural representations of racism.

Another difference between Fiske's project and mine is that Fiske draws on a large number of media outlets, ranging from the courtroom to court coverage to CNN to televised debates to amateur video. I am more concerned with how mediations on *The Real World* fit so well into MTV's identity as a cable channel. In other words, whereas Fiske explores how different social players use different discourses to mediate reality, I analyze how *The Real World* discursively constructs racism for a specific demographic: the MTV audience.

Fiske, thus, can help us see how the recording of reality on a show like *The Real World* is never neutral; its mediations draw on distinct discourses caught up in fields of social power. Yet we need to adjust Fiske's theory to suit the production practices, network goals, and textual strategies that go into a show like *The Real World* to understand its cultural resonance in a cable environment like MTV, aimed at the identity of a youthful, liberal demographic.

Given this, what is most striking about this opening incident on *The Real World* is not that Julie associated Heather's blackness with drug use and criminality. What is most interesting is why *The Real World* would use this controversial incident with conservative views to start their series on a channel that prides itself in a liberal viewership. With this in mind, just as important as Julie's claim is the way her background as a rural southerner gets associated with her statement.

Throughout its 20-season run, *The Real World* has mediated race and reality through discursive tensions between urban and rural America, as well as liberal and conservative politics. Within these tensions, white rural figures such as Julie, and later Julie from season 9 and Mike from season 10, cover significant discursive terrain in the way the show addresses racism. Through mediations of casting, filming practices, editing, and narrative strategies, *The Real World* suggests that racism is a phenomenon located within rural conservatives, not liberals with an urban feel. And here I use the phrase "urban feel" to call attention to the way the channel promotes a certain type of image so that rural viewers in the Midwest can feel urban if they buy the right clothes and have the right attitudes.

Because of this, the show constructs a reality that frees the audience of any implications in racism by blaming rural conservatives for the problem. And yet, these rural figures on the show contain a certain hip quality, both in appearance and manners, that suggests, in some ways, that they are urban and liberal. The rural characters discursively experience a dual existence on the show, partially living as members of a liberal urban clique and partly living as conservative racist outsiders. The show then constructs serial narratives to expel racism from these characters in order to make them full-fledged, city-dwelling liberals. Yet by using discourses about rural America and conservatism to construct racism as a problem of individual opinions, the show and the channel overlook the systemic nature of racism and the way it operates in liberal urban environments.

Mediating Racism as a Rural Conservative Phenomenon

From its inception, MTV has promoted itself as a hip, liberal channel with a predilection for youth. One of its earliest slogans was "MTV, some people just don't get it," a declaration implicitly naming teenagers and young adults as its target audience. Yet in these defining years, MTV faced a crisis that implicated its liberal identity in the perpetuation of racism in the United States. As Sut Jhally and Justin Lewis argue, racism "is now embedded in a iniquitous capitalist system, where economic rather than racial laws ensure widespread racial segregation and disadvantage."[3] However, white liberalism often envisions racism as a problem of individual opinions, not economic structures. This, as Jhally and Lewis argue, places a tremendous amount of blame on African Americans, who are disadvantaged by their own actions, not an unfair class system.[4]

In its early years, MTV hardly had the luxury of masking its own structural racism and relegating discrimination to the level of personal belief. The channel refused to air black music videos, claiming its white middle-class target audience lacked interest in black artists. This is a prime example of the way racism works in the U.S. economy, here disempowering a group of black artists by denying them a major market for record sales. Many black artists protested this policy, most notably Michael Jackson, whose record company threatened to pull all of its videos from MTV if the channel failed to air Jackson's *Thriller, Billie Jean,* and *Beat It* videos. Through a combination of artist, audience, and record company protests, MTV eventually decided to air black videos, fearing that their refusal to do so would hurt the channel's economic well-being.

Certainly it is a good thing that MTV lifted its ban on black artists. By doing so, the channel offered African American musicians access to a wider economic market and allowed audiences to experience the pleasures and politics of black music. As Andrew Goodwin notes, to counter its implication in explicit and systemic racism, MTV created black music programs like *Yo!, MTV Raps;* aired cutting-edge, politically controversial music videos such as Public Enemy's "By the Time I Get to Arizona," where the band assassinates white officials in Arizona, a state that fails to celebrate Martin Luther King Jr. Day; and supported a campaign to free James Brown when the singer was jailed for drug charges.[5]

At the same time, by starting a voter registration drive, campaigning for the ethical treatment of animals, and counterbalancing anti-Soviet propaganda in the 1980s, the channel increasingly looked to support liberal causes in general. According to Goodwin, these liberal specials helped MTV regiment a standardized schedule and redefine itself less as an around-the-clock video jukebox. Even music videos were organized into half-hour or hour shows.[6]

The Real World is part of MTV's explicit efforts to create a routine schedule, to promote liberal values, and to amend its previous charges of racism. It offered the channel a 30-minute weekly show for viewers to watch regularly. Yet as much as the show wants to take cutting-edge stances on race and racism, it mediates racism through discourses of ruralness and conservatism, masking the racism of liberals, propounding that racism is a matter of personal belief, and failing to address the systemic nature of racism.

This construction begins during the casting process of the show. As stated earlier, *The Real World* is not scripted, so the producers do not order the roommates to talk explicitly about racism in the United States. However, throughout the seasons Bunim and Murray have consistently cast innocent, sheltered, and young white rural Americans in houses with two African Americans from urban areas.

Certainly the seeds of a specific type of racial conflict and misunderstanding are in the house. In focusing on the culture shock these rural Americans face, the show suggests that racism is primarily a problem of misinformed individuals. For instance, early in an episode from the New Orleans season, Melissa, an African American, asks Julie, a white Mormon from Wisconsin, to pass her a paper towel. Julie responds by saying, "What color do I look?" shocking Melissa with such an offensive statement and the fact that Julie originally thinks she has done nothing wrong. The show resolves this problem with Julie claiming that her parents brought her up to say things like that, and Melissa then helps Julie try to overcome her naive and racist upbringing. As awful and hurtful as this statement is, it is fairly easy for viewers to digest, primarily because the liberal viewership of MTV is not implicated in such a racism discursively filtered through Julie's conservative upbringing in rural Wisconsin.

But the casting process is more complex than simply picking rural conservatives to mediate racism, and it speaks to the complex ways that whiteness operates in society. Richard Dyer approaches whiteness as a phenomenon of color, claiming it functions as both a visible system of privilege and an invisible regime of power.[7] Whiteness demands visibility in order to mark its subjects as empowered. Yet Dyer devotes more time to exploring how whiteness is invisible. White people tend to see themselves as unmarked or unspecified. As such, whiteness largely remains unseen, operating as a position from which a dominant social group can survey and control other races.[8] The very power of whiteness, according to Dyer, stems from its apparent neutrality and ordinariness.

Not stopping his analysis there, though, Dyer also makes several important claims about the battle over whiteness itself. Because whiteness offers power and privilege, its borders remain highly contested. The Jews, Irish, and Italians are grouped as white sometimes, but not other times, when situated in fields of social power.[9] But even within its borders, whiteness orders various levels of itself, some more acceptable than others. In these instances, certain regimes of social power graft themselves onto the skin.

For instance, working-class whites often come across as an inferior version of the race. Their lack of economic power shows up in their tainted hue, darkened because of numerous hours spent performing manual labor outside. Their whiteness is visible, and hence inferior, because their skin stands out. In this system of economic discrimination and disempowerment, middle-class and upper-class whites offer a more genuine version of the race because their labor does not tarnish the color of their skin.[10] The casting process of *The Real World* picks specific types of rural Americans, ones whose whiteness is perched between hipness and inferiority. Rural America has stereotypically been associated with the working class because of all of the farming there. The many hours in the sun because of manual labor taints the white hue of these workers. As Dyer rightly notes, this social group faces discrimination because their connection to labor somehow makes them less white.

In all of the seasons with these rural characters, the show dedicates an episode to their parents' visits. The parents are more strictly defined rural Americans, with their accents, skin color, and clothing. But the actual rural American cast members are much more urban than their family. In fact, their bodies aren't marked as an inferior version of whiteness, as Dyer would claim; rather, their mannerisms are. As college students or aspiring entertainers, their skin has not been tainted by labor, and they dress rather hip. Mike looks like a J. Crew model, and Julie is a quintessential skater girl. That said, their connection to their inferior whiteness has more to do with their relationship to their parents and their views, not their own bodies. Since MTV has always been antiparents, marking this social unit as the center of racist beliefs makes it easy for viewers to distance themselves from this social ill. By casting such people, the show says that one can shed this inferior version of whiteness attached to racism simply by changing one's views.

Beyond casting, filming practices also contribute to this specific mediation of racism and reality. The decision to film in major cities automatically positions these rural characters as outsiders. What is particularly fascinating, though, is that these supposed rural conservatives all hail from urban areas in the South or Midwest—Julie from Birmingham, the other Julie from a Milwaukee suburb, and Mike from a Cleveland suburb. Thus, the filming locale does not so much automatically or naturally function as a strange land for these characters; rather, the show discursively constructs these characters as rural Americans, positioning the city locale as another world that can cleanse their racism.

But more important than where to film is what to film. In an interview for a book on *The Real World, Chicago,* Mary-Ellis Bunim talks about the show's production practices:

> Well, it begins with the producers and directors and crew in the field as they are documenting each day in the lives of these cast members. They are watching to see if the events are more than mundane, if they have significance. So, the directors—and we have five of them who lead the crews—are focusing the cameras on any situations that are meaningful. So, it begins with the directors in the field deciding where to put the cameras because we only have one camera, maybe two, on per shift.[11]

Jonathan Murray responds to this by saying, "We have seven cast members, so if Chris and Tonya are going to the gym and Theo and some girls are going on a date, we'll go with Theo and the date, thinking that's the better story."[12]

Given this, much of the series' focus on the discursive conflicts between rural whites and urban African Americans is a result of the filming process where directors decide that shooting these roommates might eventually produce usable footage. In the case of Julie's argument with Kevin and Heather on the first season, it was logical to shoot the dinner because all seven roommates were there. Nothing else was happening. However, in the case of Julie and Melissa's conversation about the napkin on the New Orleans's season, there were only a few people in the room.

This desire to document rural conservatives with urban liberals is even more apparent on the tenth season of *The Real World,* again set in New York. In the first episode, Mike, billed as the rural American from Ohio, goes out to breakfast with Coral and Malik, two African Americans from the Bay Area of California. While there, the cameras capture Mike saying his uncle, who owns a business, will not hire black people. They are slower than whites due to their lack of education. Coral and Malik challenge Mike's racist statement, pointing out that it illuminates his uncle's own racism more than our education system's. This mixture of the rural white and the urban blacks is something to which the show always pays close attention in order to document it as much as possible.

Of course, this documented event gains significance through the editing, which positions rural conservatives as enactors of racism and urban liberals as decoders of it. While the statements made by Julie, Julie, and Mike might seem naive and blunt, they are actually more complex than they first appear. For instance, none of them explicitly states racism or demands the economic oppression of African Americans. Instead, their racisms cloak themselves in other discourses. Julie from New York addresses blacks through the discourse of criminality, while the other Julie and Mike claim their statements stemmed from their family.

This is ultimately what Stuart Hall calls "inferential racism" and what John Fiske refers to as "nonracist racism." For Hall, overt and inferential racism operate as two different modalities, the former entailing intentional statements that explicitly declare hatred against racial others and the latter functioning more dangerously because speakers do not necessarily intend their racism. In fact, people often express antiracist intent in nonracist racism, perpetuating racism in less visible and less overt ways.[13] As Fiske notes, this tactic reframes a statement about race in other discourses such as family, education, economy, or law.[14] For example, Fiske analyzes Dan Quayle's reference to the 1992 Los Angeles riots as a crisis of family values. By reframing a race problem in terms of the family, Quayle sidesteps placing blame on white hegemony in the insurgency and locates all fault within black families, which are unfairly accused of being a center or immorality.[15]

Part of what lends credence to the hipness of the liberal characters on *The Real World* is that the editing calls attention to the way they can unpack the inferential racism of the rural conservatives. After Julie comments on Heather's beeper, the show cuts in a series of personal interviews with the cast members. Both Kevin and Heather, the two African American roommates, remark that Julie's casting Heather as a criminal is trenched in racism. Moreover, Andre, a white roommate pursuing a music career in New York City, also comments on the potential offensive nature of the comment. On season 10, after Mike says that his uncle won't hire black people because they are poorly educated, editors piece together footage of Malik, Coral, and Kevin, a white roommate from the University of Texas, each separately in the confessional discussing how Mike's statement was indeed racist.

In the process of piecing together the episode, the editing uses footage that foregrounds these rural conservatives as the locus of racism in the United States, but editing choices also include clips that highlight racism as a problem of individual intentions. While there is footage of white liberal roommates decoding Julie's and Mike's inferential racism, the editors also add clips of those same roommates questioning whether or not Julie and Mike intended the statement to be racist.

According to this logic, the statement is not as racist as it seems because the individuals might not have intended it. Racism can be easily solved if roommates can make the rural conservatives aware of their statements and have them consciously change their opinions. The same issues coalesce around Julie in New Orleans when many of the roommates believe that her opinions about race stem from her parents' being conservative Mormons, not from Julie's own intentions.

If the editing plants the seeds that racism can be solved through individual attitudes, then *The Real World*'s narrative grows this idea to its fullest potential. In all of the seasons mentioned so far, the show foregrounds the friendships between a white rural conservative and a black urban liberal. While these friendships occurred through genuine interpersonal communication, they nevertheless were not the only friendships to develop in the house that season. The producers of the show gave these interracial, politically opposed friendships priority when piecing together the narrative.

Ellis-Bunim's background in soap operas is extremely useful to illuminate the way that narrative operates on *The Real World*. Soap operas resolve narrative conflicts through serial narratives. As Jeremy Butler argues, the serial provides connections between episodes as the problem/solution dilemma expands over several episodes or seasons; characters have a history as they learn from issues in previous episodes.[16]

Given this, we can see repeated narrative constructions in the way each of *The Real World* seasons develops friendships between white conservatives and black liberals. The seasons deal with these initial events of racism by having an urban black teach the rural white about black culture over the course of several episodes. For instance, Malik educates Mike about a new figure in black history each day. After hearing Julie's remark about the beeper, Heather takes Julie to a recording session for her upcoming album, allowing Julie to see African Americans working professionally, not selling drugs. Melissa teaches the other Julie that many of Julie's beliefs about African Americans are stereotypes.

The serial narrative always follows how the pedagogical nature of these relationships turns into friendships, in the process amending the rural American's personal views on racism. Most of the episodes in season 1 dedicate time to showing Julie and Heather going out and having fun together. In the very last episode, both Julie and Heather discuss how they have become best friends. On the New Orleans season, the last episode devotes time to Julie and Melissa planning to move to Los Angeles together. Mike becomes very close to Malik and eventually Coral. But *The Real World* extends its narrative issues beyond the run of the season itself by finding ways to reunite casts. On the first reunion show, which brought together the casts from the first four seasons, Julie and Heather arrived together and spoke about how they talk on the phone every day.

The producers also hold athletic challenges between the casts of *The Real World* and *Road Rules,* another reality TV show on MTV where contestants between the ages of 18 and 24 travel in a Winnebago and perform extreme stunts across the country. On one *Battle of the Seasons,* Mike and Coral represented season 10, and many of the cast members from other seasons talked about how Mike and Coral acted like a husband and wife, even though they were not married or even dating. Their friendship was that strong. By stretching these events throughout the seasons and beyond, the show foregrounds how racism can be solved by changing your opinions.

Masking Liberal Racism: Mediating Blackness through the City

In many ways, the mediations that coalesce around Julie on the first season of *The Real World* functioned as a blueprint for how later seasons would filter race and reality through rural conservative characters. The casting, filming, editing, and narratives of the ninth and tenth seasons all remain similar to the original New York show. However, the mediations of race on the first season through Kevin, an African American character, represent an important moment for *The Real World.* In casting an African American with a background in political science and a career in polemical writing, the producers of *The Real World* promised to deliver a reality about race that hardly accepted the liberal wish-wash of racism simply being a matter of personal belief.

Kevin added a different spin, insisting that racism operates through complex systems of power and economic suppression, and, for a while, it seemed as if the show was going to mediate race partly through these discourses. Kevin would write proclamations about U.S. racial orders and place them next to the entrance to the loft. In one instance, the editors show Andre, a white liberal, telling Kevin that no one in the house is racist, while Kevin claims racism exists in more complex ways than personal beliefs.

Another moment where Kevin calls attention to the racism of white liberals comes in an episode where Becky, another white liberal, states that America is a great country and everyone has the opportunity for success; Kevin insists that the economic system denies African Americans the same opportunities as whites. The show then cuts to a poetry reading of Kevin's where he recites the line, "All I want is the opportunity to have an opportunity," punctuating his point.

Yet these moments were all too unique for the show. Never again would the show cast someone who so explicitly critiques economic systems of racism in the United States or devote so much narrative time to having a character like this express his views. In fact, a character's ability to critique racism in the United States and not be represented through stereotypes would even become problematic by the end of the first season of *The Real World,* and this speaks directly to the contradictory way that the show uses discourses of urbanity to mediate race and reality to its viewers. While the city functions as a liberal location that cleanses racism from rural Americans, it also constructs African American male characters as potentially violent, hence relegating them into complex systems of stereotypes.

The second-to-last episode of the first season is particularly telling about this transition in the show. The episode opens with Julie crying, her tears brought on by a fight she had with Kevin. According to Julie, she picked up the phone, was angered that Kevin was on it, and then hung up. This led Kevin to come downstairs, say "Fuck you" and "Suck my dick," and then throw a candleholder at her. Kevin's version of the story differs, as he explains how he was on the phone with a future employer and was trying to get a job since his stay on *The Real World* and teaching gig at New York University were coming to an end. While Kevin agrees that he yelled at Julie, he insists he never said "Suck my dick" and never threw a candleholder at her.

One of the most fascinating aspects of the episode is that it never shows the fight between Julie and Kevin. Instead, it pits Julie's story against Kevin's. In the process, the episode balances Julie's turn to the other roommates for emotional support with footage of Kevin visiting the neighborhood where he grew up.

Oddly, the episode before this one is dedicated to a "homecoming" theme. Julie's family visits New York City, and so does Andre's mom. Additionally, the episode includes footage of the housemates finding a lost dog and eventually returning it to its owners. Certainly the editors could have put Kevin's story about returning home to Jersey City in the previous episode and have it fit more thematically. Moreover, there is no direct time correlation linking Kevin's going home to Julie's talking to the other roommates, and *The Real World* manipulates the timing of events to connect different stories in the same episode thematically. Why cross cut between scenes where Julie relies on the housemates for emotional support and Kevin returns home to Jersey City?

Linking Kevin's supposed threat of violence against Julie to Kevin's upbringing in a lower-class, black urban neighborhood discursively constructs Kevin's blackness in stereotypical, yet complex ways. There is a long historical trajectory connecting black sexuality to violence in the United States. According to Donald Bogle, the buck is violently sexual and ultimately a threat to white woman.[17] As Robyn Weigman argues, the buck stereotype emerged in 19th-century America after the freeing of slaves had given white and black men supposedly equal claims to citizenship. Numerous, and most often false, tales of black men raping white women circulated in order to brand African Americans as criminals and deny them citizenship. Because the buck represents a threat to white authority through his own sexuality, he needs to be disciplined, often through castration.[18]

Of course, the legacy of socially positioning black males as sexually violent is discursively complex. While whites can mobilize these fears to disempower blacks, blacks can also seize such stereotypes as sources of empowerment. As Weigman notes, the Black Panthers promoted the image of the black buck to suggest potential ways to overthrow white power.[19] Certainly urban gangs and gangsta rappers offer another instance of African Americans appropriating fears of black sexuality to represent themselves as subverting a white social system that disempowers them economically. Ice-T's song *Cop Killer* was a fitting response to the Rodney King ruling and unfair police brutality in the early 1990s. Other gangsta rappers of that period, such as N.W.A., Snoop Dog, and Dr. Dre, connected gang life to an ultrasexuality in music videos that focused on violence and sexual exploits. And yet, white institutions use these same images to dismiss African American claims and position them as socially abject.

When Kevin visits Jersey City in this episode, *The Real World* placed him in this long line of stereotypically violent black men. As Kevin walks through his neighborhood, the editors of the show play nondiegetic gangsta rap beats and cut back to Julie expressing her fear of Kevin. Kevin walks his current girlfriend through the neighborhood and points out all of its potential dangers, from violence to drug dealing. Although this discourse is available for dominant and subaltern groups to seize, this clearly is the case of the dominant using this discourse to dismiss and disempower the subaltern. Having Kevin walk through his dangerous old neighborhood cut with Julie, who claims Kevin is dangerous to her, directly goes against Kevin's own argument about the fight, where he insists he never threatened Julie and was only looking out for his economic well-being.

Even more fascinating, the show ends with Julie stating that her fight with Kevin had nothing to do with race or racism; it was only an interpersonal conflict. What the show does, then, is position Kevin, an articulate social critic of the way race operates in the United States, in the position of a stereotypical violent black male and then deny that these issues have anything to do with race, placing them within a liberal discourse of individualism.

As a pivotal moment in the history of *The Real World*, this incident set an important precedent for the ways black males would be represented through stereotypical sexuality. It also represented the last moment where *The Real World* would allow black characters to have screen time to explicitly critique the social system. Although the city functions in *The Real World* as a place that cleanses racism from rural conservatives, it also operates as a space where dangerous black sexuality lurks.

In season 2, set in Los Angeles, David, a young black male, pulls the sheets off of Tammy, another African American, and is accused of attempted rape. In Seattle, Stephen, a black male, is coded as gay throughout most of the season, and yet he is staunchly homophobic. Midway through the season, a white liberal roommate, Irene, has to leave the show because of a relapse of her Lyme disease. Although she had joked with Stephen throughout the season that they should get married, on her way out, Irene tells Stephen that a marriage between them would never work because he is a homosexual. Stephen, enraged, fakes masturbating to prove Irene wrong and then hits her in the face. Here Stephen's body is discursively positioned as sexually out of control. He has desires for men, himself, and women.

The editing of both scenes, those with David and Stephen, emphasizes how violent black sexuality can be. The editors constantly return to these events in flashbacks, often excluding the events that lead up to the violent act and just focusing on how violent these black characters are.

But if these incidents mediate race through urbanity and a historical trajectory of stereotypes, other seasons use editing to erase history and historical trauma as a source of racism. Take an episode from season 11, set in Chicago. After season 4, the show had its cast work together on a specific job throughout the season. In Chicago, midway through the season, the cast had to script and then perform a Halloween play for the Chicago City Parks District.

Keri, a white female, suggests a play where a woman becomes pregnant out of wedlock and kills the father. A jury sentences the woman to death by hanging but postpones her execution until she gives birth to her child. At that point, Theo, an African American on the show, requests that the play not involve a hanging because many of his ancestors were lynched. While Theo is willing to perform the play as long as they change the style of execution, all the white roommates who discuss the issue insist that his pleas are petty and that Keri in no way intended the story to be racist. After splicing together interview clips of Theo talking about the historical trauma of hanging and white roommates insisting Keri's story in no way relates to the history of slavery, the episode ends with an interview of Kyle, a white liberal, who frames the conflict not as a battle to define American racism but as the possible outcome of conflict on the job.

As such, *The Real World* never interrogates the inferential racism of white liberal characters on the show. Kyle's cloaking of the racism present in this scene through discourses of work goes unchecked. In fact, by giving Kyle the last word on the fight, the episode punctuates the conflict through Kyle's perspective. In this way, the rural conservatives on *The Real World* are not the only house members to expresses nonracist racism. It is just that the editing and narrative structure on the show both fixate on the rural conservatives as the source of these social ills and ignore how the liberal house members are implicated in them as well. In fact, dwelling on the racisms of the rural conservatives deflects the show's own racism.

No doubt, part of the reason why the show has remained so popular for so long on the channel is that it encourages the audience to position themselves as liberals against racism without reflecting on how this strategy for viewing race perpetuates racism itself. While it is certainly noble that MTV's audience usually does not participate in, and is in fact appalled by, explicit racism, they have certainly found rather blunt and misguided tools for combating racial oppression on *The Real World.*

Conclusion

Many of the production strategies for mediating reality that I've discussed in relationship to *The Real World* also take place on other reality TV shows. *Survivor* and *The Amazing Race* hold extensive casting calls and pointedly choose specific types of people to represent reality on their shows, and they structure interpersonal conflicts and friendships through serial narratives. Shows like these, as well as reality dating shows like *Dismissed* and *Elimidate,* edit in such a way that characters comment on the actions of other characters. And with any reality TV show, too much happens during the filming process to capture everything that every character does. Directors have to decide to film some actions and not others. What I've tried to argue is not so much that these production practices on *The Real World* are unique but that they have played a specific role in the way the show mediates race, racism, and liberal identity for a particular cable channel.

A few years ago, Ellis-Bunim and Murray's production company came to Indiana University, Bloomington, where I taught, and held an open casting call for the 13th season of *The Real World,* set in Paris. Before class one day, I was talking with my students about this open call and asked if anyone planned to audition. One student, a huge fan of MTV, admitted wanting to try out but not knowing what to say. Another student quickly chimed in with, "Just say you're a racist from a small town in Indiana and you want to expand your mind. They'll pick you." To which the student responded, "But I'm not a racist. I don't have a racist bone in my body." And the other student said, "That's okay. By the end of the show they'll portray you as a nonracist. They always do."

This incident speaks to the complex cultural operations and mediations of race on MTV. The show airs on a self-purported liberal cable channel.

My one student was an astute observer of how the me
MTV starts during the casting process, where the show
try to look for a rural American to represent racism and
racism from this person through the serial narrative. A
black and white, laughed at the comment, perhaps beca
us feel like we're not implicated in the perpetuation of
my one student thought.

Racism in this liberal cable environment discursively exists only
through rural conservatives. It's no surprise that in other classroom discussions about race, both formal and informal, students often feel more
uncomfortable and less willing to laugh. Understanding racism as systemic, subconscious, and inferential is less fun, yet ultimately necessary.
Perhaps to lead to a more critical understanding and mediation of race
and racism in the United States, MTV should make us feel a little less
comfortable.

NOTES

I thank Susan Murray and Laurie Ouellette for their insightful revision sugges-
tions. I have received feedback on many of the ideas in this article in a C190:
Introduction to Media class that I taught during the spring 2002 semester at Indiana University. I am especially grateful to Liz, Carrie, Tory, Claire, Martha, Jen,
Bria, Courtney, Christine, Kathryn, and Ali for their comments. Finally, to my
wife, Sue, who commented on this article and watched more episodes of *The Real
World* than she probably would have liked, I owe special thanks.

1. Seasons now usually film for five or six months and can also take place in a
house or, in the case of the Las Vegas season, a hotel suite. Current seasons cast
people between the ages of 18 and 24.

2. John Fiske, *Media Matters: Race and Gender in U.S. Politics* (New York:
Routledge, 1992), 2.

3. Sut Jhally and Justin Lewis, *Enlightened Racism: The Cosby Show, Audiences,
and the Myth of the American Dream* (Boulder, Colo.: Westview, 1992), 97.

4. Ibid.

5. Andrew Goodwin, "Fatal Distractions: MTV Meets Postmodern Theory," in
Sound and Vision: The Music Video Reader, ed Simon Frith, Andrew Goodwin,
and Lawrence Grossberg (New York: Routledge, 1992), 62–63.

6. Ibid., 53.

7. Richard Dyer, *White* (New York: Routledge, 1997), 44.

8. Ibid., 45–46.

9. Ibid., 51–53.

10. Ibid., 57.

11. Quoted in Alison Pollet, *The Real World: Chicago* (New York: Pocket Books, 2002), 1–2.

12. Ibid., 2.

13. Stuart Hall, "The Whites of Their Eyes: Racist Ideologies and the Media," in *The Media Reader,* ed. Manual Alvarado and John Thompson (London: British Film Institute, 1990), 8–23.

14. Fiske, *Media Matters,* 37–39.

15. Ibid., 38.

16. Jeremy Butler, *Television: Critical Methods and Applications* (Belmont, Calif.: Wadsworth, 1994), 30–33. Butler also discusses the narrative structure of a series, whose episodes are self-contained narratives. For a more detailed discussion on the difference between a series and a serial, see ibid., 25–33.

17. Donald Bogle, *Toms, Coons, Mulattos, Mammies, and Bucks: An Interpretive History of Blacks in American Films,* exp. ed. (New York: Continuum, 1989), 10.

18. Robyn Weigman, *American Anatomies: Theorizing Race and Gender.* (Durham, N.C.: Duke University Press, 1995), 90–95.

19. Ibid., 107.

"Take Responsibility for Yourself"
Judge Judy *and the Neoliberal Citizen*

Laurie Ouellette

A woman drags her ex-boyfriend to court over an overdue adult movie rental and an unpaid loan. A woman is heartbroken when her best friend betrays her and ruins her credit. A smooth-talking ex-boyfriend claims money from his ex was a gift. Welcome to *Judge Judy,* queen of the courtroom program, where judges resolve "real-life" disputes between friends, family members, neighbors, and former lovers on national television.

For critics who equate television's role in democracy with serious news and public affairs, altercations over broken engagements, minor fender benders, carpet stains, unpaid personal loans, and the fate of jointly purchased household appliances may seem like crass entertainment or trivial distractions. But such dismissals overlook the "governmental" nature of courtroom programs like *Judge Judy,* which gained cultural presence—and a reputation for "zero tolerance when it comes to nonsense"—alongside the neoliberal policies and discourses of the 1990s.[1]

Judge Judy took the small claims–based court format from the fringes of commercial syndication to an authoritative place on daytime schedules when it debuted in 1996, the same year the U.S. Telecommunications Act was passed. While the legislation has been critiqued for its deregulatory ethos and affinity with the broader neoliberal forces behind welfare reform and the privatization of public institutions from the penal system to the post office, the cultural dimensions of these parallels remain less examined.[2]

There is a tendency within policy studies to take the cultural impact of neoliberalism as self-evident—to presume that the laissez-faire principals codified by the act will erode democracy in predictable ways that typically involve the decline of journalism, documentaries, and other "substantial" information formats found unprofitable by the culture industry. While such concerns have some validity, the metaphor of subversion needs to be jettisoned, for it reifies untenable cultural hierarchies and neglects neoliberalism's productive imprint on contemporary television culture and the "idealized" citizen subjectivities that it circulates.

Reality programming is one site where neoliberal approaches to citizenship have in fact materialized on television. From makeover programs (*What Not to Wear, Trading Spaces*) that enlist friends, neighbors, and experts in their quest to teach people how to make "better" fashion and decorating choices, to gamedocs (*Survivor, Big Brother*) that construct community relations in terms of individual competition and self-enterprising—in all of these, neoliberal constructions of "good citizenship" have cut across much popular reality television. The courtroom program is a particularly clear example of this broader trend because it draws from the symbolic authority of the state to promote both the outsourcing of its governmental functions and the subjective requirements of the transition to a neoliberal society. *Judge Judy* and programs like it do not subvert elusive democratic ideals, then, as much as they *construct* templates for citizenship that complement the privatization of public life, the collapse of the welfare state, and, most important, the discourse of individual choice and personal responsibility.

In this chapter, I situate *Judge Judy* as a neoliberal technology of everyday citizenship and illustrate how the show attempts to shape and guide the conduct and choices of lower-income women in particular. *Judge Judy* draws from and diffuses neoliberal currents by fusing an image of democracy (signified in the opening credits by a gently flapping U.S. flag, a stately public courthouse, and a gavel-wielding judge) with a privatized approach to conflict management and an intensified government of the self.

Judge Judy and programs like it supplant institutions of the state (social work, law and order, welfare offices) and, using real people caught in the drama of ordinary life as raw material, train TV viewers to function without state assistance or supervision, as self-disciplining, self-sufficient, responsible, and risk-averting individuals. In this way, the courtroom subgenre of reality television exemplifies what James Hay has called a cultural apparatus for "neoliberal forms of governance."[3]

Neoliberalism and Television Culture

To understand *Judge Judy*'s neoliberal alignments, a brief detour through the concept of neoliberalism is in order. My understanding of neoliberalism begins with political economy and the activism it inspires. From this vantage point, neoliberalism is generally understood as a troubling worldview that promotes the "free" market as the best way to organize every dimension of social life.

According to activists Elizabeth Martinez and Arnaldo Garcia, this worldview has generated specific trends that have accelerated globally since the 1980s: (1) the "rule" of the market, (2) spending cuts on public services, (3) deregulation (including the deregulation of broadcasting), (4) the privatization of state-owned institutions "usually in the name of efficiency," and (5) "eliminating the concept of the public good or community and replacing it with individual responsibility."[4] For critics like Robert McChesney, the upshot of neoliberalism and the reforms it has spawned is that a "handful of private interests are permitted to control as much as possible of social life in order to maximize their personal profit."[5]

While I share these concerns, I have found Foucaultian approaches particularly useful for analyzing the subjective dimensions of neoliberalism that circulate on reality television. Drawing from Michel Foucault, Nikolas Rose theorizes neoliberalism less as a simple opposition between the market (bad) and the welfare state (good) and more as a "changing network" of complex power relations. If neoliberal regimes have implemented an "array of measures" aimed at downsizing the welfare state and dismantling the "institutions within which welfare government had isolated and managed their social problems," they still rely on "strategies of government."[6]

This manifests as various forms of "cultural training" that governs indirectly in the name of "lifestyle maximization," "free choice," and personal responsibility, says Rose. This diffused approach to the "regulation of conduct" escapes association with a clear or top-down agenda and is, instead, presented as the individual's "own desire" to achieve optimum happiness and success.[7] As Rose points out, the "enterprising" individual crafted by this discourse has much in common with the choice-making "customer" valorized by neoliberal economics. Both presume "free will," which means that those individuals who fail to thrive under neoliberal conditions can be readily cast as the "author of their own misfortunes."[8]

Rose makes several observations that can help make sense of neoliberalism's cultural manifestations. First, he contends that the ideal of citizens working together to fulfill mutual and "national obligations" has given way to the "ideal of citizens seeking to fulfil and protect themselves within a variety of micro-moral domains." Second, he observes that the requirements of "good" citizenship have come to include "adopting a prudent relationship to fate," which includes avoiding "calculable dangers and avertable risks." Finally, Rose cites the media as a technology that, operating outside "public powers," works to govern the "capacities, competencies and wills of subjects," and in so doing, translate the "goals of authorities into choices and commitments of individuals."[9]

James Hay has extended this argument to television studies specifically. Because a "neoliberal form of governance assumes that social subjects are not and should not be subject to direct forms of state control, it therefore relies on mechanisms for governing at a distance," through the guiding and shaping of "self-disciplining subjects," Hay explains. Television plays an important role in this governmental process, he contends, one that is not limited to sanctioned forms of news and public affairs. In fact, popular reality television may be better suited to the indirect, diffuse mode of cultural governmentality that Hay describes. The court program is an acute and therefore symptomatic example of popular reality television's role in mediating "a kind of state control that values self-sufficiency and a kind of personal freedom that requires self-discipline."[10]

While Hay theorizes television's role in bringing neoliberal techniques of "governmentality" into the home, feminist scholars have shown the extent to which neoliberal policies intersect with an acceleration of self-help discourse aimed at women. From advice books on intimate relationships to self-esteem-building initiatives for welfare mothers, this discourse has been critiqued for presuming to "solve social problems from crime and poverty to gender inequality by waging a social revolution, not against capitalism, racism and inequality, but against the order of the self and the way we govern the self."[11]

As Barbara Cruikshank has pointed out, the solution to women's problems is construed as having the right attitude, making smart decisions, and taking responsibility for one's life in the name of personal "empowerment."[12] In this sense, self-help is a cultural manifestation of neoliberalism, a technology of citizenship that encourages women to "evaluate and act" on themselves so that the social workers, the medical establishment and the police "do not have to."[13]

Judge Judy fuses television, neoliberalism, and self-help discourse in a governmental address to women living out what feminist philosopher Nancy Fraser has called the "postsocialist" condition.[14] The program presents the privatized space of the simulated TV courtroom as the most "efficient" way to resolve microdisputes steeped in the unacknowledged politics of gender, class, and race, but it also classifies those individuals who "waste the court's time" as risky deviants and self-made victims who create their own misfortunes by making the "wrong" choices and failing to manage their lives properly. The imagined TV viewer is the implied beneficiary of this parade of mistakes, for her classification as "normal" hinges on recognizing the pathos of "others" and internalizing the rules of self-government spelled out on the program.

For precisely this reason, the courtroom program has been institutionally positioned as a moral and educational corrective to "permissive" entertainment, suggesting that the discourse of the "public interest" in broadcasting has not been squashed but reconfigured by neoliberal reforms. Indeed, it could be that television is increasingly pivotal to neoliberal approaches to government and the citizen subjectivities on which they depend.

"The Cases Are Real, the Rulings Are Final"

Judge Judy is not the first TV program to resolve everyday conflicts within simulated courtroom settings. The genre can be traced to 1950s programs like *People in Conflict* and *The Verdict Is Yours*. In the 1980s, retired California Superior Court Judge Joseph Wapner presided over *The People's Court*,[15] while *Divorce Court* used actors to dramatize "authentic" legal proceedings.

Judge Judy did rework and revitalize the format, however, and the program's aggressive, "no-nonsense" approach to family and small-claims disputes generated immediate notoriety and scores of imitators (examples include *Judge Joe Brown, Judge Mathis, Judge Hatchet, Curtis Court,* a revitalized *People's Court,* and *Moral Court*). Well into the new millennium, courtroom programs abound on television, competing with talk shows, game shows, and soap operas for a predominantly female audience.

On *Judge Judy,* real-life litigants culled from small-claims court dockets across the United States are paid airfare, hotel, and court fees to present their cases on television. The price is to drop out of the judicial process and submit to the private ruling of Judith (Judy) Sheindlin. A former New York family court judge, Sheindlin was recruited for the "tough love" philosophy she spelled out in an influential *60 Minutes* profile and later in her bestselling book, *Don't Pee on My Leg and Tell Me It's Raining*, which faulted the overcrowded court system as a lenient bureaucracy that reflects "how far we have strayed from personal responsibility and old-fashioned discipline."[16]

Spotting ratings potential, Larry Lyttle, president of Big Ticket Television, a Viacom company, invited Sheindlin to preside over "real cases with real consequences in a courtroom on television." Called a "swift decision maker with no tolerance for excuses" by publicity, Sheindlin claims to bring to her TV show the same message she advocated in the courts: "Take responsibility for yourself, your actions and the children you've brought into the world."[17] In interviews, she situates *Judge Judy* as a public service that can solve societal problems by instilling the right attitudes and choices in individuals:

> It's a much larger audience. Whatever message I spew—"Take responsibility for your life. If you're a victim, it's your fault. Stop being a victim. Get a grip! You're the one who's supposed to make a direction in your life." All those messages I tried in Family Court to instill in people—primarily women. [The TV show] sounded like something that would not only be fun, but worthwhile as well.[18]

Like other TV judges, Sheindlin now hears noncriminal cases that rarely involve more than several hundred dollars or the equivalent in personal property. The program's governmental logic transforms these conflicts into a recurring narrative that emphasizes individual shortcomings over societal complexities and inequalities. Sheindlin's courtroom is always filled with feuding neighbors, lovers, and relations and is virtually devoid of people wishing to sue businesses, bosses, or, least of all, big corporations.

This focus makes perfect sense, for the program's impetus as a technology of citizenship is to scrutinize people who require state mediation of everyday affairs, a process that relies more on the moral radar Sheindlin claims to have developed in the public courts than on time-consuming democratic processes ("I don't have time for beginnings," she has been known to snap). While TV viewers at home are situated outside Sheindlin's disciplinary address to litigants derided as losers, cheaters, liars, and "gumbos," their status as "good" citizens presumes complicity with the advice dispensed to faulty individuals.

While the opening credits promise "real people" and "real cases," a male narrator differentiates the program from an actual courtroom by explaining that "this is Judy's courtroom" where the "decisions are final." On screen, Sheindlin plays judge, prosecutor, stern guidance counselor, and moral authority. In each 30-minute episode, she hears two cases, decides what is and is not worthy evidence ("I don't read documents," she has told litigants), and dispenses justice at "lightening speed," according to publicity. Participants must abide by the program's rules, which include speaking only when spoken to, accepting the authority of the judge ("Just pay attention, I run the show," she tells litigants), and tolerating punitive but punchy one-liners ("Are you all nuts?" and "I'm smarter than you" are typical examples).

More important than the details of any pending case is Sheindlin's swift assessment of the choices and behaviors of the people involved in them. According to Foucault, the delinquent is characterized not so much by his or her "acts" as by his or her life biography,[19] and Sheindlin routinely grills the litigants about their employment history, marital and parental status, income, drug habits, sexual practices, incarceration record, and past or present "dependency" on public welfare. Such information transcends formal evidence as the principal means whereby Sheindlin determines who is at fault in the citizenship lesson that accompanies every ruling.

In addition to this biographical scrutiny, Sheindlin mocks the accents of non-English speakers, scorns the uneducated and low-paid, accuses litigants of lying and abusing the "system," and frequently orders them to spit out gum, stand up straight, and "control" bodily functions to her liking. In one much-publicized episode, a litigant who denied her accusations of smoking pot was ordered to take a live, on-screen drug test. In these ways, *Judge Judy* mirrors and extends the surveillance of the poor and the working class carried out by welfare offices, unemployment centers, and other social services.[20]

Judge Judy is part of the current wave of reality television in that real people (not actors) involved in "authentic" disagreements are used as a selling point. While scripts are not used, reality is, as John Fiske reminds us, "encoded" at every level.[21] The program uses stringers to scour small-claims courts for "interesting" cases; potential litigants must complete a questionnaire, and only those cases that suit the program's producers are selected for presentation on television. Off-screen narration, titles, video

While *Judge Judy* condemns "dependency" on the state, its attempt to govern women indirectly is legitimated by the iconography of the formal courtroom.

replays, and teasers frame the meaning of the cases by labeling the litigants, characterizing their "real" motivations, and highlighting scenes that reiterate Sheindlin's punitive remarks and authority.

Due to increased competition for conflicts among the growing cadre of courtroom programs, viewers are now invited by bypass the courts and submit their everyday disputes directly to *Judge Judy*. On-air solicitations like "Are You in a Family Dispute? Call Judy" promise an efficient private alternative to state mediation of conflicts—and yet, those individuals who accept the invitations are ultimately held responsible for their "mistakes" on cases with names like "The Making of a Family Tragedy."

Judge Judy's focus on everyday domestic conflicts has led some critics to denounce it as a new twist on the sensational "low-brow" daytime talk show.[22] Yet Sheindlin insists that her program is a somber alternative to the participatory, carnivalesque atmosphere of the genre it now rivals in the ratings. Indeed, the courtroom setting and overtly disciplinary address of the *Judge Judy* program "code" it in distinct ways that are easily distinguishable by TV viewers. Sheindlin's strict demeanor and authoritative place on the bench are accentuated by camerawork that magnifies her power by filming her from below. The mandated silence of the studio audience; the drab, institutional-like setting of the simulated courtroom; and the constant presence of a uniformed bailiff also separate the court program from talk shows, a format that feminist scholars have characterized as a tentative space for oppressed groups (women, people of color, and the working classes) to discuss the politics of everyday life.

Jane Shattuc, for example, sees talk shows as an offshoot of the social movements of the 1960s to the extent that they draw from (but also commercially exploit) identity politics, consciousness-raising techniques, and an awareness that the "personal is political."[23] For Sonia Livingstone and Peter Lunt, talk shows offer a counterpoint to the white, male, bourgeois-dominated sphere of "serious" news and public affairs by providing a popular forum that enables women in particular to participate, however haltingly, in democratic processes.[24] Of course, talk shows also operate with their own disciplinary dynamics, as Janice Peck has shown. Relying on psychosocial experts (health workers, therapists, and self-help gurus), talk shows present a "televised talking cure" that "manages conflict and crisis" by folding women's personal stories into "confessional" discourse and "therapeutic" narratives, she contends.[25]

As Mimi White has observed in her analysis of *Divorce Court*, court programs reconfigure the confessional and therapeutic orientation of the talk show in subtle but important ways: "To the extent that the couple no longer confesses with ease, the injunction to confess must be enforced through the agencies of the . . . legal establishment."[26] On *Judge Judy*, the authority represented by the simulated courtroom setting is often enlisted to "force" such confessions. Sheindlin claims that her past experience as a frustrated state official has enabled her to "see through the bull" ("She can always tell if you're lying. All she has to do is make eye contact," reported *USA Today*).[27] Litigants who refuse to "confess" to suspected actions have been subjected to live background checks, but more often than not, Sheindlin simply discounts "false" confessions and replaces the version of events offered by the litigant with an expert interpretation gleaned through biographical information as much as "evidence."

Court programs also magnify the disciplinary logic present on the talk show by disallowing audience participation, controlling the flow of personal revelations, and fusing the therapeutic ethos of the "clinic" with the surveillance of the welfare office and the authoritative signifiers of law and order. This distinction, as much as the absence of the carnivalesque, is what has allowed courtroom programs to be institutionally positioned as a cultural corrective "tabloid" television. *Judge Judy* is the "antithesis of Jerry Springer," insists Sheindlin; "Jerry Springer encourages people to show off their filthiest laundry, to misbehave. I scrupulously avoid doing that. I cut them off."[28]

The television industry has also been quick to assert that courtroom television "educates" as well as entertains, a claim to "public service" that is rarely made of most popular reality formats. Big Ticket's Larry Lyttle contends that courtroom programs function as a positive moral force because, unlike on talk shows, where "conflicts are aired and tossed around," a court show like *Judge Judy* "ends with a decision that someone was right and someone was wrong," he explains.[29] WCHS-TV in Charlston, West Virginia, similarly praises the program's "unique ability to act as a true moral compass for people seeking guidance, insight and resolution."[30] Characterizing the courtroom genre as a technology of citizenship that can temper the "effects" of fictional television, one TV judge explained in an interview that

> America's been looking at soap operas for going on 50 some years, and they legitimize the most back-stabbing, low-down, slimeball behavior. That's gotten to be acceptable behavior. . . . We find ourselves confronted with a lot of soap-opera behavior in our courtrooms. And we resolve them and say, no, we know you may have seen this, but its not right.[31]

Privatizing Justice, Stigmatizing "Dependency"

Judge Judy's claim to facilitate "justice at lightening" speed boldly implies that commercial television can resolve problems faster and more efficiently than the public sector can. In this sense, the program affirms neoliberal rationales for "outsourcing" state-owned institutions and services. *Judge Judy* also complements neoliberal policies by conveying the impression that democracy (exemplified by the justice system) is overrun by individuals embroiled in petty conflicts and troubles of their own making.

If the program feeds off real-life microdisputes, Sheindlin chastises litigants for failing to govern their "selves" and their personal affairs. In addition to lecturing guests about their personal history, she often accuses participants of "wasting the court's time," conveying the idea that "normal" citizens do not depend on the supervision of the judiciary—or any public institution, for that matter. People who rely on professional judges (including TV judges) to mediate everyday problems are cast as inadequate individuals who lack the capacity or, worse, the desire to function as self-reliant and personally responsible citizens.

On *Judge Judy*, citizenship lessons are often directed at people who reject marriage, the nuclear family, and traditional values; unmarried couples who live together are of particular concern. While Sheindlin (who is divorced) does not condemn such behavior as moral disconduct, she does present rules and procedures for navigating modern relationships, which include getting personal loans in writing, not "living together for more than one year without a wedding band," and not "purchasing homes, cars, boats or animals with romantic partners outside of wedlock." Individuals are told that they must impose these rules on themselves—both for their own protection and because, as Sheindlin explains, there is "no court of people living together. It's up to you to be smart. Plan for the eventualities before you set up housekeeping."

When former lovers dispute an unpaid car loan, Sheindlin takes the dispute as an opportunity to explain the dos and don'ts of cohabitation without marriage. Sheindlin finds the couple incompatible and "irresponsible" and rules that it was an "error of judgment" for them to share an apartment together. This judgment is tied to a broader failure of appropriate citizenship when Sheindlin lectures the pair for then "asking the courts" to resolve a domestic property dispute. "You're not married—there is a different set of rules for people who choose to live together without marriage," she explains, reiterating that people who stray from state-sanctioned conventions have a particular duty to monitor their own affairs.[32]

If the idealized citizen subject constructed by *Judge Judy* complements the choice-making neoliberal discussed by Rose, she is also a self-supporting worker. People who receive any form of public assistance are cast as deviants in particular need of citizenship lessons. The advice they receive evokes Nancy Fraser and Linda Gordon's observation that welfare has become cloaked in a stigmatizing discourse of "dependency" that presumes gender, class, and racial parity. As Fraser and Gordon point out, women (including single mothers) are now held accountable to the white, middle class male work ethic, even as they lack the advantages and resources to perform as traditionally male breadwinners.[33]

While this marks a shift away from the patronizing assumption that all women are helpless and therefore "naturally" dependent on men or, in their absence, the state, it conceals the structural inequalities that lower-income women in particular continue to face. On *Judge Judy*, all women are presumed to be capable of supporting themselves and their children financially; accepting welfare is construed not as a reflection of gender or economic inequality but as a character flaw. Women are routinely asked to disclose their past or present reliance on government "handouts," and those who admit to receiving benefits are subsequently marked as irresponsible and lazy individuals who "choose" not to work for a living.

Welfare recipients are also constructed as morally unsound citizens who cheat taxpayers, as was the case in an episode where Sheindlin demanded to know whether an unmarried women with three children by the same father had "avoided" marriage merely to qualify for welfare benefits. In another episode, an unemployed 20-something mother being sued by her baby's would-be adoptive parents was scolded for relying on public assistance to raise the child she had decided not to give up for adoption. While adoption law doesn't allow adoptive parents to reclaim monetary "gifts" to birth mothers, Sheindlin stressed the woman's "moral" obligation to repay them. Presuming that the mother had chosen poverty, Sheindlin also sternly advised her to get a job and "not have more babies she can't take care of."

Judge Judy's disdain for welfare "dependency" extends to charity and other forms of assistance. If individuals are told to take care of themselves and their families, empathy and social responsibility for others are discouraged. "No good deed goes unpunished," Sheindlin advised a family friend who took in a homeless woman who had spent some time in jail. At the societal and community level, the "public good" is cast neoliberal terms, as a system of individual responsibilities and rewards.

According to Rose, neoliberal citizens are conceived as "private individuals" who seek to "maximize their quality of life through acts of choice while avoiding calculable dangers and advertable risks."[34] *Judge Judy* instills this template for citizenship by discouraging personal contact with deviant and "risky" individuals and by instructing women to make "smart" choices to avoid "victimization." The program functions as a "panoptic" device to the extent that it classifies and surveils individuals deemed unsavory and dangerous, a point that has also been made of reality-based crime shows like *Cops* and *America's Most Wanted*.[35]

Sheindlin contends that criminals are largely unreformable, and *Judge Judy* extends this philosophy to people who are not official criminals but are nonetheless judged to possess amoral tendencies, psychological imbalances, drug addictions, and other character flaws. The more pressing message, however, is that all citizens must take personal responsibility for protecting themselves from con artists, "manipulators," abusers, and other "risky" individuals. In this sense, one of the program's most important governmental roles is to instruct TV viewers how to detect and avoid the risks that certain individuals are shown to represent.

Since the litigants on *Judge Judy* are introduced by name and occupation—information also appears on screen titles—viewers know that individuals cast as risky are often working-class men who drive trucks, wait on tables, enter data, do construction, or perform low-paying forms of customer service. If female welfare recipients are cast as irresponsible nonworkers, men lacking middle-class occupations and salaries are routinely scorned for "choosing" a life of poverty, as was the case when Sheindlin lectured a middle-aged male WalMart cashier for failing to obtain more lucrative employment. In the adoption episode, a similar evaluation of male employment was tied to a failure of citizenship. The infant's father, who had worked on and off as a gas station attendant but was currently unemployed, was characterized as a personal failure and a societal menace, not just because he refused to admit "personal moral responsibility" to repay the money to the adoptive parents but because he "refused" to enterprise himself in accordance with the middle-class work ethic.

Cases involving men who manipulate women out of money, gifts, rent, or property are a staple on *Judge Judy*, and in these cases male unemployment and insolvency are closely tied to the detection and avoidance of romantic risk. In a case where a woman met a man on the Internet, loaned him money, and was dumped, Sheindlin fused a harsh judgement of the boyfriend's opportunism and dishonesty in his romantic relationship to an undeveloped work ethic. Demanding to know when he last "held a full-time job," she swiftly identified the man as a freeloader and a "con artist," implying that men without economic means are particularly dangerous and therefore not to be trusted when it comes to intimate relationships.

Female litigants can also be categorized as identifiable romantic risks, as was the case in "Opportunity Knocks," where Sheindlin accused an attractive young women in court to resolve whether money from her ex-boyfriend was a gift or a loan of "using" the man financially with "no intention of marrying him." In most cases, however, it is lower-income men who play this role in a gender reversal of the golddigger stereotype that complements the program's focus of solving the problem of female "victimization" through better self-management.

Women are typically cast as "self-created" victims in terms that articulate neoliberal currents to female self-help culture. Rejecting what she terms the "disease of victimization," or the tendency to blame society for one's hardships, Sheindlin claims, in her books and on her TV program, that all women can achieve happiness and success with a little knowledge and the right attitude. On *Judge Judy*, women's problems are blamed on their own failure to make good decisions, whether that means pulling oneself up from a life of poverty; "preparing" wisely for financial independence; or avoiding entanglements with unstable, manipulative, or abusive individuals. In her book *Beauty Fades, Dumb Is Forever*, Sheindlin elaborates on the value of "personal responsibility":

> Victims are self-made. They aren't born. They aren't created by circumstances. There are many, many poor, disadvantaged people who had terrible parents and suffered great hardships who do just fine. Some even rise to the level of greatness. You are responsible for nurturing your roots, for blooming. No one can take that away from you. If you decide to be a victim, the destruction of your life will be by your own hand.[36]

In some cases, female "victims" are lectured for allowing themselves to be mistreated by other women. In "The Kool-Aid Debacle," where a young waitress sued her female ex-roommate over Kool-Aid stains on the carpet and a couch that got smelly, Sheindlin scolded the plaintiff for getting herself into such a situation: "*You* make a mistake when you let someone into your house who is a slob," she explained [emphasis mine]. Other times, women are deemed responsible for making their own misfortunes.

In a case involving former lovers at odds over an unpaid loan, the program's neoliberal dismissal of female "victimization" is spelled out. The woman claims that her ex-boyfriend helped cover her hospital bill when she miscarried their baby. The man claims that she promised to pay him back. As is typical, Sheindlin focuses less on the details of the loan than on the moral and behavioral lessons she discerns from the case. She lectures the young woman (but not the man) for not using birth control and attributes her "situation" to her own unwise and irresponsible conduct.

Refusing to accept this ruling, the young woman insists that the ex-boyfriend should help pay for the cost of the miscarriage, since she was uninsured and it "was his baby too." Defying Sheindlin's orders to speak only when addressed, she demands to know what *she* as a woman would do in such circumstances. Rejecting the female litigant's appeal to a sense of female solidarity of the question—and ignoring the broader question of health care access raised by the episode—Sheindlin tells the litigant that she wouldn't be in her shoes because "she's smarter than that."

Women who claim to have been abused by men appear frequently on *Judge Judy,* where they, too, are lectured for creating their circumstances. Domestic abuse is never the basis of a legal case but is typically revealed in the course of Sheindlin's interrogation of the participants involved. In a case involving cousins fighting over a family collection of knickknacks, Sheindlin determines that the man is a deranged and unstable individual, while the woman he bullied and harassed is an "adult" who has "chosen to let someone do this to her." When Sheindlin learns that an ex-boyfriend in court over a minor car accident has battered his former teenage girl-friend, she contends that the girl made unwise "choices" and sternly advises, "Never let a man put his hands on you." In a case involving former lovers disputing overdue phone and gas bills, the woman reveals that in refusing to pay household expenses, her former boyfriend was addicted to heroin and had spent time in jail for assaulting a minor; she also implies that he physically abused her. Typifying the program's neoliberal solution of the problem of domestic violence and the complexities of gender and class, Sheindlin faults the woman for failing to accept responsibility for her own conduct. Taking the troubled relationship as the raw material for a citizenship lesson aimed at women, she determines that "being with him doesn't speak well of your judgment." As "young as you are, you allowed someone with a criminal history and no job to live with you . . . and you want the courts to fix that?"

Judge Judy seeks to instill in women a desire to avoid the "disease" of victimization and the overreliance on state assistance and intervention it is said to have spawned. This message carries traces of liberal feminist discourse to the extent that it promotes female independence and agency. Presuming that barriers to social and gender equality have long been dismantled, the program places the onus to achieve these goals on individuals. Sheindlin, who considers herself a positive female role model, contends that all "women have the power to make decisions, to call it as they see it, to take no guff."[37] She claims that all women, however positioned by an unequal capitalist society, can reap the benefits of happiness and success as long as they exercise good judgment and cultivate self-esteem.

Economic security and "feeling good about yourself" are therefore closely bound in Sheindlin's blueprint for successful female citizenship. The responsibility for cultivating self-esteem is placed not on society but on individual women, whose job it is to train themselves and their daughters "to have a profession, have a career . . . so they will never be dependent on anybody."[38] On *Judge Judy,* female litigants are advised to avoid "depending" on boyfriends and husbands for financial assistance in particular. This message has less to do with dismantling dominant ideologies and institutions and more with ensuring that women "take care of themselves" so that the state doesn't have to. Judge Judy conveys the idea that women can no longer "claim" a victim status rooted in bifurcated and hierarchical gender roles; nor, however, can they expect public solutions to the inequalities that structure women's lives.

Sheindlin presents "independence" as a responsibility that all women must strive to achieve, but she also promotes the hegemony of the nuclear family, reconstituted as a two-wage-earning unit. Family troubles underscore many of cases heard on *Judge Judy*, where mothers suing daughters, children suing their parents, and parents suing each other are the norm. This steady stream of feuding relations paints a portrait of a troubled institution that clearly isn't working, yet Sheindlin uses her authority to promote the sacred importance of family bonds. The contradiction exists in perpetual tension, as illuminated by the treatment of family in two important episodes.

In the first, a male cashier is suing his unemployed ex-fiancée for bills paid when they lived together; she is countersuing for "mental distress." Sheindlin interrogated the woman about why she wasn't working, to which the woman replies that she quit her job to "build a home together." She also tells Sheindlin that her fiancé stalked her and threatened to come after her with a gun when they broke up. Although this scenario contains the material to cast the male as a deviant individual, Sheindlin rejects the women's story as an "excuse" smacking of victimization. Contrasting her own success as a married working woman who didn't "quit her job to pick out furniture and dishes" to the failure of the "alleged victim of harassment," she ordered the woman to pay the back rent. In this episode, the female litigant's embrace of traditional family values was denounced because it included the desire for "dependency" on a male breadwinner and therefore violated the neoliberal mantra of self-sufficiency that *Judge Judy* espouses.

In a dispute involving an estranged mother and daughter, however, the nuclear family was valorized against a woman's quest for independence. The mother, who divorced her husband when she came out as a lesbian, was implicitly cast as selfish and irresponsible for abandoning the heterosexual family unit to pursue her own personal fulfillment. While Sheindlin doesn't condemn the woman's homosexuality, she harshly criticizes her performance and "choices" as a mother and recommends family counseling to repair the damage. As these examples attest, *Judge Judy*'s advice to women does not seek to expand women's choices; it merely guides them in particular directions. Operating as a technology of citizenship, the program steers women toward neoliberal reforms that are presented as their own responsibilities and "best interests." In this sense, *Judge Judy* seeks to transform what Rose calls the "goals of authorities" into the "choices and commitments of individuals."[39]

Judge Judy *and the Normative Citizen*

Judge Judy constitutes the normative citizen—the TV viewer at home—in opposition to both risky deviants and "self-made" victims. By scrutinizing the dos and don'ts of everyday life as it is presumed to be lived by "troubled" populations, it promotes neoliberal policies for conducting oneself in private. It scapegoats the uneducated and unprivileged as "others" who manufacture their hardships and require nothing more than personal responsibility and self-discipline in the wake of shrinking public services. Those who reject this logic are deemed abnormal and, often, unreformable: "I'm not going to get through to her. I have a sense that she's a lost cause at 14," Sheindlin once said of a female litigant.[40]

TV viewers are encouraged to distance themselves from the "deficient" individuals who seep into Sheindlin's courtroom, therefore avoiding any recognition of the societal basis of women's problems and concerns. While Sheindlin's harshest derision is aimed at the socially "unrespectable," her governmental advice is intended for all women—particularly middle-class viewers—for, according to the program's neoliberal logic, their happiness and success hinge on it.

It is untenable to presume that viewers respond to *Judge Judy* in seamless or uniform ways. The program can be read as an authoritarian spectacle that unravels what Foucault has called the ideology of bourgeois justice. The running parody of Judge Judy on *Saturday Night Live,* where Sheindlin is portrayed as an exaggerated version of her insulting, authoritarian television persona, suggests that *Judge Judy* may partly dislodge an image of the courts as inherently objective and fair.[41] Women on the wrong end of unequal class and gender relations may also see in *Judge Judy* a glaring example of class prejudice and professional gumption. However, these possibilities do not prevent the program from exemplifying a neoliberal form of governing that, in various dimensions and forms, cuts across the newest wave of reality television.

We can see variations of the neoliberal currents examined here in makeover programs, gamedocs, and other reality formats that "govern at a distance" by instilling the importance of self-discipline, the rewards of self-enterprising actions, and the personal consequences of making the "wrong" choice. *Judge Judy* represents one of the clearest examples of this trend because it articulates neoliberal templates for citizenship to the privatization of public life while self-consciously bringing what Foucault called "the minute disciplines" and "panopticisms of the everyday" into the home.[42]

The citizen subjectivities constructed on *Judge Judy* complement a model of government that disdains state authority and intervention but demands a heightened form of personal responsibility and self-discipline from individuals. Reality television as exemplified by the courtroom program is not outside democracy, then, but is an active agent in its neoliberal transformation.

NOTES

1. Melanie McFarland, "Tough Judges Show There's Justice in Watching Television, *Seattle Times,* 30 November 1998, at http://archives.seattletimes. The popular press has emphasized the "no tolerance" ethos of the programs, contributing to the cultural context in which they are received.

2. For critical analysis of the Telecommunications Act of 1996, see Patricia Aufderheide, *Communications Policy and the Public Interest* (New York: Guilford, 1999); and Robert McChesney, *Rich Media, Poor Democracy: Communication Politics in Dubious Times* (New York: New Press, 2000).

3. James Hay, "Unaided Virtues: The (Neo)-Liberalization of the Domestic Sphere," *Television and New Media* 1.1 (2000), 56.

4. Elizabeth Martinez and Arnoldo Garcia, "What Is Neoliberalism?" *Corpwatch,* 1 January 1997, at www.corpwatch.org.

5. Robert McChesney, introduction to Noam Chomsky, *Profit over People: Neoliberalism and Global Order* (New York: Seven Stories Press, 1999), 7, 11.

6. Nikolas Rose, "Governing 'Advanced' Liberal Democracies," in *Foucault and Political Reason: Liberalism, Neoliberalism and Rationalities of Government,* ed. Andrew Barry, Thomas Osborne, and Nikolas Rose (Chicago: University of Chicago Press, 1996), 55, 58–59. For a Foucaultian approach to "governmentality," see Graham Bruchell, Colon Gordon, and Peter Miller, eds., *The Foucault Effect: Studies in Governmentality* (Chicago: University of Chicago Press, 1991). I have also found Toby Miller's analysis of citizenship and subjectivity helpful for thinking through neoliberal modes of government. See his *The Well-Tempered Self:*

Citizenship, Culture, and the Postmodern Subject (Baltimore: Johns Hopkins University Press, 1993).

7. Rose, "Governing 'Advanced' Liberal Democracies," 57–59.

8. Ibid., 57, 59.

9. Ibid., 57, 58.

10. Hay, "Unaided Virtues," 54.

11. Barbara Cruikshank, "Revolutions Within: Self-Government and Self-Esteem," in *Foucault and Political Reason: Liberalism, Neoliberalism and Rationalities of Government*, ed. Andrew Barry, Thomas Osborne, and Nikolas Rose (Chicago: University of Chicago Press, 1996), 231.

12. In addition to Cruikshank, "Revolutions Within," see Heidi Marie Rimke, "Governing Citizens through Self-Help Literature," *Cultural Studies* 14.1 (2000), 61–78.

13. Cruikshank, "Revolutions Within," 234.

14. Nancy Fraser, *Justice Interruptus: Critical Reflections on the "Postsocialist" Condition* (New York: Routledge, 1997).

15. Judge Wapner was brought back to resolve disputes between pet owners on the Animal Channel's *Animal Court*.

16. Luaine Lee, "Judge Judy Has Always Believed in the Motto 'Just Do It,'" *Nando Media*, 28 November 1998, www.nandotimes.com; and Judy Sheindlin, *Don't Pee on My Leg and Tell Me It's Raining* (New York: HarperPerrennial, 1997), 3.

17. Quoted at www.judgejudy.com.

18. Quoted in Lee, "Judge Judy Has Always Believed in the Motto 'Just Do It.'"

19. Michel Foucault, "Complete and Austere Institutions," in *The Foucault Reader*, ed. Paul Rabinowitz (New York: Pantheon, 1984), 219–20. See also Michel Foucault, *Discipline and Punish* (New York: Random House, 1995).

20. Frances Fox Piven, *Regulating the Poor: The Functions of Public Welfare* (New York: Random House, 1971); and John Gillion, *Overseers of the Poor* (Chicago: University of Chicago Press, 2001).

21. John Fiske, *Television Culture* (New York: Routledge, 1987).

22. Michael M. Epstein, for example, argues that courtroom programs are an extension of the talk show to the extent that they use law and order to legitimate a sensationalist focus on personal conflict. Epstein also points out that the judge figure is construed as an "ultimate" moral authority less concerned with legal procedures than with the evaluation of personal behaviors. Presuming the "low" status of the genre and concentrating on its misrepresentation of the actual law, however, his critique overlooks the governmental nature and implications of this focus on everyday conduct and behavior. Michael M. Epstein, "Judging Judy, Mablean, and Mills: How Courtroom Programs Use Law to Parade Private Lives to Mass Audiences," *Television Quarterly* (2001), at http://www.emmyonline.org/tvq/articles/310101.asp.

23. Jane Shattuc, *The Talking Cure: TV Talk Shows and Women* (New York: Routledge, 1997).

24. Sonia Livingstone and Peter Lunt, *Talk on Television: Audience Participation and Public Debate* (London: Routledge, 1994).

25. Janice Peck, "Mediated Talking Cure: Therapeutic Framing of Autobiography in TV Talk Shows," in *Gender, Race and Class in Media,* ed. Gail Dines and Jean Humez (Thousand Oaks, Calif.: Sage, 2002), 538, 545.

26. Mimi White, *Tele-Advising: Therapeutic Discourse in American Television* (Chapel Hill: University of North Carolina Press, 1992), 69.

27. Elizabeth Snead, "Judge Judy Rules Courtroom TV," *USA Today,* 6 January 1998, 30.

28. Quoted in Barbara Lippert, "Punchin' Judy," *New York Magazine,* 15 June 2001, at www.newyorkmetro.com.

29. Quoted in *Judge Judy* publicity, at www.wchstv.com/synd_prog/judy.

30. Quoted at www.wchstv.com/synd_prog/judy.

31. Quoted in McFarland, "Tough Judges Show There's Justice."

32. Judy Sheindlin, *Keep It Simple Stupid* (New York: Cliff Street Books, 2000), 2.

33. Nancy Fraser and Linda Gordon, "A Geneaology of 'Dependency': Tracing a Keyword of the U.S. Welfare State," in Fraser's *Justice Interruptus: Critical Reflections on the "Postsocialist" Condition* (New York: Routledge, 1997).

34. Rose, "Governing 'Advanced' Liberal Democracies," 58.

35. Foucault defines panoptism as surveillence or "systems of marking and classifying." Michel Foucault, *Power/Knowledge: Selected Interviews,* ed. Colin Gordon (New York: Pantheon, 1977), 71. See also Elayne Rapping, "Aliens, Nomads, Mad Dogs, and Road Warriors: The Changing Face of Criminal Violence on TV," in *Reality TV: Remaking Television Culture,* 1st ed., ed. Susan Murray and Laurie Ouellette (New York: New York University Press, 2004), 214–30; and Anna Williams, "Domestic Violence and the Aetiology of Crime in *America's Most Wanted,*" *Camera Obscura* 31 (1995), 65–117.

36. Judy Sheindlin, *Beauty Fades, Dumb Is Forever* (New York: Cliff Street Books, 1999), 112–13.

37. Ibid., 105.

38. Sheindlin, quoted in Lee, "Judge Judy."

39. Rose, "Governing 'Advanced' Liberal Democracy," 58.

40. The clip was replayed during an interview with Sheindlin on *Larry King Live,* CNN, 12 September 2000.

41. Foucault, "On Popular Justice," in *Power/Knowledge,* 27.

42. Michel Foucault, "Panopticism," in *The Foucault Reader,* ed. Paul Rabinow (New York: Pantheon, 1984), 212.

12

IIIIIIIIIIIIIIIIIIIIIIIIIIIIIIIIIIIIIIIIIIIIIIIIIIII

Belabored Reality
Making It Work on The Simple Life *and* Project Runway

Heather Hendershot

> Abstention from labor is the conventional evidence of wealth and is therefore the conventional mark of social standing; and this insistence on the meritoriousness of wealth leads to a more strenuous insistence on leisure.
> —Thorstein Veblen, *The Theory of the Leisure Class*

In season 1 of *The Simple Life,* the apparently soulless Nicole Richie and Paris Hilton spend a month in rural Arkansas disappointing the Ledings, the humble, hard-working farm family that has agreed to take them in. Each day the girls ignore their chores, assemble slutty outfits, French kiss the local boys, and make a half-assed attempt to work a blue-collar job. They don't even feel gratitude for the freshly slaughtered chickens offered to them by good ol' grandma Curly, the only person in town who sees goodness in them despite the depths of bitchdom they sink to. *The Simple Life* seems to offer a Simple Moral: rich people are stupid assholes (but sexy), while working-class people are saints (but fat).

A Marxist parable? Not exactly. The "working-class" Ledings have a big house, an above-ground pool, and at least one nice car. They aren't poor, they just have working-class tastes. The show is really about Nicole and Paris, so it is hard to glean many details about the Ledings, but one has

Creative workers toil without wages as contestants on *Project Runway*.

to wonder how FOX found these farmers who seem to have no giant machinery, let their chickens breathe fresh air in outdoor coops, and manage a large farm without any hired laborers. Didn't agribusiness wipe out
this *Little House on the Prairie* lifestyle some years ago? Altus, Arkansas,
it seems, is a Southern working-class Stars Hollow, the fantasy New England town of *The Gilmore Girls*. Both towns feature quaint pie contests
and sack races, but in Altus the locals are likely to sport mullets and beer
bellies.

As on *The Gilmore Girls*, the little private dramas of *The Simple Life*
are wedged in between public dramas at work. Though TV has pictured
the workplace for years, reality TV is a genre that is obsessively focused
on labor. Indeed, it seems that there is no human activity that cannot be
turned into labor on a reality show. On *The Apprentice*, participants construct business strategies, and the effort displayed is often mental. On the
other hand, their labor also has a physical dimension, as contestants are
often asked to pound the pavement and do grunt work. (Also, one cannot fail to notice the labor of self-production on the program. Contestants
put together special outfits to catch Trump's eye, and the taut bodies of
the female participants are the visible result of hard work in the gym.)

Notwithstanding *The Apprentice,* on most programs the "work" demanded is not the kind of thing one would normally be paid for. Often, the labor is emotional: participants on *The Bachelor* are working really hard to make someone love them.

In real life, your job involves stacking things on shelves, balancing ledgers, plugging information into a database, or cleaning people's teeth. But on TV, your job is to cheat on your girlfriend, pretend to be a millionaire, eat slimy bugs, lose a ton of weight, or room with fellow washed-up celebrities. Though participants' goals may be stated loftily as "finding true love" or "resolving emotional issues," the vast majority of reality TV focuses in some way on work. Often the work is redefined as "competition," but the hoops one has to jump through to succeed on competitive reality shows are laborious. Work is work. Play is work. Banter is work. Sex is work. No one just happens to get into a hot tub because she has a sore back. Hot tubs taken in skimpy bikinis—or au natural—are used to further strategic goals in order to get the job (blow or otherwise) done.

If you do your job well, you can win a million bucks, or a Chapstick contract, or the chance to be on other reality TV shows. In regular jobs, the people who work the hardest don't necessarily advance, but if you do your job on TV, your effort is often rewarded. Even if you lose, you've gained media exposure, whatever that's worth. Moreover, in an information economy in which manufacturing has been sent overseas and minimum wage service jobs are among the few remaining jobs that require rigorous physical activity, reality TV is one of the few places where you can do hard physical labor for big bucks—if you win, that is.

"Reality TV" is, of course, a misnomer, and fans know it. At their best, the shows offer terrific melodrama and truly original dialogue, and the fact that they may picture something "really happening" seems beside the point. Reality programs are constructed by a heavy editorial hand that strives to exaggerate conflicts, amp up personality quirks, and make banal events entertaining. Watching a show like *The Girls Next Door*—about Hugh Hefner's life with his three boobilicious live-in blonde girlfriends—one can almost feel the producers' desperation to create entertainment from painfully dull source material. The show doesn't even score points for prurience—I've seen sexier infomercials.

If reality programs occasionally draw on the audiovisual conventions of documentary, they usually do not pretend to offer the putative authenticity of cinema verité—though, as Susan Murray has argued, there are certain hybrid programs that blur the boundaries between "reality TV" and "documentary."[1] If reality shows offer up a striking (and often painfully Darwinian) picture of labor in contemporary America, it is, to state the obvious, a carefully fabricated representation of labor.

At the same time, we do witness people actually working hard (or slacking off) on these programs, and there is some undeniable "realness" in play. Injuries are faked on *CSI,* but when Robert cracks his head open on season 1 of *Project Runway,* he really bleeds. And when people win reality TV contests, they are handsomely rewarded "in real life." To win, one must be evaluated by a judge or boss, in some manner that presents itself as objective or subjective. Trump as judge represents himself as methodical and fair. Flavor Flav is more, shall we say, eccentric. Either way, the judge functions like a boss doing an "annual review," assessing an employee's strengths and weaknesses and then deciding whether to grant a worker a promotion or to show him or her the door.

There is an illusion of meritocracy. Indeed, the situation of the worker-contestant on reality television closely mirrors that of the worker in today's neoliberal "talent-led economy." As Angela McRobbie argues, it is increasingly common for workers in creative industries to subsist on freelance work, to receive little or no pay and no benefits, and to work ridiculously long hours, all in hopes of being "discovered."[2]

Similarly, there is a growing number of reality TV participants (both in front and behind the camera) drifting from program to program, with little real hope of long-term stability. Consider as just one example Adrianne Curry, who won first place on *America's Next Top Model,* moved on to *The Surreal Life,* then landed on *My Fair Brady,* before a brief stint on *Celebrity Paranormal Project.* Curry is yet to emerge as a top model, but she does, for the moment, receive steady income from her short-term reality TV contracts.

In this chapter, I examine the representation of labor on two very different reality programs: one celebrating an almost puritanical work ethic, the other wallowing in lassitude. *The Simple Life* offers up a derelict work ethic by showing us rich girls who seem constitutionally incapable of work. *Project Runway,* conversely, celebrates a meritocratic work ethic. *Runway* gives us an illusion of the "American Dream" in action, as we watch talented people advance up the ladder to success. *The Simple Life,* in contrast, presents viewers with a static world in which class positions are utterly inflexible. Rich people stay rich, and poor people say poor.

Notwithstanding its contrived absurdity, then, *The Simple Life* inadvertently offers a more "realistic" lesson about work and class in America than *Project Runway* does.

Labor Is Exhausting Yet Fulfilling: Project Runway

Project Runway features aspiring fashion designers competing to win $100,000 to start their own fashion line. On each episode, designers are given a new challenge and only a short time to meet it. Some challenges have an absurdist edge, like designing an outfit made only of materials purchased from a grocery store. The dress made of flatbread and mop heads was surprisingly sexy but hardly, shall we say, functional. Other challenges are more practical, like designing a new uniform for mail carriers. Each challenge has a winner and loser, and the loser is eliminated from the program, until only three finalists remain to compete at a runway show during New York City's annual Fashion Week. The designer judged to create the best line for Fashion Week wins the show.

As season 1 develops, the personalities of the designers slowly reveal themselves.[3] Wendy Pepper is the manipulative bitch; Kara Saun, the competent, hard-working professional; Austin Scarlett, the flaming glamour queen; Robert Plotkin, the randy smooth talker. And so on. These personalities become increasingly salient as the season progresses and the melodrama builds. Viewers may briefly wonder if the show is rigged— when an early scene in an episode reveals one contestant to be manipulative and another to be a lazy designer, one can only imagine that the "bad" contestants are being set up for elimination.

But the panel of judges always appears to evaluate the outfits strictly on their own merits. As a designer, horny Robert is, as they say in England, all talk and no trousers. He charms his way out of a few sticky wickets on the runway, but he finally gets what he deserves when the judges decide that the design of his postal worker outfit is lazy, featuring an unprofessional top. Wendy is constantly plotting and strategizing, and she is certainly the show's villain, but her Banana Republic design nonetheless wins because it best matches the needs of the client. She ultimately loses during Fashion Week, not because she is a monster but because her designs are clearly inferior. The personalities add to the show's appeal, but they are, within the show's logic, secondary to talent. Good work is consistently rewarded, and bad work is punished. It is a workaholic's dream world.

On other labor-centric shows, like the *The Apprentice,* people plot and scheme to win. But *Runway* disapproves of scheming. This is perfectly illustrated by Wendy toward the end of season 1. All but the last two episodes are run on Bravo while the three finalists use their five months to create their Fashion Week lines. Then all 12 of the original designers are reunited to talk about the show, before it has actually ended. Now they have seen Wendy's true colors, as much of her duplicity is revealed through interviews that the contestants only witness in the broadcasted episodes. When they confront her, she stands firm that her behavior was logical: she was playing a game that she wanted to win.

The other designers respond that "it wasn't a game, it was just about creating the best designs and having the most talent!" Jay hits the nail on the head when he exclaims, "this isn't *Survivor!*" Wendy's behavior would be completely reasonable on a program where the contestants' "work" was expected to consist mostly of strategizing and trumping (or Trumping) others. But Wendy has played the game wrong by acknowledging that it is a game, not just an objective talent contest. In effect, she is hated because she has watched too much reality television, and she has applied what she learned from the scheming shows to her own reality show experience.

Notwithstanding Wendy's villainy, this is not a series driven first and foremost by character conflict. *Runway* producers choose to show long sewing sequences in the Parsons School of Design workrooms rather than focusing on personality issues back at the apartments that the designers share. In fact, contestants are only occasionally pictured there, especially in the first season. For viewers exhausted by the pop psychotherapy that dominates television, nothing could be more of a relief than *Runway.*[4]

Here, if people's "issues" come up, it is only a distraction from the work that must be done. On *Celebrity Fit Club,* it matters profoundly whether or not you have a good relationship with your mother. On *Project Runway,* mothers show up at the Fashion Week finale, but the program puts family issues on the back burner as much as possible.[5] (This is also, of course, the workaholic's dream—and the nightmare of the workaholic's family and friends who demand that he or she interact socially or fulfill a parental role.)

It is only on the final two-hour special episode of season 1 that we get some glimpse at the home life of our workaholic finalists. Kara lives in a small, stylish Los Angeles apartment. Since she is the consummate professional, we spend more time in a fabric shop than in her apartment. Wendy does her sewing in a cramped basement in a nice suburb in Virginia. Still playing the wrong reality TV game, Wendy is eager to rebrand herself not as villain but as nurturing mother. Viewers even see the finger painting that her daughter did for the *Runway* judges, though we are given some clue that Wendy might have persuaded her daughter to do the picture just so she could show it off to the camera. Kara Saun and Wendy Pepper seem solidly middle-class but looking to move upward by winning *Runway*.

It is Jay McCarroll who throws us for a loop. Visiting Jay in Lehman, Pennsylvania, Tim Gunn—chair of the department of fashions at Parsons School of Design, and teacher and coach to *Runway* participants—finds him enacting a full-on masquerade of redneck masculinity, pointing a gun, wearing a plaid hunting shirt, and sporting a curly wig in place of his usual stringy Jesus hair. "Don't shoot!" exclaims Tim, in high-camp mode. Jay's hetero act does more than parody "normal" masculinity; as the bumpkin "protecting his property," he also parodies a particular class position. He is playing the yokel who would creep out Paris and Nicole if this were *The Simple Life*.

But Jay introduces us to his plump, uncool family without embarrassment. Though the initial joke was that Jay was playing a working-class redneck type, it is clear that his family is middle class. Yet their tastes are "lower" than what we encountered at Wendy's and Kara's homes. Though apparently less prosperous than the Ledings, the McCarrolls, who have a successful concrete business, share their aesthetic sense. And Jay is trying to escape this small-town milieu to find success in the big city. Indeed, his sister postulates that if he wins he could "get liposuction and get the hell out of Lehman!" Though hardly destitute, Jay is clearly positioned as the finalist who has the most to gain in terms of class mobility. We feel strongly that he should win. And he does.

Runway may reward virtue, but there is a flipside to its benevolence: the program relentlessly abuses its unpaid employee-contestants. Budgets for materials are small, and the time allotted for shopping, designing, and creating new fashions is very short. Why would anyone put up with this? As per McRobbie's argument, creative expression becomes its own reward; the soul or "inner, meaningful self" has become synonymous with "talent" and "creativity."[6]

Further, as Micki McGee argues in *Self-Help, Inc.,* "the romantic myth of the artist toiling over his work alone in his garret—sequestered from the demands and rewards of the marketplace . . . encourages the pursuit of one's work out of love of the work or craft without sullying oneself with concerns about marketplace viability." This romantic, artistic ethos "provides an ideal rationale for encouraging labor without compensation."[7] Hard labor without compensation. Indeed, one often has the feeling that *Project Runway* contestants would literally die to complete their fashion designs, even though their chances of making it to the final round, much less winning the show, are slim.

The exhaustion level becomes quite palpable in season 2. In the midst of one challenge, Daniel conveys everyone's desperation: "Time is a major factor for this challenge. We have less time than we've had on almost every other challenge. This is a fucking fashion design marathon. It's the iron man triathlon of fashion." As sleep-deprived contestants frantically create dresses out of flowers and leaves, they become delirious and start doing imitations of "the bosses" cruelly judging them on the runway.

The comic relief is welcome but also disturbing, as it points to the minimal rewards that will actually come from all of this frenzied unpaid labor. The best outfit will win, and the runner-ups will be allowed to remain on the show, but one person will be made to leave, and at least one-half of the exhausted designers will be told that the fruit of their unpaid labor is crap. In other words, this apparently meritocratic world may offer dreams of success that can actually be achieved, but the show is built on a highly exploitative foundation.

In his examination of the representation of labor in Jerry Lewis films, Dana Polan explains that the Big Boss learns a valuable moral lesson when the beleaguered worker (Lewis) finally performs above all expectations. Like the greedy, uncaring capitalist of D. W. Griffith melodramas, this fellow is brought down a notch once he sees the true value of his workers. He learns that he must be a moral employer.[8] Though work clearly carries great moral weight on *Runway*, there is no room for the show's bosses (producers and judges) to become aware of their own role as exploiters. No matter how hard contestants work on *Runway*, they will inevitably be pushed harder.

Usually there is at least a semblance of good will when designers are presented with their new challenges, but in the concluding episode of season 2, the producers are simply being cruel when they force the three finalists—already working like fiends to put the finishing touches on their 12 outfits for Fashion Week—to create a 13th outfit from scratch. One contestant quite reasonably bursts into tears. The three have until 4 AM to finish, and then they have to appear at Fashion Week at 5:30 AM. This constitutes cruel and unusual punishment, to say the least. *Runway* designers convey that they are eager to work hard because they want to win, but there is a sadistic element to the show, as the producers continually push contestants to the breaking point.

Traditional Marxist notions of alienation cannot explain the situation, for these workers remain intimately connected to their own labor, as well as to the fruits of that labor. These are not assembly-line workers producing a product to which they have no personal connection. With each week's competition, the workers produce a unique object. In their wildest dreams, that object would be recognized for its potential exchange value, and anonymous workers would mass produce it. Or, better yet, produce it in very small quantities, which would make each object (piece of clothing) all the more valuable. The more personal feeling the designer puts into his or her creation—the more passionately the creator feels about the object of labor—the more likely he or she is to win, in theory, for the *Project Runway* judges will sense the personal feeling that has gone into the would-be commodity.

Labor Is Tiresome and Unrewarding: The Simple Life

The gotta-get-things-done (or die trying) work ethic that drives *Runway* is utterly lacking in *The Simple Life*. Perhaps the saddest illustration of this occurs at the Sonic fast-food restaurant in season 1, where a young manager desperately tries to get the girls to do their work. In other episodes, the older, self-employed male bosses have the option of firing the girls (after telling one of them "you're a real screw-up!"), but the fast-food manager knows that these nubile, lazy screw-ups are jeopardizing her own job, and there's nothing she can do about it. She works hard but has no money; Nicole and Paris do no work, are rich, and enjoy wasting money. Can anyone hear Thorstein Veblen shouting, "See, I told you so!" from the grave?

The Simple Life baldly manifests the shaky foundations of the American myth of class mobility. Unlike on the competitive shows, where merit is rewarded, here doing a bad job brings no real punishment, and people who work hard do not necessarily advance. At moments, season 1 offers a tepid moral lesson—it ends, for example, with the sympathetic Ledings saying that they hope the girls have benefited from the values the family has tried to teach them. But most viewers will find this about as convincing as Jerry Springer's "Final Thought," a tacked-on moral that does little to mitigate the rich-and-lazy-and-proud-of-it ethos that has preceded it.

Of course, no one is expected to take Springer's closing comments seriously. Indeed, in his study of talk show viewers, Jason Mittell notes:

> Among those who liked Springer, nobody suggested that they read the program "straight," as a representation of real people solving real problems—a more typical pleasure was "it is funny watching people that are that dumb." Fans noted that they enjoyed watching the fights, people yelling at each other, and the ridiculousness of the situations, with no presumed educational or social value.[9]

The Simple Life is even more clearly lacking in educational value than *Jerry Springer,* and the program certainly encourages us not to watch it "straight." Ironic, distanced viewing is encouraged.

Though the first three seasons of *The Simple Life* were on FOX, and the fourth on *E!,* the ridiculousness of the program and its encouragement of distanced viewing is highly evocative of *VH1*'s "celebreality" programming, where the whole point is the impossibility of accessing a celebrity's true self.[10] There is simply no there there. Paris's and Nicole's celebrity status eliminates the possibility of accessing their "genuine" selves, so we can never be certain of how slothful they actually are. Giving them the benefit of the doubt, we might wonder if perhaps these are actually wealthy young entrepreneurs cashing in on TV viewers' desires to laugh at people pretending to be dumb. Indeed, Hilton insisted over and over again when the show premiered that people needed to understand that she and Richie weren't really stupid, they were just acting. In fact, she insisted, they were "like Lucy and Ethel."

But Lucy was trapped as a housewife, dying to get a job.[11] Every time she found employment, of course, she blew it, in hilarious fashion. When she works on an assembly line making candy, for example, the belt speeds up, and she and sidekick Ethel are forced to wedge as many chocolates into their mouths as they can. It is precisely when Lucy and Ethel are in the workforce that it is clearest how different they are from Paris and Nicole. Lucy and Ethel want to work instead of being housewives. Paris and Nicole don't want to work; they will never work real jobs, and they will never be housewives, either. They are full-time socialites.

Jerry Lewis contends that "comedy is a man in trouble." In other words, comedy provokes us to laugh at the misfortune of others. Lucy and Ethel entertain us because they fail so spectacularly. Paris and Hilton do not entertain, conversely, because they are never truly "in trouble." Lucy always ended up back at home, sometimes being spanked over Ricky's knee. There are no repercussions for Paris's and Nicole's incompetence. Or none that they care about. If we are to laugh while watching this program, why, and at whom? What makes Paris and Nicole so painfully unfunny? Perhaps Lewis and Polan can provide some answers for us.

Polan observes that in Jerry Lewis films, "the comedy of laborious failure can involve derision of the disastrous efforts of the worker and achieve its comic effect at the worker's expense, but it can also rebound on the ruling class that puts the worker to work. Comedy here would be one of the ways in which the dominance of that world is defied." Further, "there can be a comic pleasure in seeing resistance to the established system of power, in seeing power's own foibles displayed in all their ridiculousness."[12] But when Paris and Nicole fail, we can't laugh at them because there is nothing at stake in their incompetence; it doesn't matter if they are fired. And there can be no comedy in the girls defeating their bosses, for the crux of that particular joke is that the boss is the enemy, the one with more power and money and privilege than the underling worker. (This is, of course, the cornerstone of much of Charlie Chaplin's humor.) Without that power dynamic, there is no fun in "putting one over on the boss." Further, the girls cannot be embarrassed, which violates all the rules of comedy. For the misfortunes of others to be funny, those subject to misfortune must be capable of feeling shame or humiliation.

Whether genuine morons or not, it is clear that Hilton and Richie are supposed to be funny. Indeed, they supply their own laugh track by giggling their way through their misadventures. Though they sometimes laugh at the earnest, hard-working, lumpen masses that they encounter in their adventures, the show itself does not seem to make fun of these folks. They are, generally, more competent and intelligent than the girls. But in scenes when the girls hang out with the local boys making small (or, rather, minuscule) talk, things become confusing. We—the middle-class people that advertisers hope are watching—are supposed to laugh at the dumb rich and the dumb working-class people trying to interact.

But this is no 1940s screwball comedy, where rich and poor meet, exchange clever banter, and fall in love. In fact, neither side has much to say, and if one were to lose the visuals of Paris's and Nicole's fancy makeup and $5,000 shoes, and just read a transcript of the dialogue, one would be hard-pressed to figure out who was rich and had attended fancy Los Angeles prep schools and who was working class and went to Midwestern public schools. The dialogue is just plain dumb on both sides of the class divide.

"Taste classifies," in Pierre Bourdieu's famous formulation, and, certainly, Paris and Nicole "know" certain things about wine and fancy designers, but they have no command of basic SAT-type words. Their intonations mark their southern California origins, but, like the white trash boys they meet, they just want to get drunk and make out. They aren't rich because they have talent or intelligence; they are rich because they were born rich. So why work?

The second season of *The Simple Life* pushes the program's celebration of Hilton's and Richie's antiwork ethic to a new extreme. They are given a huge trailer, ostensibly deprived of cell phones, credit cards, and cash, and instructed to drive across country, doing prearranged jobs along the way. In the very first episode, they find themselves scamming people for gas and toll money, and they get away with it because (1) they are celebrities (though it's not clear that everyone actually recognizes them) and (2) they are cutie-pie white girls in tight outfits who obviously don't need money.[13] Real girls on the road without cash would be seriously imperiled, eventually forced to perform sexual favors in exchange for a tank of gas.

As these special girls cross the country, though, they show over and over again how the super-rich don't actually have to work for their money. When the girls order food at Burger King even though they have no money, and they are forced by the manager to pay, they go from table to table gathering money. Their panhandling is successful precisely because their clothing and demeanor show that they are not really poor. A destitute person panhandling in Burger King would get nowhere.

This low-concept program—which certainly has no intention of saying anything meaningful about class in America—is one of the most depressing shows on television because it so aggressively and relentlessly sends the same message over and over again about class immobility. On other programs, people can win and become rich. The winner of season 1 of *Runway,* in fact, explains in an extra feature on the DVD that he wants to proceed very carefully with his reward money. He doesn't want to blow his one big chance to succeed in the fashion business. And the people who lose on the show are aware that at least they have had "exposure," which could help them succeed in fashion. Such dreams of success are not just foreign to *The Simple Life,* they are anathema to the whole ethos of the show, which wallows in the impossibility of making a better (or, if you're rich, worse) life for yourself.

That this bitter lesson is consistently delivered with a spoonful of sugar only makes it worse. For the girls are rarely overtly cruel to their hardworking inferiors. In fact, they consistently pretend to like them. One could give endless examples, but perhaps one says it all. Briefly forced to be maids at a nudist resort in season 2, the girls are left alone to clean a room. They call room service for food, charging it to the room. Then they call and demand that a maid come clean "their room." As a Colombian maid who doesn't speak English makes the bed, doing their work, they eat the food they've stolen and compliment her (obviously disingenuously) on her hair. When she's done, they tell her to charge a huge tip for herself to the room, knowing that she cannot actually understand them. Then their supervisor comes back and compliments them on doing such a great job cleaning the room. The maid has worked extra, for no tip, they have worked not at all, and they've picked up some free nachos to boot.

Since they take none of this seriously, and grin the whole time, one cannot simply dismiss them as cruel villains. It's not that they hate poor people; it's just that they hate work, and they happen to know how to make poor people work for them. In the narrative context of the show, it's not so much villainy as a life system that we are witnessing. It is the insouciance of exploitation that stings so mightily here.

Labor behind the Camera

On the face of it, *Runway* and *The Simple Life* couldn't be more different. The former presents a multicultural, homonormative world[14] in which hard work is rewarded, good generally wins out over evil, racism and homophobia have virtually disappeared, and professional advancement (and the attendant class mobility) always seem within reach, while the latter shows a world of rigid hierarchies ruled by self-centered, wealthy, white, heterosexual (and skanky) elites.

Yet the two clearly have at least one thing in common: they are TV programs and, as such, were created in order to sell advertising time. Further, as series that have continued into multiple seasons, the shows also actively sell themselves—both on the air and via DVD sales and rentals. And here is where the two actually diverge, to some extent, for *The Simple Life* never pretended to be more than it was: "hot dumb girls doing nothing, it's like watching clean porn. . . . Pure voyeuristic fun. Nothing else," as one appreciative viewer describes it on the Netflix website.[15]

As *Runway* moved into season 2, conversely, it began to take itself more seriously. Contestants spoke of what they hoped the show could do for them, and Tim Gunn started to say things that sounded scripted and trademarked, like "this is a 'make it work' time!" Notwithstanding some appealing contestants in season 2, the series felt more and more like an ad for itself (and for Saturn cars). Contestants were laboring not just to win or to further their careers but also to promote the *Runway* brand; they were insistent about their awareness of how *Runway* could change their lives for the better. Though they were all freelance, transient workers—without benefits or long-term contracts, like the creative workers McRobbie describes—they were actually expressing fierce company (brand) loyalty.

Of course, it would be naive to imply that season 1 was outside the commercial circuit. Various brands like Banana Republic were featured from the beginning. Further, contestants were laboring quite earnestly, and rewarded, for creating beautiful luxury products that were ridiculously overpriced. High fashion is beyond the reach of anyone who actually has to ask, "How much?" Though the show pictures the possibility of rewards for hard work, the commodity being created is one whose exchange value outstrips its use value by about a million to one. Although *Runway* celebrates a meritocratic work ethic, it also celebrates the fashion industry, a business that thrives on managed obsolescence—not to mention sweatshop labor.

Given reality TV's relentless focus on work, one might naively imagine a behind-the-scenes team of empathic laborers creating the shows. The BBC's scripted faux-reality show *The Office,* for example, obviously springs from an impulse of proletarian solidarity: only writers who have endured the proverbial boss-from-hell could create the monstrous David Brent. Alas, American reality programs do not spring from a similar impulse. For, in theory, reality TV has no writers. Instead, videographers shoot endlessly, and editors then step in and collaborate with "story producers" or "story editors" (actually writers) to attempt to create dramatic tension, a Herculean feat that often requires the addition of goofy sound effects, voice-overs, or music. (Witness the opening for *Strange Love,* the short-lived "celebreality" show following the romantic adventures of Brigitte Nielsen and Flavor Flav: "He's a jester, she's a fox. She likes smoking, he likes clocks.") According to a *Washington Post* article, the story editors "use the expression 'frankenbites' . . . to describe the art of switching around contestant sound bites recorded at different times and patched together to create what appears to be a seamless narrative."[16]

The premise that the people on reality shows are real translates into one thing, as far as producers are concerned: free labor. These are regular people, not actors with Screen Actors Guild cards. And once you've gotten rid of unionized actors, why not get rid of the unionized writers? In fact, though the International Alliance of Theatrical Stage Employes and the Directors Guild of America have made inroads on getting union employees on a few shows, it is more common for the workers creating reality TV—not just writers but also directors, carpenters, camera operators, and so on—to be nonunion.[17]

The Screen Writers Guild has made reality TV central to its contract negotiations with the Alliance of Motion Picture and Television Producers but has had no success in attempts to get reality writers unionized. The young reality TV workers have lower salaries than guild members, no health care, and no pension, and, of course, they don't get a writing credit for their work, since no producer wants his show tainted by a credit acknowledging that stories are managed and banter is often scripted.[18]

The shows have much shorter shooting schedules than regular programs, so writers typically work 12 to 18 hours a day, but they tolerate such conditions because reality TV is seen as a steppingstone to better gigs. Overworked, and desperate for a permanent job with benefits, these kids would be perfect candidates for a reality show. Reports one writer, "It's like guerrilla TV. . . . You have no outside life. You leave at midnight and have a 5 A.M. call."[19] Sounds a lot like *Project Runway*. This gives me a great idea: How about a reality show about workers on a reality show? I can imagine how the networks would respond to my brilliant pitch: "You're fired!"

NOTES

A much shorter version of this essay first appeared on *FLOW: An On-line Journal of Television and Media Studies* 1.11 (March 2005), at http://jot.communication.utexas.edu/flow/?jot=view&id=572. Thanks to Allison McCracken for her very helpful feedback on both that version of the essay and on this revised, expanded version.

1. Susan Murray, chapter 3 in this volume.

2. Angela McRobbie, "From Holloway to Hollywood: Happiness at Work in the New Cultural Economy?" in *Cultural Economy: Cultural Analysis and Commercial Life,* ed. Paul du Gay and Michael Pryke (New York: Sage, 2002), 97–114.

3. I center my analysis on the first season of both series, though a few examples are drawn from later seasons.

4. As Mimi White observed some time ago, the therapeutic is the "master narrative strategy of contemporary mass culture." *Tele-Advising: Therapeutic Discourse in American Television* (Chapel Hill: University of North Carolina Press, 1992), 11.

5. In season 2, contestants have a rap session about coming out to their parents. Since personal discussions on the show usually stick to crises of the moment ("Who stole my chiffon?!"), this sequence stands out as not quite fitting in with the show's ethos. In season 3, personal issues are amped up more, and one challenge requires contestants to create designs for their mothers, with the mothers wearing the outfits on the runway. This challenge is clearly designed to incite emotions from contestants and takes the program away from its previous emphasis on challenges that were about pushing creativity—not emotions—to the max.

6. McRobbie, "From Holloway to Hollywood," 109.

7. Micki McGee, *Self-Help, Inc.: Makeover Culture in American Life* (New York: Oxford University Press, 2005), 130.

8. Dana Polan, "Working Hard, Hardly Working: Labor and Leisure in the Films of Jerry Lewis," in *Enfant Terrible! Jerry Lewis in American Film,* ed. Murray Pomerance (New York: New York University Press, 2002).

9. Jason Mittell, *Genre and Television: From Cop Shows to Cartoons in American Culture* (New York: Routledge, 2004), 116–17.

10. Celebreality programs include *My Fair Brady, Flavor of Love, Strange Love,* and *The Surreal Life.*

11. Patricia Mellencamp, "Situation Comedy, Feminism, and Freud: Discourses of Gracie and Lucie," in *Studies in Etnertainment: Critical Approaches to Mass Culture,* ed. Tania Modleski (Bloomington: Indiana University Press, 1986), 80–95. On Lucy's place in the workforce in the 1960s, see Heather Hendershot, "I Love Lucy in the Sixties," *FLOW: An On-Line Journal of Television and Media Studies* (September 2005). at http://jot.communication.utexas.edu/flow/.?jot=view&id=942

12. Polan, "Working Hard, Hardly Working," 213.

13. Though Richie is biracial, everything about her self-presentation is firmly rooted in a rich, white, Southern California persona. When she and Paris stay with a black Christian family in season 2, Nicole interjects at dinner, "I'm a black folk too" [*sic*]. Though all are aware that her father is black, everyone laughs, as the statement is clearly meant as a joke.

14. In contrast to the "real" world that presumes heterosexuality, this show offers an alternate universe in which it is the straight men who seem different or strange because of their sexual orientation. Yet usually all of this remains implicit, for no one has the *time* to talk politics. There is simply too much work to be done. For a brief analysis of *Runway*'s sexual politics, see Heather Hendershot, "'Don't Shoot!' Hetero Masquerade on Project Runway," *MediaCommons,* at http://mediacommons.futreofthebook.org/node/190. On political discussion, TV, and identity politics, see Jane M. Shattuc, *The Talking Cure: TV, Talk Shows, and Women* (New York: Routledge, 1997).

15. See   www.netflix.com/Movie/The_Simple_Life_Season_2/70015742?dmode
=CUSTOMERREVIEW&lnkctr=mdpGlanceMemRev&trkid=222336   (accessed
April 18, 2000).

16. William Booth, "Reality Is Only an Illusion, Writers Say: Hollywood Scribes
Want a Cut of Not-So-Unscripted Series," *Washington Post,* 10 August 2004, C1.
This kind of labor exploitation dates back to the roots of reality television in the
1980s, as Chad Raphael explains in chapter 6 in this volume.

17. The DGA has had some success with *Last Comic Standing, Celebrity Mole,*
and *Fear Factor.* IATSE has gotten "below-the-line" union labors on the sets of
The Swan, Blind Date, Next Action Star, American Idol, The Swan, and *Queer Eye
for the Straight Guy.* Dave McNary, "Coming to Terms with Reality: Guilds Labor to Organize Workers as Genre Grows," originally published in 2004 by *Variety,* Writers Guild of America East, at www.wgaeast.org/mba/2004/article in-
dex/2004/10/13/variety3/ (accessed 19 January 2005).

18. McNary, "Coming to Terms with Reality."

19. Quoted in Booth, "Reality Is Only an Illusion."

Cinderella Burps

Gender, Performativity, and the Dating Show

Jonathan Gray

From rodent-eating contests on *Fear Factor* to *Cops* chasing naked old men, reality television offers no shortage of excess. One of its most gloriously excessive, camp, and carnivalesque beauties is that of the dating show. Take, for instance, FOX's *Temptation Island* (2001), which took four established couples to a remote island, separated them, and brought in 40 skimpy bathing suit–wearing singles to test the couples' faithfulness. Or turn to ABC's *The Bachelor* (2002–), where 25 women compete for one man. The women agree beforehand to claim him, sight unseen, as their ideal spouse, and though the game involves dating him opposite, sometimes *with,* one's competitors, the tearful professions of undying love run fast and furious. Dating shows specialize in offering us peculiar specimens of humankind, often encouraging not identification but vilification, ridicule, and sarcastic commentary. They can rely on and perpetuate some of the most backward ideas and ideals of gender, and yet they can also be such wonderfully alluring, can't-look-away, must-talk-about television.

In this chapter, I examine the oddity in the television landscape that is the dating show. Dating shows offer various viewing pleasures and strategies. Taken straight, many stage a horrific parade of patriarchal romantic fairy tale, meat-market spectacle, and the commodification of humanity. But many of them are also complex texts that simultaneously master the comic arts of carnival, opening up dialogic space for both their contestants and their viewers, creating significant fun and laughter first and foremost but also providing room to analyze and discuss the gendered performances that are required in real-world dating.

After a brief history of the dating show and an introduction to its key texts, I examine the genre's apparent reliance on disturbingly simple depictions of women in particular and then its carnivalesque play and pageantry. Although by no means do I intend to suggest that all viewers watch dating shows as play, I nevertheless focus on how these seemingly patriarchally repressive texts construct such pageantry. At times, dating shows do not so much offer depictions of the reality of gender as they offer contestants space for the performance of different, counterhegemonic scripts of gender expectations and "proper" dating behavior, and they offer audiences the space to both critically and playfully appreciate and evaluate those expectations and those performances.

A Brief History of Televised Dating

Dating is perfect fodder for reality television. Before today's reality television spectacle of screened surveillance, many dating shows expressed an early yearning to send a camera behind closed doors. America's *Dating Game* (ABC, 1975–83; syndication, 1978–80, 1986–89, 1996–99) and *Love Connection* (syndication, 1983–94, 1998–99), the Australian *Perfect Match* (Ten, 1984–89), and the British *Blind Date* (ITV, 1985–2003) all tried to match individuals through evaluation of suitors' responses to a series of silly questions. But arguably the most entertaining—if simultaneously frustrating—segment of such shows came when the host would question past show-made couples about their subsequent date, offering a playful He Said/She Said game that longed for some documentary, fly-on-the-wall evidence of "what really happened."

Meanwhile, these shows also gave the television industry an early look into audiences' capacity to root for the unhappy ending. The best laughs and fun in dating games often arise from painfully uncomfortable matches and from the ensuing tales of dating disaster, or even simply from the anticipation of such disaster. A short, half-hour program allows little time to grow attached to a character or a relationship, instead allowing the schadenfreude that would in time become a central staple of much reality television. Dating shows have always relied heavily on the pleasures of seeing a life more messed up than our own, since whatever woes a viewer suffers on the dating scene, the desperation and nationally broadcasted awkwardness of dating game contestants reassure one that life could be worse.

Audiences' voyeuristic desires to go along with a couple on their date were finally realized with the broadcast in 1999 of the American *Blind Date*, sold in first-run syndication by Universal. *Blind Date* paired couples and then let the cameras follow them. Learning from VH1's *Pop-Up Video* (1996–2002), *Blind Date* included constant sarcastic commentary on the date in the form of pop-up thought bubbles for the couple and cartoon or text-bar additions to the scene. The show gave birth to legions of followers, many of which added a competition element. Hence, as their titles suggest, *Fifth Wheel* (syndication, 2001–4) added three more suitors to the date, and *Elimidate* (syndication, 2001–6) required the bachelor or bachelorette to cut three of four suitors all on the same date.

Just as dating games had helped lead the way for reality television with regard to the genre's frequent enjoyment of personal failure, this new brand of dating game also became a forerunner in sexing up reality television: dates tended to involve plenty of drinking, competitive stripping, making out, bumping and grinding, and hot tubs. Typically, such programs played well in late evening time slots, presumably when real-life dates had ended prematurely or had never even occurred. Aimed at younger viewers, they both teemed with pent-up sexual energy and allowed for the vicarious release of such energy.

Then, with the turn of the century, the genre moved into the flashy mainstream of prime time. After FOX had already set the ethical bar for reality television so low in 2000 with *Who Wants to Marry a Multi-Millionaire*, it returned for another try at "real" romance in primetime with *Temptation Island*, which serialized the dating game genre. The setup and characterization were so perverse that they inspired a camp, distanced viewership, and yet through actually stringing out its rather vapid characters over a season, *Temptation Island* also gestured toward opening the genre up to greater viewer identification with particular individuals or couples.

Temptation Island's ratings were quite poor but clearly not bad enough to detract from more successful foreign versions or from each major American network fashioning their own serialized hour-long dating games. Hence the next few years saw CBS's *Cupid* (2003), NBC's *Average Joe* (2003–5) and *For Love or Money* (2003–4), FOX's *Joe Millionaire* (2003), UPN's *The Player* (2004), and by far the most successful of the group (and the model for the rest), ABC's *The Bachelor*. Mixing *Big Brother* with *Elimidate*, these shows established the prime-time reality dating show as a major entity on the televisual landscape.

Each of these shows chooses a single bachelor or bachelorette and surrounds him or her with many singles of the opposite gender, often in a huge mansion in an exotic location. The bachelor/ette goes on multiple dates and gradually eliminates all of the suitors but one. Many of these shows or their subsequent seasons failed to impress in the ratings, but *The Bachelor* has continued to attract viewers and, as with most reality shows, benefits from being cheap to produce.

Meanwhile, with MTV's conversion in recent years from broadcasting music videos to peddling reality television, the dating game has continued to thrive in its nonserialized, half-hour episodic form. Outrageous gimmicks have become a hallmark of many dating shows, from *Average Joe*'s use of a "fat suit" to disguise its bachelorette, to *The Player*'s pimping-out of *The Bachelor*, but MTV and VH1 have specialized in wild premises and a carnivalesque atmosphere.

Starting in 2004, *Date My Mom* allowed a mother to go on three "dates" to check out and select from three suitors for her daughter. In 2005, *Next* brought the world of speed dating (and speed dumping) to reality television, allowing the bachelor/ette to replace their date at any time. In 2006, *Parental Control* gave parents the opportunity to replace their son or daughter's current partner, and 2006 also introduced *Flavor of Love*, with VH1 trying to find love for questionable "catch" Flavor Flav. In 2007, the *Flavor of Love* spinoff *I Love New York* was born.

MTV's shows are cheap, simple, and yet over-the-top, offering ludicrous dates (such as having a frog race), larger-than-life characters, plenty of sarcastic commentary from competitors, and absurdly manufactured situations and scripting.

Making the Shoe Fit: Dating Show as Fairy Tale

A casual look at reality dating shows might suggest an appalling gallery of female stereotypes and a patriarchal, fairy-tale ethos. According to this ethos, Girl (not Woman) meets Man in a magical setting, and Man eventually chooses her above all other suitors, thereby validating her as a person, completing her, rescuing her from a humdrum life, and giving her the chance to become a princess of Reality TV-Land.

The Bachelor serves as the archetypal example, offering all the accoutrements of modern-day fairy-tale romance, from evening gowns to extravagant dates, and even, in *The Bachelor: Rome*, a "real" prince (by way of New

Jersey) as bachelor. Alison Graham-Bertolini poses that in *Bachelor*-with-a-twist *Joe Millionaire*, "editing convincingly establishes that the women consider this opportunity more important than anything else in their lives. Their degrees, careers, and loved ones are marginalized for their chance to accomplish what is being touted as women's primary objective, marriage."[1]

Certainly, *Joe Millionaire* and *The Bachelor* in particular highlight the apparent desperation behind many of their female contestants' choices to come on reality television to find a (rich) mate, and they squeeze maximum mileage out of depicting the women as highly competitive and conniving. Each week, *The Bachelor* climaxes with the "rose ceremony," in which the bachelor selects his top picks by offering them roses, resulting in a 10-minute showpiece full of, first, expectant and, then, joyous or crushed reaction shots. The ceremony gives the women very little power, reducing them to waiting on their man, and to being given identity via the bachelor's gaze.[2]

Such programs would seem to require that the women play along and subject their sense of individuality and personal agency to the rules of this very patriarchal game. Even their gender-flipping variants, such as *Cupid, The Bachelorette*, and *Average Joe*, often made the single female appear more desperate than the cool and collected men, and they allowed the men considerably more power and agency in the process.

This power play extends to many dating games' ambivalence with regard to the rules of fairy tale, for while many shows peddle fairy-tale romance, some also distance themselves with "twists" that mock the women placed in this fairy tale. For instance, in *Joe Millionaire*, contestants were told that the handsome-but-poor bachelor was a millionaire. Thus, the show invited viewers to enjoy the site of "gold diggers" being "put in their place," positing all of the women as either shallow or likely to become so upon revelation of the truth, and setting the entire season up to punish the ultimate "winner." *Average Joe*, meanwhile, took a young woman and filled her mansion with awkward geeks, encouraging viewers to regard her subsequent grimaces as she was introduced to them, and her ultimate choice of a hunky Prince Charming when finally offered some beefed-up suitors, as signs of the supposedly inherent shallowness of the fairy-tale woman.

Apparently, then, these women cannot win—they are encouraged to reduce themselves to dutiful waifs dreaming of Prince Charming on *The Bachelor*, and then are attacked for doing so on *Joe Millionaire* and *Average Joe*. Taken as representational and as reality, those shows that rely heavily on a fairy-tale ethos can render women inevitable losers.

Bikinis and Hot Tubs: Dating Show as Spectacle

Dating shows also all too often render the date, and more specifically the woman, as spectacle. Justin DeRose, Elfriede Fürsich, and Ekaterina V. Haskins, for instance, have observed that the pop-up text and graphics on *Blind Date* frequently judge women solely based on looks: "Cartoon-like bugging eyes or a panting tongue are placed over the face of a male participant who seems to be particularly pleased with his date's appearance. Conversely, such cartoonish emotions do not appear on the faces of female participants."[3] Or, when thought-bubbles are added to the screen, the men's comments often focus on women's breasts, while thoughts ascribed to female contestants concern the man's fashion and financial standing. On *Fifth Wheel* and *Elimidate,* winning usually requires women to strip the quickest, kiss the sloppiest, and perform for the man, expectations that are rarely attached to male contestants.

My students often mistakenly believe that Laura Mulvey was writing about dating shows when she first wrote of the voyeuristic male gaze,[4] since few genres illustrate the camera's masculinization of the audience as perfectly as can the dating show. *Elimidate* and *Fifth Wheel* commanded particularly high viewership among 18–34-year-old men, with especially high ratings for late-night slots,[5] no doubt in part because their visual reduction of women to performing objects came as close as basic cable could to porn. Beauty pageants and *Victoria's Secret Lingerie Show* only happen once a year, but dating shows have made gratuitous displays of women cavorting for the camera's pleasure a regular occurrence.

The rose ceremony in particular is a set-piece that gives the bachelor or masculinized viewer the chance to pick women as if from a mail-order catalogue. Since part of the "game" for the viewer at home lies in guessing who will win, such shows can actively encourage viewers to criticize the women's relative style and looks, hence adding considerable scrutiny to the voyeurism of the male gaze. Certainly, a browse through *Television Without Pity*'s (www.televisionwithoutpity.com) *Bachelor* discussion pages offers one ample criticism, frequently of the likes of "ohmigod—she'll never get a man with hair like *that!*" Moreover, dating shows commonly dedicate considerable time to scenes of the female contestants criticizing each other in secret, and in doing so, they further establish a secondary sport of encouraging viewers, too, to criticize the women's looks.

Given such texts, many critics worry about the patriarchal messages and reinforcement being offered to audiences. DeRose et al. declare that *Blind Date* invites the audience "to join the comic 'chorus,' represented by the [pop-up] supertext, and thus to adopt a dominant ideological subject position."[6] DeRose et al. respond in part to John Fiske's judgment of dating games as opening up room for audiences to challenge hegemonic notions of how men and women should behave. Instead of seeing an "open text" that allows viewers to make sense of it in various different ways, they argue that *Blind Date*'s pop-ups close down viewers' chances to view against the textual grain, making it harder for inherent challenges to dominant notions of gender roles to actually rise to the surface of the text.[7]

Similarly, Myra Mendible notes with frustration that her female students "casually agree that women are ruthless when vying for male attention. To these young women, RTV [reality TV] shows such as *For Love of Money* or *Joe Millionaire* simply reflect 'reality.'"[8] Many reality dating shows' structures appear to reward women for relishing the roles of sexual object and spectacle and of the old duality of madonna or whore.

Playing at Dating: Performances of Gender

However, dating shows have long been about more than Cinderella in lingerie. Rather, key to their success has been their playful atmosphere that frequently celebrates bad connections and suitors and puts humor front and center. First, as Fiske observes of *Perfect Match,* many dating games are all about fun and pleasure, not about fairy tales and marriage. In such a zone of fun and play, "sexuality is understood as the source of equally valid pleasure for both genders, not, more 'responsibly,' with the gender-power differential inevitably inherent in it." In this, he sees an "egalitarian" spirit that allows women powers of choice and options of behavior that go against traditional, patriarchal norms and expectations.[9]

Certainly, many of the half-hour shows privilege fun and casual hook-ups. On MTV in particular, marriage is for old people (i.e., those in their 30s), not its young participants. Dates on *Next* and *Parental Control* are also notoriously silly, allowing for some sexual tension and chemistry but rarely providing either a natural habitat in which to grow. With fun at the forefront, and with women (not just men) choosing, the fairy-tale dynamics dissipate somewhat, leaving men and women on a more level footing and allowing space for more varied forms of female behavior. Even on the hour-longs, most reality television watchers know that both the failure rate of dating show relationships and the desire for fame of the average contestant are high.

Thus, while contestants talk a good "I want a soul-mate" game, most of us know that it is just a game—complete with rules, costumes, a game-master/host, and plenty of artifice—and one in which savvy female contestants can play both the bachelor and the network. Semblance of fairy tale notwithstanding, most dating shows operate within a frame of being just for fun, and women can participate in the fun, too.

All dating shows require a high level of performativity. Gender is fundamentally performative, as writers such as Judith Butler and Candace West and Don Zimmerman have famously observed.[10] We might see dating show women not so much as being forced to conform to fairy-tale performances of femininity, though, as *playing* with this role in the game-like atmosphere of reality television. They go on sunset hang-gliding dates and win diamond earrings, or, alternatively, they pick their dates off a busload of hopefuls and get paid $1 per minute spent on the date—events marked as uncommon, *unreal.*

As Butler observes of drag, then, when the very artificiality of gender performances is highlighted—when one observes the performance of a performance of gender—the performance carries with it subversive potential, as the spectator's eye is directed to the contortionist act that some performances of gender (here, of Cinderella and Prince Charming) require.[11] Hence, to criticize dating shows for asking women to play Cinderella may be to fall in the trap of believing that the *game* is real, or at least regarded as real, when much of the fun of many dating shows is permissible because of their clear pronunciations that they are not real but play.

In due form, MTV and VH1 in particular enjoy flipping or flouting gender roles. In one episode of *Next,* the bachelorette makes a hopeful take off his shirt and turn around so that she (and the camera) can inspect him. She then waxes his armpits and gives him a spray-on tan, in the process ordering him to put on a skimpy, unflattering pair of Speedos. On this date, the voyeuristic, scrutinizing gaze is female, the woman is in control, and though she hardly uses this control for any wonderfully progressive purpose, the man's submissiveness in the face of this power is neither mocked nor even overtly sexualized. Especially when the women are left to select dates, dating shows can give their female characters considerable power and agency to dictate what constitutes an appropriate performance of gender.

Next, Parental Control, Flavor of Love, and *I Love New York* are particularly keen to play with gender roles, but all dating shows offer some level of dialogism, hence heightening the power of certain performances. Mikhail Bakhtin first used the term "dialogism" to describe how novels allow multiple characters to speak for themselves, and in so doing, they offer various competing points of identification for readers.[12] Reality television, too, is notoriously dialogic. Hence, we must avoid assuming that the genre's seemingly more patriarchal texts will necessarily be consumed as such by all audiences.

In particular, the large stable of contestants common to most reality shows opens up space for viewers to identify with or against characters as they see fit, not necessarily as the program asks them to. Indeed, when reality shows have allowed audience voting, results have often shown viewer support for unlikely heroes, as when judge favorites are eliminated in *American Idol* and as when *Cupid* saw viewers nearly hijack the fairy tale by voting for the "worst" bachelors to stay in the show. Editing and producer commentary by way of interviews or on-screen supertext in *Blind Date* provide something of an authorial voice, limiting possibilities for identification, as do elimination and other rules of the game.[13] But through a dialogic mode of delivery, most dating shows nevertheless give their nonnormative underdogs some room for movement.

As George Lipsitz's discussion of Fredric Jameson insists, although popular texts often grab our attention by opening up unresolved cultural tensions, or what Lipsitz dubs "the hurts of history," solely with the purpose of closing them up again, still the process of resealing is never guaranteed: for some readers, it is the hurts of history that will remain the most salient parts of the text.[14] A dialogic reading of the seemingly patriarchal rose ceremony, therefore, would observe that the tension and discomfort of a public dumping ceremony may dominate many viewers' experience of this set-piece. Nobody likes to be picked last or to be dumped, and thus while some viewers will watch the rose ceremony for their favorites, the scene also opens up a "hurt of history" for other viewers, implicitly calling for us to identify with the underdogs and to resent the patriarchal system behind this selection process, doubly represented by the bachelor and the frat brother–like male host. Rather than encourage one to criticize the women's looks, then, *The Bachelor* may instead encourage a rejection of the entire setup, from the bachelor's supposedly "dreamy" quality, to the legitimacy of the game, and even to the producers' casting and editing decisions.

During the Rose Ceremony on *The Bachelor,* the women line up to see who will make it to the next round.

Similarly, viewers are welcome to watch the rest of the "fairy tale" unfold with a critical eye, favoring underdogs, adding their own voice to the dialogue by playfully yelling at the screen, or cheering on the eventual union as one in which the rent-a-hunk bachelor and dainty waif "deserve each other." As noted earlier, dating shows have long relied on the pleasures of mocking those on screen, not celebrating them. Viewers can quite easily perform a dialogic recoding of the text as morality play of an outdated mode of romance, identifying *against* the protagonists and their gender performances, just as, for instance, one is encouraged to revile the shocking specimens of humanity on shows such as *My Super Sweet Sixteen* and *The Simple Life.*

Women Who Cuss: Dating Show Carnivals

Most of the MTV shows have also included gay or lesbian episodes, hence challenging the heteronormativity of romance elsewhere in the dating show genre (especially noteworthy on *Date My Mom* and *Parental*

Control, since the parents' presence serves as implicit acceptance of, and participation in, their children's gay or lesbian dating lives). Bravo even offered an all-gay reality show, *Boy Meets Boy* (2003). And these shows also frequently present "unruly women" who, as Kathleen Rowe notes of the figure of the unruly woman, buck the expectations of "ladylike" behavior, make a spectacle of their performance of power, and loudly resist traditional gender expectations.[15]

In one episode of *Parental Control,* for instance, a young man explains to a date that his parents dislike his girlfriend because she "cusses" and burps too much. We cut back to his parents' living room, where his girlfriend and parents are watching, and his girlfriend responds, "I have just one thing to say about this date," after which she releases a huge trucker's burp. She peppers her comments—about the boyfriend, the date, and the parents—with expletives. The parents chastise her for never cooking for their son or "taking care of him," to which she bluntly responds, "I don't need to cook. He cooks." When her boyfriend's father overzealously expresses admiration of the date's looks, she instructs him to "keep it in your pants."

By the show's end, she is dumped, which could be read as the show's disciplining of her failure to conform to a feminine norm—except for the fact that the young man's dates proved remarkably dull. Put simply, "good" dates make for boring television, suffering in reality television's dialogic space, whereas this young woman's glorious performance becomes the highlight of the episode: an unruly woman whose behavior violates norms but with great comic results, hence encouraging us to like her, not to disapprove of her.

Similarly, much of *Flavor of Love*'s 500-plus pages worth of fan commentary at *Television Without Pity* are filled with expressions of admiration of and comic appreciation for the show's unruly women and their outrageous behavior. One contestant in particular, dubbed "New York" by Flavor Flav, became a quick fan favorite for her continued refusal to behave in appropriate *Bachelor* contestant style. New York frequently tested the veracity of VH1's bleeper machine, would yell down anyone who crossed her, and loved to eat—she was anything but the dainty Cinderella. Her sheer self-confidence and verve made for an immensely likeable comic star, as she upstaged the show, leading to VH1 centering a spinoff program on her. Thus, this unruly woman joined a pantheon of other unruly women favorites, including Mae West, Miss Piggy, Roseanne Arnold, and Sarah Silverman as women who use their power and transgressive performance of gender as "a weapon for feminist appropriation" that encourages similar acts of rebellion from the unruly women's admiring viewers.[16]

New York's transgressions risk being racialized, stereotypical behavior of a sassy African American woman, and hence they are bound to render her anything but transgressive to some viewers; at the same time, the supreme excesses of her performance reference the genre of blaxploitation and its campy over-the-top quality,[17] so that to others, they might draw as much attention to the artificialities of performing race and racialized gender as of performing gender itself.

Meanwhile, though *The Bachelor* has yet to offer us a New York, when inevitably one woman steps out of line and behaves "inappropriately" by refusing to play the role of doting, quiet, floor-scrubbing Cinderella, although she may mark herself for elimination and for ridicule by fellow contestants, hence moving her quickly into the role of villain, in truth reality television's "villains" are often our heroes, the reasons to watch, the catalysts of all activity, and hence much-loved.

Ultimately, many dating shows follow carnivalesque rules that privilege indecorum and perform a reversal of power structures. As explained by Michel Bakhtin, medieval carnival represented a "temporary liberation from the prevailing truths and from established order" and "from norms of etiquette and decency imposed at other times."[18] Serfs would toil in the fields for most of the year, but when carnivals came, they could engage in all manner of mockery, drunkenness, debauchery, high performativity, and mayhem. Bakhtin's notion of carnival has often been used to explain humor, especially due to its echo of Sigmund Freud's famous writings on jokes.

To Freud, many jokes display a "disguised aggressiveness" that provides "a liberating pleasure by getting rid of inhibitions" and hence that "affords assistance against suppression."[19] Freud saw "tendentious" jokes as those that offer us the means to play with or attack those forces that control us and our behavior. Similarly, Bakhtin wrote of carnival as providing a zone in which tendentious jokes and "inappropriate," unsanctioned behavior is allowable. Laughter, to both Bakhtin and Freud, can be "liberatory" because, in Bakhtin's romantic terms, "Laughter purifies from dogmatism . . .; it liberates from fanaticism and pedantry, from fear and intimidation, from didacticism, naïveté and illusion, from the single meaning."[20] In effect, then, both figures discuss the potential for comedy and carnival to release anxiety and to empower us to laugh at and critique the rules by which we more normally live.

If such is carnival, MTV and VH1 in particular provide glorious carnivals, as their dating shows open up significant room for the trouncing of expected "normal" behavior. *Parental Control,* for instance, is most amusing not during the actual dates, which are fairly mundane and which occupy comparatively little screen time, but, instead, during the parental interviews of prospective dates and when the parents and unwanted boyfriend or girlfriend watch the dates together. These scenes are marked by heavily scripted and outrageous behavior. In one episode, the mother asks candidates, if they were a love doctor, what they would prescribe for their daughter.

The editors string together a litany of trite, cheesy answers before cutting to a geeky looking candidate, who straightfaces, "I'd recommend 300 milligrams of hot beef injection." In another episode, the parents ask candidates how long their average relationship lasts, to which an odd-looking hopeful replies, "It depends: How long does the average orgasm last?" The same candidate's interview ends with his closing pitch to the parents that if they don't like him, "you can go fuck yourselves." The utter inappropriateness of offering such responses to a prospective date's parents, and of behaving in such a way in an interview of any sort, invites a laughter of release, especially for young viewers who might be particularly anxious about "meeting the parents" or about job interviews.

Later in each episode, *Parental Control* offers yet more comic release when it quite clearly scripts fights between the parents and the unwanted boyfriend or girlfriend in front of the television monitor. The combatants trade insults and gibes more becoming of *The Jerry Springer Show* than of a meeting with a boyfriend or girlfriend's parents.

Next opens up similar space for the violation of expected norms. In particular, each date is introduced to us in absurd terms, so that, for instance, one suitor's onscreen fact sheet lists that she thinks David Blaine is hot, that she is obsessed with *The Golden Girls,* and that she sold male-enhancement pills. Another suitor introduces himself by doing a monkey dance, while his fact sheet tells us that he shaves his arms; one of his rivals introduces himself by saying that his "collar isn't the only thing that's stiff." From the outset, then, such disjunctive collections of factoids and blatantly inane statements work to create playful humor, not declarative statements on the real. Rarely are we given either enough information or favorable enough editing to root for *any* contestant on either *Parental Control* or *Next,* as, instead, the attention is deflected away from who will "win" to the general sense of play, performance, fun, and absurdity.

Parental Control and *Next* offer themselves more as light-hearted silliness than as statements on anything.

If such shows operate by creating such a ludicrous realm of comedy and absurd spectacle, though, we must ask whether they completely abdicate their claim to represent and speak of reality. For the purposes of classification, such shows are *called* "reality television," but do they actually even *pretend* to speak of the real? And do audience members regard them and their "depictions" as in any way real?

Though a more complete answer to these questions would require production and reception analysis, to scratch the surface of especially the latter question, one could read one's way through the abundant ironic and playful audience commentary of the MTV and VH1 shows at *Television Without Pity*. Of particular interest, one poster excitedly writes of how s/he knew the family in one of the episodes of *Parental Control*, elaborating:

> It is painfully obvious the show is scripted but it was so interesting to hear how very contrived it really is. Calyse and Tyler aren't even really dating. . . . The [parents' objection to the boyfriend's] clothes-stealing and cigar-smoking was totally made up. And the producers picked the dates for the parents, picked the house they "lived" in, and made the mom say all those ridiculous "douchebag" comments. . . . Some of the guys tried to refuse to do the humiliating stunts during the interview section—like act like a dog. The producers told them if they didn't crawl around on the floor they would be pulled from the show entirely.

Assuming that this poster is telling the truth, s/he proves that the show is scripted from beginning to end: there is little "reality." However, equally telling is that nobody on the discussion board responds with either disappointment or surprise. Conspiracy theories regarding scripting run rampant with reality shows, often fueling considerable debate, but here *Parental Control*'s manufactured nature is so obvious that other posters seem unfazed, while the poster presents the information more for the sake of detail than as shocking news. Indeed, the "fakeness" of the show receives compliments from some posters, who enjoy how some participants constantly look off-set for cue cards, and who realize that surely nobody would talk to a loved one's parents in such a way, yet they relish the camped-up, over-the-top quality of the show.[21]

In this regard, we can compare *Parental Control* and *Next* (similarly scripted to the point of absurdity) to the World Wrestling Federation

(WWF) before it finally admitted that its bouts were entirely scripted and choreographed. No official confirmation of *Parental Control* or *Next*'s scripting has been forthcoming, but none is needed for many of its viewers.

Ultimately, though, if *Parental Control* and *Next* are both distanced from reality, and if many of their pleasures are based precisely on their absurdity, might attacking their depictions of women and men—or anything, for that matter—be akin to fishing through a black hole? We can still find certain *images* of men and women, male- and female-gendered behavior, and so on, but, surely, for an image to actually tell us something about the realities *of gender,* we must read and regard it as depicting reality in the first place. Thus, when shows that are so brazenly carnivalistic step outside of and away from reality, they are reality television no more and, arguably, are depicting and representing reality no more.

As with their fellow carnivalesque WWF, *Jerry Springer,* and supermarket tabloids, the shows are badly put together, badly scripted, and littered with absurdly overt stereotypes.[22] But this means that, to many viewers, they have lost the power to depict. Just as we would not look to a *Weekly World News* article on human babies with duck bills to tell us about possible birth defects, the carnivalesque absurdity of some dating shows announces loudly and clearly that we should not look to them for much accurate information on gender, dating, or romance.

Carnivals are not wholly divorced from the real, however, for that from which they provide release exists in reality and works as the vital prerequisite of the possibility of fun, release, and laughter. If burping in a boyfriend's parents' faces wasn't such a clear violation of the expected performance, it wouldn't be funny. Hence, of continuing interest to scholars of humor, especially in the wake of Bakhtin's theory of carnival, has been an interrogation of what import, if any, carnival can have on the realm of the real.

Bakhtin himself was reasonably ambivalent, for while he recognized the liberatory function of carnival and the subversive potential of a mode of literature that would develop its audience's critical capabilities, he also recognized that those in power use carnivals precisely to allow frustrations to vent and dissipate. Other critics have suggested that carnival merely reifies the rules that it violates, our laughter at abnormality perpetuating a strict sense of what is normal and accepted.[23]

Here again, Lipsitz's commentary on the "hurts of history" is relevant, for we can never be sure that the carnival will end. This terminal opening seems especially likely when the text's play with the "hurts of history" is what makes the text entertaining, and hence that which pleases the audience.

Conclusion

Ultimately, then, the performativity, unruly women, play with expected and traditional dating behavior, and camp vulgarity common to dating shows might open up room for subversion of gender expectations. How much the individual audience member will allow such play and performance to force reflective reevaluation of his or her own performance of gender in the real world is open to debate and impossible to declare in the abstract.

Nevertheless, at their most progressive moments, dating shows might provide not only fun but also negation and a humorous way of ridiculing and undermining traditional performances of gender. The more overtly carnivalesque dating shows such as *Next* and *Parental Control* might even condition viewers to expect the carnivalesque from all dating shows. Hence, even if, in its heart of hearts, *The Bachelor* wants to be read as fairy tale, and though *Fifth Wheel* offers itself as voyeuristic spectacle, their own distance from reality provides all the necessary ingredients for one to read them as camp silly carnival and thus to turn their more nightmarish depictions of women into blatantly obvious and ludicrously constructed carnivalesque figures, to be laughed at and enjoyed as bad television, as marionette shows of televisual stereotyping, and as playgrounds for evaluating gender performance.

I do not suggest that this reading strategy is one shared by all readers; on the contrary, the fairy tale and spectacle strands of the dating show are clearly alive and kicking. A sobering reminder of how dating shows can create misogynist representations of the real comes to us from a reviewer of *The Bachelor* on *The Internet Movie Database* (www.imdb.com), who disturbingly notes that "I'm still a youngster, and was led to believe that women gradually grew out of their shallowness as they got older and more realistic about their future partner. This show is proving otherwise." Moreover, while a carnivalesque reading strategy might allow one to enjoy *The Bachelor* as camp, being an active, resistant audience takes effort.[24]

A reading strategy of negation may work for only a few episodes before boredom sets in, the carnival ends, and one is left with a pageant of poor depictions. Fairy tale told, spectacle staged, or carnival enacted, it can often be hard not to feel jilted and dumped by the dating show, which perhaps explains the average dating show's short shelf-life. But the discursive possibilities are rich, and some carnivals more riotous than others, as dating show performances and their brief respites of play and of silliness can offer many more versions of femininity, gender, and reality than a shocked first glance might suggest.

NOTES

1. Alison Graham-Bertolini, "*Joe Millionaire* as Fairy Tale: A Feminist Critique," *Feminist Media Studies* 4 (2004), 342.

2. Ibid.

3. Justin DeRose, Elfriede Fürsich, and Ekaterina V. Haskins, "Pop (Up) Goes the *Blind Date*: Supertextual Constraints on 'Reality' Television," *Journal of Communication Inquiry* 27.2 (2004), 178.

4. Laura Mulvey, "Visual Pleasure and Narrative Cinema," *Screen* 16.3 (1975), 6–18.

5. Paige Albiniak, "Dating Service," *Broadcasting and Cable*, 22 March 2004, 23.

6. DeRose et al., "Pop (Up)," 176.

7. John Fiske, *Reading Popular Culture* (London: Unwin Hyman, 1989).

8. Myra Mendible, "Humiliation, Subjectivity, and Reality TV," *Feminist Media Studies* 4 (2004), 337.

9. Fiske, *Reading Popular Culture*, 141.

10. Judith Butler, *Gender Trouble: Feminism and the Subversion of Identity* (New York: Routledge, 1990); Candace West and Don Zimmerman, "Doing Gender," *Gender and Society* 1.2 (1987), 125–51.

11. Butler, *Gender Trouble*, 176–177; and Leila J. Rupp and Verta Taylor, *Drag Queens at the 801 Cabaret* (Chicago: University of Chicago Press, 2003).

12. Mikhail Bakhtin, *The Dialogic Imagination,* trans. Caryl Emerson and Michael Holquist, ed. Michael Holquist (Austin: University of Texas Press, 1981).

13. DeRose et al., "Pop (Up)."

14. George Lipsitz, *Time Passages: Collective Memory and American Popular Culture,* (Minneapolis: University of Minnesota Press, 1990); and Fredric Jameson, "Reification and Utopia in Mass Culture," *Social Text* 1.1 (1979), 7–39.

15. Kathleen Rowe, *The Unruly Woman: Gender and the Genres of Laughter* (Austin: University of Texas Press, 1995).

16. Ibid., 3.

17. Yvonne D. Sims, *Women of Blaxploitation: How the Black Action Film Heroine Changed American Popular Culture* (Jefferson, N.C.: McFarland, 2006); and Ed Guerrero, *Framing Blackness: The African American Image in Film* (Philadelphia: Temple University Press, 1993).

18. Mikhail Bakhtin, *Rabelais and His World,* trans. Hélène Iswolsky (Cambridge: MIT Press, 1984), 10.

19. Sigmund Freud, *Jokes and Their Relation to the Unconscious,* trans. James Strachey (London: Hogarth, 1960), 108, 134, 136.

20. Bakhtin, *Rabelais,* 123.

21. On camp, see Susan Sontag, *Against Interpretation, and Other Essays* (New York: Delta, 1967), 275–92.

22. Kevin Glynn, *Tabloid Culture: Trash Taste, Popular Power, and the Transformation of American Television* (Durham, N.C.: Duke University Press, 2000).

23. Umberto Eco, "The Frames of Comic 'Freedom,'" in *Carnival!,* ed. Thomas A. Sebeok (New York: Mouton, 1984), 1–9; and Chris Powell, "A Phenomenological Analysis of Humour in Society," in *Humour in Society: Resistance and Control,* ed. Chris Powell and George E. C. Paton (New York: St. Martins, 1988), 86–105.

24. Celeste Condit, "The Rhetorical Limits of Polysemy," *Critical Studies in Mass Communications* 6 (1994): 103–22.

||||||||||||||||||||||||||||||||||||||||||||||||||||||

14

The Comedic Treatment of Reality
Kathy Griffin: My Life on the D-List, Fat Actress, and The Comeback

Heather Osborne-Thompson

In 2005, three reality-inflected series featuring female comedians appeared on American cable networks: Bravo's *Kathy Griffin: My Life on the D-List,* a six-part "special" based on the life of stand-up comedian Kathy Griffin, and Showtime's *Fat Actress* and HBO's *The Comeback*—two half-hour comedies about fictional former sitcom stars featuring actual former sitcom stars Kirstie Alley and Lisa Kudrow.[1]

Their appearances came in the wake of two closely related trends in post–network television comedy: a renewed interest on the part of the traditional networks in inexpensive and unscripted reality television formats that began with the introduction of such popular programs as *Survivor* (CBS, 2000–) and the so-called death of the traditional sitcom format lamented by critics and industry professionals at approximately the same time. In this respect, they could be interpreted as benefiting from the critical and popular success of reality-sitcom hybrids, such as the Larry David–centered *Curb Your Enthusiasm* (HBO, 2000–), the British (and later American) series *The Office* (BBC, 2001–3, and NBC, 2005–), and the FOX dysfunctional family sitcom, *Arrested Development* (2003–6).

With their cinema verité aesthetic, reliance on improvisation, and focus on comedy that comes from the myriad shortcomings and outright hostility of their main characters—a form that Walter Metz has designated the "cringe-com"[2]—such programs were often credited as reviving the flagging situation comedy form and providing the model for a spate of comedy programs popping up on both traditional networks and the cable landscape.[3]

However, while this industry and critic-based definition of comedy-reality hybrids might well explain the appearance of *The D-List, Fat Actress,* and *The Comeback* on cable schedules at this particular moment, a more careful assessment of their generic roots would also have to acknowledge the gendered dimensions of what Jason Mittell calls the "conventions and assumptions from a range of genres" that reality TV hybrids draw from more generally.[4] For what distinguishes *The D-List, Fat Actress,* and *The Comeback* from their celebrated male counterparts is their investment in foregrounding the often humiliating processes by which "real" female comedians attain visibility on television.

For example, *D-List*—the only show out of the three that purports to be a "straight-up" reality program—fashions cinema verité–style footage of Kathy Griffin's everyday life as a stand-up comedian into a first-person narrative about her status as a "D-list" celebrity. Typical episodes might include sequences in which Griffin "bombs" on the stand-up stage or is snubbed by other, more successful celebrities.

Similarly, as a sitcom-based rendering of *Cheers* and *Veronica's Closet* star Kirstie Alley's well-publicized battle with her weight, *Fat Actress* employs a roving single camera that lingers on the faces of horrified onlookers—including network presidents and Alley's celebrity pals—as the once trim and sexy star lumbers past in seeming oblivion.

Finally, *The Comeback*'s Valerie Cherish is based on a character that Lisa Kudrow reportedly created during her tenure in the L.A. improvisational comedy troupe The Groundlings—a character whom she has referred to ironically as "your favorite actress on a talk show."[5] Significantly, despite Kudrow's protestations, critics repeatedly sought to make a connection between the talented actress who had recently finished working on the enormously successful and long-running *Friends* (NBC, 1994–2004), and Cherish, a cloying, narcissistic has-been who unwittingly alienates nearly everyone she comes into contact with and who never was able to duplicate the success of her own enormously successful sitcom *I'm It.*

This seemingly stubborn impulse to ferret out the true connections between female comedians and their humiliating/humiliated on-screen personae is not particularly new; it informs the history of women and comedy both on television and within the culture more generally. As a number of feminist studies of women's humor (including Linda Martin and Kerry Segrave's survey of female comedians from 1860 to the mid-1980s, Nancy A. Walker's analysis of American women humor writers, and Frances Gray's discussion of American and British women's humor in television and stand-up comedy) have indicated, comedy—whether stand-up, slapstick, or satire—was commonly considered by philosophers, writers, and cultural critics to be "male terrain," as the female "nature" was invariably characterized as devoid of humor and better suited to "passive" pursuits, such as homemaking and motherhood.[6] As those aforementioned scholarly works have also indicated, however, funny women have nonetheless maintained a presence in popular culture, despite being fewer in number than their male counterparts.

Historians Robert C. Allen and Susan A. Glenn have demonstrated in their studies of late-19th- and early-20th-century popular comedy that the typical strategy of mainstream cultural critics was to explain the existence of such performers as "aberrations" that resulted from their "failures" as women.[7] Indeed, many of these performers, including singer Sophie Tucker and film comedian Marie Dressler, made their "shortcomings" as women—which included their girth and their various appetites—part of their acts.

This "unruliness," or publicly laying claim to all of those unfeminine or grotesque characteristics that have historically been attributed to female comedic performers, is, according to Kathleen Rowe, part of a much longer tradition of women who provoke ambivalent responses in observers because of their penchant for transgressing boundaries of feminine taste and decorum by being too loud, too physical, too fat, or too ugly.[8] Citing an array of diverse figures from more contemporary popular culture, such as Miss Piggy and Roseanne Barr, Rowe argues that these women's expressions of "gargantuan" female desire—often indicated by their loose bodies, big mouths, and even bigger appetites—unsettle even as they delight and therefore must be carefully "emplotted" in narratives which contain the threat of that desire.[9]

Quite understandably, then, histories of the relationship between female comedians and American television have tended to focus on the ways such age-old characterizations of these women have influenced the terms by which they were allowed to be visible on the small screen. Many such histories point to a 1953 piece on female television comedians by *New York Times* critic Jack Gould, suggesting that, as a domestic medium, television was the perfect showcase for female comedians, who often had trouble being as successful as male comedians because of the cultural constraints that governed their reception in the more public venues of vaudeville stage and film screen.[10]

Indeed, as Denise Mann, Mary Desjardins, and Susan Murray have pointed out, a number of the most popular female comedians of early television, such as Martha Raye, Imogene Coca, and Lucille Ball, had already made their careers on radio and vaudeville stages and in Hollywood cinema before making the transition to television.[11] According to these scholars, part of the task of adapting their often spectacular performance styles to the new medium involved carefully navigating the intimate relationship that television networks sought to foster with their viewers.[12]

In practice, this sometimes meant cultivating less-glamorous personae by emphasizing the stars' "ordinary" qualities, as well as developing narrative formats in which their outrageous physical comedy could be both showcased and "explained" by narrative conceits. In this context, for example, the famously "rubber-faced" Martha Raye (of *The Martha Raye Show* [NBC, 1952–54]) and Imogene Coca (of *Your Show of Shows* [NBC, 1950–54]) were positioned as "fans" of more glamorous celebrities or the "sidekicks" of more famous male comedians, respectively,[13] and the once-celebrated Hollywood glamour girl Lucille Ball became an ordinary housewife and "'real' American woman" both on and off the set of *I Love Lucy* (CBS, 1951–57).[14]

Regardless of the realities of their personal lives, female comedians like Raye, Coca, and Ball helped to "sell" the new medium as a domestic one, in part by selling versions of themselves that highlighted the ways in which they and their unruly comedy had been literally or figuratively "domesticated" by television.[15] In turn, according to Patricia Mellencamp, such early representations of zany but domesticated female comedians ultimately helped to usher in an even more "pacified" version of femininity in situation comedies of the late 1950s and early 1960s, such as Laura Petrie of *The Dick van Dyke Show* (CBS, 1961–66).[16]

Although the degree to which such outrageously funny women can be said to be "contained" by the medium has certainly diminished since the early years of television—particularly with respect to powerful and popular figures like Barr, who, as Rowe has suggested, is able to "author" herself in ways that her predecessors were not[17]—the question of why women continue to be disproportionately likely to appear on television in comedic formats where they tend to perform their "failures" as women still haunts critical appraisals of their work.

This is where I want to situate my discussion of the three programs in question. For while they are undoubtedly capitalizing on the vogue for reality-based situation comedies whose humor comes from making people uncomfortable, they are also in dialogue with a much longer tradition of female television comedians who have always foregrounded their perceived shortcomings for their audiences' pleasure. The difference between these earlier performers and the stars of *D-List, Fat Actress,* and *The Comeback* is one of degree. In many ways, the three programs echo earlier televisual attempts to use comedy as a space in which to perform women's struggles for visibility and equality; however, their relative proximity to "reality" (made possible by camera and editing techniques, among other things) creates a startling sense of urgency that arguably highlights the stakes of the comedy in a qualitatively different way.

That is, by linking the history of women's television comedy—which is itself defined by a series of compromises designed to domesticate the more culturally undesirable aspects of female comedians—to production techniques that connote "reality" in televisual terms, these programs engage in what Jason Mittell might refer to as an "escalation" of the emotional stakes associated with their respective genres.[18] Like all reality shows, they are generic amalgams whose particular combinations are designed to "press the boundaries of audience tolerance and pleasure" by removing the "fictional frame" or distance between actors and audiences that more traditional genres hold in place.[19]

But unlike many celeb-reality shows like *The Surreal Life* (WB and VH1, 2003–) and *My Fair Brady* (VH1, 2005–), which are ostensibly structured to "catch" their protagonists behaving badly on the fly, the raison d'être of *D-List, Fat Actress,* and *The Comeback* is to *invite* viewers to witness the process by which their stars craft the "raw" material of their difficulties with age, weight, and sexism into comedic narratives. And it is this sense of intentionality that both suggests a development of the forms women's comedy can take on television and helps to explain the critical reception of the programs and their relatively short lifespans.[20]

My Life on the D-List

Of the three programs in question, *Kathy Griffin: My Life on the D-List* gets its dominant sensibility from stand-up comedy. Indeed, although she has worked in narrative genres on television, such as situation comedy,[21] Griffin mainly works as a stand-up comedian who appears in nonfiction formats such as comedy concerts and "red-carpet coverage" segments of celebrity awards shows.

From the moment its opening credits begin, then, *My Life on the D-List* is presented as the distilled version of a comedian's real life that characterizes most stand-up comedy acts. Standing before a red velvet curtain and behind a microphone, Griffin utters a typical monologue opener—"Okay, here's the thing . . ."—as if she is speaking to one of her stand-up audiences. Before she can continue, however, the curtain is pulled aside to allow a moving camera to enter an animated world of the celebrity red carpet. Griffin stands off to the side as images of glamorously dressed, anonymous starlet "types" emerge from limousines and make their way along the fabled path to fame. On the soundtrack, the theme song, which is performed by a woman in the manner of a white soul singer, belittles the starlets as "bores," while a cut-out version of Griffin kicks and claws her way, *South Park*-like, along the carpet to a fictional comedy club called the Hoo-Hah Hut:

> Get out of my way,
> you A-List bores. [male voice shouts "Bor-ing!"]
> My Prada shoes are as good as yours.
> I worked twice as hard to get half as far as you
> 'cause there ain't no ass to kiss
> when you're livin' life on the D-list.

By constructing the opening credits—which will mark the beginning of every new episode—as a stand-up monologue about Griffin's struggle to "screw her way to the middle," the program alerts viewers to the idea that the reality of her life they are about to gain access to is a continuation of her stand-up shtick.[22] Rather than consume the thumbnail sketch of her life that comprises a single evening of stand-up, however, viewers are invited to watch Griffin's endlessly repeatable *lack* of ability to get beyond the status of middling celebrity who makes a nice living but nonetheless works tirelessly to maintain her public visibility.

To make that symbiotic relationship between her comedy and her "real" life clear, the first episode of the series begins with a typical reality show sequence that connects footage of Griffin interacting with her rather anemic entourage: her husband, Matt Moline, with whom she is pictured at home, at celebrity events and comedy gigs, and in the backs of limousines; her assistant, Jessica Zajicek, who is quoted as saying, "When I tell people I work for Kathy Griffin, they either say, 'Who's that?' or 'Does she suck?'"; Griffin's elderly parents, who are often pictured drinking wine in the afternoon and questioning (as doting, biased parents might) whether their daughter is really on the "D-list"; and her two closest friends, Dennis and Tony, whom Griffin calls "her gays." Laid over the entire sequence, Griffin's voice explains how much of a "job" her job is and saying how grateful she is to have those people to help her through it.

In this respect, we might understand *My Life on the D-List* as a narrative version of the troubled relationship between the shockingly personal stand-up style adopted by many female comedians and network television that polices the boundaries of middle-class taste. Historically, the strategy for navigating this relationship has been either to formulate stand-up routines that *do* conform to stereotypical notions of what makes women funny on the small screen or to work outside the realm of television altogether.

As examples of the former option, one might think of personalities like Totie Fields and Phyllis Diller, who crafted very recognizeable personae on such programs as *The Ed Sullivan Show* and talk and game shows as fat, ugly, or undesirable women and whose jokes were often contained within discussions or images of more normative femininity. The latter option is embodied by figures like Margaret Cho, who produced several successful concert films that document her antagonistic relationship to television, and of older comics like Belle Barth and Moms Mabley, who were largely excluded from network TV because of their decidedly nontasteful, nonwhite, or non-middle-class material.

By linking the somewhat sarcastic characterization of her celebrity life as a job with verité-style footage that follows Griffin as she navigates red carpets, radio interviews, and book tours; performs tasks like searching her closet for an outfit that doesn't make her look fat and driving herself to appearances; and suffers the indignities of being misidentified with other mid-level celebrities, such as Kathie Lee Gifford, *My Life on the D-List* appears to take stand-up comedy's confessional mode beyond the narrative or fictional "frame" that television typically allows women's comedy.[23]

That is, rather than employing the stereotypical strategy of presenting her failures as a woman/celebrity/comedian via a carefully timed stand-up routine, Griffin offers these usually mundane, sometimes painful, sequences as hard evidence of the difficult and lonely work involved with becoming a comedian and celebrity with a recognizable persona. Hence, rather than choosing the above-named options of conforming to televisual standards of the way female comedians should behave or working outside of television altogether, Kathy Griffin takes the "middle road" in that she documents the process by which she fails to connect with "mainstream" audiences through material that seems to delight in attacking "mainstream" sensibilities.

A particularly good example of this alienation occurs in the first episode of the show when Griffin has been tapped to host a charity event at the Beverly Hilton Hotel for the John Wayne Cancer Institute. This sequence is constructed in the manner of an instant replay, cutting back and forth between a medium shot of Griffin being interviewed at home about the numerous humiliations of the evening and the documentary footage of those humiliations. After explaining that she knew that the people attending this event did not comprise her core audience (and would therefore not find her comedy accessible), she maintains that her dual interest in charity work and in public visibility (illustrated by her excitement about the possibility of having a photo taken with Warren Beatty) compelled her to accept the gig. This prefatory statement then gives way to evidence of Griffin's D-list status: long shots of her on stage rattling off jokes about PETA and Brooke Shields are cut with medium and close-up shots of guests not connecting with her act by talking through it, rolling their eyes, and picking their teeth as her voice echoes around the seemingly cavernous room.

In the face of what is designed to show her humiliation as a "fish-out-of-water" female comic, then, Griffin's postmortem session—in which she drops one-liners like, "The silent auction was deafening compared to the reception I got"—functions as a corrective stand-up routine. Through her narrativization of what comedians refer to as "dying" on stage, which is made possible by the cameras that seem to follow her everywhere, Griffin is able to demonstrate both the scope of the failure she often experiences (despite her tireless efforts) and the process by which that failure becomes comedy.

In this way, the program, which presents stand-up comedy as a process of instant replay and revision, uses documentary conventions to highlight its connection to the pleasures of reality TV. That is, by "pulling back the curtain" on a performance that usually begins and ends on a stand-up stage,[24] *My Life on the D-List* offers a privileged, almost illicit view of the work and pain that goes into Kathy Griffin's life as a female comedian beyond that stage.[25] Hence, Griffin is able to integrate the part of being a comedian that many longtime performers allude to but never show—the "dying" and the subsequent "rebirth" that often comes with that—into her comedy in the most immediate way possible.

Fat Actress

If *My Life on the D-List*'s "reality" takes its cue from the travails of a female celebrity who uses stand-up comedy as her weapon of choice against
invisibility, *Fat Actress* has more in common with the star-centered, spec-
tacle-focused domestic situation comedy à la *I Love Lucy* (CBS, 1951–57).
Whereas the central problematic that structured the Lucille Ball–Desi Arnaz vehicle had to do with whether or not the ambitious, but homebound
Lucy would ever break into show business, the question driving the narrative of *Fat Actress* has to do with whether the former situation comedy
star Kirstie Alley can get a job in Hollywood despite her obesity.

   Indeed, Alley's problem is not that she has a husband who wants to
prevent her from breaking into show business but that she has an agent
who is unable to help her break *back into* show business because she no
longer resembles the physical ideal for women in Hollywood. This fact,
which had been established in the "real world" of supermarket tabloids
long before *Fat Actress* began production, is taken up by the program in
spectacular fashion in every one of its seven episodes.

   Through sequences where Alley falls on the bathroom floor weeping
operatically after weighing herself; secretly feasts on Sirloin Burgers in her
car and, in between bites, screams at her agent for suggesting she take a
job as a spokesperson for Jenny Craig; and engages in a *9 ½ Weeks*–like
food orgy with a black NBC programming executive (played by comedian
Mark Curry) who appreciates her largesse (set to the music of The New-
beats' "Bread and Butter," of course),[26] Alley—much in the way Lucy Ricardo's spectacular physical performances represented a female body that
would not conform to expectations about the way middle-class housewives should behave—addresses the "problem" of the body that will not
assent to the pressures of an industry obsessed with thinness and youth
through performative excess.

   Not only does Alley eat constantly in each episode, but also she takes
up space in other ways: she sings, dances, swears, and talks about sex constantly. Nor does she give up her quest to work in television again, cajol-
ing her agent and eventually blackmailing NBC president Jeff Zucker into
a long-term development contract in the program's finale.

   What disturbed many critics and audiences about *Fat Actress* was perhaps the same question that scholars like Patricia Mellencamp have described as the "double bind" that makes spectacular performances by

sitcom stars like Lucille Ball both pleasurable and disturbing.[27] That is: the pleasure that we as audience members receive from watching Lucy try and fail to become something other than a housewife is achieved through a kind of sublimation of her desire.[28]

So what does it say about the terms by which funny women attain visibility on television that they do so through a kind of spectacular failure that, by virtue of the narrative structure of the sitcom form, they are doomed to repeat during the very next episode? This seeming "replacement" of anger with comedy[29] was especially pronounced in the case of Kirstie Alley, who, unlike Lucille Ball, was not the head of a TV studio or one of the most powerful women in television but, rather, someone who *was* offered the chance to be a spokesperson for the Jenny Craig weight-loss plan and lobbied to appear on *The Oprah Winfrey Show* to discuss her weight-loss battle. So while the diegetic world of *Fat Actress* repeatedly portrays these aspirations as comical failures, the "real" Alley accepted the Jenny Craig offer (and lost more than 60 pounds), appeared on *Oprah* twice, and published a 2005 autobiography called *How to Lose Your Ass and Regain Your Life: Reluctant Confessions of a Big-Butted Star.*

Such relentless cross-promotion *was* clearly designed to repackage and sell a "new" version of Kirstie Alley that would help to jump-start her flagging career. But it's significant that it does so via *Fat Actress*'s hybridization of "reality" (the true story behind Alley's struggle to regain visibility in Hollywood as represented stylistically through cinema verité) and the somewhat formulaic, episodic spectacle of situation comedy. As opposed to the melodramatic narratives favored by other "documentary" forms, such as reality programs that focus on "has-been" celebrities, which position audiences to pity or condemn their subjects,[30] *Fat Actress* effects the same kind of relationship between Alley and her TV counterpart that Kathleen Rowe claims characterized the sitcom version of the much-maligned comedian Roseanne Barr in the 1980s and 1990s.[31]

In Rowe's view, while the cruel headlines splashed across supermarket checkstands allowed tabloid reporters to "write" the story of Barr's off-screen/offstage life in the excessive mode of melodrama, her stand-up comedy and her successful production of *Roseanne* allowed Barr to create an alternative, more empowering comedic version of that story (of which Barr is the author). And the interaction between those two modes is what created the ambivalent charge that is attached to Barr's persona.

While *Roseanne* focused on a character that was similar to her in terms of class background and motivations, however, *Fat Actress* uses a number of devices to indicate that Alley's character *is* Alley. Aside from the verité aesthetic, in which a camera follows the fictional Alley closely to capture every humiliating moment in her ongoing quest for a job and a love life, the program features some of the "real" Alley's closest friends and professional colleagues, such as John Travolta, Merv Griffin, and the aforementioned Jeff Zucker. In each case, they speak both *to* Alley when she is in frame and *about* her when she is out of earshot (typically offering harsh assessments of her "ruined" body).

For example, in the first episode of the program, John Travolta rushes to Alley's home in a panic after he phones and reaches a distraught, incoherent Alley (who has just stepped off the scale). Although she has sobbed, "They're killing me" into the phone because she has just been asked to take a job as a Jenny Craig spokesperson, Travolta thinks someone is actually killing her and calls the police. He discovers everything is all right when he meets Alley—who has just returned from a trip to the local Sirloin Burger wearing a peignoir and sporting bad bedhead—in her front yard. Once he sees that Alley is all right, Travolta leaves and chats with the police officers he has summoned. They ask, "Hey man, that's not the same chick from *Cheers,* is it?" and he answers, "Fellas, I knew this chick since she was boning cowboys in Wichita. She was an athlete, a swimmer. But . . . you go to flesh when you stop working out." Travolta's use of crass language—which is possible only because of the program's airing on Showtime—and the cavalier attitude he takes about the pain his friend is going through create the sense that there is a side to Hollywood that none of us—including the "fictional" Alley—knows. The conceit of the narrative is that it's only because she doesn't know all of what's being said about her by the press, her friends, and her colleagues that allows her to persevere in her attempts to get back to work and to be taken seriously as an actress.

But, of course, the "real" Kirstie Alley, who, along with Brenda Hampton and Sandy Chanley, produced the program, *does* know this. And *Fat Actress* offers a number of clues that this is the case, both in its publicity and the lampooning of Hollywood that occurs throughout the episodes. As part of her quest to lose weight, for example, Alley does everything from hiring a group of "little people" to help her "feel" smaller at the recommendation of former child star Mayim Bialik to consulting Quinn Taylor Scott, a fictional actress who is depicted getting collagen shots in her lips, prancing around in a pink tutu à la Lara Flynn Boyle, and espousing the benefits of eating cigarettes, scarfing laxatives and bulimic purging using a "beautiful" object ("like a MontBlanc pen or a cloisonné chopstick or something").

While comedically broad, characters like Scott, who is played by John Travolta's wife, actress Kelly Preston, are typical of the way *Fat Actress* offers special pleasure for those who are "in the know" about the pitfalls of Hollywood celebrity. At other times, this critique of that culture and its biggest stars is more pointed. This is illustrated in the first episode by the cell phone conversation Alley has with her agent Sam about Hollywood's double standard regarding overweight actors while she is camped out in her Bentley outside of Sirloin Burger. When he explains to her that he cannot help her get her own television show unless she is willing to lose weight, she counters with a list of heavy male actors whose careers have not suffered because of their weight:

Alley: I mean, look, John Goodman's got his own show. And Jason Alexander looks like a frickin' bowling ball. And how 'bout James Gandolfino [*sic*]? He's like the size of a whale—he's way, way, way fatter than I am, all right? . . . Do you think they said to Marlon Brando, "Listen, hey, Marlon, you're a little bit too fuckin' fat to do *Apocalypse*"?

Sam: They are all men . . .

Alley: I can *play* a man. I am an actress. I think that you're forgetting the fact that I have won, what, two—three Emmys and Golden Globes and many, many People's Choice Awards. . . . They can choose—they have a choice—and you know what? They choose me. So you need to choose me. Choose me, Sam! Choose me!

Although the sequence is meant to be humorous—particularly because the audience has a privileged view of Alley devouring a burger and searching her bra for stray French fries while making her impassioned speech— the scene provides a distilled example of the program's perspective on the limited, painful, and hypocritical options available for successful comedic actresses when they are no longer young and thin. However, unlike Lucy Ricardo, who seems doomed to repeat her spectacular but ultimately futile physical performances, and Roseanne Barr, whose more "realistic" program was liberated by the influence of her stand-up comedy yet framed by the narrative constraints and conventions of the sitcom,[32] through *Fat Actress*, Kirstie Alley is able to take advantage of the possibilities that Jason Mittell claims reality TV as an inherently hybridized form offers.[33]

By fusing the formal elements of reality shows and the situation comedy with the intertextuality of her star persona, *Fat Actress* tests the boundaries of what both Alley and prospective audiences can laugh at with regard to the plight of "fat actresses." And this is made clear by the way Alley moves between the narrative proper and the credits sequence of the program in which the camera follows the "real" her, dancing with her costars as songs about fat women play on the soundtrack. This ability to move between such spaces—arguably made possible by the mixing of generic elements—demonstrates that the option for Kirstie Alley, who knows she "is good writer, smart gal" and an actress, is to continue to demand that someone choose her, "no matter the size of butt" (and to keep dancing in the meantime):

> Decided to write book today. Thought am good writer, am smart gal, have interesting, sex-filled (lie) life.
>
> Thought can write about men, life, love, family, food, sex, and fat assedness.
>
> Thought can share stories with tiny-butted and big-butted alike.
>
> Can tell people why fat, why (was) cokehead, why traffic jams and herbal laxatives don't mix, and why suede pants and sprinklers have same rule. . . . More important . . . can show world how life is beautiful and funny, no matter size of butt.[34]

The Comeback

The Comeback is slightly different from the other two programs discussed so far. Situated as it was within the quality environment of the heavily promoted "not-TV" HBO and focused on a fictional television comedy actress, it was not overtly about Lisa Kudrow's failures on the small screen.

Indeed, perhaps as a way of distinguishing *The Comeback* from titles like *Kathy Griffin: My Life on the D-List* and *Fat Actress,* HBO characterized the program as "an original and timely look at the humor and humiliations that often accompany the single-minded pursuit of the limelight, and what passes for entertainment and 'reality' in the meat-grinder that is modern-day television."[35] Aside from including *The Comeback* in the company of what HBO's promotional spots referred to as its many "groundbreaking, critically acclaimed, smash hits," then, the channel (and

Kudrow, to some degree) sought to position protagonist Valerie Cherish as a *meditation* on the self-imposed humiliation of aging female stars that often occurs in the *non*-HBO arena of network television.

In this respect, although I think it shares some similarities with *Fat Actress*'s approach to comedic spectacle, *The Comeback*'s roots are in variety and sketch comedy, which is most closely associated on television with virtuoso performers like Carol Burnett. Like Burnett's long-running program did, *The Comeback* constructs a televisual space composed of multiple modes of representation and performance. As a "show-within-a-show," it is a fictional reality series about one of the stars of a fictional situation comedy, who, like Kathy Griffin in *D-List* and Kirstie Alley in *Fat Actress*, is trying to rebuild and maintain her career in television. What makes *The Comeback* more similar to the sketch comedy of Burnett (and, later, Lily Tomlin and Gilda Radner), however, is the program's ambivalence toward its protagonist, Valerie Cherish.

Like many of Burnett's characters, including Eunice from *Mama's Family,* and any number of disgruntled housewives, who were often parodies of female types that were layered with pathos, and, at times, anger, Cherish is not easily dismissed as totally ridiculous, nor is she totally likeable. Alternating between the cinema verité style in which Cherish addresses the reality show's cameras directly and the multicamera aesthetic and line readings of a traditional sitcom, *The Comeback* offers a double view of her. On one hand, the reality show consistently reveals her irritatingly fake demeanor and delusions about her own importance (for which she is marginalized and treated badly by the producers of her sitcom), and on the other, her work in front of the sitcom cameras is depicted as that of a highly competent comedic actress who is willing to work hard to get a laugh.

In this respect, perhaps the most significant moment of *The Comeback* occurs during episode 12 (entitled "Valerie Shines under Stress"). As the second-to-last episode of the series, it marks a breaking point for Valerie in which she has decided she can take no more of the abuse that Pauly G., one of *Room and Bored*'s head writers, has heaped on her over the course of the sitcom's development. In contrast to Tom, his co-head writer, who tries to be respectful to the overbearing Cherish, Pauly G. is unabashedly ugly to her, refusing to speak with her, glaring at her, and deliberately leaving her out of off-the-set social gatherings. In this way, he operates as the "surrogate contempt provider" for the other characters in the show, as he says and does what no one else has the guts to do.

Programs like *Fat Actress* and *The Comeback* craft the "raw material" of famous women's insecurities as comedic narratives.

From the perspective of the faux-reality program, the stakes in this episode are high because *The Comeback*'s producer Jane has informed Pauly G. and Tom that, since they are contractually obligated to give Valerie a certain number of lines, they can no longer write her out of scripts and out of the visibility that she so desperately craves. Although this sequence occurs on camera but out of range of the sound people, the only audible sound is Pauly G.'s "No fucking way," which sets the tone for the rest of the episode. Once it has been decided that Valerie's character, Aunt Sassy, who is the "chaperone" to a group of 20-something coeds to which she rents a condominium, will be given an episode that will require her to do a pratfall dressed as a giant cupcake, Valerie begins to prepare for her "big" scene. She consults her former director on *I'm It* (who is played by comedy writing legend Jim Burrows) for tips on the best way to do the fall and practices for hours on pillows in her bedroom—caught on tape by the surveilling eye of the reality show camera.

Concurrent with these plot developments, Jane learns (accidentally) that Valerie—who was diagnosed with scoliosis as a teenager—has a metal rod in her back. When Jane asks Valerie to comment on this on camera, the episode experiences a shift in tone. As Valerie talks about suiting up for every field hockey game, despite her inability to play because of her back brace and her subsequent exclusion from the team picture, she begins to weep and waves the camera off. As the camera pans to the side, it catches a glimpse of Jane in a dressing room mirror, and we discover that she is also weeping and also waves the camera off.

By the time the final taping of Aunt Sassy's cupcake episode rolls around, the mood of the reality show is apprehensive, both because of the worry that Valerie will not fall properly and injure her back and because Pauly G. will be the sole head writer on set for the evening. For most of the taping, he is captured by the reality camera downing tequila shots and snarfing pizza, while Valerie tries in vain to do a take of her pratfall that will impress him. After numerous equipment problems and multiple takes, Valerie decides to try something new and fall on her back, which is risky and none-too-popular with the reality show and sitcom crews. When she completes the take and asks once more for Pauly's approval, he shrugs and she snaps:

Valerie [trying to catch her breath]: Good, okay, yeah. . . . I think that was the one. Right Pauly?
Pauly [sullenly]: I liked the first one.

Valerie: Then why did I do all those other takes?

Pauly: Because you like throwing yourself on the ground?

Valerie: You know . . . I could have really hurt myself [sounds as though she might begin to cry]

Pauly: Relax! It was a joke! What? Does that rod in your back go all the way up your ass?

Valerie [turns to walk away]: All right . . . well [at the last second, whirls around and punches Pauly in the gut].

Pauly: Fuck! [vomits]

Valerie [vomits in response]: Blahhh!

Pauly: Turn the fucking camera off!

Valerie: Get it off! No!! Augh! [runs off set]

[Camera follows Pauly G. as he exits the set, cuts to Jane who is flab-bergasted but half-smiling, then pans to puddles of vomit and zooms in.]

The elaborate setup that was necessary to explain the effect of this se-quence is typical of reality shows, whose structures are built out of lay-ers of fleeting encounters between their "actors" and usually culminate in highly edited moments of surprise, crisis, or revelation. What makes this sequence powerful is its uncharacteristic view of the sitcom and its grue-some "behind the laughter" perspective of its subject, Cherish, whose car-toonish self-centeredness has, if only momentarily, given way to pathos. Like Carol Burnett's character of Eunice—who is both a grating drama queen and a woman tragically trapped within the bickering, stifling, dead-end world of her brutally critical mother and ambitionless husband—Val-erie is represented here as vulnerable in a way that causes others (Jane) to empathize with her.

Whereas the sympathy that Eunice might have evoked in audiences at the time would not be easy to quantify, *The Comeback*'s reality aesthetic attempts to provide such evidence through the surreptitious glances of its camera. Even as the camera settles its gaze on the vomit, however, the feeling is gone. Despite the fact that the people closest to Valerie—Jane; Valerie's hairdresser, Mickey; and Wagner, the director of the cupcake episode—seem satisfied with, if shocked, by her display, Valerie is only horrified that she vomited on camera and violated the idealized image of herself that she had been so carefully trying to craft.[36]

Ironically, this sequence—which caused Valerie so much personal pain—would also be the one that made her reality show a ratings success, and *The Comeback* ends with her on *The Tonight Show,* basking in the applause for her humiliation. As HBO's publicity for *The Comeback* suggests, such moments are staples of reality programs and perhaps a key to understanding the specific kind of celebrity that comes with them. However, by combining the "reality" mode with the improvisational or sketch comedy character of Cherish, *The Comeback* engages in and extends the kind of comedic balancing act—between the "real" and constructed—that characterizes the female characters created by such gifted comedians as Carol Burnett in the variety programs of the 1960s and 1970s. Through their emotional volatility and broad physical comedy, Burnett's characters critiqued images of women as comfortable in domestic roles that circulated within television and popular culture of the time, yet they were limited by the spatial and narrative frames of the variety theater and the comedy sketch.

The Comeback's use of reality TV conventions allow it to transcend such limits by subjecting Cherish to 24-hour video surveillance and by voyeuristically looking to capture painful private moments with all available technology. The lead-up to the vomiting scene, with its stealthy "peeks" at Valerie's personal and workplace crises and the zoom in on the puddles of vomit display a contempt for the intrusiveness and indignity of reality shows and provide a comedic perspective on the humiliating options available to female celebrities of a certain age who crave visibility on television.

And I think this was a sticking point for many critics and potential viewers of the program, who felt that *The Comeback* was too "real" in its abuse of both the Cherish character and the sitcoms on which the show is based.[37] As one of many bewildered reviewers who couldn't quite get behind the Kudrow vehicle, *Entertainment Weekly* television critic Gillian Flynn claimed that *Entourage* (HBO, 2004–)—"a series about a pack of voracious, womanizing, party-hopping dudes"—was "both smarter and more humane" than *The Comeback.*

The fairly short life (by American television standards) and "means-to-an-end" aspects of *D-List, Fat Actress,* and *The Comeback* beg the question of exactly where in the post–network TV landscape such experiments with the "reality" of women's comedy can attract sustained interest. As the continued popularity of *Entourage* suggests, the "warts and all" promise of reality-comedy hybrids is a gendered one. Some warts—the "boys will be boys" variety, in particular, in which too many people want to sleep with you and you can't decide between acting in a blockbuster or an independent feature—foster palatable and marketable illusions about celebrity. Other warts, like the ones exhibited by Griffin, Alley, and Kudrow, create a sense of reality that is so intimate and humiliating, you eventually have to turn away.

NOTES

1. *D-List* continued for a fourth season and episodes of the program continue to air on Bravo.

2. Walter Metz, "Big Man on Campus Ladies," *Flow* 3.11, at http://jot.communications.utexas.edu/flow/.

3. A typical example of the critical perspective on these types of programs appeared in a review of FOX's *Free Ride* and ABC's *Sons and Daughters,* which traced the roots of these now-defunct programs to the "openly hostile family show" *Arrested Development* and the vogue for "reality" ushered in by *American Idol* and others. Paul Brownfield, "In Sitcoms, Hostility Trumps All," *Los Angeles Times,* 1 March 2006, E1+.

4. Jason Mittell, *Genre and Television: From Cop Shows to Cartoons in American Culture* (New York: Routledge, 2004), 197.

5. Alynda Wheat, "Lisa Kudrow's New Reality," *Entertainment Weekly,* 3 June 2005, 54.

6. Linda Martin and Kerry Segrave, *Women in Comedy: The Funny Ladies from the Turn of the Century to the Present* (Secaucus, N.J.: Citadel, 1986); Nancy A. Walker, *A Very Serious Thing: Women's Humor and American Culture* (Minneapolis: University of Minnesota Press, 1988); and Frances Gray, *Women and Laughter* (Charlottesville: University Press of Virginia, 1994).

7. Robert C. Allen, *Horrible Prettiness: Burlesque and American Culture* (Chapel Hill: University of North Carolina Press, 1991); and Susan A. Glenn, *Female Spectacle: The Theatrical Roots of Modern Feminism* (Cambridge: Harvard University Press, 2000).

8. Kathleen Rowe, *The Unruly Woman: Gender and the Genres of Laughter* (Austin: University of Texas Press, 1995), 30–31.

9. The two types of narratives Rowe claims best accommodate such transgressive female desire are melodrama and comedy. *Unruly Woman,* 99.

10. Jack Gould, "TV's Top Comediennes," *New York Times Magazine,* 27 December 1953, 16–17.

11. Denise Mann, "The Spectacularization of Everyday Life: Recycling Hollywood Stars and Fans in Early Television Variety Shows," in *Private Screenings: Television and the Female Consumer,* ed. Lynn Spigel and Denise Mann (Minneapolis: University of Minnesota Press, 1992), 41–69; Mary Desjardins, "Lucy and Desi: Sexuality, Ethnicity, and TV's First Family," in *Television, History, and*

American Culture: Feminist Critical Essays, ed. Mary Beth Haralovich and Lauren Rabinovitz (Durham, N.C.: Duke University Press, 1999), 56–74; and Susan Murray, *Hitch Your Antenna to the Stars: Early Television and Broadcast Stardom* (New York: Routledge, 2005), particularly 139–87.

12. Lynn Spigel also addresses this point in her book on the myriad strategies by which television was introduced and marketed to consumers. Lynn Spigel, *Make Room for TV: Television and the Family Ideal in Postwar America* (Chicago: University of Chicago Press, 1992), particularly 136–80.

13. Mann, "Spectacularization of Everyday Life," 59.

14. Murray, *Hitch Your Antenna,* 163, 168.

15. Ibid., 167–68.

16. Patricia Mellencamp, "Situation Comedy, Feminism and Freud: Discourses of Gracie and Lucy," in *Feminist Television Criticism: A Reader,* ed. Charlotte Brunsdon, Julie D'Acci, and Lynn Spigel (Oxford: Clarendon, 1997), 62.

17. Rowe, *Unruly Woman,* particularly 76–82.

18. Mittell, *Genre and Television,* 198.

19. Ibid.

20. Each series had short seasons—lasting between 7 and 13 episodes—and only one (*D-List*) is still on the air. *Fat Actress* had a "means to an end" quality, in that Kirstie Alley lost the weight that made her a "fat actress" as part of her duties as spokesperson for the weight-loss company Jenny Craig. *The Comeback* was the only one of the three to be cancelled due to low ratings.

21. Griffin played Susan Keane's (Brooke Shields) wacky office pal Vicki Groener on *Suddenly Susan* (NBC, 1996–2000).

22. In episode 1 of the series, Griffin claims to have done this.

23. Mittell, *Genre and Television,* 198.

24. David Marc refers to stand-up comedy as "presentational comedy" that occurs on a stage "in front of the curtain." David Marc, "Television Comedy," in *What's So Funny? Humor in American Culture,* ed. Nancy A. Walker (Wilmington, Del.: Scholarly Resources, 1998), 262.

25. Mittell, *Genre and Television,* 198.

26. The subplot surrounding Alley's fling with Mark Curry is typical of many reality-sitcom hybrids that seem intent on transgressing certain notions of "politically correct" behavior by depicting overly frank conversations about such topics as race. In this context, Alley's openly stated and problematic search for a black male lover—because "black men like big women"—is presumably meant to signal her general unruliness.

27. Mellencamp, "Situation Comedy, Feminism and Freud," 73.

28. Ibid.

29. Ibid.

30. Both Bill Nichols and Brian Winston have written about nonfiction that exhorts audiences to feel sorry for (but not intervene on behalf of) its subjects.

Bill Nichols, *Blurred Boundaries: Questions of Meaning in Contemporary Culture* (Bloomington: Indiana University Press, 1994), 43–62; and Brian Winston, "The Tradition of the Victim in Griersonian Documentary," in *New Challenges for Documentary,* ed. Alan Rosenthal (Berkeley: University of California Press, 1988), 269–87.

31. Kathleen Rowe, "Roseanne: Unruly Woman as Domestic Goddess," in *Feminist Television Criticism: A Reader,* ed. Charlotte Brunsdon, Julie D'Acci, and Lynn Spigel (Oxford: Clarendon, 1997), 75.

32. Kathleen Rowe claims that one of the distinguishing features of Roseanne was its more "realistic" feel that was made possible by Roseanne Barr's persona and feminism-inflected stand-up routines. *Unruly Woman,* 82.

33. Mittell, *Genre and Television,* 198.

34. Promotional insert.

35. HBO, *The Comeback*—About the Show, at http://www.hbo.com/comeback/about/.

36. According to the DVD commentary for this episode, which was done by Kudrow and producer Michael Patrick King, Kudrow was not pleased with this sequence, either, and resented having to do so many "vomit" takes. Commentary for "Valerie Shines under Stress," *The Comeback: The Complete Only Season,* HBO Video, 2006.

37. Gillian Flynn, "Ego Trips," *Entertainment Weekly,* 10 June 2005, 91–92.

Part IV

||||||||||||||||||||||||||||||||||||||||||||||||||||||||||

Interactivity

15

||||||||||||||||||||||||||||||||||||||||||||||||||||||||||

Melancholy, Merit, and Merchandise
The Postwar Audience Participation Show

Amber Watts

Between 2003 and 2005, American reality television experienced a significant shift in tone. While castaways continued to backstab one another on
Survivor, neighbors glued hay onto one another's living room walls while
Trading Spaces, and Simon Cowell lambasted untalented *American Idol*
auditioners, a slew of other shows premiered with the ostensible goal of
helping people in need. Writing about the premiere of *Wife Swap* in 2004,
New York Times television critic Alessandra Stanley declared, "The revolution known as reality television has reached its Thermidor: pathos, verg-
ing on bathos, is the ruling fashion."[1]

Indeed, this period saw the debut of many "feel-good" reality shows
that set out to transform their subjects inside and out, while tugging at
America's heartstrings. Programs like *Miracle Workers, Supernanny, Nanny
9-1-1, The Biggest Loser, Extreme Makeover: Home Edition,* and *Renovate
My Family* sought to transform real Americans in real need—be it of
medical, economic, psychological, or behavioral support—into healthy,
attractive, and financially stable citizens. And, with *Extreme Makeover:
Home Edition* leading the way, all these programs framed their subjects'
transformations as narratives of misery and redemption, with the shows
themselves playing the role of altruistic benefactors to the downtrodden.

Time magazine's James Poniewozik praised this turn away from reality TV's earlier cynicism, saying that it was "good to see TV using its resources for an act of charity other than giving Jenny McCarthy a sitcom"
and commending the shows' abilities to help others and to inspire viewers to do the same.[2] This charitable programming borne of real people's
troubles proved to be a successful formula, resonating with the American

The studio audience voted on *Queen for a Day,* an antecedent of today's inter-active reality programs.

audience. In 2005, *Extreme Makeover: Home Edition* was the second high-est-rated reality show on television and the seventeenth highest-rated show overall for the season,[3] suggesting a broad appeal for both audience and producers trading in these fantasies of melancholy and metamorphosis.

Despite Stanley's revolutionary prose, though, the association between television and real-life pathos predated the millennium. Fifty years earlier, the American airwaves were as full of misery and the promise of trans-formation as the 2004 prime-time schedule, if not even more so. The postwar "audience participation" genre, including shows like *Queen for a Day, Strike It Rich, The Big Payoff,* and *High Finance,* featured individuals disclosing real-life troubles on-air in hope of receiving some reward in return. Audience participation programs situated their subjects' stories of hardship within various types of quiz and talk show formats, offering cash and prizes as the solution to personal tragedy. Much like contemporary "feel-good" reality programming, these shows promised to transform the lives of participants in significant ways.

On *Queen for a Day* (1945–56, Mutual; 1956–60, NBC; 1960–64, ABC), four women chosen from the studio audience told their hard-luck stories and explained how one desired item could assuage their troubles. At the end of the show, the audience voted by applause-o-meter for the most deserving contestant, who received her requested item, in addition to thousands of dollars of other sundry goods. *Strike It Rich* (1947–58, CBS) contestants described a product or service they desperately needed and answered quiz questions to win enough money to pay for it. Even if they failed, viewers could call the show's "Heart Line" and offer the contestants money, merchandise, housing, or even jobs. *The Big Payoff* (1951–53, NBC; 1953–59, CBS) had male contestants describe why their wives, mothers, or daughters deserved a reward. While the woman in question sat off to the side, her champion narrated her story and then answered a series of questions for prizes, ultimately aiming for the grand prize—a mink coat and trip to Paris.

Even boxer Joe Louis got into the act when he appeared on *High Finance* (1956–57, CBS). On this show, contestants answered current events questions to build a jackpot to fund their life's ambitions. This usually involved start-up money for a business, as was the case on the 1956 premiere for a retired Navy commander who wanted to open a miniature golf course. Louis's ambition was less entrepreneurial, though, and his narrative about why he needed money sounded more like that of a *Queen for a Day* contestant than a former heavyweight champion. Due to poor financial management, as he told the *High Finance* audience, Louis owed the IRS over $1 million in back taxes. He had turned to professional wrestling to try to pay the bills but sustained heart damage when he continued to wrestle after a brawny opponent jumped on his chest and broke three of his ribs. Unable to work, he turned to *High Finance* as his fiscal savior. For eight weeks in 1956, Louis and his wife appeared as special guests on the show, answering quiz questions for Uncle Sam. They accrued $41,000 in cash and prizes, all of which went to the IRS, and they only stopped when they arrived at a double-or-nothing round.[4]

While this is one of the stranger examples of the "needy" competing on quiz shows, it is nonetheless emblematic of the way televised competition and personal hardship came together in postwar America. The way audience participation shows combined narratives of melancholy and financial or merchandise-based relief directly spoke to a number of common anxieties Americans felt. Hearing about real people's difficulties—whether celebrity or civilian, and their problems resulting from tragedy or bad decisions—was compelling television, particularly when viewers could subsequently watch them repair the damage. And all of the shows offered a clear solution to their subjects' problems: entry into the consumer marketplace. The fiscal and material transformations on the shows structured consumer society as the resolution to complicated issues. By playing off the audience's fears and insecurities, they helped rewrite the role of personal consumption to be more than a means of achieving luxury. Rather, it became the path to happiness and social and financial security.

The confessional audience participation show first emerged on radio in the years leading up to the end of World War II and remained popular on radio and TV throughout the 1940s and 1950s. *Queen for a Day*, for example, was the highest-rated daytime program in 1957, averaging a 12.3 rating for the year—and other shows were close behind.[5] The ubiquity of these programs in the postwar daytime schedule is especially telling. In the mid-1950s, all four television networks ran at least an hour a day of audience participation programming, a clear staple of daytime television.[6] While these programs resembled the equally popular question-and-answer-based quiz shows of the era like *Twenty-One* (1956–58, NBC) and *The $64,000 Question* (1955–58, CBS), the two genres differed greatly in tone and, often, structure. *Queen for a Day* and *Glamour Girl* (1953–54, NBC), for example, were competitions, but instead of being rewarded for skill or knowledge, women won for having the saddest life story, expressing the greatest need, and generating the most audience applause and sympathy.[7]

Other shows forewent any competitive elements. Participants on *Stand Up and Be Counted* (1956–57, CBS) described a difficult dilemma they were facing, and the studio audience offered feedback and advice. Participants returned the next day to announce their decision, and they received prizes based on their choices. *It Could Be You* (1956–61, NBC) surprised unsuspecting studio audience members with gifts and, frequently, reunions, based on touching or humorous stories their friends and families sent the show. Some programs like *Welcome Travelers* (1947–54, NBC; 1954–55, CBS) and *On Your Account* (1953–54, NBC; 1954–56, CBS) resembled talk shows more than quiz shows. On these programs, guests—ordinary people—chatted with the hosts about their troubles and received merchandise that would help them out.

On all of these "giveaways," demonstrating personal hardship (rather than any particular form of intelligence, skill, or talent) justified the prizes that participants received, and even when contestants were competing against one another, it was a compelling backstory rather than a particular skill that helped them win.

On the other hand, a number of programs like *Strike It Rich, The Big Payoff, High Finance,* and *On Your Way* (DuMont, 1953) were fundamentally straight game shows, closely resembling the more traditional quizzes of the era. On all of these shows, contestants answered a series of questions to win cash or prizes. Where the "misery" quizzes differed from more conventional shows was not so much structurally but more in the implications of contestants' introductory narratives, which altered the meaning of the competitions as a whole. Contestants on both types of programs appeared on camera with hopes of winning cash or prizes, but audience participation shows framed prize-giving within discourses of need, as opposed to contestants on more straightforward quiz shows who won luxuries due to knowledge, skill, or luck.

Most quiz show hosts introduced contestants by name, occupation, and hometown and asked several questions about their backgrounds; the fundamental difference between *Strike It Rich* and *The $64,000 Question* lay in the contestants' descriptions of themselves and their reasons for appearing on the show. Whereas a *$64,000 Question* contestant might be asked what she would do with her prize money, a *Strike It Rich* contestant's interview focused almost entirely on why she *needed* the prize money. In both cases, the interview served as an entry point for audiences to understand and root for contestants, and a *Strike It Rich* participant's tragic backstory would almost certainly enhance a viewer's emotional investment in her overall success in the game.

But misery quizzes evoked something closer to pity than identification. Even though contestants on both types of shows answered questions for cash and prizes, misery quiz participants—no matter how impressive their displays of intellect may have been—were usually framed as disadvantaged rather than venerable, based on the fact that they were playing for necessities, not luxuries.[8] Although their winnings did not solely depend on the successful articulation of personal tragedy, as in the giveaway shows, contestants nonetheless became defined by their problems, not their achievements.

While the audience participation show's focus on real people's troubled lives appears to be at odds with familiar images of postwar domesticity, this fusion of misery and financial relief nonetheless speaks to very real social and economic changes affecting Americans in the postwar era. Beginning in World War II, both marriage and birth rates climbed steadily for all social groups in the United States.[9] The number of new families, coupled with the mass migration to the suburbs, led to an increased focus on domesticity. At the same time, the percentage of Americans in the middle class rose just as steadily.

In *The Mass Consumption Society,* behavioral economist George Katona showed how class mobility became much more possible for all Americans in the years after World War II. According to Katona, almost everyone from every class improved their economic positions after the 1930s depression (if not their percentage of the total collective American income), but the most notable increases were within what he calls "the discretionary-income group," or the middle class. Between 1929 and 1961, the number of family units in America increased by 55 percent and the overall national income by 60 percent, but the percentage of those with discretionary income—families with the power to purchase more than basic needs on a regular basis—increased 400 percent.[10] The result, Katona said, was a new kind of affluence—a firmly middle-class society, where most people had the ability to buy what they wanted rather than solely what they needed to survive.[11] Because of their numbers and their purchasing power, the middle class became both the ideal representation of American families and the target demographic for advertisers.

Despite the fact that Americans were more family-bound and financially stable than ever before, the postwar era was nonetheless marked by feelings of anxiety. As Elaine Tyler May has demonstrated, a major factor influencing the return to domesticity was the perceived need for security in an uncertain political era. In the 1950s, adults had distinct memories of the depression and World War II, and the postwar era offered relative tranquility in comparison with previous decades. Americans sought to keep it that way, both internationally and domestically, desiring, above all, "secure jobs, secure homes, and secure marriages in a secure country."[12] Thus, as May explains, many postwar families applied the cold war foreign policy of containment as protection against communism, with a slightly different inflection, to the domestic sphere.

The cold war produced its own anxieties for Americans, but the cohesive nuclear family with its rigid social roles became its own protection against—as well as something to protect from—the uncertainties of the outside world.[13] Despite the relative stability of many Americans' social and economic realities, postdepression and postwar individuals knew how easily tranquility could become chaos; their goal became protecting that stability however they could.

The stories of contestants on audience participation shows represented precisely the types of insecurity many Americans feared and illustrated the difficulties many women experienced trying to maintain their social roles. A typical episode of *Queen for a Day* from 1958, for example, featured four or five contestants, all in conspicuous financial or emotional distress. One asked for her trailer home to be furnished with bunk beds for her four daughters who currently slept in one bed. Another requested a transistor radio and a hospital gurney for her bedridden son recovering from polio, while a third asked for a set of encyclopedias for *her* bedridden son recovering from rheumatic fever, which she could not afford because her husband had a "rheumatic heart" and could not work. A fourth contestant, pregnant with her second child, needed stock for the grocery store she and her husband owned, for they could not afford both to pay the bills and fill the shelves. The store had 64 cents in the till and no inventory when it opened the morning of the show, and her family was in serious financial trouble.

The winner, Ruth Kliczkowski from Toledo, Ohio, had the saddest story of them all. Her husband had died several months previously in a hunting accident, her two young daughters were severely depressed, and Mrs. Kliczkowski had no means of supporting her family because she had never finished high school. She asked for some form of vocational training so she could feed her children and get her family back on its feet. The audience voted her the winner, and she received a full scholarship to beauty school in addition to several thousand dollars worth of other prizes, which would—at least theoretically—pave the way for a more secure financial future for her and her children.

All of the contestants on this episode described unfortunate situations that conflicted with images of postwar domestic tranquility. Ruth Kliczkowski's life story, however, exposed the seams of the ideal image—showing how quickly circumstances could wear away at an apparently stable foundation. Especially for women who married young and did not complete their educations, the realities of postwar life would be particularly bleak if their husbands died or left them without a means of support.

That these were all typical *Queen for a Day* pleas begins to explain the dynamics of audience participation shows. As Georganne Scheiner points out, most candidates on the show were lower-middle or working class, a large number of the women worked, and many were in severe financial distress. Their stories showed that not everyone had attained—or could attain—the security that middle-class suburbia offered and that finding oneself in a vulnerable position could happen very easily. In addition, they demonstrated the dearth of options for women, particularly single mothers and widows, to fix unacceptable domestic and economic situations—as did Ruth Kliczkowski's narrative.[14]

In the sampled episodes of *Queen for a Day*, candidates' wishes included several radios and record players to entertain invalid children, two wheelchairs, a wedding dress for the contestant's daughter, two hospital gurneys, and a hole in the ceiling to heat the contestant's children's bedrooms. All of these pleas were for specific material goods or services, but at the same time, they hint at much larger concerns for all of the candidates. Each woman, whether as a result of tragic, unforeseen circumstance or of personal failure, was in some way unable to maintain her proper social role of wife, caregiver, and mother of happy, healthy children. The poor financial planning by the contestant with the empty grocery store and her husband had put their family's secure future at risk. The candidate asking for the ceiling hole was unable to provide a warm house for her family, and the woman who needed a wedding dress did not have the means to launch her daughter into the social sphere. Women with disabled children frequently appeared on the show, as did political émigrés who had been forced to leave their children behind the Iron Curtain.[15]

Although neither disability nor politics was within a woman's control, the contestants' inabilities to ameliorate their situations (obtaining the equipment to help the child in one case, or physically obtaining the child in the other) signified a general powerlessness within their capacities to be the best mothers possible. While their difficulties in providing for their families in extreme circumstances may not have indicated a lack of foresight, they did demonstrate how easily one could lose control of the domestic sphere, particularly without a financial cushion on which to fall back.

These types of stories were by no means limited to *Queen for a Day* contestants. In the "Helping Hand" segment of a 1956 *Strike It Rich* episode, for example, actor Richard Dern appeared on behalf of an army veteran in Texas who was injured during active duty and could not perform physical labor once he returned home. Dern answered a series of questions and earned enough prize money for his beneficiary to raise rabbits and support his family. A 1953 episode of *On Your Account* featured a widow whose six children had been taken away from her when she could not support them after her husband's death. She wanted money to bring them home, and the show did her one better by reuniting the entire family on air. On *Strike It Rich* in 1952, a woman won $500 to help pay for her husband's medical bills. He had been in a car accident and would likely never walk again; she had to quit her job in order to care for him, because they could not afford a full-time nurse. Stories about losing control in some way of one's financial, social, or domestic spheres drove the majority of narratives on audience participation programs, and appearing on television in the hopes of receiving money or prizes seemed to be one of the few available means of repairing the breach for many participants.

While some shows like *High Finance* and *Strike It Rich* aired in prime time,[16] most were daytime programs aimed at a female audience—largely of a demographic strikingly similar to the shows' (mostly female) contestants. According to one 1954 audience study, the majority of audience participation show viewers were lower-class or working-class women between 30 and 60 who were seven times as likely to have an elementary school education as a college degree.[17] That these women, by and large, had backgrounds comparable with those who appeared on the programs complicates the shows' appeal—for the contestants' stories warned the audience that they, too, could be one accident, illness, or other unforeseen setback away from financial distress. While these narratives were often dismal, the genre's popularity and longevity indicate that audiences nonetheless experienced very real pleasures in hearing them.

That audience participation shows allowed American women to hear types of stories that were normally ignored by mainstream media, spoken by and about people much like them, is likely part of their allure. Marsha Cassidy has argued that *Glamour Girl* and other daytime postwar programming opened up the possibility for mediated "feminine discourse," where women spoke to other women about their troubles in a public forum—a form of power that emerged through the recognition and validation of the difficulties of living in a patriarchy.[18] These programs represented a site where normally invisible social contradictions could become visible, and the inconsistencies of postwar social ideals were evident. While audience members may have empathized with participants' stories, a number of elements within the shows created an emotional distance that deflected the stories' effect. Audience participation shows, both structurally and affectively, mitigated the potential for defiance that feminine discourse can offer by placing the audience in a position of judgment, framing the stories within a light game show format, and offering easy material solutions to difficult problems.

In 1946, CBS consulting psychologist Ernest Dichter explained the appeal of giveaway shows as "a chance to portray yourself" in a spectacular way, since a broadcast microphone could make even the most mundane details of a life story sound like "an accomplishment."[19] And for viewers at home, particularly those with backgrounds similar to those of the contestants, there was likely a multitiered feeling of achievement that came from identifying with them. On the one hand, everyday lives like their own became noteworthy enough to be broadcast, and the contestants' accomplishments of being mothers and housewives added a layer of nobility onto viewers' own everyday lives. On the other hand, viewers—at least those *not* in dire straits—could feel comparatively content about their own social and financial conditions. A working-class housewife without any significant life crisis could feel like she was coming out ahead, at least compared with her pitiable peers on *Strike It Rich,* while still identifying with their stories.

Such reassuring reflexivity has larger implications, considering that not all 1950s housewives were happy with their social roles. The secure home was for women the site of both work *and* leisure—and, as Elaine Tyler May indicates, much unspoken isolation and discontent. Women were much more likely than men to report dissatisfaction with their marriages, for example, and much less likely to rate their mental health as "excellent" on survey questions.[20] Even if a housewife was unhappy, though, contestants' sob stories on audience participation shows could assuage her by demonstrating that there were clearly worse positions in which she could find herself. *Queen for a Day* and *Glamour Girl,* in particular, invited such comparisons by placing the audience in a literal position of judgment, both as virtual jury members assessing the merits of each candidate's story and as spectators assessing their own lives against those of the candidates.

While not necessarily mean-spirited, this type of judgment depended on a viewer's sense that her circumstances and life choices were better than the candidates.' Such valuation, however, was contingent on the viewer believing that she would not fall into the same types of hardship, for doing so would mitigate the power of her judgment. Contestants' stories showed that living up to the postwar ideal may have been a difficult prospect for many Americans. However, the reality of contestants' hardships appeared to be much worse than struggling to maintain the ideal, which therefore reaffirmed the importance of trying to do so. Being able to compare one's own life favorably to audience participation show contestants' could thus make even the most disgruntled housewife complicit with her social role by allowing her to relish details about the harsh reality of the alternatives.

Even though these alternatives may have appeared bleak, it was not necessarily easy to become overly emotionally invested in any one contestant. Despite the shows' lachrymose reputation and structural dependence on contestants' stories of woe, they rarely let the misery get out of hand.[21] *Queen for a Day* host Jack Bailey, for example, told a *TV Guide* interviewer that, regarding the "sob stuff," "I just don't let it happen if I can possibly help it."[22] Indeed, Bailey and the show's producers tried to keep the show as "light" as possible, notwithstanding the nature of the candidates' stories. Women who looked like they might cry were not chosen to be on the show, and producers also shied away from contestants with stories that may have been *too* depressing for daytime television, such as those involving rape or domestic abuse.[23] This aversion to emotional excess was evident on other programs as well. *It Could Be You* host Bill Leyden's recital of humorous anecdotes about the show's guests defused the emotion of tearful reunions. *Strike It Rich* host Warren Hull would draw out contestants' stories to elicit as much sympathy as possible, but his constant complimenting of and joking with the storytellers inevitably gave even the most dismal stories a positive spin.

An even greater factor mitigating the misery, though, was the competitive nature of many audience participation shows, which refocused attention from the stories themselves to the candidates as game show contestants vying for prizes. *Strike It Rich* made this shift explicit through its use of separate spaces for interviews and game play. Warren Hull chatted with contestants on a living room set located on the left side of the soundstage. When the interview was complete, Hull and the contestant walked to a scoreboard in the center of the stage—a literal movement away from the site of misery, toward the actual quiz. This physical shift also indicated a shift in tone, for Hull rarely mentioned a contestant's troubles as he asked them trivia questions. Instead, attention refocused on the size of the jackpot contestants were able to build.

On *Queen for a Day*, this movement was not quite so literal. However, the show's format encouraged viewers to rank the candidates on the basis of need and to root for one at the expense of others. The more stories one heard, the less impact each one seemed to have, for each functioned as a basis of comparison with the other candidates' in the viewers' attempts to predict the day's winner. The focus, then, became more about the *idea* of misery-as-merit than the particular implications of each contestant's misery, neutralizing the potential power of each story. The result was sob stories about social insecurity that would not create any outright moral or social anxiety for the audience. Contestant narratives were necessary as an excuse for prize-giving, and defusing their sadness made the prizes' impact that much more credible.

Indeed, all the giveaway shows offered an easy solution to their candidates' often complex problems: merchandise. Despite the fact that a mink coat and a Hawaiian vacation would likely be of little use to a widow with hungry children and no job prospects, the narrative structure of most shows nonetheless posited that the consumer goods they gave away would be the participants' ticket to a stable, happy future. This equation of prizes and financial relief was most explicit on *Queen for a Day,* where every contestant wished for one specific product to alleviate her misery. Of course, on this sponsor-driven show, the producers' desires for greater advertising revenue underwrote the connection. Although many potential candidates needed doctors or lawyers, producers could never find any medical or legal professionals who would work in exchange for a plug, so these women were never chosen as contestants. Rather, in order to be selected, women had to want something that could be given away in exchange for free advertising.[24]

Eliminating the possibility of nonpluggable wishes resulted in a narrative where commodity consumption solved all problems. Each contestant claimed to need only one commercial product, the lack of which encapsulated, and the acquisition of which would surely fix, the major problems in her life. Her specific issue could thus be instantly taken care of with a phone call to "Carl Woodall, maker of artificial limbs,"[25] for example. As a bonus, her acquisition of the myriad other prizes—usually including several major appliances, a new wardrobe, a vacation, and assorted medium-ticket home goods like cookware and tableware—would, in theory, secure her future happiness and ensure that her problems would not resurface. The products plugged on the show were thus intertwined with the contestants' hard luck stories into a seamless narrative, presenting a problem and offering a clear solution.

This link between merchandise and security was not unique to *Queen for a Day* but was a common thread that ran through almost all of the audience participation shows. *Bride and Groom* (1946–53, CBS; 1953–54 and 1957–58, NBC), for example, was in many ways the antithesis to the misery-based audience participation show, since a couple got married live on the show every weekday for a dozen years. Every half-hour episode ended with the couple's "reception," where they received thousands of dollars worth of wedding gifts to start their happy future on secure footing. On a

1956 episode of *Stand Up and Be Counted,* a middle-aged widow chose to continue with her church and community work in her hometown instead of moving away to marry a man she did not love, despite the secure future he offered.[26] In honor of her decision, she received a prize package consisting of an air conditioner, a recliner, and a refrigerator. None of these may have offered the fiscal stability of the marriage she turned down, but the combination of the three prizes, as host Bob Russell indicated, would help ensure her future ease and comfort.

Even shows with cash prizes linked participants' financial relief to consumer culture. While these programs were not sponsor-driven in the same way as giveaway shows, they nonetheless implied that it was not so much the money that helped contestants but, rather, the opportunity to purchase items that fulfilled their particular needs. As long as a contestant's troubles defined her more than her achievements did, and as long as she played *for* something specific (whether it was tuition money, cash for a needed appliance, or medical care), the implication was that her winnings would rectify her problem by allowing her to reenter consumer culture.

In 1964, George Katona named postwar America a "mass consumption society," in which, as never before, consumers themselves were a major factor in economic growth.[27] Kiminori Matsuyama describes the mechanisms driving the development of mass consumption societies as cyclical, whereby the rapid takeoff of the market for one consumer good is followed by equally rapid increases in the markets for other goods.[28] Matsuyama argues that such patterns of overall increased consumption are tied to upswings in productivity, which decrease the value of products, making them more affordable to a greater number of consumers. As more people purchase a broader range of goods, the expanded consumer market further increases productivity, which keeps the cycle intact.[29]

As Gary Cross and George Lipsitz have noted, certain changes in federal economic practices and citizens' status as consumers drove this cycle, in an attempt to transition successfully from a booming wartime economy to one equally successful in peacetime. Business leaders sought to invigorate the postwar economy primarily through increased federal spending, exports, and consumer debt. They believed a 30 to 50 percent growth in consumer spending was necessary in order to jump-start the economy. Increased consumption allowed for the creation of new jobs and would eventually offset consumers' initial postwar debts—largely mortgages—and stabilize the federal economy.[30] Personal spending thus became "a patriotic duty."[31] And consumption did increase dramatically in the postwar era, particularly in terms of household goods. Consumer spending itself increased 60 percent between 1945 and 1950, but purchases of household goods went up 240 percent.[32] Buying household goods could embody national security while simultaneously providing consumers with secure home lives.

As Matsuyama explains, the changing nature of the meaning of each product as its use penetrates into larger markets is key to the development of a mass consumption society. It is not just that the availability of goods themselves trickles down from upper-class to lower-class citizens but that the goods' relative priority within the running of a household changes as well. What starts out as a luxury for a lower-class consumer—highly desirable but largely out of reach—becomes rewritten as a necessity as its price drops, its market penetration increases, and a consumer's relative income rises.[33] Such rewriting of any given product's relative importance not only fuels its own market penetration but also can jump-start the same cycle for other consumer goods—for there will always be luxuries one aspires to own.

Audience participation shows, where products could resolve any problem, enacted this cycle in a very literal way. While home viewers likely saw many of the shows' prizes as desirable luxuries—particularly the appliances—the programs framed them as necessities, at least for the contestants who received them. Because participants were defined by their particular needs, the specific products that fulfilled them—no matter how lavish—were therefore rewritten as essential. A 1960 *Queen for a Day* contestant, for example, asked for a washing machine so she could take in laundry and help pay the bills that accrued during her husband's unemployment. While the appliance was a luxury for her, since she could not afford it on her own, it was simultaneously a necessity, since owning one would solve her financial issues.

The effect of such a connotative shift was that a viewer could see not just how desirable a product was but also why she, too, needed it for her own home—if not to resolve a specific dilemma, then at least to prevent one from happening in the future. If a washing machine or a new wardrobe could solve the problems of the truly needy participants on audience participation shows, then owning one could keep the same problems at bay for the less needy viewer at home. Within the programs' narratives, then, what appeared to be "luxuries" were actually necessary to enter into a middle-class lifestyle and consequently keep oneself afloat. The self-control and security audience participation show contestants lacked could therefore be purchased by viewers at home.

That so many programs centered on questions of merit—showing why contestants deserved the products they received—further enhances this blurring of luxury and necessity. While quiz-type shows like *Strike it Rich* and *High Finance* allowed their contestants to earn their way back to fiscal security by answering questions successfully, participants on giveaways had to justify their need in order to win merchandise. The interview portions of chat-show giveaways, for example, made the eventual sponsor-driven prize-giving appear less gratuitous by allowing participants to demonstrate why they were worthy recipients of the prizes. *Queen for a Day* and *Glamour Girl* centered on finding the most deserving contestant of the day, usually the one who needed the most help. Even on *The Big Payoff*, where a man answered questions on behalf of a beloved female, the contestant's interview focused solely on why she deserved the prizes he was about to win for her.

While participants' sad life stories were a necessary setup for prizes and product plugs—albeit a powerful one that underscored the importance of the products—this fusion of melancholy, merit, and merchandise delivered a clear message about consumer culture. Whereas the "earning" shows were about working one's way through a financial crisis—demonstrating that with enough effort, one could buy material goods to ensure a stable future—these "deserving" shows eschewed the idea of effort. Rather, they seemed to assert that owning the right merchandise could help one avoid both crisis and the labor of recovery and that every woman deserved to own the right merchandise. By rewriting the meaning of "need" to universalize contestants' specific desires, the shows also universalized the idea of merit, so that all women could feel that they deserved the same consumer goods, whether to solve problems or ensure their families' future security.

George Lipsitz has identified the urban ethnic sitcoms popular on both radio and television in the postwar era as a key site for teaching the American audience about the new rules of consumer culture without patronizing them.[34] And much like the immigrant characters on ethnic sitcoms, contestants on audience participation shows often needed instruction in how to be successful economic citizens; however, they never received lessons in financial management or the credit process. Rather, the less transparently pedagogical audience participation shows encouraged the desire to consume while eliding the practicalities of doing so. Buying into the subjects' problems meant literally buying into the solutions. And by equating the benefits of a middle-class lifestyle with proper consumption and allowing every woman to feel that she both needed and deserved these benefits, audience participation shows promoted an overall fantasy of consumerism. Even if one did not require an economic transformation, audience participation programs showed how new products could make dreams come true or prevent nightmares from happening.

In May 1964, Lyndon Johnson gave the commencement speech at the University of Michigan in which he announced his plan for a series of domestic programs he called the "Great Society." The central themes of the Great Society involved abolishing racial injustice and poverty, and when Johnson was reelected that same year, he pushed a series of social programs, including Medicare, increased welfare benefits, and the Civil Rights Act of 1964 through Congress. That same year, 1964, was also when *Queen for a Day* went off the air and the audience participation show disappeared from American broadcasting for almost four decades.

The two are perhaps not coincidental. The audience participation show, while a product of the postwar mass consumption society, is also emblematic of a pre-welfare state, in which very few social programs existed to help people out of desperate situations. For some women, going on these shows may have been their only means of getting help with everyday hardship. During the early 1950s, stories abounded of wannabe *Strike It Rich* contestants stranded in New York and *Queen for a Day* hopefuls stuck in Los Angeles when they could not get on the shows. In 1953, the New York Department of Welfare attempted to shut down *Strike It Rich*, claiming that the show—and the audience-driven "Heart Line" in particular—was functioning as a "charitable organization."[35] While the Department of Welfare action elicited certain changes in the structure of *Strike It Rich* (afterward, for example, contestants were preselected, to avoid the stranded traveler problem), the show stayed on the air for another five years and remained exceptionally popular, because of both the problems and solutions presented on air.

The popularity of audience participation shows is emblematic of certain aspects of the postwar social climate—namely, the fact that many people could not attain the ideal lifestyle, or even a minimally comfortable one, but had no real recourse for help. In 1962, the *Los Angeles Times* ran a series of stories about Teresa Tarrants, a mother of five who hitchhiked to the Moulin Rouge Theater in an attempt to appear on *Queen for a Day*. Her husband had been laid off, the family had lost their house, and they learned that the only way they could receive any form of public aid was if her husband was to desert his family. Winning *Queen for a Day* was the only solution she could come up with to keep her children from starving; unfortunately, however, she was not chosen as a contestant. Columnist Paul Coates, outraged at the fact that Public Aid suggested a husband leave his family, took up their cause, and after the first article ran on January 18, the Tarrants family received an outpouring of support, including food, clothing, money, and job offers from hundreds of local readers.[36]

While the Tarrantses may have been able to get back on their feet (albeit thanks to a media intervention), other families in similar situations more often than not remained helpless. The fascination with and fear of stories like the Tarrants family's drove the postwar audience participation show, which, because they played on fears of insecurity, could only exist when such circumstances were possible. Changes in the American social climate, however, may have mitigated audiences' desire to hear others' pitiful stories—especially once there were greater resources available to help those truly in need and other means of changing their financial situations.

When ABC cancelled *Queen for a Day* in 1964, the audience participation show largely disappeared from the American airwaves for almost four decades, only reemerging with the premiere of *Extreme Makeover: Home Edition*, which reunited pathos and primetime television. *Extreme Makeover: Home Edition* premiered in February 2004, at the same time that George W. Bush's Republican Congress was cutting Medicare and welfare benefits and implementing new deregulatory policies. If the postwar shows were a product of a pre-welfare state, then perhaps the contemporary philanthropic reality genre represents a post-welfare society, where neoliberal ideals of self-reliance can only get one so far. Katherine Sender has called *Queen for a Day* contestants "passive," particularly in contrast to makeover subjects on *Queer Eye for the Straight Guy*, who must put significant effort into their transformations—and this passivity holds true for *Extreme Makeover: Home Edition* as well.[37] Making the effort to ask for a new iron lung on *Queen for a Day* or a new house on *Extreme Makeover: Home Edition* may be a roundabout way of taking personal responsibility, but it is nonetheless a reliance on outside institutions to repair one's personal problems. Personal responsibility and self-sufficiency are noble principles, but when circumstances occur that even the most forward-thinking individual would not anticipate, other recourse may be necessary.

However, the shows' messages are directed just as much to the audience as they are to the contestants, focusing on the perils of financial and material instability and delineating what one can do to stave off insecurity. While postwar audience participation show subjects and *Extreme Make-over: Home Edition* families ask for help they cannot provide themselves, the home viewers learn how to be self-sufficient through the subjects' own pitiful circumstances.[38] Forcing subjects to ask for help, diverting potential sympathy into consumerist fantasy, and illustrating the effects of self-insufficiency all work together to create viewers who want to consume because they do not want to ask for help. The televised transformation thus becomes more than a means to help struggling families; rather, it becomes a lesson in self-reliance.

NOTES

1. Alessandra Stanley, "The Latest Reality Show Twist: Take My Wife, Please," *New York Times*, 29 September 2004, E7.

2. James Poniewozik, "When You Wish upon TV," *Time*, 6 June 2005, at http://www.time.com/time/magazine/article/0,9171,1069080,00.html.

3. Nielsen Media Research, "TV Ratings: 2004–2005 Season," *zap2it.com*, 24 July, 2005, at http://v.zap2it.com/tveditorial/tve_main/,1002.272111 season,00.html2 (accessed 24 July 2005).

4. John Barrington, "Joe Needs Fair Deal on Taxes," *Chicago Daily Defender*, 30 August 1956, 20; "Joe Louis, Uncle Sam Win $41,000," *Chicago Daily Defender*, 15 October 1956, 17.

5. "TV's Hottest Battleground," *Sponsor*, 14 May 1957, 38–40.

6. "Monday Television Programs," *Washington Post*, 12 October 1953, 21; "Monday Television Programs," *Washington Post and Times Herald*, 10 January 1955, 31.

7. A *TV Guide* interview with *Queen for a Day* host Jack Bailey described how the show's producers would wager each day on who would win. One episode's backstage favorite was the elderly schoolteacher who wanted books and records for her students. Ralph Widman, the still photographer, disagreed. He favored the mother of three with the ill husband who wanted groceries for a month, saying, "Woman can't stand to see kids go hungry." He was right; she, with the saddest story, won. "Jack Bailey: Mesmerizer of the Middle Aged," *TV Guide*, 11 March 1961, 15–19.

8. Of course, not all *Strike It Rich* contestants competed for personal gain. People frequently came on the show to win money for a favorite charity, and the "Helping Hand" segment featured a celebrity answering questions for a home viewer nominated by a friend or family. The dynamics remained similar, however, since even celebrity contestants were playing for someone who did very much need the money.

9. Elaine Tyler May, *Homeward Bound: American Families in the Cold War Era* (New York: Basic Books, 1988), 20, 137.

10. George Katona, *The Mass Consumption Society* (New York: McGraw-Hill, 1964), 13–14.

11. Ibid., 5–6.

12. May, *Homeward Bound,* 13.

13. Ibid., 13–36.

14. Georganne Scheiner, "Would You Like to Be Queen for a Day? Finding a Working Class Voice in American Television of the 1950s," *Historical Journal of Film, Radio and Television,* 23.4 (2003), 380–81.

15. "Queen for a Day," *Variety,* 11 January 1956, n.p.; "Those 800 Babies," *TV Guide,* 28 June 1958, 16.

16. *Strike It Rich* aired simultaneously in daytime and prime time on CBS during the summers of 1951–55, but for the rest of its 11-year run on both radio and television, it was a daytime program.

17. Quoted in "Does Your Show Reach People—Customers?" *Sponsor,* 18 October 1954, 83–84.

18. Marsha F. Cassidy, "The Cinderella Makeover: *Glamour Girl,* Television Misery Shows, and 1950s Femininity," in *The Great American Makeover: Television, History, and Nation,* ed. Dana Heller (New York: Palgrave MacMillan, 2006), 135.

19. Jean Meegan, "It's Psychology That Pays Off on Radio Quiz, Giveaway Shows," *Washington Post,* 21 July 1946, S6.

20. May, *Homeward Bound,* 193–203.

21. Critics of these shows tended to point out the tearful nature of both the programs and their contestants. For example, Cleveland Armory, "Queen for a Day," *TV Guide,* 7 March 1964, 23; John Crosby, "It's Been a Wet Summer, and It's Getting Wetter," *Washington Post,* 15 August 1953, 29; "The Stuff That Tears Are Made Of," *TV Guide,* 22 June 1957, 17–19; and "Troubles and Bubbles," *Time,* 15 April 1957, at http://www.time.com/time/magazine/article 0,9171,862558,00.html.

22. "Stuff That Tears Are Made Of."

23. Ibid. See also Howard Blake, "An Apologia from the Man Who Produced the Worst Program in TV History," in *American Broadcasting: A Source Book on the History of Radio and Television,* ed. Lawrence W. Lichty and Malachi C. Topping (New York: Hastings House, 1975), 418–19.

24. Blake, "Apologia," 417.

25. This occurred on the July 4, 1955, episode. To enhance the product plug, guest host Adolphe Menjou added, "You can be assured that if Mr. Woodall makes it, it's going to be right."

26. This was against the advice of the studio audience, 87 percent of whom said she should marry.

27. Katona, *Mass Consumption Society,* 25.

28. Kiminori Matsuyama, "The Rise of Mass Consumption Societies," *Journal of Political Economy* 110.5 (2002), 1037. In postwar America, for example, the percentage of households with television grew from 9 percent in 1950 to 87.1 percent in 1960, a rise concomitant with the increased growth of myriad other household products. Between 1940 and 1954, the proportion of American households with telephones rose from 36 percent to 80 percent, those with refrigerators increased from 44 percent to 91 percent, and indoor plumbing became part of 80 percent of American homes as opposed to 65 percent in 1940. Nielson Media Research–NTI, "TV Basics: Television Households," September 1950 and September 1960, Television Bureau of Advertising Inc., at http://www.tvb.org/rcentral/mediatrendstrack/tvbasics/02_TVHouseholds.asp; Gary Cross, *An All-Consuming Century: Why Commercialism Won in Modern America* (New York: Columbia University Press, 2000), 89.

29. Matsuyama, "Rise of Mass Consumption Societies," 1038.

30. George Lipsitz, *Time Passages: Collective Memory and American Popular Culture* (Minneapolis: University of Minnesota Press, 1990), 44–47.

31. Cross, *All-Consuming Century*, 138–139.

32. May, *Homeward Bound*, 165.

33. Ibid., 1035–40.

34. Lipsitz, *Time Passages*, 39–57.

35. Jack Gould, "TV's Misery Shows," *Sunday New York Times*, 7 February 1954, xii.

36. Paul Coates, "Poverty-Stricken Mother of Five Tried to Hitchhike to Happiness," *Los Angeles Times*, 18 January 1962, B6; Paul Coates, "Mother Thanks Kind Folks Who Turned Sad Story to Happy One," *Los Angeles Times*, 16 February 1962, A6; and Paul Coates, "Royal Ending to Story of Woman Who Tried to Be Queen for a Day," *Los Angeles Times*, 21 September 1962, A6.

37. Katherine Sender, "Queens for a Day: *Queer Eye for the Straight Guy* and the Neoliberal Project," *Critical Studies in Media Communication* 23:2 (2006), 134.

38. Laurie Ouellete and James Hay, *Better Living through Reality TV: Television and Post-Welfare Citizenship* (Malden, Mass.: Blackwell, 2008).

ll

Visceral Literacy
Reality TV, Savvy Viewers, and Auto-Spies

Mark Andrejevic

Reality TV, we are told insistently by pundits, critics, and assorted pop culture gurus, caters to the viewer as voyeur. The popular genre is, as media historian Neal Gabler put it, "above all . . . about old-fashioned voyeurism—providing us the entertainment of seeing something and imagining something that television had never allowed us to see or imagine."[1] In one sense, such observations are hard to dispute; clearly there is an element of voyeurism in the appeal of shows that allow us to observe first-hand the personal lives of others—their loves and losses, their fights, their grief, rage, and individual triumphs. But the ready invocation of the timeless human appeal of voyeurism rings thin. It sounds like more of an explanation than it is. After all, Gabler's formulation falls a bit short: much of what takes place on reality TV is eminently imaginable, and we may have seen much more revealing scenes of love and rage in fictional formats. FOX's *Temptation Island,* despite the titillating title and the provocative promotions provided less in the way of graphic fare than *Sex in the City* or MTV's *Undressed.*

Even assuming that these shows are documentary rather than fiction, thereby rendering such formats truly voyeuristic, the question remains as to why voyeurism suddenly took hold of the TV industry at the turn of the millennium. The ready explanation for the genre's appeal does little to provide any convincing answer to the questions, "Why reality TV? Why now?" Instead, it reinforces the tendency to abstract media phenomena from the rest of society according to what might be described as a form of media determinism: the notion that a medium develops autonomously according to its own internal logic and then imparts its influence on viewers.

In this essay, I situate the voyeuristic element of reality TV within the broader social context of an era characterized by both a canny skepticism toward the contrivance of public images and the proliferation of technologies and techniques that promise behind-the-scenes access. If we all know that celebrities' public lives are carefully stage-managed for public consumption, reality TV formats promise to show us the seams in the public facades of their cast members, the traces that guarantee, as one popular celebrity magazine puts it, they are "just like *us*." And by logical extension, we are just like them: our public images are also a matter of performance, stage management, and artifice. Contemporary image culture teaches both the inevitability of contrivance and, paradoxically, the need to penetrate it—not just out of casual curiosity but in order to avoid the risk of being seen to be a dupe who is taken in by the lure of the image.

If, as the invocation of voyeurism suggests, there is pleasure to be taken in the act of seeing behind the scenes, there is also a certain pleasure to be derived from the performance of the savvy subject—the one who isn't taken in by the performance of others, who insists for all to see that he or she "gets it."

This is a pleasure that is becoming increasingly available, thanks to what might be described (misleadingly) as the democratization of surveillance in the interactive era. Thanks to the widespread distribution of increasingly sophisticated digital devices, it is becoming easier for us to spy on one another—to capture, record, or stumble across behind-the-scenes glimpses and information. In addition to routine forms of monitoring such as Googling one another, tracking each other's Facebook or MySpace sites, and so on, we have access to a proliferating array of devices specifically designed to allow us to watch (over) one another. Shopping malls sell home surveillance cameras alongside clock radios and massage chairs, while concerned parents can buy "nanny-cams" concealed in stuffed animals, as well as software to track everything from their children's web surfing to their driving.

Such devices are marketed online and off as tools that combine security with the entertainment of high-tech gimmickry and the thrill of voyeurism. As one online ad put it, "With X10 surveillance cameras, we've made it extremely easy and affordable to look after your loved ones, home and possessions—or even just to have fun."[2] Surveillance has become such an integral part of the twenty-first century lifestyle that the home design and repair section in O, *the Oprah Magazine* includes tips on motion detectors and digital surveillance cameras with its advice on interior decorating.[3]

Such is the twenty-first-century version of the beautiful people's fashion mantra: it's all about seeing and being seen.

In an era of postmodern boundary blurring, the combination of security and entertainment (securitainment?) is becoming increasingly familiar. On the one hand, we are confronted with surveillance-based entertainment in the form of reality TV shows that promise to instruct us in matters ranging from personal safety to professional and romantic fulfillment.[4] Such shows may be entertainment, their promoters tell us, but they also supply us with invaluable information about how to take care of ourselves and our loved ones. On the other hand, our tools for communication and entertainment can be enlisted for personal and national security. In the public sphere, for example, we are urged to use our cell phones to report risky or suspicious behavior in post-9/11 antiterrorism campaigns. As Senate Majority Leader Bill Frist urged citizens in his how-to guide for protection from terrorist attack, we should "become the eyes and ears of our law enforcement agencies": "You know your communities better than anyone else. You know when something looks out of place, whether it's a package left on the subway or someone acting in an unusual or suspicious manner in your neighborhood."[5]

The blurring of public and private uses of surveillance has implications for both realms. Even as private citizens are invited to adopt the monitoring priorities of the state—to use their personal communication technologies for homeland security—they are simultaneously urged to incorporate policing techniques into their personal relationships. In an increasingly mediated world in which people are not always who they say they are, monitoring and background checking techniques are portrayed as ways of navigating the risks of interpersonal relationships. The Internet and other new media technologies at our disposal increase both the potential for deceit (on the Internet, we can be whoever we say we are, at least for a while, and cell phones make it possible to disguise our locations, at least for now) and for new forms of monitoring one another. As the subsequent sections argue, these monitoring strategies come to be portrayed in both popular culture and in the marketing of new technologies as prudent strategies for personal—and not just homeland—security.

Consider the example of two testimonials for the online background check website, NetDetective.com. The first highlights the crucial importance of good "intel" about one's love life: "Net Detective stopped me from making a grave error. The woman I almost married had a dark past that included fraud and other marriages she never mentioned. . . . Thank you for helping me."[6] The second celebrates the entertainment value of peer monitoring: "I've been bragging to my friends about Net Detective. I've also tracked down information on friends, and they are not even aware of it. One of my neighbors has serious credit problems, and I also found out how much child support and alimony my next-door neighbor is paying every month. Simply *incredible!*"[7]

The overtones of schadenfreude and downward comparison combined in this gleeful testimonial echo those discerned in the appeal of reality TV by commentators who refer to it with sympathetic or scornful disparagement as "voyeur TV." In the interactive era, the promise that anyone can be Big Brother coincides with the promise that anyone can be *on Big Brother,* a show described by one commentator as responsible for transforming the "multitude into voyeurs."[8] Whether voyeur TV made us that way or just found us out, the predominant pop culture narrative relies on a suspiciously convenient coincidence: the predilection for voyeurism on the part of TV audiences emerges alongside a seemingly endless supply of celebrity-hungry exhibitionists, who are only too willing to trade in their privacy for the chance of a brief flirtation with fame.

This neat coincidence is an apparent boon for producers, who need only marry the complementary trends by putting the exhibitionists to work for the delectation of the voyeurs. But there is something a little too neat about this story—it overlooks or suppresses the underlying connection between voyeurism and exhibitionism in a culture in which savvy skepticism might be understood as a self-conscious performance: the persistent attempt to be seen as *not* a dupe. Reality TV offers a rather straightforward version of this default of voyeurism to exhibitionism or, rather, of the intertwined nature of these two aspects of what Sigmund Freud termed "the scopic drive." In the following sections, I draw on examples from reality TV as a means of considering the relationship between voyeurism and exhibitionism in the information age—an age in which both practices are facilitated by interactive communication technologies.

My intent is not to interpret reality TV formats per se but to offer an interpretation of contemporary social practices through the lens of popular culture. Reality TV provides a pop-culture paradigm of the logic that links voyeurism and exhibitionism—a logic captured by Jacques Lacan's description of a drive that enacts not the desire to see and control as much as the drive to "make oneself seen."[9] Here I consider some of the ways in which reality TV enacts this Lacanian formulation and shed light on the connections between a culture of savvy skepticism and the proliferation of monitoring techniques and technologies.

Rather than describing the cultural moment of reality TV simply in terms of voyeurism—what Clay Calvert has dubbed "Voyeur Nation"—in the following analysis I suggest an alternative formulation in which the savvy voyeur is caught up in a performance for the gaze of an imagined other.[10] Viewers who strive to see behind the curtain of facades are simultaneously engaged in displaying themselves as "unduped" by appearances. The pleasure of voyeurism and that of self-display, in other words, are intertwined. The role of the savvy voyeur defaults to what the philosopher Slavoj Zizek describes as a form of active submission—participatory passivity—that fits neatly with an increasingly surveillance-based economy, one in which the voyeuristic "appeal" of reality TV serves as a means of enticing submission to the increasingly monitored activity of viewing.[11]

To develop this argument, I trace the relationship between surveillance and a savvy form of self-display (which I describe, following Lacan, as "the drive to make oneself seen") through several reality formats. Taken as persistently recurring repetitions of the promise of participation and access to authentic, verifiable experience, these formats might be treated as cultural symptoms that lend themselves to what Theodor Adorno described as a "micrological" approach to cultural analysis.[12] The purpose of running the argument through several examples taken from reality TV, therefore, is not to argue that such programs directly influence audience attitudes and behavior; rather, it is to explore "microcosmic" cultural representations of surveillance relations in the information society: instances of the social writ small.

Seeing through the Facade: Room Raiders *and the "Active" Form of the Scopic Drive*

The MTV dating show *Exposed* caters to the savvy, skeptical single while tracing its default to brute, bodily empiricism. As the show's description puts it, "One hot SINGLE. Two unsuspecting DATERS. What the DATERS don't know is that every word they speak is being processed through a lie detector."[13] If self-presentation is one more performance, why not put prospective dates to a bodily test? In this marriage of generalized skepticism (self-presentation as a series of performances—the metastasis of the facade) with the return to the body as site of truth, postmodern and pre-modern skepticism overlap.

If, then, what people say is potentially inaccurate, uninterpretable, or illusory, the body is offered as a guarantee of some surplus beyond the manipulations of discourse—what John Peters has described as "the retreat to the body as the haven of truth."[14] Slavoj Zizek diagnoses this default to bodily empiricism as a symptom of the demise of what, following Claude Levi-Strauss, he terms "symbolic efficiency."[15]

The efficacy of the symbolic—of the shared system of representations according to which we organize our world—relies on an acceptance of the nonidentical and contradictory character of the symbol itself: the fact that, for example it can be inadequate to the reality it designates, or vice versa. Zizek uses the example of the Groucho Marx question, "Who do you believe, your eyes or my words?" to illustrate the role that symbolic efficacy plays in opening up a space of possibility beyond the seemingly irrevocably given character of directly experienced reality.[16]

It is not, of course, an uncommon experience to trust the evidence of the symbolic over our direct experience, as when, for example, we concede that the earth orbits the sun. Symbolic efficacy has, Zizek suggests, an important role to play at the level of social and political institutions in which,

> the symbolic mask-mandate matters more than the direct reality of the individual who wears this mask and/or assumes this mandate. This function involves the structure of fetishistic disavowal: "I know very well that things are the way I see them [that this person is a corrupt weakling], but none the less I treat him with respect, since he wears the insignia of a judge, so that when he speaks it is the Law itself which speaks through him."[17]

Postdeferential authenticity, reality TV–style, short-circuits this logic, brushing aside the symbolic mandate to get directly to the "corrupt weakling" behind the black robe. It is, as Zizek suggests, the space of the symbolic, and its productive contradictions that are foreclosed by the cynicism of the "nonduped."

The attempt to bypass mediation—the symbolic register—remains an incoherent one: the danger always remains that even the "corrupt weakling" is no more than a facade—another layer of performance that only a dupe would be willing to misrecognize as the "real." The debunking of symbolic efficiency results not just in generalized skepticism but, consequently, in the multiplication of paranoiac possibilities. The uncanny persistence of the debunked (ideology, capitalism, artifice) combines with the removal of any grounds for distinguishing among competing inter- pretations to create a hospitable climate for conspiracy theory and what might be described as savvy paranoia.

Such is the substance of Bruno Latour's lament regarding the effects of a generalized skepticism that coincides with the proliferation of con- spiracy theory: "Things have changed a lot, at least in my village. I am now the one who naively believes in some facts because I am educated, while the other guys are too *un*sophisticated to be gullible: 'Where have you been? Don't you know the Mossad and the CIA did it [a reference to the September 11 attacks]?'"[18] Savviness, pushed to its limit, threatens to default to an ostensibly democratic gullibility: no interpretation is inher- ently better than any other.

The stage is thus set for the return of the symbolic in the register of "the real." The reflexive mistrust of mediation defaults to a search for some im- mediate trace that might arbitrate among proliferating narratives, perfor- mances, and interpretations. If all media are biased, as it were, selecting among competing narratives requires a leap into the realm of immediacy: the extraction, via torture, surprise, or perhaps intuition, of a "sign" that might not be consigned to the realm of the arbitrary.[19] Thus, the emer- gence of the lie detector, the hidden camera (penetrating into the back- stage realm), and other similar tactics in reality TV might be considered part of a larger pattern pairing savvy skepticism with naive empiricism.

Consider, for example, the recently hyped trend of neuromarketing. Bypassing the standard approaches of survey research and focus-group interviews, neuromarketers promise to tap directly into the brain, relying on MRI scans to evaluate consumer response to products and ads. As one news account puts it, "brain scans, unlike focus groups, can't lie."[20]

Tellingly, the mystical power of the brain scan or the lie detector to "cut through" the deceptive layer of discourse aligns itself with its seem- ing opposite: a reliance on intuition, or gut instinct. In a world in which a critical skepticism toward the staging of public facades and spectacles is fostered by an ongoing fascination with the "behind-the-scenes" access provided by an increasingly pervasive and invasive mass media, reliance on both intuitions and skills of detection are portrayed as an increasingly necessary supplement to public discourse.

No less a public figure than George W. Bush framed his image as a leader in terms of his finely honed instincts and his ability to "read" character.

Recall, for example, his highly publicized first meeting with Russian leader Vladimir Putin, when Bush, famous for both his creative awkwardness with words and his evident mistrust of them, noted that he had been able to bypass speech and cut straight through to the essence of his interlocutor: "I looked the man in the eye; I found him to be very straightforward and trustworthy. . . . I was able to get a sense of his soul."[21]

It bears reemphasizing that this soul-seeing skill goes hand in hand with savvy skepticism. The hallmark of Bush's putative honesty during the 2000 campaign was, of course, his willingness, in a flight of self-fulfilling prescience, to highlight the untrustworthiness of politicians themselves: "We don't trust bureaucrats in Washington, DC. We don't believe in planners and deciders making decision on behalf of America."[22] Trust me, he seemed to proclaim cannily, because at least I concede the untrustworthiness of political discourse itself.

Even that is not quite enough—such trust requires a further warrant, an appeal that sidesteps the tangle of a self-undermining savviness. Such was the carefully managed message of what came to be known as "Ashley's Story," a 2004 campaign ad built around the much-circulated image of Bush comforting the daughter of a September 11 victim with a cradling embrace. The response of the young lady's father to this gesture of presidential consolation is featured in the ad, alongside an image of the hug: "What I saw is what I want to see in the heart and in the soul in the man who sits in the highest elected office in our country."[23]

Soul-seeing is not just the province of the savvy political leader but of those who recognize his talents. In an era of generalized risk—in which politicians, like peers, are not necessarily who they seem—the rest of us need a crash course in visceral literacy: the ability to cut through the facade, whether by investigation or intuition.

The point of assembling these disparate examples, from the realms of dating, marketing, and politics (perhaps not quite as disparate as they might seem), is to suggest that the familiar pattern of reality TV serves as a variety of cultural shorthand for the identification of broader social trends. It is with this in mind that I now turn to a consideration of another MTV reality series, *Room Raiders,* that provides a pop-culture portrayal of do-it-yourself detection in practice: viewers get to watch the spies as they "investigate" the bedrooms of potential dates before meeting them.

The show offers a distillation for mass consumption of the promise that if appearances can be deceiving, one way of accessing the behind-the-facade reality of potential dates is to bypass face-to-face meeting and conversation by performing a surprise forensic examination instead. In this regard, the show represents the investigatory subgenre of dating shows, one in which those searching for dates subject them to forms of interrogation, behind-the-scenes monitoring, and lie-detection technology.

As if highlighting the privatization and internalization of police-state protocols, each episode begins with a ritual kidnapping: anonymous figures knock on the front door, forcefully grab the targets, and unceremoniously frog march them into the back of an "undercover" panel van. Describing the element of surprise as a means of extracting some traces of a "behind-the-scenes" reality, the introductory voice-over announces, "They have no idea the crew is on the way, by catching them off guard they'll have no time to clean up or hide anything."

In its emphasis on policing techniques, detection, and deduction—the reliance on traces and glimpses behind the scenes—*Room Raiders* self-consciously enlists the appeal of the ubiquitous genre of the police procedural: *CSI* MTV. The new crop of detection shows focus attention on the techniques and technologies of empirical evidence gathering: not on piecing together the intricate interaction of character and motive but on black-light body-fluid illumination.

One of the supervising producers of *CSI: Miami* noted that "in the old shows, no one could figure out how to make the analysis of evidence interesting. . . . What we did was slow things down to say, 'This is cool stuff.' . . . We wanted them to look through the microscope."[24] As the *Room Raiders* website notes, this is precisely what the "raiders"—equipped with a "trusty" spy kit complete with portable UV light, tongs, and rubber gloves—do: "No drawer will be left unopened and no bed stain unexamined as each victim—or potential date—is mercilessly scrutinized without advance warning."[25]

The remainder of the show is devoted to following the "searcher" as he or she (the show mixes up the genders) conducts an investigation of three bedrooms and provides a running monologue of observations and often obscure, Sherlock-Holmes-for-the-MTV-generation deductions ("I like that he had a surfboard, it shows he has hobbies and some goals for himself") as they go.

For the most part, the show portrays the "raider" in the guise of investigator/voyeur. That is, although the raiders provide a running explanation of their observations for the benefit of the imagined audience on the other side of the cameras, the performative aspect of their investigation is not directly staged (in contrast to the shows that are discussed in the following sections). We don't see any of the camera operators trailing the raider, and we are invited to follow the progress of their search much as we would a fictional police investigation. As in the case of the detective show, we are treated to findings that purportedly reveal hidden aspects of the characters under investigation—the clean and dirty little secrets concealed by the veneer of their public personas.

In this respect, the show provides a pop-culture echo of the findings of psychologist Samuel Gosling, who had students fill out a standard personality test and then compared how well friends evaluated the students' personalities with evaluations made by strangers who had only inspected the students' rooms. He found, as one account puts it, that "it is quite possible for people who have never met us and who have spent only 20 minutes thinking about us to come to a better understanding of who we are than people who have known us for years."[26] Similarly, the abbreviated investigations on *Room Raiders* purportedly unearth elements of the targets' personalities that might well have remained obscured in face-to-face encounters during which prospective dates presumably engage in selective self-disclosure and impression management.

Indeed, the risk-averse raiders place a premium on ferreting out clues to character traits that might spell relationship disaster down the road. Telling details were singled out to help screen potential dates and prevent wasted emotional investment. For example, the failure of one young man to put away his ironing board was taken as a sign that he was "lazy and disorganized." A box of memorabilia from old boyfriends became evidence that one prospective date "is living in the past . . . and I need someone who's going to push on the present." One young woman's overnight bag condemned her, in the eyes of her would-be paramour to a state of moral laxity and, perhaps even worse, clinginess: "If I was dating her, she'd be sleeping in my room, and I'm a pretty independent guy, so I'm going to have to let her go."

The search is part social-sorting—an attempt to rule out incompatibles—and part market research and risk management, designed to help the raiders figure out how best to court their potential dates. The finale of each episode features—in the form of "the reveal"—the judgment of the "raider," along with an elaboration of the reasons for selecting one and disqualifying the others. When raiders are allowed the opportunity to exclude those whose rooms exhibit traces of deviance and dishonesty—or just improper conduct—both raider and target are implicitly ensured that the correct choice has been made.

Only two of the 20 episodes viewed for this chapter ended with the *Room Raiders* expressing any misgivings about their final choices. For the most part, the show repeatedly confirms investigation and detection as effective tools for prescreening dates. In this regard, the gaze of the voyeur detective has hit its mark: examination and surveillance have proven themselves to be useful techniques in penetrating the potentially deceptive facades of appearance and performance, and the savvy subject escapes the fate of the dupe.

One Bad Trip: *The Passive Form of the Drive*

If the exhibitionistic character of the spies on *Room Raiders*—the fact that they are performing their investigations for the audience's gaze—remains a subtext, it becomes the central theme of yet another, somewhat shorter-lived, MTV format called *One Bad Trip.* The show might be considered a response to the question that cannot fail to pass through viewers' minds at one point or another during the course of the network's more outrageous youth-oriented reality shows: "How on Earth are the people who know these kids going to react when they see what they're doing on national TV?"

One Bad Trip provides the answers by bringing friends, significant others, and parents along for the ride as the cameras document the antics of what the network fondly terms its "elite party animals." The latter are told that they are going to be featured in an MTV show about youth gone wild in locations such as Las Vegas, New Orleans, and Lake Havasu City. What they don't know is that people from back home are going to be along for the ride, in disguise, spying on them as they drink, flirt, and party. The premise of the show recapitulates in slightly different form one of the central themes of this chapter: that people are not always who they seem. The prim and proper daughter may cut loose in ways her parents never expected when (seemingly) freed from their monitoring gaze and fixed by that of the MTV cameras.

As in the case of *Room Raiders,* the format promises privileged access to a behind-the-scenes reality obscured by the forms of impression management that characterize face-to-face encounters. Also as in the case of *Room Raiders,* the behind-the-scenes voyeurs narrate their reaction to the hidden "truths" they discover about their targets along the way.

We are presented, for example, with the spectacle of two fathers spying on their college-aged daughters as they frolic on Lake Havasu, drinking, making out with one another, flashing the crowd, and so on. "This might be too much information," says one father peering through binoculars from a nearby boat; "I don't think she's going to end up being a school teacher."

Finally, intriguingly, the "reveal" and debriefing at the end of the show, in which the spies reveal themselves to their targets, is portrayed as a learning experience and a bonding experience. In the case of the Labor Day party episode, one father describes the experience as an ordeal he underwent to get closer to his daughter: "I know Mindy will think if anyone was willing to go through all this, 'it would be my dad.'" Even in the cases in which the surprise surveillance leads to conflicts or a probable breakup, the targets, in keeping with long-standing convention, refer to the show as a learning experience that helped clarify their relationship—even if that clarification led to (a probably inevitable) clash. As Anna Mc-Carthy notes in chapter 1 in this volume, the "reveal" which comes in the form of "unmasking the hoax" serves as "a way of affirming the fact that it was mounted not out of cruelty or sadism but rather in the interest of knowledge."

The function of the reveal, then, is not just to placate the victim but also to assure viewers of the innocuous, perhaps even salutary, character of their own voyeurism. The reveal absolves them of complicity in any resulting trauma or embarrassment. As the cultural critic Slavoj Zizek has suggested, insofar as the audience is positioned in the role of "pure gaze" it is invited to overlook the desire at work in its ostensible neutrality and thereby to background its complicity in the onscreen action.[27] Indeed, the fly-on-the-wall, verité style of such shows, which typically forego the intrusive character of a third-person narrator, help sustain the fiction that allows the viewer, "the true addressee," to "mistake his/her position for that of an accidental bystander."[28]

Furthermore, as McCarthy suggests, with her invocation of reality TV's "operational aesthetic" (its implicit or explicit claim to inform or educate, as well as to entertain) the voyeurism of the audience parallels that of the on-screen spy, insofar as both are in pursuit of behind-the-scenes access to potentially useful information.[29] Both are positioned as the savvy viewers for whom the backstage view they have attained serves as evidence that they are not duped by appearances. The typical savvy reaction to reality TV is both an invocation of its contrived character ("it's not really real") and an attempt to wrest some shred of authenticity from the web of artifice. As Annette Hill noted in her study of British reality TV viewers, "part of the attraction in watching BB [*Big Brother*] is to look for a moment of authenticity in relation to selfhood. . . . The 'game' is to find the 'truth' in the spectacle/performance environment."[30]

The twist introduced by *One Bad Trip*—precisely because of the savvy character of its audience-based talent pool—is to reveal the exhibitionist character of the voyeur, or what might be described, drawing on Freud, as the reflexive or passive form of the scopic drive. In particular, Freud notes that every active form of drives, including scopophilia (voyeurism), is "accompanied by its passive counterpart": "The most striking peculiarity of this perversion lies in the fact that its active and passive forms are regularly encountered together in the same person"—the voyeur doubles as exhibitionist.[31] The goal here is not to vindicate Freudian theory through recourse to reality TV but to enlist it as a means of reflecting on the emerging cultural logic of the interactive information age.

There is a particular fruitfulness to the notion of the overlapping character of voyeurism and exhibitionism—an overlap that is staged quite clearly in the investigative formats described above. If the room raiders conduct their investigation with an eye to the camera, on *One Bad Trip,* the relationship is inverted, so that the spies become the explicit object of the gaze and the targets of the investigation. The turning point came during an episode of the second season when the targets, who were familiar with the show, started to suspect they were not on MTV's *Ultimate Party Show* after all—it was bound to happen eventually. In a hyperreflexive, media-saturated culture, prank shows like *One Bad Trip* may have a built-in expiration date: the moment at which they become so well known that the pool of contestants who haven't heard of the show dries up.

However, as *One Bad Trip* demonstrates, formats can adapt to changing circumstances. The producers logged the show for another season by adapting to the new circumstances: if the targets knew they were being spied on, why not get them to *stage* outrageous behavior for the express purpose of testing the limits of the would-be spies who were following their every move? Precisely because they were undercover, in other words, the spies could be tricked into believing they were getting a behind-the-scenes glimpse of their loved ones. This twist had the added appeal of pranking the pranksters, of paying back the spies for their willingness to dupe their children, friends, siblings, and significant others. It simultaneously realized the truth of the position of the spies "for itself" (to borrow a Hegelian formulation) in the form that it had been all along for the audience: that of exhibitionistic target of the monitoring gaze. It is precisely the introduction of this third-person position, that of the audience "Other" which reveals the reflexive character of voyeurism.

As Freud notes in "The Instincts and Their Vicissitudes," the progression to exhibitionism passes through voyeurism—indeed, scopophilia defaults to a form of exhibitionism insofar as it is to be understood in terms of the introduction of a "new" subject—an external other to whom the active role of voyeuristic watcher is ceded. The result is "a transformation to passivity and the setting up of a new aim—that of being looked at."[32] What MTV's producers described as *One Bad Trip*'s script "flip" turns the would-be spies into the dupes of the camera: the experimental subjects submitting to the machinations of the observers, who, in turn, seek to gain information about their behavior in simulated circumstances they mistake for reality.

This exhibitionistic default is not a simple toggle from active to passive. In Freud's formulation, it is characterized by the interplay or layering of active and passive forms of the drive: "To some extent its earlier active direction always persists side by side with the later passive direction. . . . All phases of its development . . . co-exist alongside one another."[33] Zizek describes this doubling of active and passive drive, with respect to voyeurism, as a process of "actively sustaining the scene of one's own passive submission"—a formulation that invokes not simple, hermetic, self-control but a self-mastery that internalizes the control exercised by an other (to whom the active role is ceded).[34] Thanks to the introduction of the camera as an "other" on *One Bad Trip*, the spies find themselves revealed to be the objects of the gaze of the very people on whom they sought to spy.

Thus the "reveal" segment of the show's second season rebounds onto the spies themselves, who in the closing sequence are presented with the "real" behind-the-scenes footage that escaped their monitoring gaze: the scenes that unmask the staged character of what they took to be reality. For example, a young woman who, on a holiday trip to Vegas, was tailed by her mother and boyfriend in disguise, reveals at the end of the show how her aggressive flirtation with another man was merely a setup—a ruse to test the reactions of her loved ones. The takeaway lesson of the reveal recapitulates Baudrillard's description of simulation as deterrence: the simulated infidelity is offered up as proof that what was portrayed could never be realized.[35] As Crystal, the woman in the Vegas episode, put it, she staged the scene of her infidelity to prove to her boyfriend that "I would never leave you for anyone else. . . . I'm grown up and can do the things that I want to do. . . . I did it because I love you."

The claim that the goal of the deception was, paradoxically, to prove the trustworthiness of the deceiver is a recurring theme in the second season reveals. The reflexive turn reveals a world in which all appearances are deceiving, even those culled from behind the scenes. Given the uncertain circumstances, it is the ostensibly caring effort that goes into demonstrating the ubiquity of manipulation that serves as evidence of affection and warrant for trust. The moment of reconciliation during the reveal takes place when the victims accept the hoax to which they've been subjected as a sign of affection—and an implicit admonishment for not having trusted their loved ones.

For example, a young woman whose boyfriend has just treated her to the spectacle of an extended flirtation with a stripper in New Orleans finds herself marveling that he devoted so much effort to duping her in order to prove his affection: "I just can't believe that you pulled this off. . . . I'm impressed that you can plan something like this: you got me good!" Thus, in the show's second season, the ultimate behind-the-scenes spectacle is portrayed as the revelation of the scene of contrivance itself, and the surveillance targets are transformed into stage-managers of the spectacle.

As in the case of *Room Raiders,* the central role of the show's actual producers is relegated to the background, while the camera focuses on the active role played by the exhibitionist turned voyeur. The elite party animals who agreed to have their antics broadcast to the nation become the investigators crafting experiments to test the reaction of the spies whose cover has been blown. Every suggestive comment, every calculated moment of excess (down to acquiring fake tattoos and drinking fake, nonalcoholic shots), is performed with an eye to the spies' reactions.

The script flip thereby results in an all-too-neat role reversal: the savvy voyeur turns out to be the actual target of the monitoring gaze—and the exhibitionist is revealed as the savvy manipulator. It turns out, in what is hard not to read as a rather unsubtle form of promotion for the emerging era of interactive surveillance, that the target of the monitoring gaze has seized control. To the extent that contrivance is at work here, it is overseen by the targets themselves.

Strategically excluded from the binary role reversal in this formulation is the role played by the gaze of the camera and its imagined audience. On *One Bad Trip,* the default of spy to exhibitionist revolves around the vortex of the audience gaze—for which the entire spectacle is staged. The ostensible goal of each cast member's voyeurism is, precisely, to see from the position of the other/audience: to discover the objective truth of the significant other's intentions (and thereby to see oneself as one is seen). This implicit positioning of the audience/camera as neutral observer is reinforced by the structure of the reveal in which spies and exhibitionists alike accept their submission to the monitoring gaze as a learning experience and a reconfirmation of their relationships to one another.

Crafting a position for audience members as innocent (but interested) bystanders not only fails to implicate the audience desire in the "self-inflicted" torment of the cast members, it simultaneously backgrounds the cycle of voyeurism within which the audience participates—this time, as exhibitionist. Just as the voyeurism that takes place within the diegetic action of the series revolves around the vortex of the audience gaze, so, too, does the voyeurism that takes place in the relation between viewer and spectacle revolve around a third, excluded gaze: that which monitors and surveys the audience. The result is two interlocking triads (target/spy/audience and spectacle/viewer/producer) in which the audience plays the double role of voyeur/viewer and object of the monitoring gaze.

The overlapping positions of voyeur and exhibitionist are redoubled: in the first instance the subject position of the savvy voyeur (on, for example, *One Bad Trip*) is revealed as a self-conscious performance for the imagined gaze of the other; in the second, the audience serves as both the source and object of the monitoring gaze (for cast members and media marketers, respectively). Interactive shows like *American Idol* push this double role a step further: the audience becomes a monitored target market (a nationwide focus group), actively participating in the process of generating information about their viewing habits and preferences.

Spying on Myself: *The Reflexive Form of the Drive*

The final figure of this discussion of the relationship between voyeurism and exhibitionism in reality TV combines both roles in one and is featured in the short-lived A&E series, *Spying on Myself*. If the voyeurs on *One Bad Trip* had to be caught "in the act" in order for the performative character of their spying to be revealed, the "spies" in *Spying on Myself* embrace from the start the double role of target and voyeur. As the show's description put it, the show "gives participants the chance to infiltrate their own lives" and, in so doing, to transform themselves into "a completely different person."[36]

The premise of the show is that participants attempt to see themselves as others do—to adopt the gaze of the audience as other—by disguising themselves and then engaging in videotaped conversations with friends, family members, and former employers in order to see how they are seen. As the show's melodramatic introductory voice-over puts it, cast members are on an undercover mission "in their own life to find out the truth at any cost."

Admittedly, the show remained little more than a cheap one-season series whose claim to novelty lay in its ability to add one more predictable twist to the already terminally reflexive subgenre of "spy"-themed reality shows—shows, that is, about people watching people watch people. At the same time, the attempt to push the format to its somewhat absurd limits yields up a figure that is suggestive for a consideration of the shifting role of surveillance in the information society: that of the "auto-spies" who are consciously submitting to the monitoring gaze for their own good.

This is arguably the ideal type of the citizen consumer envisioned by the interactive information economy, as well as by the participatory security programs of the post-9/11 era and the neoliberal regimes of responsibilization invoked by Laurie Ouellette in chapter 11. Consider the example provided by Bill Gates of the "intelligent agents" he imagines will one day populate our personal computers: programs that allow us to learn about ourselves by quizzing us from time to time about our habits and preferences—in order to facilitate customized forms of consumption.[37] Benign spyware, as it were. Similarly, one of the requirements of post-9/11 security is not just willing submission to unaccountable forms of government monitoring but reflexive self-monitoring: all our habits and practices become redoubled via the mediation of the Department of Homeland Security.

In his book on preparing for the threat of terrorism, former Senate Majority Leader Bill Frist makes clear the connection between bioterror and biopower (the management of the life processes of the populace): we need to watch over our own hygiene practices (exercising, sleeping, and cleaning ourselves properly) as a matter of national security.[38] In a range of spheres of social life, from those of economics, politics, and personal relationships, the interactive era offers up the same injunction: watch (over and out for) yourself.

The fantasy of such regimes of self-scrutiny, which enact the overlap between spy and willing target, voyeur and exhibitionist, is that they are simply self-reflexive—purely about the subject's relationship to himself or herself. The example of reality TV, insofar as it offers a pop-culture representation of contemporary forms of savvy surveillance, provides a more appropriate metaphor: that of mediated self-surveillance which incorporates the imperatives of those who control the monitoring apparatus.

As in the case of the reality shows described in previous sections, *Spying on Myself* legitimates itself to viewers (as well as participants and producers) with the closing "reveal" that highlights the salutary effects of infiltrating one's own life. We see friends, family members, and coworkers estranged by some mysterious misunderstanding reunited in the closing scenes, thanks to the mysterious alchemy of the surveillance cameras. At times, unsurprisingly, the producers have to intervene to calm the emotions of the unpleasantly surprised victims of the hoax by insisting that anyone who was willing to go to such lengths just to deceive someone must truly care about him or her.

As one man who hadn't spoken to his brother for years put it after the producers calmed down his estranged brother, "Once he found out it was a really big production that went into it and the steps that I took to make the whole process happen, I think he really softened up." The closing voice-over drove the point home: the brothers, who had been part of a musical act, "are singing together now," reunited by *Spying on Myself.*

The producers take a much more important role in the diegetic action of *Spying on Myself:* they are shown coaching the "spies" alongside a team of experts who provide training in the arts of interrogation and dissimulation. As the show's description puts it, cast members, "undergo rigorous training by acting coaches and CIA operatives on how to speak, walk and behave with a new identity. Finally the person is sent out on the mission: to find out the truth about themselves in their own world." The difference between self-reflection and self-surveillance, reality TV style, is that the latter entails the *realization* of the imagined gaze of the other by the introduction of a media apparatus that allows cast members to learn about themselves, express themselves, and, in so doing, become someone new.

Reality TV, in other words, thematizes the agency of this figure of the other that intervenes in our self-observation. To take reality TV as one more manifestation of the interactive "democratization" of culture—a format that allows selected members of the audience to learn about themselves by participating in the rarefied realm of cultural production from which the masses have been largely excluded—is to run the danger of downplaying the imperatives that producers bring to bear in shaping the desires, actions, and transformations of the savvy spies they recruit for their shows.

By extension, when viewed from the perspective of the relationship between the audience and the market apparatus that mediates its self-monitoring activity, such an approach backgrounds the mediating role of the market in shaping rather than merely reflecting consumer desire and behavior. This means that the figure of the auto-spy has much in common with that of the interactive citizen consumer. Both are promised self-expression, self-realization, and security through active submission to structured forms of interactive monitoring.

In an interactive era, the attitude of the savvy voyeur is a reflexive one. Insofar as it recognizes its own default to an exhibitionistic performance with an eye to the gaze of the other, it remains susceptible to the invitation to see itself through this gaze and thereby to incorporate the imperatives and desires structured for it by the means of self-surveillance. Like the reality TV cast members laboring for producers in the name of their own self-expression and transformation, the denizens of the interactive era find themselves taking on the duties and imperatives of marketers—contributing to the process of marketing to themselves: actively staging the scene of their own submission.

Todd Gitlin's formulation of savvy voyeurism similarly describes it as a form of surrender: "Savviness . . . transmutes the desire to participate into spectacle. One is already participating, in effect, by watching. 'I like to watch' is the premium attitude."[39] To update this formulation for the interactive era, we might invert it: savviness transmutes the spectacle into an invitation to participate. In one more reflexive twist, this participation becomes itself a form of manipulation insofar as it is portrayed as a form of empowerment—not just what Reg Whitaker calls a "participatory panopticon" but a participatory *spectacle*—in the sense of self-alienation and separation invoked by Guy Debord.[40] The effort to gloss over the process of manipulation is, in the interactive era, displaced by its spectacular *celebration* as a form of participatory passivity available to the exhibitionist-voyeur.

All of which is not to denounce the promise of interactive participation per se but to point out that the deployment of interactivity is not automatically empowering. The figure of the auto-spy providing cheap labor for reality TV producers in the name of an ersatz form of self-discovery and cultural collaboration serves to direct our attention to the imperatives structured by the means of mediated interactivity and those who control them. Lurking in the background of this figure is the recognition that although democracy cannot do without participation, participation is not inherently democratic. As Walter Benjamin noted, "the masses have the right to a change in property relations; Fascism seeks to give them a form of self-expression in the preservation of those relations."[41]

NOTES

1. Neal Gabler, "Behind the Curtain of TV Voyeurism," *Christian Science Monitor,* 7 July 2000, C1.

2. "X10 Home Security," *X10.com,* at http://www.x10.com/homepage.htm (retrieved 4 January 2007).

3. Al Corbi, "Secure a Home from Inside Out," *Oprah.com,* at http://www.oprah.com/foodhome/home/repair/home_20030213_inside.jhtml (retrieved 12 January 2007).

4. For more on reality TV as mode of governance, see Laurie Ouellette and James Hay, *Better Living through Reality TV: Television and Post-Welfare Citizenship* (Malden, Mass.: Blackwell, 2008).

5. Bill Frist, *When Every Moment Counts: What You Need to Know about Bioterrorism from the Senate's Only Doctor* (Boulder, Colo.: Rowman and Littlefield, 2002), 26.

6. *Official Net Detective Site,* at http://netdetective.com/ (retrieved 2 February 2007).

7. Ibid.

8. Alan Mulholland, "Exercise Self-Control—and the Remote Control," *Courier Mail* (Queensland, Australia), 13 June 2002, F11.

9. Jacques Lacan, *The Four Fundamental Concepts of Psychoanalysis: The Seminar of Jacques Lacan, Book XI* (New York: Norton, 1998), 195.

10. Clay Calvert, *Voyeur Nation: Media, Privacy, and Peering in Modern Culture* (Boulder, Colo.: Westview, 2000).

11. Slavoj Zizek, "In His Bold Gaze My Ruin Is Writ Large," in *Everything You Always Wanted to Know about Lacan but Were Afraid to Ask Hitchcock,* ed. Slavoj Zizek (London: Verso, 1999), 294.

12. Theodor Adorno, "The Actuality of Philosophy," in *The Adorno Reader,* ed. Brian O'Connor (Oxford: Blackwell, 2000), 23–29.

13. "MTV Exposed," *MTV.com,* at http://www.mtv.com/ontv/dyn/mtv_exposed/series.jhtml (retrieved 10 January 2007).

14. John Durham Peters, "Witnessing," *Media, Culture and Society* 23 (2001), 712.

15. Slavoj Zizek, *The Ticklish Subject* (London: Verso, 2000), 248.

16. Ibid., 323.

17. Ibid.

18. Bruno Latour, "Why Has Critique Run out of Steam? From Matters of Fact to Matters of Concern," *Critical Inquiry* 30 (2004), 228.

19. In a related context, one account of an anecdote recounted at the Oscars of pornography, the Adult Video News Awards, recapitulates this logic of the search for an elusive, flickering trace of authenticity. One porn fan explains (to a journalist acquaintance) the appeal of sex films. As the fan, who happened to be a police detective and family man, put it, what drew him to the films was not the sex per se but "the faces": "Sometimes—and you never know when, is the thing—sometimes all of a sudden they'll kind of reveal themselves. . . . Their what-do-you-call . . . humanness. . . . In real movies, it's all on purpose. I suppose what I like in porno is the accident of it." David Foster Wallace, "Big Red Son," in *Consider the Lobster and Other Essays* (New York, Little, Brown, 2005), 16. On this account, the appeal of the contrivance of porn is its ability to yield up fleeting traces of facade-dropping authenticity, perhaps because of the very strain of attempting to sustain a simulacrum of desire.

20. Samantha Ellis, "You've Seen the Movie, Now Take the Brain Scan," *Guardian* (London), 3 June 2001, 8.

21. G. Robert Hillman, "Bush, Putin Swap Praise after Meeting," *Seattle Times,* 17 June 2001, A2.

22. Quoted in Alison Mitchell, "The 2000 Campaign," *New York Times,* 7 September 2000, A27. This was, of course, long before George Bush dubbed himself the "decider" in the face of mounting criticism of Secretary of Defense Donald Rumsfeld.

23. Eric Boehlert, "The TV Ad That Put Bush over the Top," *Salon.com,* 5 November 2004, at http:// dir.salon.com/story/news/feature/2004/11/05/bush_ads/ index.html (retrieved 2 June 2006).

24. Stefan Lougren, "'CSI Effect' Is Mixed Blessing for Real Crime Labs," 23 September 2004, at http://news.nationalgeographic.com/news/2004/09/0923-040923_ csi.html.

25. See http://www.mtv.com/ontv.dyn/room_raiders.

26. Quoted in Malcolm Gladwell, *Blink: The Power of Thinking without Thinking* (New York: Little, Brown, 2005), 36.

27. Zizek, "In His Bold Gaze."

28. Ibid., 225

29. Anna McCarthy, chapter 1 in this volume.

30. Annette Hill, "*Big Brother:* The Real Audience," *Television and New Media* 3.3 (2002), 337.

31. Sigmund Freud, "Three Contributions to the Theory of Sex," in *The Basic Writings of Sigmund Freud,* ed. A. A. Brill (New York: Random House, 1938), 576, 570.

32. Sigmund Freud, "Instincts and Their Vicissitudes," in *Sigmund Freud: Collected Papers*, Vol. 4, ed. Jacques Riviere (London: Hogarth Press, 1950), 72.

33. Ibid.

34. Zizek, "In His Bold Gaze," 284.

35. Jean Baudrillard, *Simulacra and Simulation* (Ann Arbor: University of Michigan Press, 1992).

36. *AETV Community Center*, at http://boards.aetv.com/category.jspa?categoryID=500000007 (retrieved 18 December 2006).

37. Bill Gates, *The Road Ahead* (New York: Penguin, 1996).

38. Frist, *When Every Moment Counts*, 40–41, 38.

39. Todd Gitlin, "Blip, Bites, and Savvy Talk: Television's Impact on American Politics," in *State of the Art: Issues in Contemporary Mass Communication*, ed. David Shimkin, Harold Stolerman, and Helene O'Connor (New York: St. Martin's, 1992), 217.

40. Reg Whitaker, *The End of Privacy: How Total Surveillance Is Becoming Reality* (New York: New Press, 1999); and Guy Debord, *The Society of the Spectacle* (New York: Zone Books, 1995).

41. Susan Buck-Morss, "Aesthetics and Anaesthetics: Walter Benjamin's Artwork Essay Reconsidered." *October* 62 (1992), 3.

17

‖‖‖

Buying into *American Idol*
How We Are Being Sold on Reality Television

Henry Jenkins

Who would have predicated that reality television series, such as *Survivor* (2000) and *American Idol* (2002), would turn out to be the first killer applications of media convergence—the big new thing that demonstrated the power that lurks at the intersection between old and new media? Initial experiments with interactive television in the mid-1990s were largely written off as failures. Most people didn't want to stop watching television just to buy the clothes one of the *Friends* (1994) was wearing. Few were interested in trivia quizzes flashing up at the bottom of the screen during sportscasts or James Bond movies. Critics argued that most of us simply wanted to sit back and watch television rather than interact with it. The current success of reality television is forcing the media industry to rethink some of those assumptions. The shift is one from real-time interaction toward asynchronous participation.

Few can argue with *American Idol*'s success. By the final weeks of its second season in 2003, FOX Broadcasting Company was receiving more than 20 million telephone calls or text messages per episode, casting verdicts on the *American Idol* contestants.[1] This made the phone companies happy because they have been trying to find a way to get Americans more excited about text messaging, which hasn't taken off in the United States the way it has in Asia and northern Europe. Of the 140 million mobile phones in the United States today, only 27 million are being used for text messaging.[2] AT&T Wireless reported that roughly one-third of those who participated in *American Idol* through text messaging had never sent a text message before.[3] As an AT&T spokesman explained, "Our venture with FOX has done more to educate the public and get people texting than any marketing activity in this country to date."[4]

American Idol commanded two of the top five time slots throughout the important May 2003 sweeps period. More than 40 million people watched the final segment of the final episode of *American Idol*'s second season. By the third season, FOX devoted 13.5 hours to *American Idol* during the crucial May sweeps period, representing nearly one-quarter of their total prime-time schedule for the month.[5]

This made advertisers happy. As MediaCom chief executive Jon Mandel explains, "We know when people are watching a show they care about, they tend to watch commercials more. Unfortunately, there aren't that many shows people care about."[6] *American Idol*, based on the successful British series *Pop Idol*, was sold to FOX through an aggressive campaign by the Creative Artists Agency, which saw the series as an ideal match for their client, Coca-Cola, and its 12–24-year-old target audience.[7] And what a match it has been. For those of you without a television or a teenage offspring, *American Idol* is a showcase of unknown singers—some good, some very bad—from around the country. Each week, the finalists perform and the audience votes out one contestant. In the end, the surviving performer gets a record contract and a promotion deal. *Forbes* ranked *American Idol* as the most profitable of all reality series, estimating that it had netted the network more than $260 million in profits by the end of its third season.[8] [. . .]

American Idol was from the start not simply a television program but a transmedia franchise. The show's first season winner, Kelly Clarkson, signed to RCA records and had an immediate number 1 hit single on the Billboard Hot 100, "A Moment Like This." The song went on to become the top-selling U.S. single for 2002. Kelly's initial singles got played more than 80,000 times on radio stations in 2002. An *American Idol* book made the bestseller list,[9] and the *American Idol* contestants played to sold-out houses on their nationwide concert tour. Production began immediately on a feature-length movie, *From Justin to Kelly* (2003), though the film ultimately generated low box-office returns.

Not everyone, however, was enchanted with *American Idol*'s success. Speaking for so many critics of reality television, Karla Peterson ranted in the *San Diego Union-Tribune:*

> *American Idol* was not a dumb summer fling, but a conniving multimedia monster. Shameless product placement. Bloodless nostalgia. Incestuous corporate hype. Like the show's Stepford divas—who dutifully parroted

every shriek, quiver and growl from the Mariah Carey catalog—*American Idol* has absorbed the sins of our debauched culture and spit them out in a lump of reconstituted evil. And because we were so dazzled by its brazen lack of redeeming qualities, we stepped over the mess and happily followed it over the abyss.[10]

Peterson is correct that *American Idol* was shaped at every level by blatant commercial calculations. Yet, her moral outrage doesn't take us very far toward understanding its appeal to the networks, advertisers, or consumers.

To understand *American Idol*'s success, we need to better understand the changed context within which American broadcasting is operating and the changed model of consumer behavior shaping programming and marketing strategies. We need to know more about what I am calling "affective economics." By affective economics, I mean a new configuration of marketing theory, still somewhat on the fringes but gaining ground within the media industry, which seeks to understand the emotional underpinnings of consumer decision making as a driving force behind viewing and purchasing decisions. In many ways, affective economics represents an attempt to catch up with work in cultural studies over the last several decades on fan communities and viewer commitments. There is a crucial difference, however: the cultural studies work sought to understand media consumption from the fan's point of view, articulating desires and fantasies that were ill-served by the current media system; the new marketing discourse seeks to mold those consumer desires to shape purchasing decisions.

While they are increasingly interested in the qualities of audience experience, the media and brand companies still struggle with the economic side of affective economics—the need to quantify desire, to measure connections, and to commodify commitments—and, perhaps most important of all, the need to transform all of the above into return on investment. These bottom-line pressures often deflect attempts to understand the complexity of audience behavior even when such knowledge is desperately needed by companies that want to survive in the coming decades. Rather than rethinking the terms of their analysis, they are struggling to fit these new insights into familiar economic categories. It is still a world where what can be counted is what counts most.

Arguably, fans of certain cult television shows may gain greater influence over programming decisions in the age of affective economics. From time to time, networks reprioritize certain segments of their audience, and the result is a shift in program strategies to more fully reflect those tastes. For example, a shift from rural to urban viewers changed television content in the 1960s, a renewed interest in minority viewers led to more Afrocentric sitcoms throughout the 1990s, and a shift toward an emphasis on loyal viewers has been changing what reaches the air in the early twenty-first century. Fans are seeing more shows reflecting their tastes and interests reaching the air; those shows that fans like are apt to remain on the air longer because they are more likely to get renewed in border-line cases.

Here's the paradox: to be desired by the networks is to have your tastes commodified. On the one hand, to be commodified expands a group's cultural visibility. Those groups that have no recognized economic value get ignored. That said, on the other hand, commodification is also a form of exploitation. Those groups that are commodified find themselves targeted more aggressively by marketers and often feel they have lost control over their own culture since it is mass produced and mass marketed. One cannot help but have conflicted feelings because one doesn't want to go underrepresented—but one doesn't want to be exploited, either.

For years, fan groups seeking to rally support for endangered series have argued that networks should be focused more on the quality of audience engagement with the series and less on the quantity of viewers. Increasingly, advertisers and networks are coming to more or less the same conclusion. Marketers seek to shape brand reputations, not through an individual transaction but through the sum total of interactions with the customer—an ongoing process that increasingly occurs across a range of different media "touch points." They don't simply want to get consumers to make a single purchase but, rather, want them to build a long-term relationship with a brand. New models of marketing seek to expand consumers' emotional, social, and intellectual investments with the goal of shaping consumption patterns.

In the past, media producers spoke of "impressions." Now, they are exploring the concept of audience "expressions," trying to understand how and why audiences react to content. Marketing gurus argue that building a committed "brand community" may be the surest means of expanding consumer loyalty and that product placements will allow brands to tap some of the affective force of the affiliated entertainment properties. For this reason, shows such as *American Idol* are being watched closely by advertisers, marketing companies, television networks, and trade press reporters, all eager to understand how corporate convergence strategies may be reshaping the branding process. Early evidence suggests that the most valuable consumers are what the industry calls "loyals," or what we call fans. Loyals are more apt to watch series faithfully, more apt to pay attention to advertising, and more apt to buy products.

For the moment, I want readers to bracket their anxieties about consumerism and their fear of Madison Avenue. I do not intend this chapter to be in any simple sense an endorsement of or apology for the changes that are taking place. My own view is that this emerging discourse of affective economics has both positive and negative implications: allowing advertisers to tap the power of collective intelligence and direct it toward their own ends, but at the same time allowing consumers to form their own kind of collective bargaining structure that they can use to challenge corporate decisions.

Even if you want to criticize the way American capitalism works, you need to recognize that the models of marketing depicted in classic accounts, such as Vance Packard's *Hidden Persuaders* (1957), no longer adequately describe the way the media industries are operating.[11] Even if you believe that fan and brand communities lack the clout to significantly alter corporate behavior, you still need to understand the way participation works within this new effective economy so that you can direct criticisms at the actual mechanisms by which Madison Avenue seeks to reshape our hearts and minds.

At industry gatherings around the country, corporate visionaries and brand gurus are promoting what I am calling affective economics as the solution to a perceived crisis in American broadcasting—a crisis brought about by shifts in media technology that are granting viewers much greater control over the flow of media into their homes. Affective economics sees active audiences as potentially valuable if they can be courted and won over by advertisers. In this chapter, I am looking more closely at the ways that advertisers and networks think about their audiences in the age of media convergence and the ways those assumptions about branding, audience commitment, and social viewing are shaping series such as *American Idol*.

American Idol offers up a fantasy of empowerment—"America" gets to "decide" who will be the next Idol. This promise of participation helps build fan investments, but it may also lead to misunderstandings and disappointments as viewers feel that their votes have not been counted. [. . .]

Lovemarks and Emotional Capital

Delivering the keynote address at *Advertising Age*'s Madison + Vine conference on February 5, 2003, Coca-Cola president Steven J. Heyer outlined his vision for the future relations between the advertising ("Madison") and the entertainment industries ("Vine). His speech offers a glimpse into the thinking of one of *American Idol*'s primary sponsors.[12]

Heyer opened by identifying a range of problems that "demand a new approach to connecting with audiences" and force a rethinking of the old mass media paradigm:

> The fragmentation and proliferation of media, and the consolidation in media ownership—soon to be followed by a wholesale unbundling. The erosion of mass markets. The empowerment of consumers who now have an unrivaled ability to edit and avoid advertising and to shift day parts. A consumer trend toward mass customization and personalization.

Confronting profound shifts in consumer behavior, Heyer then outlined what he saw as his "convergence" strategy—the greater collaboration between content providers and sponsors to shape the total entertainment package. The focus, he argued, should be less on the content per se than on the "why, where and how" the various entertainment media are brought together and the relationship that gets brokered with the consumer. As he explained, "Imagine if we used our collective tool kit to create an ever-expanding variety of interactions for people that—over time—built a relationship, an ongoing series of transactions, that is unique, differentiated and deeper" than any the entertainment industry has offered before.

Heyer's speech evokes the logic of brand extension, the idea that successful brands are built by exploiting multiple contacts between the brand and the consumer. The strength of a connection is measured in terms of its emotional impact. The experience should not be contained within a single media platform but should extend across as many media as possible. Brand extension builds on audience interest in particular content to bring them into contact again and again with an associated brand. Following this logic, Coca-Cola sees itself less as a soft drink bottler and more as an entertainment company that actively shapes and sponsors sporting events, concerts, movies, and television series. This intensification of feelings enables entertainment content—and brand messages—to break through the "clutter" and become memorable for consumers:

> We will use a diverse array of entertainment assets to break into people's hearts and minds. In that order. . . . We're moving to ideas that elicit emotion and create connections. And this speeds the convergence of Madison + Vine. Because the ideas which have always sat at the heart of the stories you've told and the content you've sold . . . whether movies or music or television . . . are mo longer just intellectual property, they're emotional capital.

Kevin Roberts, the chief executive officer worldwide of Saatchi and Saatchi, argues that the future of consumer relations lie with "lovemarks" that are more powerful than traditional "brands" because they command "love," as well as the "respect" of consumers: "The emotions are a serious opportunity to get in touch with consumers. And best of all, emotion is an unlimited resource. It's always there—waiting to be tapped with new ideas, new inspirations, and new experiences."[13] Arguing that only a small number of customers make purchase decisions based on purely rational criteria, Roberts urges marketers to develop multisensory (and multimedia) experiences that create more vivid impressions and tap the power of stories to shape consumer identifications.

For example, Coca Cola's corporate website includes a section where consumers can share their own personal stories about their relationship with the product, stories that get organized around such themes as "romance," "reminders of family," "childhood memories," "an affordable luxury," "times with friends," and a "memory of home." These themes merge core emotional relationship with core promotional themes, helping people not simply to integrate Coca-Cola into their memories of their lives but to frame those memories in terms of the marketing pitch.

American Idol wants its fans to feel love or, more specifically, the "love marks." Audience participation is a way of getting *American Idol* viewers more deeply invested, shoring up their loyalty to the franchise and its sponsors. This investment begins with the turnout of millions of would-be contestants at auditions held in stadiums and convention hotels across the country. Many more people watch the series than try out; many more try out than make the air; many more make the air than become finalists. But, at every step along the way, the viewers are invited to imagine that "it could be me or someone I know." From there, the weekly votes increase the viewer's engagement, building a strong allegiance to the individual performers. By the time the records are released, many of the core consumers have already endorsed the performers, and fan clubs are already involved with grassroots marketing.

For example, fans of Clay Aiken, the runner-up on season 2, turned their disappointment into a campaign to ensure that his album, *Measure of a Man* (2003), outsold first-place finisher Ruben Studdard's *Soulful* (2003). Clay's album sold more than 200,000 more copies than Studdard's in its opening week on the charts—though one suspects that the record executives would have been happy whichever way the sales contest went.[14]

Coca-Cola, in turn, brands key series elements: contestants wait in the "red room" before going on stage; judges sip from Coca-Cola cups; highlights get featured on the official program website surrounded by a Coca-Cola logo; soft drink promotions reward tickets to the finales; Coca-Cola sends *Idol* performers to NASCAR races and other sporting events that it sponsors; and Coca-Cola's sponsorship figures prominently at the *American Idol* finalist's national concert tour.[15]

Heyer spoke of a shift "away from broadcast TV as the anchor medium" and toward "experience-based, access-driven marketing" as the ideal means of reaching the emerging generation of consumers. *Cokemusic.com* further aligns the soft drink company with people's enjoyment of popular music, allowing for a range of different participatory and interactive options. Members can pay for downloads of popular songs or redeem coupons that allow them to download songs for free. Members can create their own music mixes, share them with one another, and receive ratings from other site visitors. Ratings points reward "decibels" that can be redeemed to purchase virtual furnishing for their "pads," allowing further customization and a deeper sense of belonging in the world of Coca-Cola. "Performers" develop reputations and followings, which provide emotional incentives for them to spend even more time working on their "mixes."

More casual site visitors can participate in a range of quizzes, games, and contests. *Cokemusic.com* has become the third most popular website among teens, registering more than 6 million users who spend an average of 40 minutes per visit. As Carol Kruse, the director of interactive marketing for the company, explains, "They're having fun, they're learning about music, they're building a sense of community . . . and it's all in a very safe and friendly Coke environment.[16]

Brand loyalty is the holy grail of affective economics because of what economists call the 80/20 rule: for most consumer products, 80 percent of purchases are made by 20 percent of their consumer base. Maintaining the allegiance of that 20 percent stabilizes the market and allows them to adopt an array of other approaches to court those who would make the other 80 percent of purchases.[17] Corporations are turning toward active consumers because they must do so if they are going to survive; some have learned that such consumers can be allies, but many still fear and distrust them, seeking ways to harness this emerging power toward their own ends.

Something of this ambivalence can be seen in Roberts's description of what he calls "inspirational consumers" and others call "brand advocates":

> They are the ones who promote and advocate for the brand. The ones . . . who suggest improvements and refinements, who create websites and spread the word. They are also the people who act as moral guardians for the brands they love. They make sure the wrongs are righted and hold the brand fast to its stated principles."[18]

Roberts acknowledges that these inspirational consumers, individually and collectively, place demands on corporations, citing the example of the outcry when Coca-Cola sought to replace its classic formula with "New Coke" and was forced within two months to back off from that decision. Roberts argues that companies need to listen closely when these inspirational consumers speak—especially when they criticize a company decision. A company that loses faith with its inspirational consumers, he argues, will soon lose its core market: "When a consumer loves you enough to take action, any action, it is time to take notice. Immediately."[19]

Roberts praises companies that actively court such fans, to continue the Coca-Cola example, by hosting events and conventions where their collectibles are appraised and showcased. The first fan club for Coca-Cola formed in 1974, a grassroots effort by a small group of enthusiasts. Today, fan clubs operate in 28 different countries around the world and host a global network of local and national conventions that the company uses to bring together and address its most dedicated consumers.

Roberts's advice about courting inspirational consumers is echoed across a range of other business best-sellers, such as Marc Gobé's *Emotional Branding: The New Paradigm for Connecting Brands to People* (2001), Mathew W Ragas's *The Power of Cult Branding: How Nine Magnetic Brands Turned Customers into Loyal Followers (and Yours Can, Too)*

(2002), and John Hagel III and Arthur G. Armstrong's *Net.Gain: Expanding Markets through Virtual Communities* (1997).[20] They point toward a world where the most valued consumer may be the one who is most passionate, dedicated, and actively engaged. Far from marginal, fans are the central players in a courtship dance between consumers and marketers.

As one noted industry guide explains, "Marketing in an interactive world is a collaborative process with the marketer helping the consumer to buy and the consumer helping the marketer to sell."[21] This search for "inspirational consumers" is starting to impact the way television audiences are appraised and the ways advertisers think about selling products.

Zappers, Casuals, and Loyals

Industry insiders often deploy the distinction among zappers, casuals, and loyals: this distinction manages to blur together how, why, and what consumers watch. Zappers are people who constantly flit across the dial—watching snippets of shows rather than sitting down for a prolonged engagement. Loyals actually watch fewer hours of television each week than the general population: they cherry pick those shows that best satisfy their interests; they give themselves over fully to them; they tape them and may watch them more than one time; they spend more of their social time talking about them; and they are more likely to pursue content across media channels. Loyals watch series; zappers watch television. Loyals form long-term commitments; zappers are like the folks at cocktail parties who are always looking over their shoulders to see if someone more interesting has just entered the room. Casuals fall somewhere in between; they watch a particular series when they think of it or have nothing better to do. They gradually watch it from start to finish but are more apt to wander away if it starts to bore them. They may be more likely to conduct conversations or do other household activities over the show rather than give it their full attention.

No given viewer is exclusively a loyal, a casual, or a zapper; most watch television in different ways on different occasions. The most discriminating viewer will zap around the dial in a hotel room or at the end of the day. And sometimes zappers get hooked into a series and watch it every week. Nobody knows for sure yet whether the new media environment has produced more zappers, casuals, or loyals. For one thing, A. C. Neilsen's continued focus on entire program blocks rather than more microscopic units of time means that they have no real way of measuring zapping or, indeed, the fluctuating loyalties of more casual viewers.

Throughout much of the 1990s, industry analysts overstressed the significance of the zappers. For example, Phillip Swann asserts in his book *TV.Com: How Television Is Shaping Our Future:* "Few viewers today can sit through an entire program without picking up the remote and checking out another channel. . . . Today's viewer needs constant gratification: if she's not entertained or intrigued for any stretch of time, she will flip the dial."[22] Swann thinks interactive television should and will be designed for zappers. In Swann's future, variety and magazine shows will almost entirely displace dramas, and the few remaining series will be shrunk to 30 minutes or less. According to Swann,

> [There will be] fewer occasions where people sit down and watch a show from beginning to end without interruptions. People will start watching TV shows the way they read books: a little at a time. . . . The concept of "appointment television"—arranging to be home at a precise time to watch a particular program—will soon be a thing of the past.[23]

Refusing to bow out just yet, the networks want to hold on to appointment viewing by constructing new forms of programming that demand and reward immediate attention, and they want to build up viewer loyalty by intensifying the affective appeal of their programs.

Industry research now suggests that loyals are much more valuable than zappers. According to a study done by Imitative Media, the average network program was identified as a "favorite series" by only 6 percent of its viewers. But, in some cases, as many as 50 or 60 percent of viewers may rank a program as their favorites. Early evidence suggests that these loyals have a higher rate of brand recall (a key concern of advertisers) and are much less likely to be lured away from the networks toward competing cable content (a key concern of programmers). Loyals are twice as likely to pay attention to advertisements and two to three times more likely to remember product categories than more casual viewers. And they are between 5 to 20 percent more likely to recall specific sponsors—not huge numbers, perhaps, but big enough that they can give a competitive edge to advertisers who consistently target shows with a high degree of viewer loyalty.

Historically, networks ignored those fan bases in making decisions about renewing series, seeing fans as unrepresentative of the general public; but advertisers are increasingly realizing that they may be better advised investing their dollars behind shows that have a high favorability than shows that have high ratings. As this research impacts programming decisions, the media industry is trying to generate content that will attract loyalists, slow down zappers, and turn casuals into fans.

At first glance, *American Idol* looks like it was designed for zappers. Each episode breaks down into bite-size units of only a few minutes' duration as each of the competing performers sings and is judged. To some degree, reality series are built up of "attractions," short, highly emotionally charged units that can be watched in or out of sequence. But the series is designed to support and sustain multiple levels of engagement.

American Idol is designed to pull in every possible viewer and to give each a reason not to change the channel. Many elements that loyals find repetitive ensure the program's continued accessibility to casuals—things like the recaps of the previous episodes, the recurring profiles of the contestants, the rereading of key quotes from the judge's assessments. Each of these segments reorients casuals to the contest's basic mechanics or provides the background that's needed to appreciate the dramatic conflict in that night's episode. As they move into their final weeks and more casuals are drawn into the snowballing phenomenon, *American Idol* and many other reality shows may devote an entire episode to the season's highlights, designed to provide an easy entry point. Beyond this, each episode is constructed to allow a satisfactory entertainment experience. In *American Idol,* each Tuesday night episode includes performances by all of those contestants still in the competition. Each episode also includes a cliffhanger, so *American Idol* viewers are encouraged to tune in the following night to see how the voting went. These unresolved elements are intended to pull casuals toward a more committed relationship.

As for loyals, perhaps the single most important factor separating reality from other kinds of nonfiction programming is serialization. Talent contests are a well-established pattern in American broadcasting, going back at least as far as Major Bowles's *Original Amateur Hour* on radio in the 1930s. What *American Idol* added to the mix, however, was the unfolding of the competition across a season, rather than in the course of a single broadcast. Or to be more accurate, serialized talent competitions had already sprung up on cable networks, such as MTV and VH1, but FOX brought them over to the major networks and made them prime-time entertainment.

In serializing the talent competition, *American Idol* is simply following a trend that runs across all contemporary television—a movement away from the self-contained episodes that dominated broadcasting for its first several decades in favor of longer and more complicated program arcs and more elaborate appeals to series history. Serialization rewards the competency and mastery of loyals. The reason loyals watch every episode isn't simply that they enjoy them; they need to have seen every episode to make sense of long-term developments.

Every reality series starts out with a cast larger than most audience members can grasp, and most of those characters will receive relatively limited airtime. As the winnowing process occurs, however, certain characters will emerge as audience favorites, and a good producer anticipates those interests and rewards them by providing those characters with more airtime. Viewers move from thinking of the characters as generic types toward thinking of the characters as particular individuals. Viewers get to know the contestants: learn their personality, see their motives for competing, view their backgrounds, and, in some cases, meet other members of their families. In *American Idol*, viewers watch them improve or crash and burn. This may be why *American Idol* has become such a powerful marketing tool for launching the careers of young performers compared with earlier televised talent competition. [. . .]

Contesting the Vote

So far, we have focused our discussion on those factors that ensure viewer loyalty to *American Idol*, but as Heyer's speech suggests, sponsors are seeking to transfer viewer loyalty from entertainment properties onto their brands. The majority of the people interviewed by a research study conducted by MIT's Comparative Media Studies Program and Initiative Media of audience response to the second season of *American Idol* were acutely aware that the show was serving as a testing ground for branding strategies and were eager to offer their opinions about the experiments as they unfolded. Product placements and program-themed commercials became an acknowledged part of the *American Idol* phenomenon, something people, in some cases, turned in to see—much as the Super Bowl has become as much a showcase for advertising as a sporting event.

Coca-Cola spoofed the uncompromising honesty of judge Simon Cowell, depicting him as forced by a mobster to read an endorsement for Vanilla Coke; Ford created new musical segments each week featuring the program contestants; AT&T created a campaign that mimicked *Legally*

Blonde (2001) and showed an airheaded teenager going around the country encouraging people to participate in the call-in voting process. Sponsors are not simply seeking the chance to advertise their products; they are seeking to brand the content so that the red of the *American Idol* set becomes inseparable from Coca-Cola's sponsorship of the series, so that the Ford spots featuring the contestants become part of the evidence fans mobilize in support of their favorite performers, and so that AT&T's text-messaging system becomes the preferred vehicle for voting.

Viewers are more accepting of product placements in reality programming than in any other genre (they are least comfortable with product placements in drama, news, and children's programming). Some are turned off by this hypercommercialism, but for others, recognizing marketplace interventions has become part of the "game": "I find myself trying to pick out products placed in shows and get an a-ha moment when I find one." Even those who claim not to watch commercials are drawn toward series-targeted spots: "You know what I do in the commercial breaks? Refill my popcorn bowl. Go to the bathroom. Bake a cake. Sing a song. Dance a dance. I refuse to be made to sit through that crap!!! However, I really liked the Simon/Vanilla Coke commercial."

Even many of those who refused to watch the show because it was overcommercialized still accurately named its sponsors. In some cases, sponsors improved public perception of their brand, whereas others potentially damaged their standing. As one regular viewer told our researchers, "Now I know for sure that AT&T Wireless and Ford and Coca-Cola advertise with them, but it's to the point of being annoying and I want nothing to do with those particular brands now." Others couldn't separate consumerism from their participation in the series: "*Sigh*. Yes, I purchased a sweatshirt from Old Navy because Aiken wore it in the studio recording of 'God Bless the USA' and I loathe Old Navy. Normally I hate that kind of stuff." The early evidence, however, suggests that as a general rule, the more invested viewers became in *American Idol*, the more committed they became to its sponsors.

Such a tight integration of advertising and content is not without its risks, since the credibility of the sponsors became closely linked with the credibility of the competition itself. Marketing researcher Robert Kozinets warns that participation in a consumption community heightens one's awareness of the consumption and marketing process and reaffirms feelings of resentment if a company exploits that relationship. The collective voice speaks louder and often more decisively than its individual members.

Such expressions reach the ear not only of the companies being challenged but also the mainstream media; consumer backlashes are increasingly being covered as "scandals," which puts further pressure on the companies to respond. In some cases, Kozinets notes, the corporations, angry over their loss of control, threaten or punish their most loyal consumers, undermining valuable relationships. Kevin Roberts argues that companies need to see such scandals as opportunities to listen and learn from their most hard-core consumers, building up greater loyalty through their responsiveness rather than tearing it down through indifference or overreaction.

The down-to-the-wire contest between Clay Aiken and Ruben Studdard turned out to be almost as close as the 2000 presidential election, with the two finalists separated by a little more than 100,000 votes out of 24 million votes cast. The text message votes all got through and were counted—several million worth—whereas millions of telephone callers faced endless busy signals. As one fan explained in our survey, "Hanging chads in Florida is nothing compared to this stupid voting procedure." Clay supporters were particularly vocal about the degree to which clogged phone lines made it impossible to get an accurate count, and some argued that the lines may have been arbitrarily restricted to ensure a close race. The *American Idol* producers had raised expectations about responsiveness to audience feedback and thus faced a backlash when they failed to meet those expectations.

By the third season, inconsistencies in the voting made headlines in national newspapers, with the network forced to acknowledge that significant numbers of callers were not able to register their votes because local phone lines were being flooded. The result was an uneven counting of votes from one region to another. For example, viewers in Hawaii, an area where there were relatively few people competing for access to the local connection, could have cast as much as one-third of the total votes in the third season, an imbalance which some have argued accounted for the prolonged run of a Hawaiian contestant.[24] As the controversy intensified, they expanded voting hours and added more phone lines to try to lower public disappointment. An editorial in *Broadcasting and Cable* warned: "Viewer loyalty is hard to build and tough to maintain. . . . With AT&T one of the show's sponsors, FOX needs to go out of its way to avoid the appearance that it could be in cahoots with the phone company to drive as many calls as possible, whether or not they get through."[25]

Despite such scrutiny, FOX has refused to release the actual vote counts, offering only partial information on a selective basis during the broadcasts. Many fans argue that such selective reporting makes it hard for them to put much faith in the reliability and impartiality of the process.

Complaints went beyond the voting mechanism to include concerns about how particular contestants were "pushed" by the judges and the producers, given higher prominence on the show and more supportive comments, or, in some cases, intentionally attacked to inspire audience backlash against the judging. Cynics saw the producers as more interested in generating controversial and compelling programming than in recognizing talent. Much as the spoilers sought to thwart Mark Burnett's efforts to keep the *Survivor* outcome a secret, the *American Idol* online community took pleasure in trying to read through the "mechanisms" by which the producers "engineer" the results. As one fan explained, "I like seeing Simon trying to figure out the power of saying evil things to create a backlash, and saying to a so-so performer that they are amazing."

For many, such efforts to shape public response were seen as an extension of the sponsor interference into program content. The performers, they argued, were becoming so "packaged" that they were no different from the other products being advertised. In some cases, the "Idols" became models who displayed new fashions, new makeup, and hair-styling products. Fans suggested this refashioning of their images was simply the first step in what would result in overprocessed versions of their performances when their albums were released.

This degree of anger suggests that product placements might be a double-edged sword—on the one hand, higher consumer awareness and, on the other, higher consumer scrutiny. Virtually every research participant had some criticism of the ways that commercialism tainted the series, complicating arguments that might see media-savvy marketers manipulating naive and gullible consumers. Even loyals complained that the series was sometimes nothing more than a "merchandise machine."

These online communities gave "inspirational consumers" a place to talk about their resistance to these new forms of commercialism. In critiquing the results, fans often focused on the corporate interests they saw as shaping the outcome. Through this process, more economically conscious participants could educate others about the commercial structures shaping American broadcasting. In some cases, *American Idol* fans used the resources of these online communities to identify flaws in the voting system. This summary from one fan site suggests the sophistication with which they were collecting information:

Most text messages go through—according to message board posts, websites maintained by the text messaging company, and through news articles. But viewers pay a small fee to send a vote in text—so paying for the vote does give you leverage. Yet last year when Ruben Studdard won, texters on an *American Idol* message board reported some of their messages didn't go through. Hours after the calls, people said their phone companies sent back text error messages from their phone carriers saying some messages failed. Up till that point, texters were reporting 100 percent completion.[26]

American Idol fans discussed voting strategies they felt would counter such distortion in the competition. Their efforts might be aimed at supporting the best singer, balancing out negative comments, or undermining "heavily marketed" contestants. From day 1, the producers had sought to position the third season as a battle between three black "divas," and the judges had all but proclaimed Fantasia Barrino the likely winner. As the other two black "divas" went down and as Fantasia ranked near the bottom of the vote counts across several weeks, guest judge Elton John denounced America's voting patterns as "incredibly racist."[27] Such seemingly erratic voting patterns, however, make more sense if we see them in the context of a growing backlash among the most hard-core viewers to what they saw as open attempts to take away their right to choose the Idol.

Sponsoring such a show ensures that companies will get talked about, but it doesn't guarantee what the audience is going to say about them. In much of this chapter I look at *American Idol* in terms of the behind-the-scenes calculations of media companies such as FOX, consumer brands such as Coca-Cola, and marketing researchers such as Imitative Media. Yet, we must also take seriously the backlash of Roberts's "inspirational consumers." Who wins *American Idol,* in the end, doesn't matter that much in the great scheme of things. But, the debates about *Idol* voting are debates about the terms of audience participation in American media. At a time when networks and sponsors are joining forces to shape the emotional context through which we watch their shows, consumers are also scrutinizing the mechanisms of participation they are being offered. If the rhetoric of Lovemarks emphasizes the audience's activities and investments as a central source of value in brands, then the consumption community may well hold the corporations accountable for what they do in the name of those brands and for their responsiveness (or lack thereof) to consumer demands. Such disputes generated considerable "heat" around the series, drawing in many new viewers, but they also alienated and disenfranchised many of the most dedicated ones.

Too much backlash can damage ratings or hurt sales of the products. The Initiative Media study found that AT&T, the company that had branded the voting mechanism, was damaged by the public backlash and that the other key sponsors—Coca-Cola and Ford—may have been hurt as well. No one would imagine that viewers might translate bad will to one advertiser in a traditional segment of commercials toward another advertiser. Yet in a world where sponsors are more closely associated with the content, all of the hosting companies may be negatively affected by any negative perceptions that emerge around the series. It is through struggles that the relationship between media producers and consumers will get redefined in the coming decades.

Understanding when audience backlash hurts companies—or, for that matter, how far companies can go in shaping the nature of audience participation—is central to what I have been calling affective economics. If a program is going to become, in Hoyer's terms, the "emotional capital" of its consumers, then we can expect consumers to make different investments in the program than the producers do, and for the love behind the Lovemarks to turn into hate when producers alter something the brand community sees as fundamental to their experience. For the moment, the marketing industry still has a long way to go if it wants to understand the complexity of audiences' emotional investments in entertainment properties and brands. And audiences have a long way to go if they are going to exploit the points of entry that affective economics offers them for collective action and grassroots criticism of corporate conduct.

NOTES

1. Jefferson Graham, "*Idol* Voting Strained Nerves, Nation's Telephone Systems," *USA Today,* 27 May 2003, at http:www.usatoday.com/life/television/news/2003–05–26-idol_x.htm.

2. Jeff Smith, "Getting the Mssg: U.S. Wireless Carriers Mining the Airwaves for Ways to Profit from Text Messaging," *Rocky Mountain News,* 19 May 2003.

3. Ibid.

4. Quoted in "AT&T Wireless Text Messaging Takes Center Stage with Unprecedented Performance on FOX's *American Idol,*" *PR Newswire,* 16 April 2003.

5. Scott Collins and Maria Elena Fernandez, "Unwanted Wrinkles for *Idol*," *Los Angeles Times*, 25 May 2004, 1.

6. Quoted in Stuart Elliot, "The Media Business: Some Sponsors Are Backing Off to Fine-Tune the Art of Blending Their Products into Television Shows," *New York Times*, 22 January 2003.

7. Jennifer Pendleton, "*Idol* a Standard for Integration," *Advertising Age*, 24 March 2003.

8. Penelope Patsuris, "The Most Profitable Reality Series," *Forbes*, 7 September 2004, at http://www.forbes.com/home_europe/business/2004/09/07/cx_pp_0907 realitytv.html.

9. Carla Hay, "Idol Ups Stakes for TV Talent," *Billboard*, 26 April 2003.

10. Karla Peterson, "False Idols: How to Face down a Media Monster So We No Longer Worship Moments Like This," *San Diego Union-Tribune*, 16 December 2002.

11. Vance Packard, *The Hidden Persuaders* (New York: Bantam, 1957).

12. Steven J. Heyer, keynote remarks delivered before *Advertising Age*'s Hollywood + Vine Conference, Beverly Hills Hotel, Beverly Hills, California, 5 February 2003. For a transcript of the remarks, see http://egta.com/pages/News letter%20-%20Heyer.pdf. All subsequent references to Heyer refer to these remarks.

13. Kevin Roberts, *Lovemarks: The Future beyond Brands* (New York: Power House, 2004), 43.

14. Joe D'Angelo, "Ruben Debuts at #1 but Can't Match Clay's First Week Sales," *VH1*, 17 December 003, at http://www.vh1.com/artists/news/1482928/12172003/ aiken_clay.jhtml.

15. Theresa Howard, "Real Winner of 'American Idol': Coke," *USA Today*, 8 September 2002; Wayne Friedman, "Negotiating the *American Idol* Product Placement Deal," *Advertising Age*, 29 September 2003.

16. Sara Wilson, interview with Carol Kruse, *Media Connection*, 2 October 2003, at http://www.imediaconnection.com/content/1309.asp.

17. Robert V. Kozinets, "E-Tribalized Marketing? The Strategic Implications of Virtual Communities of Consumption," *European Management Journal* 17.3 (1999), 252–64.

18. Roberts, *Lovemarks*, 170.

19. Ibid., 172.

20. Marc Gobé, *Emotional Branding: The New Paradigm for Connecting Brands to People* (New York: Allworth, 2001); Mathew W Ragas, *The Power of Cult Branding: How Nine Magnetic Brands Turned Customers into Loyal Followers (and Yours Can, Too)* (Roseville, Calif.: Prima, 2002); and John Hagel III and Arthur G. Armstrong, *Net.Gain: Expanding Markets through Virtual Communities* (Cambridge: Harvard University Press, 1997).

21. Quoted in Don Peppers, Introduction to Seth Gordon, *Permission Marketing: Turning Strangers into Friends and Friends into Customers* (New York: Simon and Schuster, 1999), 12.

22. Philip Swann, *TV.Com: How Television Is Shaping Our Future* (New York: TV Books, 2000), 9–10.

23. Ibid., 31.

24. Wade Paulson, "Distorted *American Idol* Voting Due to an Overtaxed American Power Grid?," *Reality TV World,* at http://www.realitytvworld.com/index/articles/story.php?s=2570.

25. Staff, "The Right Fix for FOX," *Broadcasting and Cable,* 24 May 2004, 36.

26. Joan Giglione, "What's Wrong with the *American Idol* Voting System," 24 May 2004 (no longer on the web).

27. Wade Paulson, "Elton John Calls *American Idol* Voting 'Incredibly Racist,'" *Reality TV World,* 28 April 2004, at http://www.realitytvworld.com/index/articles/story.php?s=2526.

About the Contributors

MARK ANDREJEVIC is Associate Professor in the Department of Communication Studies at the University of Iowa. He is the author of *iSpy: Surveillance and Power in the Interactive Era* and *Reality TV: The Work of Being Watched*, as well as several articles and book chapters on surveillance and popular culture. He is also a Postdoctoral Research Fellow at the Centre for Critical and Cultural Studies at the University of Brisbane.

JOHN CORNER is Professor in the School of Politics and Communication Studies at the University of Liverpool. He has written extensively on television and media culture in books and journals and is an editor of *Media, Culture and Society*. Recent work includes *Public Issue Television* with Peter Goddard and Kay Richardson, and he is currently researching aspects of documentary aesthetics.

NICK COULDRY is Professor of Media and Communications at Goldsmiths College, University of London. He is the author or editor of seven books, including most recently *Listening beyond the Echoes: Media, Ethics and Agency in an Uncertain World* and (with Sonia Livingstone and Tim Markham) *Media Consumption and Public Engagement: Beyond the Presumption of Attention*.

JONATHAN GRAY is Assistant Professor of Communication and Media Studies at Fordham University. He is author of *Watching with* The Simpsons: *Television, Parody, and Intertextuality* and *Television Entertainment*. He is coeditor of *Fandom: Identities and Communities in a Mediated World*; *Battleground: The Media*; and the Taylor and Francis journal *Popular Communication: The International Journal of Media and Culture*.

ALISON HEARN teaches media theory and cultural studies in the Faculty of Information and Media Studies at the University of Western

Ontario. She is coauthor of *Outside the Lines: Issues in Interdisciplinary Research* and has published in such journals as *Topia, International Journal of Media and Cultural Politics,* and *Bad Subjects.* She is currently completing a book on reality television, promotional culture, and the will to image.

HEATHER HENDERSHOT teaches film and media classes at Queens College, City University of New York, and at the CUNY Graduate Center. She is the author of *Saturday Morning Censors: Television Regulation before the V-Chip* and *Shaking the World for Jesus: Media and Conservative Evangelical Culture.* Hendershot is also the editor of *Nickelodeon Nation: The History, Politics and Economics of America's Only TV Channel for Kids.*

HENRY JENKINS is the Co-Director of the MIT Comparative Media Studies Program. He is the editor or author of 12 books, including *Textual Poachers: Television Fans and Participatory Culture; Convergence Culture: Where Old and New Media Collide;* and *Fans, Bloggers, and Gamers: Exploring Participatory Culture.* He blogs regularly on reality television, media education, and fan culture, among other topics, at henryjenkins.org

DEREK KOMPARE is an Assistant Professor in the Division of Cinema-Television in the Meadows School of the Arts at Southern Methodist University, where he teaches courses on media history, media theory, film and television genres, and media globalization. He has written about television history and form in *Flow, Media History, Television, and New Media,* and in anthologies. His recent book *Rerun Nation: How Repeats Invented American Television* was runner-up for the Katherine Singer Kovacs Book Award from the Society for Cinema and Media Studies.

JON KRASZEWSKI is Assistant Professor in the Department of Communication at Seton Hall University. His essays have appeared or are scheduled to appear in journals such as the *Quarterly Review of Film and Video,* the *Journal of Film and Video,* and the *Velvet Light Trap.* He is currently writing a book that examines the relationship between postwar theater and early television drama and, with Victoria E. Johnson, is coediting an anthology about the cultural geography of sports media.

TED MAGDER is Chair of the Media, Culture, and Communication Department at New York University. He is the author of two books, *Canada's*

Hollywood: Feature Films and the Canadian State and *Franchising the Candy Store: Split-Run Magazines and a New International Regime for Trade in Culture,* as well as numerous articles on the political economy of the cultural industries and international trade in media products.

ANNA MCCARTHY is Associate Chair of Cinema Studies at New York University and coeditor of the journal *Social Text.* She is the author of *Ambient Television* and with Nick Couldry is coeditor of the anthology *MediaSpace.* Her publications include articles in the *Journal of Visual Culture, October, GLQ,* the *International Journal of Cultural Studies,* and *Montage A/V.* She is currently working on a book about experiments in governing by television in the 1950s.

JOHN MCMURRIA is Assistant Professor of Communication at DePaul University. In addition to his published articles in book anthologies and journals, he is coauthor, with Toby Miller, Nitin Govil, Richard Maxwell, and Ting Wang, of *Global Hollywood 2.* He is currently working on a critical cultural policy history of cable television in the United States.

SUSAN MURRAY is Associate Professor of Media, Culture, and Communication at New York University. She is the author *of Hitch Your Antenna to the Stars: Early Television and Broadcast Stardom.*

HEATHER OSBORNE-THOMPSON is Assistant Professor of Radio-TV-Film at California State University, Fullerton. She teaches courses in television studies and is currently working on a textbook about television and cultural studies.

LAURIE OUELLETTE is Associate Professor in the Department of·Communication Studies at the University of Minnesota, Twin Cities. She is author (with James Hay) of *Better Living through Reality TV* and *Viewers Like You? How Public TV Failed the People.*

CHAD RAPHAEL is Associate Professor of Communication at Santa Clara University. His articles have appeared in journals such as *Jump Cut* and the *Quarterly Review of Film and Video,* and the University of Minnesota anthology *Culture Works: Essays on the Political Economy of Culture.* He is the author of *Investigated Reporting: Television Muckraking and Regulation.*

AMBER WATTS is Visiting Assistant Professor in the Department of Communication Arts at the University of Wisconsin–Madison. Her research examines schadenfreude and humiliation within contemporary media culture.

Index